THE CLASSICAL MUSIC BOOK

THE
CLASSICAL
MUSIC
BOOK

DK LONDON

PROJECT EDITOR
Sam Kennedy

SENIOR ART EDITOR
Gillian Andrews

SENIOR EDITOR
Victoria Heyworth-Dunne

US EDITOR
Jennette ElNaggar

US EXECUTIVE EDITOR
Lori Cates Hand

ILLUSTRATIONS
James Graham

JACKET EDITOR
Claire Gell

JACKET DESIGNER
Stephanie Tan

JACKET DESIGN
DEVELOPMENT MANAGER
Sophia MTT

PRODUCER, PRE-PRODUCTION
Jennifer Murray

PRODUCER
Mandy Inness

MANAGING EDITOR
Gareth Jones

SENIOR MANAGING ART EDITOR
Lee Griffiths

ASSOCIATE PUBLISHING DIRECTOR
Liz Wheeler

ART DIRECTOR
Karen Self

DESIGN DIRECTOR
Philip Ormerod

PUBLISHING DIRECTOR
Jonathan Metcalf

DK DELHI

SENIOR EDITOR
Rupa Rao

PROJECT ART EDITOR
Vikas Sachdeva

ART EDITOR
Sourabh Challariya

ASSISTANT ART EDITORS
Anukriti Arora, Monam Nishat

JACKET DESIGNER
Suhita Dharamjit

JACKETS EDITORIAL COORDINATOR
Priyanka Sharma

SENIOR DTP DESIGNERS
Shanker Prasad, Neeraj Bhatia,
Harish Aggarwal

DTP DESIGNER
Vikram Singh

PICTURE RESEARCHER
Sakshi Saluja

MANAGING JACKETS EDITOR
Saloni Singh

PICTURE RESEARCH MANAGER
Taiyaba Khatoon

PRE-PRODUCTION MANAGER
Balwant Singh

PRODUCTION MANAGER
Pankaj Sharma

MANAGING EDITOR
Kingshuk Ghoshal

SENIOR MANAGING ART EDITOR
Arunesh Talapatra

TOUCAN BOOKS

EDITORIAL DIRECTOR
Ellen Dupont

SENIOR DESIGNER
Thomas Keenes

SENIOR EDITOR
Dorothy Stannard

EDITORS
John Andrews, Rachel Warren Chadd,
Abigail Mitchell, Larry Porges

ASSISTANT EDITOR
Michael Clark

INDEXER
Marie Lorimer

PROOFREADER
Marion Dent

ADDITIONAL TEXT
Dr. Anthony Alms, Katy Hamilton,
Andrew Kerr-Jarrett, Gavin Plumley,
Marcus Weeks, Philip Wilkinson

original styling by
STUDIO 8

This American Edition, 2022
First American Edition, 2018
Published in the United States by DK Publishing
1450 Broadway, Suite 801, New York,
NY 10018

Copyright © 2018, 2022
Dorling Kindersley Limited
DK, a Division of Penguin Random House LLC
22 23 24 25 10 9 8 7 6 5 4 3 2 1
015–326981–Aug/2022

A catalog record for this book
is available from the Library of Congress.
ISBN: 978-0-7440-5633-4

DK books are available at special discounts
when purchased in bulk for sales promotions,
premiums, fund-raising, or educational use.
For details, contact: DK Publishing
Special Markets, 1450 Broadway, Suite 801,
New York, NY 10018
SpecialSales@dk.com

Printed and bound in China

For the curious
www.dk.com

This book was made with Forest Stewardship
Council™ certified paper – one small step in
DK's commitment to a sustainable future.
For more information go to
www.dk.com/our-green-pledge

CONTRIBUTORS

DR. STEVE COLLISSON, CONSULTANT

British cellist, lecturer, and examiner Dr. Steve Collisson has taught at the Royal Birmingham Conservatoire, the University of Birmingham, and the Open University. He has adjudicated at many music festivals and competitions, including the BBC Young Musician competition.

LEVON CHILINGIRIAN

Founder of the Chilingirian Quartet with the pianist Clifford Benson, renowned violinist Levon Chilingirian performs worldwide and teaches at London's Royal Academy of Music and Guildhall School of Music & Drama.

MATTHEW O'DONOVAN

Head of Academic Music at Eton College, in the UK, Matthew O'Donovan writes extensively about music. He is also a founding member of the vocal ensemble Stile Antico and a published arranger.

GEORGE HALL

A former editor for Decca and the BBC Proms, George Hall is now a full-time music critic. He writes for a wide range of UK music publications, including *The Stage*, *Opera*, and BBC *Music Magazine*.

MALCOLM HAYES

Composer, writer, and broadcaster Malcolm Hayes has written biographies of Anton Webern and Franz Liszt and edited *The Selected Letters of William Walton*. His Violin Concerto premiered at the BBC Proms in 2016.

MICHAEL LANKESTER

Educated at the Royal College of Music, Michael Lankester enjoys an international conducting career. He has been Music Director of the Hartford Symphony Orchestra, Connecticut, and Conductor-in-Residence of the Pittsburgh Symphony Orchestra.

KARL LUTCHMAYER

An international concert pianist, Karl Lutchmayer holds a professorship at Trinity Laban Conservatoire in London and is guest lecturer at various music colleges, including the Juilliard and Manhattan Schools.

KEITH MCGOWAN

Early music expert Keith McGowan has worked with most of the major early music ensembles in the UK and was Master of Music on several productions at Shakespeare's Globe in London.

KUMI OGANO

Adjunct Associate Professor in Music at Connecticut College, Kumi Ogano is an authoritative performer of the work of Japanese composers Toru Takemitsu and Akira Miyoshi.

SOPHIE RASHBROOK

Sophie Rashbrook writes and presents on classical music for Sinfonia Cymru and the Royal College of Music.

DR. CHRISTINA L. REITZ

Dr. Christina L. Reitz is an Associate Professor of Music at Western Carolina University (North Carolina), where she teaches courses in music history and American music.

TIM RUTHERFORD-JOHNSON

A teacher at Goldsmiths College, University of London, Tim Rutherford-Johnson blogs about contemporary music and is the author of *Music after the Fall: Modern Composition and Culture since 1989*.

HUGO SHIRLEY

Hugo Shirley is a music journalist and critic based in Berlin. He is a regular contributor to *Gramophone* and *Opera* magazines.

KATIE DERHAM, FOREWORD

Host of the BBC Radio 3 programs *Sound of Dance* and *In Tune*, Katie Derham is one of the station's best-known voices. She has been the face of the BBC Proms since 2010 and hosts the weekly magazine show *Proms Extra* during the season. Katie also fronts television documentaries, including *The Girl from Ipanema: Brazil, Bossa Nova, and the Beach* for the BBC, and hosted the programs *All Together Now: The Great Orchestra Challenge* and *Fine Tuned*. In 2015 Katie was a finalist on *Strictly Come Dancing*, and she won the Christmas *Special* in 2017.

6

CONTENTS

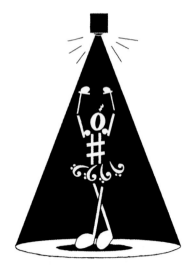

NATIONALISM
1830–1920

CONTEMPORARY

FOREWORD

Music has a certain magic. It can transport us to a different world, drive us to dance, or remind us of lost loved ones. A single chord can reduce us to tears. Far from being an exclusive, elite preserve, the kind of music that provided people in the Western world with pleasure and inspiration for most of the past 1,000 years—and now commonly known as classical music—is still delighting listeners today. It toys with our emotions in our favorite movies; its symphonic swells add drama to the action of computer games; and it hides in the structure and melodies of everyday pop songs. Its magic is of a very special sort—one that has grown and evolved over the centuries, shaped by politics, geography, religion—and the particular genius of a multitude of great composers.

Sometimes it's enough just to listen and let the music wash over and through you without asking why, when, or how, this piece originated. However, the classical music canon can seem intimidatingly vast, encompassing many different styles and genres. For example, the early music of the medieval church—plainsong and chant—is a sonic world away from the waterfalls of sound created by the 19th-century symphony orchestras employed by romantic composers, such as Tchaikovsky and Brahms, or the atonal experimentation of Schoenberg in the early 20th century. At times exploring new sound worlds can be unfamiliar, or even a little uncomfortable, as the composer may have intended.

With *The Classical Music Book,* you will discover the context of the great musical works of the last 1,000 years. Understanding who the composers were and why they were writing can be a revelation and can add a new layer of enjoyment and insight to your listening. A familiar piece such as Vivaldi's *Four Seasons* takes on a whole new resonance when you learn that Vivaldi demonstrated the true potential of the concerto form for the first time and that his reputation spread from Italy to Germany, where he inspired a young organist named Johann Sebastian Bach.

You might know that Beethoven was deaf later in life, but learning which of his works he composed yet never actually heard adds a poignancy and an increased sense of wonder to the listening experience. Realizing that Mozart was effectively an 18th-century pop star might convince you to give the *Marriage of Figaro* another try. Power, patronage, and censorship have each played a part in the genesis of some of the best-loved pieces of music. As you will discover, the real-life drama and scandals often kept pace with the musical dramatics on the stage and in the score.

These, then, are the worlds that the book you are holding invites you to explore. It will be an invaluable companion as it takes you on a journey through the different periods of musical history, deepening your understanding and appreciation of some of classical music's greatest works. It will delight those of you who already love classical music but may have never—until now—come to grips with the component elements of musical vocabulary and theory. And best of all, it will, I hope, encourage endless hours of new listening.

Classical music, like all music, has passion at its heart. It's why the great works of the past have endured for centuries, why contemporary composers still strive to match and challenge that beauty, and why millions of us love to play, listen, and be transported by it today. There is so much wonderful, passionate music out there—let this book open your eyes and your ears to it.

Katie Derham
Classical music commentator

INTRODU

CTION

A vital part of human culture, at least since Neolithic times, music has been a feature of every civilization, as cave paintings, frescoes, and archaeology show. What is loosely referred to as "classical music" is the music of Western civilization as it evolved from medieval times to the present day. In its broadest sense, it covers a wide spectrum of music and not just the orchestral or piano music that some people imagine. This book explores how classical music developed as an essential part of European culture and then spread across the world, delighting, surprising, and sometimes perplexing audiences as it evolved through the centuries.

Bold leaps

The development of a musical tradition, from medieval church music and courtly *trobadors* to the avant-garde music of the 21st century, was often incremental, but it has also been punctuated by exciting innovations. The first operas, staged at the end of the 16th century, for example, revolutionized sacred as well as secular music, while Beethoven's "Eroica" Symphony shocked early 19th-century audiences with its groundbreaking structure and

disregard for Classical conventions, just as Igor Stravinsky's *Le Sacre du printemps* (*Rite of Spring*) astounded those who attended its Paris premiere a century later.

Such leaps have defined the main periods of classical music—Early Music, Renaissance, Baroque, Classical, Romantic, Nationalist, Modern, and Contemporary—though these are broad distinctions, with different styles within each one, and the dividing lines are not clear-cut.

The role of the Church

Like other art forms, music has been shaped by external influences as well as by brilliant individuals.

Music is the social act of communication among people, a gesture of friendship, the strongest there is.
Malcolm Arnold

The first of these was the Church. Western classical music originated in a Europe dominated by the Church. In addition to wielding considerable political power, the clergy provided the only source of learning in society. For the educated, music was part of an act of worship, not entertainment. It was sung by monks without instrumental accompaniment.

The "New Art"

For hundreds of years, the Church resisted any change to the simple chanting of sacred texts, the rise and fall of which was represented on manuscripts by "neumes" (inflective marks). Eventually, however, new ideas found their way in. With the invention of a system of notation by Guido d'Arezzo, a monk in 11th-century Italy, choristers began to sing simple harmonies to the tunes. They later embellished them with other melodies, creating polyphony, a new sound that, in the 14th century, was hailed as the *Ars nova*, the "New Art." Composers soon introduced other innovations, such as an organ accompaniment.

The Church began to lose its control over music, and culture in general, a process helped along by the birth of a new cultural

movement, the Renaissance. As the taboo surrounding secular music disappeared, composers expressed themselves more freely, and their music spread through Europe, especially after the invention of a method for printing and therefore distributing music. No longer controlled by the Church, musicians sought employment in the aristocratic courts of Italy, France, Britain, and the Netherlands, where they made a comfortable living providing entertainment.

The Church still wielded some power, however, and after the Reformation, a more austere musical style was imposed on the Protestant churches in northern Europe, and even the Catholic authorities looked to curb the complexity of polyphony. Composers thus developed a simpler yet more expressive harmonic style. Monteverdi's *Vespers* of 1610 broke new ground for sacred music by incorporating elements of this exciting new style.

Musical explosion

Around the same time, in Florence, a group of intellectuals called the Camerata de' Bardi came up with a new form of entertainment, combining music and drama to create opera. This was a success in the aristocratic courts, which continued to act as patrons to composers and performers, but there was also an increasing public demand for opera and music in general, prompting investment in opera houses, concert halls, and public theaters.

As the Baroque period progressed, composers such as J.S. Bach and George Frideric Handel created works of increasing complexity, taking advantage of the orchestras provided by their aristocratic patrons. The music of the "High Baroque" era was particularly expressive, often ornamented with trills and other embellishments, and sometimes dazzlingly virtuosic.

For a while, the concertgoing public flocked to hear the latest orchestral showpieces, operas, and choral works, but then the Enlightenment, the Age of Reason, dawned, and fashions changed. There was suddenly a demand for more elegant music emphasizing balance and clarity, leading to the Classical period from which "classical music" gets its name.

In a short time, Classical composers, such as Mozart, Haydn, and Beethoven, established the musical forms that are the staple of modern concert repertoires, including the four-movement symphony, the solo concerto, and the string quartet. Music also became popular in the home as the swelling middle class acquired leisure time and musical instruments, including the piano, became more affordable.

The Romantic period

Despite its enduring influence, the Classical period gave way to a new cultural movement almost as soon as it had begun. As Romanticism, with its emphasis on the individual, swept through Europe, expression took precedence over clarity. Composers stretched the Classical forms to their limits in the quest for new sounds. They looked to extramusical sources of inspiration, such as art, literature, landscapes, and human experience. »

What passion cannot music raise and quell.
John Dryden

Romanticism was essentially a Germanic movement, yet its emphasis on the individual provoked a wave of nationalist composers who wanted to distance themselves from Austro-German dominance of the musical *ancien régime* and champion the music of individual nations. Russian and Czech composers began to integrate elements of folk music and themes into their work, a trend later explored by composers in other parts of Europe.

By the end of the 19th century, the excesses of German Romanticism also precipitated a breakdown of the very foundations of Western music—a structure based on the harmonies of the major and minor keys. What followed was a century of composers seeking not just a fresh style but a completely new musical language. Two of the many strands that emerged were particularly influential: 12-note "serialism," pioneered by Arnold Schoenberg and refined by Pierre Boulez, and "aleatoricism"—in which chance played a role in the composition or performance of music.

New influences
These musical experiments coincided with the evolution of jazz and later the explosion of pop and rock music, whose rhythmic beats had instant appeal, causing audiences to turn away from the unfamiliar sounds of new classical music, and even classical music in general. Nonetheless, popular music also influenced and inspired classical composers, producing a cross-fertilization of ideas that brought new life to classical forms, as did the harnessing of modern technology. Composers such as Karlheinz Stockhausen exploited the potential of the electronic studio and the huge advances in recording equipment.

Today, some composers, more conscious of public tastes, are writing in a more accessible style than was the case 50 years ago, but composers continue to experiment, producing music incorporating video, theater, and global influences.

The elements of music
In order to understand the ideas and innovations described in this book, it is useful to be familiar with the "building blocks" of Western classical music, many of which were devised by medieval monks, drawing on concepts formulated by the Ancient Greeks.

Notes are the fundamental material of all music, either sung or played on an instrument. The pitch of an individual note, how high or low the sound is, especially in relation to others, is represented by a letter (A, B, C, and so forth), sometimes modified by "accidentals" (sharp or flat) that raise or lower the note by a half step. For much of the history of classical music, melodies (patterns of notes) were composed using the notes of the major and minor scales, or keys, which help to determine the mood of a piece of music. The key also governs the harmony, when two or more notes are played at the same time. Certain combinations of notes—chords—are consonant, or harmonious, and others more dissonant, harsher; major chords tend to sound brighter, while minor chords are more mournful.

Rhythm and harmony find their way into the inward places of the soul.
Plato

A feature of the Baroque, Classical, and Romantic periods was the system of major-minor tonality in which a key note, called the tonic, is the gravitational center around which a composition revolves—moving away from the tonic to create tension and toward the tonic to resolve it.

Musical forms

Different styles of music emphasize particular aspects of its structure. Some focus on melody, perhaps with a harmonic accompaniment, as was common during the Early Baroque period; others employ counterpoint, the interweaving of two or more melodies in a complex form of polyphony that is one of the defining characteristics of Western classical music.

Also important is the musical form, or shape, of a piece of music: it may comprise recognizably different sections, perhaps in contrasting keys. For example, in a simple "ABA" form, a musical idea is presented, followed by a second idea, and then the opening idea is repeated. Musical forms range from simple songs, such as the *Lieder*, made popular by Franz Schubert and Robert Schumann, to the complexity of a multimovement symphony.

For listeners, the most noticeable difference between a Renaissance song and a full-blown 19th-century symphony is the sound of the voice and/or instruments. Throughout history, new musical instruments have been invented and existing ones refined, giving composers and musicians new sounds with which to work.

Each of these instrument has its own distinctive timbre, or tone, and different combinations of instruments and voices have evolved over time. These range from a cappella (the unaccompanied voice), through solo instruments, like the piano, and small chamber groups, such as the string quartet, to the full concert orchestra of more than 70 players of stringed,

The time is past when music was written for a handful of aesthetes.
Sergei Prokofiev

woodwind, brass, and percussion instruments, and—since the 1950s—electronic technology.

This book

How composers put these musical elements together to develop different genres of classical music, and the factors that influenced them, is explained in this book. It presents significant milestones in the history of Western classical music: not only the great composers and their works but also some lesser-known figures whose music exemplifies a style or period. They are arranged in chronological order, placing them in a wider historical context to show how they reflect society and culture.

Each article focuses on a piece of music that illustrates a particular development in music, discussing its salient features and its significance in relation to other works by the same composer, or in the same style. An "In Context" sidebar and a "See also" section refer to other pieces of music that are relevant to the one under discussion. As not every major composer, let alone all the great pieces of music, could be featured, a Directory section at the end of the book details other significant composers and their work. ∎

EARLY MUSIC
1000–1400

Pope Gregory I gathers plainchant traditions from across the Church in an attempt to unify them.

Frankish ruler Charlemagne instructs his musicians to employ the nuances of Roman singers, leading to the development of **neumatic notation**.

The anonymous treatise *Musica enchiriadis* is published, the first publication to name **musical pitches** with the letters A to G.

Hildegard of Bingen's musical play *Ordo Virtutum* depicts a war between the Virtues and the Devil over the human soul.

c.600   **c.800**   **c.875**   **c.1151**

c.750   **c.850**   **c.1026**

Gregorian chant, a synthesis of Roman and Gallican chants, is commissioned by French Carolingian rulers.

The development of the **sequence**, text associated with a particular chant melody of the Latin Mass, redefines liturgical music.

Guido d'Arezzo pens his treatise *Micrologus* and dedicates it to Tedald, Bishop of Arezzo, in Tuscany, Italy.

What is now known as Western Classical music evolved from the music of the medieval Church in Europe, which in turn had its roots in Jewish religious music and the music of classical Rome and Greece. Our knowledge of this early music is limited, however, as it was an oral tradition, memorized by musicians and passed down from generation to generation. The little that is known for certain comes from contemporary accounts, which almost exclusively describe sacred music, as the Church effectively had a monopoly on literacy.

The role of the Church

The story of classical music begins with sacred Latin texts sung by monks as part of acts of worship. The performance was simple—

it was exclusively vocal music, without accompaniment, and consisted of a single line of music, known as monody, which could be sung by one voice or a choir singing in unison. The tunes they sang are called "plainchant," and each region had its own collection of chants. At the beginning of the seventh century, however, Pope Gregory attempted to collect, categorize, standardize, and teach these regional variations of plainchant as part of his efforts to unify liturgical practice.

In order to guarantee that performance of these plainchants was standardized across the whole of Christendom, a form of music notation was developed. This used symbols, known as "neumes," written above the text to give a graphic indication of the shape of

the melody. At this point, some time in the ninth century, the pace of change began to accelerate: a standardized form of church service, the Mass, was established, and specific plainchants were assigned to its various sections. Notation also became more sophisticated, with a horizontal line to clarify the pitch of the notes, showing how high or low they are.

Most significant musically was the introduction of "organum," a simple form of harmony. Where plainchant had consisted of a single line of music, organum had two, and later three or even four, lines. One voice would sing the plainchant, and the other a parallel line of music a few notes higher or lower.

As the music became more complex over the years, the means of writing it down also evolved,

Adam de la Halle's *Le Jeu de Robin et de Marion*, regarded as the first secular French play, is premiered in Naples.

The *Tournai Mass*, composed by several anonymous authors, is the first known **polyphonic setting** of a Mass transcribed to a manuscript.

French composer **Guillaume de Machaut's** polyphonic mass *Messe de Notre Dame* is composed.

c.1280–1283

c.1320

c.1360–1365

c.1170

c.1300

c.1350

In Paris, **Léonin** bridges the gap between plainchant and polyphony in his *Magnus liber organi.*

Music theorist **Johannes de Garlandia's** *De mensurabili musica* explains modal rhythmic systems.

The Toulouse Mass assembles **polyphonic Mass movements** adapted from existing motets for three voices.

and in the 11th century a system of differently shaped dots written on a staff of four or more horizontal lines was established this way—the forerunner of our modern system of music notation.

Music spreads

Notation not only helped standardize performance but also enabled musicians to write new music, which they did from the 12th century onward, marking the beginning of classical music as it is known today. Music was no longer anonymous and passed on orally, and this led to the emergence of composers and compositions. This new breed of composer was keen to try out innovatory techniques. The simple harmony of organum, with voices singing in parallel with the melody

of the plainchant, was succeeded by a more complex style, polyphony, in which each voice has its own melody. This new technique was pioneered by Léonin and Pérotin in Paris and rapidly caught on across Europe.

At the same time, secular music was flourishing, too, in the form of traveling minstrels who entertained in the aristocratic courts and on the street. Known as *trobadors*, *trouvères*, or similar regional variations, they were poets as well as composers and performers and, unlike church musicians, sang their songs with an instrumental accompaniment. It is likely that these entertainers also played purely instrumental music for dancing, but as such secular music was still an oral tradition, none has survived.

By the mid-14th century, polyphonic music with interweaving vocal lines had become known as *Ars nova*, the "New Art," and composers who had mastered the technique were commissioned to write Masses for the cathedrals.

The new style was not exclusively developed for the Christian Mass. Composers also wrote shorter settings of words in the same polyphonic style called "motets." Some were settings of sacred texts, but a number of "serious" composers were also writing polyphonic motets on secular poems. As the medieval period drew to a close, and the Renaissance got under way, the Church's monopoly on music was on the wane. Sacred and secular music were about to flourish side by side. ■

PSALMODY IS THE WEAPON OF THE MONK

PLAINCHANT (6TH–9TH CENTURY), ANONYMOUS

IN CONTEXT

FOCUS
Plainsong

BEFORE
c.1400 BCE A clay tablet from the ancient city of Ugarit in northern Syria records the hymn of a religious cult, with fragmentary musical notation.

c.200 BCE–100 CE Found on a tombstone in a town near Ephesus, in Turkey, the "song of Seikilos" is the earliest complete, notated musical composition.

AFTER
1562–1563 The Catholic Church's Council of Trent bans the singing of the medieval embellishments of plainchant known as "sequences."

1896 The monks of the Benedictine Abbaye de Solesmes publish their *Liber usualis*, an attempt to restore Gregorian chant, distorted by centuries of use, to a more pristine and standardized text.

The early Christian Church began as a Jewish sect, so the evolving liturgy, or forms of service, of the new faith shared many traits with Jewish worship, including the repeated speaking, or chanting, of scripture and prayer. Specifically, Christian aspects focused on particular types of observance, such as the reenactment of the Last Supper (later to become the Mass) and psalm-singing, scripture readings, and prayer to mark the new Church's holy days and feasts. Over time, these rites evolved

into the Divine Office or Liturgy of the Hours—the basis of Roman Catholic worship.

The singing of rites

As Christianity spread from the Holy Land, so did its rites and ceremonies, celebrated in the languages of the communities where it took root, such as Aramaic in Palestine and Greek in Rome. As a result, different chant styles evolved, including the Mozarabic in Iberia, the Gallican in Roman Gaul, and Ambrosian, after St. Ambrose, a 4th-century bishop of Milan.

Of these earliest liturgies, only the Roman and Ambrosian chants have survived in a recognizable form. They became known as "plainsong" (a direct translation of the Latin *cantus planus*) for the simplicity of their unaccompanied melodies, which were sung in a free, speechlike rhythm, reflecting the unmetrical prose of prayers, psalms, and the scriptures. This music, though unstructured, largely

A wooden sculpture of St. Ambrose (c.1500) shows him in his study. The Roman bishop championed the hymn, or "sacred song," as a key part of church worship.

See also: *Micrologus* 24–25 ▪ *Magnus liber organi* 28–31 ▪ *Messe de Notre Dame* 36–37 ▪ *Canticum Canticorum* 46–51 ▪ *Great Service* 52–53

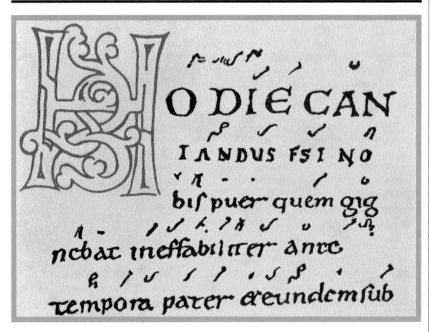

This Gregorian chant, *Hodie Cantandus* ("today we must sing"), by St. Tuotilo, a 10th-century Irish monk, has neumes on the upper lines and Latin script underneath.

The Mass

It took until at least the 11th century for the Mass to reach a final form. Its music became known as the Gradual, a book divided into the Ordinary (the elements that remain the same every week) and the Proper (the parts that are particular to the time and day in the Church calendar).

The Ordinary of the Mass has five parts. The first, *Kyrie eleison* ("Lord, have mercy"), *is an* ancient text in Greek (the language of Roman services until about the 4th century); the second, *Gloria in excelsis Deo* ("Glory to God in the highest"), was introduced in the 7th century; the third, the *Credo* ("I believe") was adopted in 1014 (though is believed to date from the 4th century); and the fourth, the *Sanctus* ("Holy"), rooted in Jewish liturgy, had become part of the Roman rite before the reforms of Pope Gregory I. The fifth section, *Agnus Dei* ("The Lamb of God"), was added to the Roman Mass in the 7th century, originating from a Syrian rite.

The ritual of the Mass was based on the Last Supper, shared by Christ and His disciples, seen here in this detail from a 6th-century manuscript.

followed the ancient Greek modal system of seven-note octaves made up of five tones and two semitones, and consisted of two types of chant: the responsorial and the antiphonal. The former involved more elaborate, solo chants, with a response from the choir. Antiphonal chants, where singing alternated between choir and congregation, consisted of simpler melodies.

These forms were shared by Roman and Ambrosian plainsong, but Ambrosian chant was smoother in its note progression and more dramatic than Roman chant. It also made greater use of melisma, in which a string of notes was sung on one syllable—a style still used in Middle Eastern and Asian song.

By the middle of the first millennium, thousands of chants existed across the different rites. The sheer variety of unique styles and traditions was addressed by Gregory I (Pope 590–604 CE), who wished to unify liturgical practice.

Gregory consolidated the music of the Roman rite and is said to have instigated a papal *schola cantorum* ("choir school") to do justice to the evolving repertoire.

Expanded repertoire

Under the rule of Charlemagne (742–814), the first Holy Roman Emperor, Roman chants were synthesized with elements of the Gallican style, which was also in common use. This expanded collection formed the basis of Gregorian chant, which remains at the heart of Catholic Church music. Plainsong was also the foundation for medieval and Renaissance music and its notation, based on the staves and neumes, or notes, of written chants. ∎

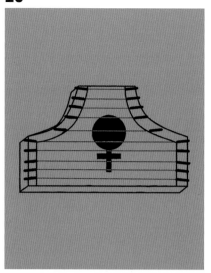

WE SHOULD SING PSALMS ON A TEN-STRING PSALTERY
ORDO VIRTUTUM (c.1151), HILDEGARD OF BINGEN

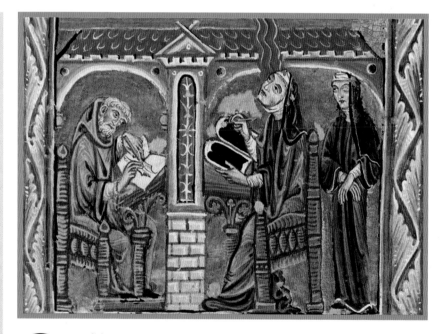

Hildegard receives a divine vision in an image from a 13th-century manuscript. She is accompanied by Volmar of Disibodenberg (left) and her confidante Richardis von Stade.

One of the most original voices in sacred music of the early Middle Ages was that of the female cleric Hildegard of Bingen in Germany. Her musical output is also one of the largest of any single identifiable medieval composer. Her collection entitled *Symphonia armonie celestium revelationum* ("The symphony of the harmony of celestial revelation"), for example, includes more than 70 plainchant compositions.

Hildegard grew up under the tutelage of a young visionary called Jutta of Sponheim. With support from Jutta and a monk named Volmar at the abbey of Disibodenberg, Hildegard learned the psalms and practiced the

See also: *Le jeu de Robin et de Marion* 32–35 ▪ *Messe de Notre Dame* 36–37 ▪ *Missa l'homme armé* 42 ▪ *The Wreckers* 232–239 ▪ *blue cathedral* 326

chant repertory of the church year, studied the playing of the psaltery (a stringed instrument), and learned to write Latin. Like Jutta, Hildegard professed to be divinely inspired, claiming to have "never learned neumes, or any other part of music." While the truth of this assertion is unknown, it may have been an attempt to disassociate herself and Jutta from an education that ordinarily would not have been available to women. For women in the 12th century, to profess knowledge of the *trivium* (the rhetorical arts) or *quadrivium* (the sciences and music theory) or to provide interpretation of the Bible might be considered a direct threat to male authority.

Magnum opus

The earliest extant morality play, and one of the first musical dramas to be recorded, Hildegard's most well-known work, *Ordo Virtutum* ("The play of the Virtues"), contains more than 80 melodies that form a musical drama most likely intended to be performed by the nuns of Hildegard's order. The play calls for a cast of more than 20 singing roles and concerns the struggle for a soul (*Anima*) between 17 "Virtues" (Humility is the Queen of the Virtues) and their adversary, Diabolus (the Devil). Diabolus, perhaps originally spoken by Hildegard's friend and scribe Volmar, lacks all harmony and articulates in spoken interjections.

The accompanying melodies in the manuscript indicate when the Virtues sing as a chorus and gives more florid music to the solo voices. As the Virtues step forward to introduce themselves, the music

Heaven was opened and a fiery light of exceeding brilliance came and permeated my whole brain … and immediately I knew the meaning of the exposition of the Scriptures.
Hildegard of Bingen

becomes more expressive and animated, the sweeping vocal lines of *Humilitas* (Humility), *Fede* (Faith), and *Spes* (Hope) inspiring the sister Virtues to respond with ardor. However, the original notation is little more than the barest of bones: recordings with fiddles, flute, and harmonized accompaniments represent the modern interpretation of this sketch.

Writings and divinity

Hildegard's letters reveal her status as "seer and mystic," which allowed her not just the freedom to offer stern advice (even to the pope) but opportunities for musical expression. She often emphasized the transcendent origin of her works. Music connected her to a lost Eden, before Adam and Eve precipitated the Fall of humankind by eating the forbidden fruit. She envisaged her texts being at the service of the music, so that "those who hear might be taught about inward things." ▪

Hildegard of Bingen

Born in 1098 as the youngest child in a large family of lesser nobility, Hildegard spent her early childhood in Bermersheim, south of Mainz, in Germany. She suffered from ill health, and even before the age of five began to see visions, drawing the family's attention to her spiritual acuity by predicting the color of an unborn calf. At about the age of eight, she was placed in the care of Jutta of Sponheim, a visionary who lived as a recluse in a hermitage near the abbey at Disibodenberg.

The women's hermitage was later opened to monastic aspirants, and at the age of 14 Hildegard devoted her life to God as a Benedictine nun. On the death of Jutta in 1136, and at the age of 38, Hildegard was elected to lead the religious community. She performed this role until her death in 1179 but also found time to write three volumes of visionary theology, scientific works, and religious verse.

Other key work

c.1150s *Symphonia armonie celestium revelationum*

TANDARADEI, SWEETLY SANG THE NIGHTINGALE

LE JEU DE ROBIN ET DE MARION (1280–1283), ADAM DE LA HALLE

IN CONTEXT

FOCUS
Secular medieval music

BEFORE
c.1160 *Festum stultorum* (Feast of Fools) appears in Paris and Beauvais as an opportunity around Christmas for clerics to indulge in a parody of the liturgy.

c.1230 *Ludus Danielis* (*The Play of Daniel*) is written in Beauvais as a liturgical drama in Latin.

AFTER
Late 14th century The annual cycle of Mystery Plays (performances of biblical scenes set to music) begins in York and Wakefield, England.

Diverse musical traditions are known to have flourished in European towns and villages in the Middle Ages, as they did in the courts of noble families, yet almost none of this popular music survives in notation. While the Church used scribes to regulate and record its own repertoire for posterity, much secular music was passed on orally.

However, the lack of written sources among common people is not just the consequence of poor literacy. For many dance musicians and the singers of epics, a written text would not have reflected the skilful, improvisatory nature of their profession, honed by generations of hereditary entertainers. Furthermore, by recording their works in a manuscript, they risked handing their cherished repertoire to rivals.

See also: *Missa l'homme armé* 42 ▪ *Water Music* 84–89 ▪ *Musique de table* 106 ▪ *The Magic Flute* 134–137 ▪ *Die schöne Müllerin* 150–155

Le Jeu de Robin et de Marion was performed in St. Petersburg, Russia, in 1907. Its set design was recorded in watercolor by Mstislav Dobuzhinsky.

The sources of European secular music tended to be found where popular styles aroused the interest of the Church or nobility. The crusading knights of southern France found the highly developed styles of instrumental and vocal music they encountered on Crusades in the Holy Land particularly appealing, this being a period of great cultural exchange as well as of conflict and hostility.

Languages and influences

Medieval secular music features distinct poetic identities linked to regional languages. Two medieval French languages emerged from Latin: *langue d'oc* or *Occitan* in Southern France and Northern Spain (where *oc* meant "yes"); and *langue d'oïl*, north of the Loire (where *oïl* meant "yes"). Each of these languages had its own bardic tradition: the south had the music of the *trobador* and female *trobairitz*, while the north used the word "*trouvère*," both of which may have come from the Early French word *trobar*, meaning "to find or invent" (a song). An alternative root may be the Arabic word *tarab*, meaning "source of joy." One of the earliest troubadours, William IX, Duke of Aquitaine, was said to have sung "in verse with pleasant tunes" about his experience of leading the so-called "Crusade of the Faint-Hearted" into Anatolia (now Turkey) in 1101. His songs are clearly influenced by Arabic poetic conventions, in particular the popular song-forms of *muwashah* and *zajal*.

A play with music

The 13th-century musician Adam de la Halle has been described as a trouvère. De la Halle probably wrote

Adam de la Halle

French musician Adam de la Halle was born in the cloth-working city of Arras in 1222, and grew up learning about music as part of his theological education at the abbey of Vaucelles, founded only a century before. De la Halle's father expected him to enter the Church, but he chose a different path. After a short-lived marriage, he enrolled at the University of Paris, where, among other things, he learned the polyphonic techniques that he would later apply to popular musical genres.

De la Halle initially used his verse to speak out against the corrupt administration of Arras but later entered into noble service. It was in the service of Charles of Anjou, who became king of Naples, that he wrote *Le jeu de Robin et de Marion*. Halle died a few years later, sometime between 1285 and 1288.

Other key works

Date unknown *Mout me fu grief/Robin m'aime/Portare (Great was my sadness/Robin loves me/Portare)*
Date unknown *A jointes mains vous proi (Take my hand, I pray)*

Le jeu de Robin et de Marion ("The Play of Robin and Marion") for his fellow Frenchmen as part of a Christmas celebration in Naples in 1284. The French noblemen had taken refuge there after the island of Sicily had overthrown the rule of Charles I of Anjou (Adam's patron) in a bloody Easter coup. The *Jeu* tells the story of a country maid who is wooed by a lustful knight yet remains true to her lover »

MUSIC IS A SCIENCE THAT MAKES YOU LAUGH, SING, AND DANCE
MESSE DE NOTRE DAME (c.1360–1365), GUILLAUME DE MACHAUT

IN CONTEXT

FOCUS
Polyphony and the notation revolution

BEFORE
c.1320 The *Tournai Mass* is the first known Mass that uses polyphony—"many sounds."

c.1350 The *Toulouse Mass* assembles polyphonic Mass movements arranged from existing motets (short, unaccompanied choral pieces).

AFTER
1415–1421 *The Old Hall Manuscript* contains several polyphonic settings of the *Kyrie* to suit the English fashion for elaboration of that section of the Mass.

1440s *Missa Caput* is an early Mass by an English composer using a *cantus firmus* ("fixed song") around which other melodies are based. It includes a bass voice below that of the tenor—one of the first compositions with a bass part.

The 14th century was one of the most turbulent periods of medieval history. The "Little Ice Age," which began around 1300, resulted in crop failures and famines, including the Great Famine of 1312–1317, and the Black Death killed up to 60 percent of Europe's population.

Such extreme social, economic, and environmental upheaval shook religious certainties. Scholars, such as the French scientist-cleric Nicole Oresme (c.1320–1382), began to envision a more complex universe than the faith-based view of the natural world. Music, already embracing polyphony, was also influenced by this way of thinking and exploded into new metrical complexity when Oresme's fellow Frenchman, the mathematician-composer Philippe de Vitry (1291–1361), devised a precise method to notate rhythm.

A new order of rhythm
The new style became known as *Ars nova* after de Vitry's treatise *Ars nova notandi* ("The New Art of Notation"), published in 1322. Vitry composed vocal pieces to demonstrate the novel notation in the form of motets (polyphonic compositions based on one melody and text, with other voices bringing in different words and melodies). Each of Vitry's motets, only 12 of which survive, displayed different aspects of a technique known today as isorhythm (from the Greek for "same rhythm"), which aimed to give structure to extended compositions.

Musicians illuminate a 1316 manuscript of *Le Roman de Fauvel*, a French poem by Gervais du Bus, which is interspersed with some of the first Ars nova music.

See also: *Magnus liber organi* 28–31 ▪ *Missa l'homme armée* 42 ▪ *Missa Pange lingua* 43 ▪ *Canticum Canticorum* 46–51 ▪ Monteverdi's *Vespers* 64–69

> Certain disciples of the new art are preoccupied with their measured dividing up of beats … We forbid these methods.
> **Pope John XXII**

Vitry took a series of notes in the tenor voice (called the *color*) and applied a rhythmic pattern (called a *talea*) to it. The *talea* (rhythm) was usually shorter than the color (melody) so it might require several cycles of the talea to equal one repetition of the color.

The Church was not enamored of Ars nova, and Pope John XXII condemned it in a decree of 1323. The clergy were alarmed by the style's role in the secularization of the once purely sacred motet, which was now appropriated as a way to comment on events of the day. The satirical poem *Le roman de Fauvel* (c.1316), for example, contains 130 musical works, including five motets by de Vitry.

Despite the religious opposition, the precision of the new notation opened the door to experiments in rhythm and meter. These can be heard in the intricate and shifting rhythms of the songs of the Italians Matteo da Perugia and Philippus de Caserta and the French composer Baude Cordier (all working around 1400), in a style that is now known as *Ars subtilior*

("even more subtle art"). Ars nova had become established and went on to form the basis for the development of rhythmic notation in Western music.

Changing the Mass

De Vitry's ideas found perhaps their greatest flowering in the music of Guillaume de Machaut, a 14th-century composer and poet. Machaut used the same isorhythmic techniques in his own motets and in the *Kyrie, Sanctus, Agnus Dei,* and *Ite, missa est* movements of his *Messe de Notre Dame,* the first known setting of polyphonic music for a complete Mass cycle by a single composer. As well as using isorhythm to unify elements of the Mass, Machaut also employed a plainsong *cantus firmus* ("fixed song") as a linking melody for each movement, from which other melodies develop, and added a *contratenor* to raise the number of voices from three (the traditional number) to a richer and more expansive four.

Machaut secured his artistic heritage by carefully managing his own output, collecting his works in manuscripts that he compiled during his lifetime. Besides his importance as a composer, Machaut was one of the greatest French poets of the medieval period, producing extensive poetic narratives in the form of *lais* (lines of verse with eight syllables) and *dits* (verse without music). He also developed shorter poetic genres with repeated phrases, or refrains, such as the *ballade, rondeau,* and *virelai,* which became popular vehicles of expression for poets and composers of subsequent generations. ▪

Guillaume de Machaut

Born in the Champagne region of France around 1300, Machaut spent much of his life in and around the nearby city of Reims. After taking holy orders, in 1323 he joined the household of John of Luxembourg, King of Bohemia, traveling with him around Eastern Europe and Italy as his chaplain and secretary. Through King John, Machaut acquired lucrative benefices as canon of the cathedrals at Verdun in 1330, Arras in 1332, and in Reims in 1337.

After King John's death at the Battle of Crécy in 1346, Machaut found further patronage from Bonne of Luxembourg, the second daughter of King John the Blind, and Charles II, King of Navarre in Spain. The composer's final years were spent in Reims, overseeing the compilation of his works. He died in 1377 and was buried in Reims cathedral.

Other key works

c.1330s *Douce dame jolie* (virelai)
c.1340s *Rose, liz, printemps, verdure* (rondeau)
c.1340s *Voir dit*

RENAIS

1400–1600

SANCE

Missa Rex seculorum is written as a cantus firmus Mass in the influential English style, attributed either to **John Dunstaple** or **Leonel Power**.

Franco-Flemish composer **Josquin Desprez** sets music to the Ordinary of the Mass in his *Missa Pange lingua*.

Thomas Tallis's 40-part motet *Spem in alium*, is composed, featuring eight choirs of five voices each.

c.1430

c.1515

c.1570

c.1460

1568

1572

Guillaume Dufay composes the Mass *L'Homme armé*, employing the third interval in the scale to create a sweet sound.

Italian composer and diplomat **Alessandro Striggio** premieres his motet *Ecce beatam lucem* in Munich, Germany.

Spanish composer **Tomás Luis de Victoria** writes his first collection of motets while working in Rome.

The cultural movement known as the Renaissance emerged in Italy as early as the 14th century. However, a distinctively Renaissance style of music did not manifest itself until some years later. It first flourished in the Netherlands, at the court of Philip the Good of Burgundy (1396–1467). The composers there, although Franco-Flemish by birth, were cosmopolitan by nature. The leading light of the Franco-Flemish school, Guillaume Dufay, inspired by the Ars Nova polyphony that he had heard while in Italy, found a way to break with the medieval style and began to redefine Renaissance music.

One of Dufay's innovations was his use of the *cantus firmus*, the technique of composing a polyphonic piece around a plainchant melody. Echoing the Renaissance trend toward increasing secularization, he started to use secular melodies instead of plainchant as a basis for his Masses, which were in a richly expressive polyphonic style. He and other composers at the Burgundian court, including Gilles Binchois, Johannes Ockeghem, and one of the finest composers of the early Renaissance, Josquin Desprez, did not restrict themselves to sacred music and also wrote secular motets and chansons.

New challenge

The Franco-Flemish school of polyphony dominated the music of the early Renaissance, but in the 16th century, things changed dramatically. The power that the Catholic Church had wielded in medieval times was being challenged, and in 1517 Martin Luther triggered the Reformation. Much of northern Europe converted to the Protestant Church, which had a very different attitude to music for their services, preferring simple hymns and melodies for the congregation to sing rather than polyphonic Masses sung only by the choir. Such music became the foundation of a distinctly Germanic musical tradition.

The Reformation had, however, provoked a reaction in the Catholic world—the Counter-Reformation—in which the Church defended some of its practices while examining and reforming others. One of the things that came under scrutiny was the music for church services. Many in the Catholic Church were uncomfortable

William Byrd composes *Great Service* for use on state occasions at Her Majesty's Chapel Royal at Hampton Court Palace.

Venetian composer **Giovanni Bassano** publishes his four-part collection *Ricercate, passaggi et cadentie*, to be played in the style of an *étude*.

Thomas Weelkes pens *O care, thou wilt despatch me* as part of his most famous work—his collection of madrigals.

c.1580–1590

1585

1600

1584

1597

1604

Giovanni Pierluigi da Palestrina writes the *Canticum Canticorum*, a collection of motets based on excerpts from the biblical Song of Songs.

Italian organist **Giovanni Gabrieli** uses loud and soft dynamics in *Sonata pian' e forte*.

John Dowland's *Lachrimae* uses dissonance to conjure an atmosphere of melancholy.

with the complex polyphony that had become fashionable, as so many voices singing different lines of melody made the words unintelligible. Composers were told to moderate their style, precipitating the adoption of a relatively simple polyphony that avoided the sometimes dissonant harmonies that occur in polyphonic music and emphasized the clarity of the words. This clearer and sweeter-sounding style characterized what came to be regarded as the musical "High Renaissance."

Among the first composers to adopt the style was Giovanni Pierluigi da Palestrina, who wrote numerous motets and Masses for churches in Rome. Composers from across Europe gravitated to Italy to absorb the new sound, before taking it back to their native lands.

In England, it was adopted by composers such as Thomas Tallis and William Byrd.

Instrumental music

It was not just church music that was changing. By the end of the 14th century, traveling minstrels had all but disappeared thanks to the ravages of the Black Death. They gravitated instead to the aristocratic courts, where they provided entertainment, singing chansons and playing instrumental music for dancing and for civic ceremonies, such as the installation of a new Doge in Venice.

In a more secularized society, instrumental music became popular not only in the courts but also among an increasingly educated middle class, creating a demand for music to play at home,

either in consorts of instruments, such as viols or recorders, or for solo keyboard instruments, such as the harpsichord. Thanks to the development of a mechanical technique for printing, sheet music was readily available, and the new style spread through Europe. Madrigals, for small groups of singers, became a popular form of home entertainment, especially in Italy and England.

However, composers and the public were experimenting with another form by the end of the 16th century, and a dramatic new style was heralded by the works of Giovanni Gabrieli in Venice. The last great works to be composed in the Renaissance style were Tomás Luis de Victoria's *Officium defunctorum* and John Dowland's *Lachrimae*, fitting ends to an era. ∎

NOT A SINGLE PIECE OF MUSIC COMPOSED BEFORE THE LAST 40 YEARS ... IS WORTH HEARING
MISSA L'HOMME ARMÉ (c.1460), GUILLAUME DUFAY

IN CONTEXT

FOCUS
New harmonies

BEFORE
1430 Englishman Leonel Power composes *Alma redemptoris mater*, possibly the first Mass to use an identified *cantus firmus*—a "set song"—as the basis for its melodic framework.

1430 *Rex seculorum* is written as a cantus firmus Mass in the English style, either by John Dunstable or Leonel Power.

AFTER
1570 Italian Giovanni Palestrina publishes a five-voice setting of the Mass on the *L'homme armé* melody.

1999 Welsh composer Karl Jenkins incorporates the *L'homme armé* folk song into the first and final movements of his Mass *The Armed Man*.

From Franco-Flemish composer Guillaume Dufay onward, the harmonic language of music begins to sound more familiar to modern listeners. Earlier composers had followed the harmonic ideals worked out by the ancient Greek philosopher and mathematician Pythagoras, based on the "perfect" consonance of octaves and fourth and fifth intervals. Dufay's innovation was to use chords featuring the third interval in the scale as a harmony note (*mi* in the sol-fa singing scale, following *do* and *re*). Historically, the harmony of third intervals had been seen as somewhat dissonant, to be used sparingly.

Secular sounds in church
Dufay's masses made much use of the *cantus firmus* technique, which built a piece around an already existing melody, such as a well-known sacred composition or a plainchant. In *L'homme armé*, Dufay chose a popular French folk song with a distinctive melody that lent itself well to a polyphonic layering of voices. Following the lead of English musicians, who had already embraced the use of third intervals, Dufay allows the music to dwell on the interval's sweet, less hollow sound. This extended the harmonic vocabulary and created room for more voices. ∎

Master of melody Guillaume Dufay stands beside a portable organ in an illumination from the 15th-century poetic work, *Le champion des dames*.

See also: *Micrologus* 24–25 ▪ *Magnus liber organi* 28–31 ▪ *Missa Pange lingua* 43 ▪ *Canticum Canticorum* 46–51 ▪ *St. Matthew Passion* 98–105

TONGUE, PROCLAIM THE MYSTERY OF THE GLORIOUS BODY
MISSA PANGE LINGUA (c.1515), JOSQUIN DESPREZ

IN CONTEXT

FOCUS
Dissemination of music

BEFORE
c.1415–1420 The largest collection of 14th-century Italian music, the *Squarcialupi Codex* illuminated manuscript, is compiled in Florence.

1457 The *Codex Psalmorum*, produced in the German city of Mainz, is the first printed book to contain music, although the notation is handwritten.

AFTER
c.1520 English printer John Rastell produces the first music where the staves, notes, and text are printed in a single impression.

1710 The Statute of Anne, enacted in Britain, gives authors copyright over their printed work for the first time, a right finally extended to music composition in 1777.

J osquin Desprez, born in France around 1450, was an early beneficiary of the printing press. Until the invention of the technology in the mid-15th century, music was copied out by hand, by professional copyists. According to the 16th-century Swiss music theorist Heinrich Glarean, Desprez "published his works after much deliberation and with manifold corrections." This care and attention made his compositions a favorite in the emerging music publishing market.

Now that Josquin is dead, he is putting out more works than when he was alive!
Georg Forster
German composer (1510–1568)

Desprez's contemporary, the Italian printer Ottaviano Petrucci, perfected a method for printing music in three passes: the staves, followed by notes, and then the words. Petrucci's first publication, *Odhecaton*, a selection of nearly 100 secular pieces, mostly by Franco-Flemish composers, including Desprez, Alexander Agricola, Antoine Busnois, and Jacob Obrecht, appeared in 1501. To meet the challenge of a first collection of polyphonic music for the Mass with underlayed text, Petrucci chose to devote his *Misse* (1502) to works solely by Desprez.

A late Mass
Missa Pange lingua was one of Desprez's final compositions, taking its central melody from a hymn for the Feast of Corpus Christi written by the 13th-century Italian friar and theologian Thomas Aquinas. The work was not ready in time for Petrucci's final book of masses in 1514, but it survived in manuscript form and was finally published in 1532. ∎

See also: *Messe de Notre Dame* 36–37 ▪ *Missa l'homme armé* 42 ▪ *Canticum Canticorum* 46–51 ▪ *St. Matthew Passion* 98–105

HEARE THE VOYCE AND PRAYER

SPEM IN ALIUM (c.1570), THOMAS TALLIS

IN CONTEXT

FOCUS
Large-scale choral music

BEFORE
c.1500 French composer Antoine Brumel writes a Mass in 12 parts, *Missa Et ecce terrae motus*, known as the "Earthquake Mass."

1568 Alessandro Striggio's motet *Ecce beatam lucem* for 40 voices with instruments is performed in Munich.

AFTER
1682 Heinrich Biber composes his *Missa Salisburgensis* in 53 parts arranged in six choirs of singers, strings, recorders, cornetts, and sackbuts, with two ensembles of trumpets and timpani, and at least two organs—probably the largest work in the Colossal Baroque style, the name given to large-scale, poly-choral works.

The composition of the great 40-voice motet *Spem in alium* by Thomas Tallis marked a pinnacle of early English Renaissance choral music and was an inspired response to a continental challenge. In 1567, the composer Alessandro Striggio had arrived in England on a diplomatic

A chapel choir sings from sheet music displayed on a lectern in the frontispiece of *Practica musicae* by the Italian music theorist Franchini di Gaffurio, published in 1512.

mission from the Medici court in Florence, bringing with him the parts for his recent compositions for 40 or more independent voices. These were musical manifestations of influence and power, and some wondered what the result might be if an English composer were to attempt such a composition. They turned to Tallis, who had been the foremost court composer under four monarchs—Henry VIII, Edward VI, Mary I, and Elizabeth I. Tallis's Roman Catholic patron, Thomas Howard, Fourth Duke of Norfolk, commissioned the work.

A long choral tradition

The English had long excelled at choral music. In the 15th century, John Dunstable established the *contenance angloise* ("English manner"), a distinctive, richly harmonic polyphonic style. Flemish music theorist Johannes Tinctoris described Dunstable as "the fountain and source" of musical innovation.

A generation before Tallis, Robert Fayrfax was the leading English composer and a favorite of Henry VIII. He was the organist and Master of the Choristers at St. Albans Abbey from 1498 to 1502

See also: *Messe de Notre Dame 36–37* ▪ *Missa l'homme armé 42* ▪ *Missa Pange lingua 43* ▪ *Canticum Canticorum 46–51* ▪ *Great Service 52–53* ▪ *St. Matthew Passion 98–105*

and composed the complex five-voice Mass *O quam glorifica* for his doctorate in 1504.

Masters of sacred music

In the early 16th century, John Taverner emerged as a significant composer of English sacred music after his appointment in 1526 as Master of the Choristers at Thomas Wolsey's newly founded Cardinal College, Oxford (the future Christ Church). There he composed three six-voice Masses, *Corona spinea*, *Gloria tibi Trinitas*, and *O Michael*. The tenor part from the "In nomine Domini" section of the *Benedictus* of his *Gloria tibi Trinitas* became widely used by other composers as the basis of vocal and instrumental arrangements. This was the origin of the English fantasia genre known as *In nomine*, which was popular until the late 17th century.

Taverner moved back home to Lincolnshire after Wolsey's downfall and produced little more music. John Sheppard was perhaps more adept at tailoring his output to the tastes of Roman Catholic and

The Duke hearing of the song [*Spem in alium*] took his chain of gold from of his neck and put it about Tallis his neck and gave it him.
Thomas Wateridge
Letter (1611)

Protestant monarchs. He was the choirmaster at Magdalen College, Oxford, for three years, and then, from 1552, a Gentleman of the Chapel Royal under Edward VI and Mary I. He died on the eve of Elizabeth's succession in 1558. Much of Sheppard's Latin-texted church music survives. His responsory *Media vita* for six voices is a Lenten work of monumental status: the slow statement of the *Nunc dimittis* chant running through the work adds to its impact.

An extraordinary response

Thomas Tallis was a member of the Chapel Royal when Striggio visited and unfurled his multipart scores. The Italian's works were in the polychoral style, with voices grouped into self-contained choirs that came together in a grand sound at crucial points in the score.

Tallis's response in his motet *Spem in alium* was quite different: it dipped back into the soaring sound of Taverner's and Sheppard's music to create an unmistakably English piece. The 40 voices of *Spem in alium* seldom gather in the same groupings, but each follow their own paths. One voice may maintain a steady pace on the beat but will have a counterpart that achieves something similar in syncopation, adding a scintillation to the steady voice. Like a gradual murmuration of birds, the voices gather, separate, and finally assemble to exhilarating effect. ▪

Thomas Tallis

Little is known of Tallis's early life, but by 1532 he was the organist of Dover Priory, on England's south coast. After the priory's dissolution three years later, he worked at the church of St. Mary-at-Hill in London, Waltham Abbey, and Canterbury Cathedral, before becoming a member of the choir ("Gentleman") of Henry VIII's Chapel Royal, where he later became the organist.

Queen Elizabeth granted Tallis and William Byrd a patent to print music in 1572, and in 1575 they jointly published *Cantiones sacrae*, a collection of Latin motets. Tallis was also one of the first to set English words to psalms, canticles, and anthems. Centuries later, his setting of Psalm 2 was used by Vaughan Williams for his *Fantasia on a Theme of Thomas Tallis* (1910).

Tallis died peacefully at home in 1585. It is thought he was around 80 years of age.

Other key works

1560–1569 *The Lamentations of Jeremiah*
1567 Nine psalm settings for Archbishop Parker's Psalter.

THE ETERNAL FATHER OF ITALIAN MUSIC

CANTICUM CANTICORUM (1584), GIOVANNI DA PALESTRINA

IN CONTEXT

FOCUS
Simplification of polyphony

BEFORE
c.1540 In the motet *Inviolata, integra et casta es Maria*, the Italian composer Costanzo Festa uses canonic Flemish style to great effect. Festa was much admired and imitated by Palestrina.

1545 Franco-Flemish composer Nicolas Gombert publishes *Musae Jovis*, a deliberately archaic piece, as a tribute to Josquin Desprez.

AFTER
1610 Claudio Monteverdi returns to polyphony and the *stile antico* ("old style") with *Missa in illo tempore*.

c.1742 J.S. Bach performs his arrangement of Palestrina's *Missa sine nomine* (1590).

The Protestant reformer Martin Luther influenced sacred music not only in the new Protestant churches, but also, as a result of the Counter-Reformation, in Roman Catholic rites. The Council of Trent, an ecumenical meeting of senior members of the Church in the northern Italian town of Trent between 1545 and 1563, issued guidelines for sacred music that restrained dissonance, curbed excessive ornamentation, and refined liturgical polyphony. The composer who responded most exquisitely to this new call for purity was Giovanni da Palestrina.

New demands
Luther was an accomplished singer and loved music, which, together with the power of the printing press to disseminate his ideas, was key to the success of his reforms. In 1524, his first published hymn, *"Ein newes Lied wir haeben an"* ("We're raising a new song") was a street ballad about the death at the stake in Brussels of two adherents to Protestant reform. Set to a familiar tune, it was far removed from the rich polyphony and instrumental brilliance of Roman Catholic music. Its simple appeal spoke directly to many who felt alienated by the Church's love of wealth and lavish ritual.

Popular, accessible music became a potent vehicle for spreading ideas and rallying support and was also the hallmark of services in the new reformed church. Luther and the French Protestant reformer John Calvin encouraged the singing of hymns to tunes that everyone knew.

Old traditions
This emphasis on simplicity was in sharp contrast to Roman Catholic practice. The less educated would have had the greatest difficulty in following the Masses in a cathedral or ducal chapel of the time. This was a problem that the Roman Catholic churchman, humanist, and scholar Bernardino Cirillo recognized. In 1549, he wrote: "In our times musicians have put all their work and effort into the composition of fugues (where the voices make staggered entries), so that while one voice sings 'Sanctus' another has 'Sabaoth,' and yet one more sings 'Gloria tua.' Howling,

Giovanni da Palestrina

Probably born in the Italian town of Palestrina in 1525, Giovanni Pierluigi da Palestrina had strong family connections to nearby Rome. After his mother's death when he was about 11, he became a chorister at the city's Santa Maria Maggiore church.

In his late teens, Palestrina returned to his hometown to become the organist at the cathedral. When the Bishop of Palestrina, Cardinal Giovanni Maria del Monte, was elected Pope Julius III in 1550, the composer went back to Rome as director of the Capella Giulia: he dedicated his *Missa Ecce sacerdos magnus* to Julius in 1554. The next year he gained a place in the papal choir at the Sistine Chapel and went on to hold several top musical posts. His music includes madrigals and more than 105 masses and 50 motets.

Other key works

1562 *Missa Papae Marcelli*
1570 *Missa brevis*
1572 *Missa Tu es Petrus*
1584 *Pulchra es* (motet)
1590 *Stabat Mater* (motet)

See also: *Messe de Notre Dame* 36–37 ▪ *Missa l'homme armé* 42 ▪ *Missa Pange lingua* 43 ▪ *Spem in alium* 44 ▪ *Great Service* 52–53 ▪ *Ein feste Burg ist unser Gott* 78–79

bellowing, and stammering, they more closely resemble cats in January than flowers in May."

The reform of notation in the 14th century had, for the first time, given composers the ability to set down almost any musical idea with precision. Since then, the Catholic Church had at times encouraged, and at other times censured, their tendency to embellish music and add ever-increasing degrees of complexity and subtlety.

At the end of the 15th century, the daily Mass was usually sung to plainchant. However, if the institution hosting the service had the resources, the Ordinary of the Mass (the *Kyrie*, *Gloria*, *Credo*, *Sanctus*, *Benedictus*, and *Agnus Dei*) might be treated to many varieties of embellishment. In the 1490s, several writers noted the presence of a cornett player at High Mass as part of the chapel of Philip IV of Burgundy. They do not mention what he played; his mere presence, as a wind player in the chapel, was enough to be remarkable. Wind players, who had previously improvised, began to hone their skills in reading music and accompanying such choirs,

so that by the 1530s their presence at a polyphonic High Mass became less unusual to congregants.

While the contribution of wind players to church music would have been impressive, the resonance of a brass ensemble, if badly handled, might hinder the clear delivery of the text. The Spanish composer Francisco Guerrero encouraged his cornett players to improvise florid ornaments but to take turns, as "when they ornament together it makes such absurdities as would stop up the ears."

Little thought for the text

Even when a Mass was sung as unaccompanied polyphony, the clarity of expression favored by

The Council of Trent met 25 times in 18 years to discuss its response to the "heresies" of Protestantism and to clarify Catholic doctrine and liturgy.

Cirillo was not always uppermost in a composer's mind. Franco-Flemish musicians often paraded their skill in handling complex polyphonic structures in compositions of extraordinary virtuosity. In a Mass in four parts, for instance, certain sections might be written in the manuscript with only three parts notated, so that the singer had to "find" the fourth part by following the logic of the other three parts—effectively solving a riddle. The composer might make the singers' job even »

[Palestrina's] *Stabat Mater* ... captivates the human soul.
Franz Liszt

Musical textures

Degrees of complexity
Renaissance composers, aided by more precise notation methods and encouraged by wealthy patrons, produced increasingly multilayered music.

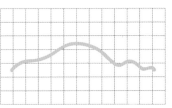

Monophony
Sung by a single singer or single choir in unison. Examples include plainchant and most troubadour songs.

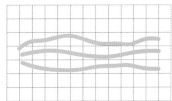

Homophony
Melody supported by chordal harmony and solid bass in the same rhythm. Often used in the singing of hymns.

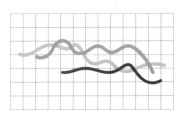

Polyphony
Several parts, which are independent and of equal importance. Forms include the canon, fugue, and motet.

---

harder by writing canonic voices that moved at different speeds from the original. The tour de force here is Johannes Ockeghem's *Missa prolationum*, in which each of the four movements of the Mass explores a different canonic scenario. The interval separating the voices of the canon becomes progressively longer in each consecutive movement

Josquin Desprez's *Missa l'homme armé super voces musicales* provides only one line of music for an elegant and varied three-voice setting of the second repeat of the *Agnus Dei*. The result of three voices singing polyphony woven from a single melody sung at different speeds is extraordinary for its audacity, but the emphasis is not on easily discernible words.

An official response
The Catholic Church dealt with the mounting crisis precipitated by Luther's reforms with a series of meetings to decide what the official response should be. After many delays, the Council convened in the town of Trent in northern Italy in 1545. By the time of the final meeting (1562–1563) overseen by Pope Pius IV, positions had reached a deadlock, and it was

clear that reconciliation between Rome and the Reformers would be impossible.

Yet the Protestant reforms had forced the Roman Catholic Church to introduce changes to doctrine and practice, which included purifying its sacred music. In 1562, a resolution of the Council of Trent laid down guidelines for musicians. This stated: "All things should indeed be so ordered that the Masses, whether they be celebrated with chant or chorally, may reach the ears of listeners and gently penetrate their hearts, when everything is executed clearly and at the right speed. In the case of those Masses, which are celebrated

The Renaissance fostered the growth of personality, an idea fundamentally opposed to the selflessness and objectivity of the old polyphony.
Zoë Kendrick
Biographer of Palestrina

with polyphony and with organ, let nothing profane be intermingled, but only hymns and divine praises." Composers needed to respond to this new directive.

Enhancing the words
Giovanni Pierluigi da Palestrina had published his first book of Masses in 1554 and had returned to Santa Maria Maggiore, where he had first served as a choirboy, as *maestro di cappella* (music director) in 1561. The story runs that he anticipated complete papal censure. Fearing the reduction of music in Catholic liturgy to plainchant alone (a reform a few zealots had called for), he stood ready with a Mass in four voices to demonstrate that polyphony could serve the text in a way that would please even the harshest critics.

The *Missa Papae Marcelli* does appear to date from 1562, the year of the Council's resolution concerning music. It is said that the cardinals found this Mass especially pleasing, approval that gave Palestrina status as the savior of polyphony. It seems, in fact, that the Mass was probably written for Holy Week and complied with Pope Marcellus II's desire for a restrained setting that could be clearly understood in mind.

Palestrina's work fulfils much of what was expected of polyphony in the era after the Council of Trent, with his targeted approach to dissonance, clarity of declamation, and refined command of polyphonic writing. Yet Palestrina did not shy away from taking the new precepts to their limits: his *Missa repleatur os meum* in five voices, published in 1570, shows complete control of the virtuoso "canonic" style favored by the Franco-Flemish composers but with such clear handling of the text that even Cirillo might have approved.

In his *Canticum Canticorum*, composed in 1584, an acclaimed cycle of 29 motets based on the Old Testament's "Song of Solomon,"

Palestrina spent five years as *maestro di cappella* (music director) at St. John Lateran in Rome, depicted in this 17th-century Dutch print.

Palestrina was even more daring. While he referred to it as a sacred piece, he unashamedly embraced a more passionate style, explaining in his dedication to Pope Gregory XIII that this was in keeping with its subject matter.

Elsewhere in Europe

Palestrina was one bright star in a constellation of great polyphonists of the Counter-Reformation. In Spain, the orthodox zeal of Philip II encouraged a strong school of polyphonic composition in its cathedrals. Tomás Luis de Victoria, a prolific composer of sacred works, was renowned for the intense drama of his music. He had been a choirboy and organist in Ávila, before going to Rome, where he may have studied with Palestrina. Later returning to Spain, he spent most of his working life at Madrid's convent of the Descalzas Reales.

The German states were greatly split in their religious allegiance; the Southern principalities still adhered to Rome. Duke Albrecht V of Bavaria, a leading figure of the German Counter-Reformation, for example, employed many musicians including Orlande de Lassus, a Flemish composer renowned as a child for the beauty of his singing voice. Under generous ducal patronage, Lassus directed the Hofkapelle, combining voices, violins, viols, lute, a variety of brass and woodwind instruments, and even a rackett (a newly invented, gently buzzing bass reed instrument). Such a large ensemble of almost orchestral ambition would have been highly unusual for the time. If the Catholic Church looked askance at such instrumentation, its guidelines were obviously open to a degree of local interpretation. ∎

THAT IS THE NATURE OF HYMNS—THEY MAKE US WANT TO REPEAT THEM

GREAT SERVICE (c. 1580/1590), WILLIAM BYRD

IN CONTEXT

FOCUS
English Protestant church music

BEFORE
1558 John Sheppard composes his *Second Service*, a setting for five voices of the "full" service (rather than the customary short service comprising only settings of the *Magnificat* and *Nunc dimittis*) and precursor to Byrd's 10-voice *Great Service*.

c.1570 William Mundy composes his Evening Service *In medio chori* for a choir in nine parts, expanding to 11 parts at times.

AFTER
c.1620 Thomas Weelkes publishes *Evensong for Seven Voices*, a Great Service in up to 10 parts.

c.1630 Thomas Tomkins's *Third or Great Service* for 10 voices is the grandest work in the genre.

Although William Byrd is believed to have been a Catholic for most, if not all, of his life, he composed music for the Anglican Church in addition to motets and Masses in Latin for the Catholic rite. He lived through three eras of religious revisionism in England. Under Henry VIII and then Edward VI, the country had been Protestant since 1534, but in 1553 Mary Tudor acceded to the throne with her husband Philip II of Spain and reinstated Catholicism. When Mary died in 1558, Elizabeth I returned England to Protestantism. However, Elizabeth was tolerant of Catholicism among the country's gentry if they were loyal and practiced it discreetly. She sanctioned the use of Latin for services at the Chapel Royal, and

The seeds of Protestantism in England were sown by Martin Luther, the architect of the Reformation in Germany, shown here playing music with his children.

See also: *Missa l'homme armé* 42 ▪ *Missa Pange lingua* 43 ▪ *Canticum Canticorum* 46–51 ▪ *Ein feste Burg ist unser Gott* 78–79

To a man thinking about divine things … the most fitting measures come, I know not how, as if by their own free will.
William Byrd

composers were permitted to use Latin as well as English when writing liturgical music.

Byrd flourished under Elizabeth's patronage. By 1565, he was the organist and master at Lincoln Cathedral, where he produced his *Short Service*, settings for Matins, Communion, and Evensong, amounting to the greater part of music in English for the Anglican liturgy. Later, when Byrd was a Gentleman of the Chapel Royal, Elizabeth granted Byrd and his fellow composer Thomas Tallis, who was also a Catholic, a monopoly on music production in England.

God and queen

Concern about Byrd's religious adherence did become an issue, however, in 1577, when Byrd's wife, Julian, was accused of failing to attend a service by the Bishop of London, John Aylmer, a rigorous enforcer of the Act of Uniformity of 1559, which aimed to unify the Anglican Church. From then on, Byrd did not make a secret of his Catholic faith, and the reception for the first publication of Latin "sacred songs" in 1575 was lukewarm, perhaps because of the Catholic sentiment of some of the texts.

In spite of his Catholicism, Byrd's loyalty to queen and country appears to have taken precedence over his religious adherence. In thanksgiving for the victory of the English fleet over the Spanish Armada in 1588, Elizabeth composed a song titled "Look, and Bow Down Thine Ear, O Lord." It is thought that she chose William Byrd to set it to music. Although the anthem is now lost, it would have been a clear demonstration of her high regard for him.

Last Anglican work

In 1580, Byrd published his *Great Service*, his last work for the Anglican rite. A monumental composition, the *Great Service* comprises seven sections for an Anglican celebration of the mass in English for two five-voice choirs. It is not known if Byrd wrote his *Great Service* with any particular choir or occasion in mind. However, the sheer scale of the piece and the technical requirement of the writing would have put it beyond the reach of all but the largest choirs. Some hear it as a farewell to colleagues, or a last act of contrition to a monarch who had chosen to overlook Byrd's Catholicism.

In 1605, a messenger carrying a copy of Byrd's newly published *Gradualia* (a collection of settings of movements of the Mass for the Catholic church year, for three to five voices) was apprehended and thrown in Newgate gaol. The composer, however, avoided imprisonment, facing only pressure in the courts and heavy fines. ▪

William Byrd

Born into a large merchant family in London in 1540, William Byrd most likely gained his musical training as one of 10 boy choristers at London's St. Paul's Church (the Gothic predecessor of St. Paul's Cathedral), before going on to sing for Catholic ceremonies at the Chapel Royal under Queen Mary. Later, in 1572, during Elizabeth I's reign, Byrd became a Gentleman of the Chapel Royal, a post he held for more than 20 years.

While Byrd composed much secular music, including works for virginals, he is best known for his religious music. In 1575, he and Thomas Tallis published a first volume of Latin motets, *Cantiones Sacrae* (Sacred Songs). After Tallis's death, Byrd continued the series with two volumes of his own Cantiones in 1589 and 1591. Byrd published his last work, *Psalmes, Songs, and Sonnets* in 1611, 12 years before his death in 1623.

Other key works

1589 *Cantiones sacrae, Book 1*
1591 *Cantiones sacrae, Book 2*
1605 *Gradualia*

ALL THE AIRS AND MADRIGALS ... WHISPER SOFTNESS

O CARE, THOU WILT DESPATCH ME (1600), THOMAS WEELKES

IN CONTEXT

FOCUS
Madrigals

BEFORE
1571 Thomas Whythorne publishes *Songes*, the first collection of English madrigals.

1594 Thomas Morley publishes his *First Book of Madrigals to Four Voices*, the first collection to use the Italian description of the style.

AFTER
1612 Orlando Gibbons publishes his *First Set of Madrigals and Motets*; it includes "The Silver Swan," a short madrigal but one of the best known today.

1620–1649 The fashion for the English madrigal waned, giving way to the lute song, and the style vanished with the establishment of the Commonwealth of England from 1649.

I n 1544, at a time when England was hungry for Continental fashions, the composer and poet Thomas Whythorne toured Europe and wrote sonnets that he later set to music in *Songs*, the first book of English madrigals.

In Italy, the masters of the madrigal style included Philippe Verdelot and Jacob Arcadelt, whose works appeared in the earliest book of Italian madrigals, published in Rome in 1530. In 1588, Nicholas Yonge published his *Musica transalpina*, a collection of Italian madrigals reworked with English texts, whetting an appetite for homegrown songs sung in parts.

Illustrating the words

Many English collections followed, often arranged for voices and viols to satisfy a growing middle-class taste for after-dinner music making. In 1595, Thomas Morley introduced the ballett, a rustic madrigal with a *fa-la-la* chorus in imitation of an instrumental refrain. Thomas Weelkes, among others, began to use musical effects to illustrate the text—known as "word painting." In *O Care, Thou Wilt Despatch Me* (1600), Weelkes describes the poet's disturbed state of mind in sliding semitones (chromaticism) at odds with the cheerful *fa-la-la* refrain.

In Italy, the madrigals of Carlo Gesualdo da Venosa use extreme harmonic shifts and dissonance to paint words, while the *Madrigali guerrieri et amorosi* (1638) of Claudio Monteverdi lift the form to theatrical heights. ∎

Madrigal ... music made upon songs and sonnets ... to men of understanding most delightful.
Thomas Morley

See also: *Le jeu de Robin et de Marion* 32–35 ▪ *Musique de table* 106 ▪ *Die schöne Müllerin* 150–155

THIS FEAST ... DID EVEN RAVISH AND STUPEFIE ALL THOSE STRANGERS THAT NEVER HEARD THE LIKE
SONATA PIAN' E FORTE (1597), GIOVANNI GABRIELI

The Basilica of St. Mark's in Venice provides a dramatic setting for composers exploring instrumental timbre and the use of space. The Flemish composer Adrian Willaert was the first to exploit its potential when he became musical director there in 1527. His chori spezzati ("split choirs") style divided the ensemble around the galleries, giving performances a greater theatricality. Learning the chori spezzati style from Willaert, Andrea

Renaissance recorders were often used to accompany songs. This image from *Musica getutscht* (1511), a treatise on music theory by Sebastian Virdung, illustrates fingering on the instrument.

Gabrieli, appointed organist of St. Mark's in 1566, and his nephew Giovanni Gabrieli, employed the Venetian ensembles of *pifferi* (civic wind players) both to reinforce a vocal ensemble or for purely instrumental purposes.

Dramatic impact
In the past, civic trumpeters had mostly just sounded the curfew and played for dances. As Renaissance cities and nation-states jostled for power, the role of their instrumentalists became more important. Music making of the highest order was encouraged, and in this Venice became preeminent.

Giovanni Gabrieli's *Sonata pian' e forte* (1597), for six trombones, a cornett, and a *viola da braccio* (early violin), was the first work for specific brass instruments and the first to include dynamic indications of loudness and softness for the players, adding dramatic light and shade effects. In the shimmering shadows of St. Mark's, such an intense sonata might accompany the consecration of the Host. ∎

See also: *Canticum Canticorum* 46–51 ▪ *Water Music* 84–89 ▪ *The Four Seasons* 92–97 ▪ *St. Matthew Passion* 98–105 ▪ *Elijah* 170–173

MY LUTE, AWAKE!

LACHRIMAE (1604), JOHN DOWLAND

FOCUS
Renaissance instrumental music

BEFORE
1507 Francesco Spinacino's *Intabulatura de lauto* is published in Venice—the first printed collections for solo lute.

1545 The appointment of "Mark Anthony Gayiardell and George Decombe, viallines" as court musicians marks the debut of the violin in England.

AFTER
1611 Giovanni Girolamo Kapsberger publishes his *Libro primo d'intavolatura de lauto*, music for the theorbo—a lute with an extended neck to hold additional bass strings.

c.1630 English composer John Jenkins produces his pavans and *In nomines* for viol consort in up to six parts, continuing an English interest in music for viol consort that lasts into the time of Henry Purcell.

M usical instruments developed rapidly from the late 14th century onward, as musicians refined their skills and emulated court style to attract patronage. The first organ with pedals and 12-note chromatic keyboard was recorded in the German town of Halberstadt in 1361. Around 1440, while working in the Burgundian court, Dutch organist Arnaut van Zwolle drew a diagram of the earliest harpsichord, with keys that lifted vertical pieces of wood, called jacks, fitted with

Blame not my lute,
for he must sound
Of this or that as liketh me;
For lack of wit with
the lute is bound
To give such tunes as
pleaseth me.
Thomas Wyatt

plectrums that then plucked strings. Zwolle also described the *dulce melos*, a keyboard instrument in which the strings were struck by metal mallets, the earliest recorded use of a piano-style action.

The rise of the lute
Beyond these innovations, the more portable lute evolved to become the emblematic instrument of the Renaissance. Pietrobono, a much-feted musician to the Este family of Ferrara around 1450–1470, had played virtuosic streams of melody (not unlike fast electric guitar solos) with a quill plectrum, while an accompanist called a *tenorista* played the slow, accompanying lower parts on another lute. The addition of gut frets, tied around the neck of the lute, facilitated left-hand speed and accuracy.

A more significant stylistic change occurred when the lutenist put down the plectrum. Stroking the strings with the thumb and fingers of the right hand, the soloist could play all the voices of a polyphonic piece. By the late 15th century, the lute was no longer simply the companion of minstrels but had moved to the heart of court music and composition.

See also: *Le jeu de Robin et de Marion* 32–35 ▪ Gabrieli's *Sonata pian' e forte* 55 ▪ *Le bourgeois gentilhomme* 70–71 ▪ Stamitz's Symphony in E-flat major 116–117

Renaissance consort instruments, including the lute and strings, are shown in *Hearing* (c.1617–1618), a collaboration between Jan Brueghel the Elder and Paul Rubens.

The 16th-century lute at first had six courses (a single string for the highest note, then five pairs of strings tuned in unison or octaves), then gained extra courses in the bass called diapasons, tuned diatonically (by steps of one tone).

The English connection

By the turn of the 17th century, John Dowland was one of a number of composers who were writing for a lute with nine courses. England excelled in the new style of lute playing, which was also popular with amateur players, including Elizabeth I, who is shown playing the instrument in a miniature painted by Nicholas Hilliard.

Dowland composed around 90 works for the lute alone but also incorporated the instrument into a wider ensemble, known as a consort. His collection *Lachrimae* (1604) develops the composer's own *Lachrimae* pavan (a dance with stately music often treated to instrumental elaboration) to create seven melancholy variations, scored for a string ensemble with solo lute. Renaissance ensembles usually comprised consorts of the same instrument, but Dowland imagined for his *Lachrimae* pavans either six viols or six violins, including the bass violin, forerunner of the cello.

Dances like the pavan and the triple-time galliard were used by keyboard players and composers to show their skill at improvisation, usually playing "divisions" (variations) on the repeat of a section. *My Ladye Nevells Booke* (1591) by the English composer William Byrd contains 10 pavan—galliard pairs with variations for the virginal, an instrument related to the harpsichord. ▪

John Dowland

It has been variously claimed that Dowland was born in 1563 in Westminster (London) or Dalkey (Ireland), and his early life remains obscure. He spent his late teens in service to the English ambassador in France, where he embraced Catholicism, later claiming that this conversion prevented his appointment as lutenist at the English royal court in 1594. Dowland then set off for three years on a European tour, before finding an appreciative patron in Christian IV of Denmark. The relationship later soured, and Dowland was dismissed in 1606.

Although his son, the composer and lutenist Robert Dowland, described his father in 1610 as "being now gray, and like the Swan, but singing toward his end," Dowland was, within two years, made one of the lutenists of King James I of England and Scotland. Between that appointment and his death, in 1625, few compositions survive.

Other key works

1597 *Firste Booke of Songes or Ayres*
1612 *A Pilgrim's Solace*

BAROQ

1600–1750

The earliest surviving opera, **Jacopo Peri's** *Euridice*, is composed in honor of King Henry IV of France and his marriage to Maria de' Medici.

Jean-Baptiste Lully's *Le bourgeois gentilhomme* satirizes social climbing and the snobbish aristocracy of France under Louis XIV.

Danish-German composer **Dieterich Buxtehude's** organ prelude *Ein feste Burg ist unser Gott* greatly influences the chorale genre.

Handel premieres his suite of short pieces *Water Music* on a barge on the Thames River, hosted by King George I.

1600   **1670**   **c.1690**   **1717**

1610   **1689**   **1714**

Claudio Monteverdi's *Vespers* incorporates polyphony and monody, bridging the Renaissance and Baroque styles.

Henry Purcell's opera *Dido and Aeneas* relates the mythical love affair between the Queen of Carthage and the Prince of Troy.

The publication of **Arcangelo Corelli's** *Twelve concerti grossi,* Op. 6, establishes the concerto grosso as a style of composition.

The Baroque period of music started dramatically, with the performance of the world's first opera, Jacopo Peri's *Dafne*, staged in Florence in 1598. The opera illustrates the dramatic change in musical style from polyphony to something more expressive—a change exploited to great effect in Monteverdi's *Vespers*, which contrasts sections in the old and new styles.

Key developments

One of the main features of the Early Baroque period, and one that must have been startling at the time, was a rejection of polyphony in favor of a single line of melody with a simple accompaniment. This "monody," as it was called, was an attempt to reproduce the style of Classical Greek drama. The accompaniment was of particular significance: in the recitative sections of early opera—the freely composed expositions of the plot that connected the arias—the voice was accompanied by a single bass instrument, such as a cello, and an instrument capable of playing chords, such as a harpsichord or lute. This accompaniment, known as the "basso continuo," or simply continuo, became a key feature of music in the Early Baroque period.

The importance of the continuo was that it provided a harmonic base for the melody. While Renaissance music had been characterized by polyphony, the new style was defined by harmony. In place of interweaving melodies based on the ancient Greek scales or modes, early Baroque composers built their music on major and minor chords. Dramatic and contrasting effects were achieved by varying the loudness and tempo, moving the music between keys and instruments, and sometimes adding embellishments such as trills.

The revolutionary new style and the idea of a drama set to music proved very popular, especially among the aristocracy in Italy and France, who employed a staff of musicians and a resident composer to provide entertainment in the courts. In addition to operas, they performed instrumental music, and in the royal court at Versailles, Jean-Baptiste Lully assembled an orchestra to provide incidental music and dances for the performance of the latest comedies by playwrights such as Molière. This form of light

Antonio Vivaldi's *Le quattro stagioni* (*The Four Seasons*) is published with accompanying program notes to critical acclaim.

Georg Philipp Telemann handles a diverse range of musical genres in his celebrated *Musique de table*.

In the last decade of his life, **J.S. Bach** writes *The Art of Fugue*, comprising 14 fugues and four canons.

1725

1733

c.1742–1750

1717–1723

1727

1733

François Couperin, of the renowned Couperin family of musicians, publishes four volumes of harpsichord orders in the *Pièces de Clavecin*.

J.S. Bach's sacred oratorio *St. Matthew Passion* sets chapters 26 and 27 of the Gospel of Matthew to music.

The success of **Jean-Philippe Rameau's** *Hippolyte et Aricie* challenges the dominance of Italian opera.

---

entertainment caught on elsewhere and influenced the development of the musical drama known as a "masque" in England.

Since the Reformation, opera had been frowned upon by Protestants, and in the Germanic countries, musical activity was largely restricted to the Church. Gradually, though, a distinctly German Baroque style, very different from the Italian and French, evolved from the chorale, the hymn tunes of the Lutheran Church, uniting the harmonic treatment of the new style of vocal music with some elements of the old Italian polyphony.

This hybrid style was more suited to the northern European temperament and soon became accepted into Protestant church music. It inspired the development of the instrumental chorale prelude, a sometimes florid setting of a chorale melody, usually for organ.

High and Late Baroque

As time passed, many elements of the Early Baroque period disappeared. By about 1700, the period referred to as the "High Baroque" had begun. What had been a small accompanying group for opera singers had taken on a life of its own as an orchestra of stringed, woodwind, and brass instruments, playing a new form of music, the "concerto grosso," made popular by Arcangelo Corelli and Antonio Vivaldi. The continuo, while still acting as the harmonic backbone of the orchestra, had also become an independent chamber ensemble, playing a form of music known as the "trio sonata." Opera itself had been hijacked, appearing instead as unstaged choral works such as the secular cantata and the sacred oratorio.

The Late Baroque period was dominated by three composers born in Germany in 1685. The first, Georg Philipp Telemann is often overshadowed by his contemporaries but was by far the most prolific. The second was George Frideric Handel, a populist who made his name in England with his oratorios and orchestral music. The third, regarded by musicians as the greatest of the three, was Johann Sebastian Bach: a conservative composer but a consummate craftsman. During a lifetime of employment by courts and the Church, Bach's sacred and secular music represented the high point of the Baroque period. ∎

ONE OF THE MOST MAGNIFICENT AND EXPENSEFULL DIVERSIONS
EURIDICE (1600), JACOPO PERI

The conditions for the birth of opera were right in Florence in the 1590s. Large-scale theatrical entertainments utilizing music, known as *intermedi*, often performed as interludes during spoken plays, were commissioned for dynastic celebrations, such as weddings and baptisms. Their musical sections—songs (or "arias"), dances, and choruses—were themselves interspersed with spoken dialogue. It was the

Orpheus and Eurydice climb out of the Underworld in Edward Poynter's painting of 1862. The Greek myth was a particularly apt subject for opera because Orpheus was a musician.

introduction of recitative (*recitar cantando*), the art of speaking in song, that defined opera.

Florentine intellectual societies, most notably the Camerata de' Bardi, which met at the house of patron, playwright, and composer Giovanni de' Bardi, had included in

See also: *Le bourgeois gentilhomme* 70–71 ▪ *Dido and Aeneas* 72–77 ▪
Orfeo ed Euridice 118–119 ▪ *The Magic Flute* 134–137 ▪ *The Barber of Seville* 148

their humanist debates discussions about the nature of Greek drama, which they concluded was sung throughout. Peri wrote *La Dafne* (1598) with composer Jacopo Corsi and poet Ottavio Rinuccini in an attempt to revive this practice.

Elements of opera

While only fragments of *La Dafne* exist today, Peri's second work, *Euridice*, survives intact. The libretto of *Euridice* tells the Greek myth of Orpheus, who enters the Underworld to retrieve his wife Eurydice after her death from snakebite. *Euridice* offers the standard *intermedio* combination of songs alternating with choruses and instrumental passages, but these are linked by recitatives— the new style of sung speech. In his preface to the work, Peri described his intention of "imitating speech with song," which was the bedrock of the new genre. He also listed some of the instruments played in the original production, such as harpsichord, chitarrone (bass lute), violin, lyre, and lute, although other

It creates a coherent world, highly charged with a distinctive atmosphere. It is simple without being vapid, and dignified without being portentous.
Stephen Oliver

Singing his works composed with the greatest artifice ... moved and disposed every stony heart to tears.
Severo Bonini

instruments may also have been used. The performance included sections composed by Peri's rival at court, Giulio Caccini, who had trained several of the singers. Caccini even made his own musical setting of the libretto and had it printed prior to Peri's. The publication of these scores ensured the opera's survival.

In Peri's footsteps

The new form represented by *Euridice* was repeated in Florence and emulated elsewhere. In Mantua in 1607, Claudio Monteverdi, master of music at the city's ducal court, produced *L'Orfeo*, which is regarded as the first operatic masterpiece. Monteverdi later composed three further works for the Venetian opera houses—*Il ritorno d'Ulisse in patria*, *L'incoronazione di Poppea*, and one now lost—exemplifying the new style. Soon Monteverdi's followers, such as Francesco Cavalli and Antonio Cesti, were producing operas in Italy and abroad, with the basic construction blocks of recitatives and arias holding the structure together. ▪

Jacopo Peri

Born into a noble family in 1561, Jacopo Peri grew up in Florence. As a teenager, he played the organ and sang at various churches and monasteries in the city before beginning a lifelong association with the Medici court as singer, accompanist, and composer. In 1598, he produced *La Dafne*, followed two years later by *Euridice* for the wedding festivities of Maria de' Medici and Henry IV of France. Peri also composed for the musically distinguished Mantuan court.

Peri often collaborated with other composers, such as the brothers Giovanni Battista da Gagliano and Marco da Gagliano. While only a small handful of these works survive as testament to Peri's talent, they nonetheless laid down the template that later opera composers would follow. Peri died in Florence in 1633. His gravestone in the Florentine church of Santa Maria Novella describes him as the inventor of opera.

Other key works

1598 *La Dafne*
1609 *Le varie musiche*

MUSIC
MUST MOVE
THE WHOLE MAN
VESPERS (1610), CLAUDIO MONTEVERDI

Monteverdi's *Vespers for the Blessed Virgin* of 1610 is one of the most influential collections of sacred works for voices and instruments of the 17th century. No larger choral work had been written before, and none as long nor as innovative appeared again until J.S. Bach's Passions and Handel's oratorios in the 18th century.

Choral leap

Written for vespers, the early evening service in the Catholic Church, in particular vespers in honor of the Virgin Mary, Monteverdi's *Vespers* marks the transition from the old polyphonic ("many voices") style known as *prima pratica* ("first practice") of the Renaissance, in which all voices are equal, to the freer Baroque style

Cremona Cathedral, where the young Monteverdi is thought to have studied composition under the choirmaster Marc'Antonio Ingegneri.

known as *seconda pratica* ("second practice"), with its emphasis on solo voice. In the latter, harmonies became more adventurous, with greater use of monody, in which a melody was underpinned by an instrumental "continuo," or bass line, in the form of the organ, harpsichord, or lute. The bass lines also became more melodic. Embellishments, which had previously been improvised by the performer, were more elaborate and often fully notated by the composer.

These developments led to the distinct musical characteristics of the Baroque period, in which irregularity and extreme expression sometimes disturb the smooth musical flow, compelling the attention of listeners. Contrasts of melody, texture, timbre, tempo, and rhythm abound in Baroque music. In addition, instruments assumed a more important role and their music was more idiomatic, reflecting greater technique and better-made, more reliable instruments.

See also: Plainchant 22–23 ▪ *Magnus liber organi 28–31* ▪ *Messe de Notre Dame 36–37* ▪ *Missa Pange lingua 43* ▪ *Canticum Canticorum 46–51*

> The end of all good music
> is to affect the soul.
> **Claudio Monteverdi**

The new style was taken up in most forms of music. The greater use of figured bass (numerals and symbols, indicating the harmonies to be played by the continuo player) lent themselves to opera and oratorio. In vocal music, the melody projected the thoughts, emotions, actions, and reactions of a character in an opera, or even in an accompanied song.

The new emphasis on character led to the development of the accompanied sonata (including the trio sonata, comprising two violins and a cello), the solo recitative and aria, and the concerto—indeed, any musical form showcasing one particular performer among a group. This stylistic development emphasized contrast, allowing for wider emotional expression in vocal music and for more rhythmic variation in expressing and projecting the text. It stimulated experimentation among composers, who explored increasing instrumental virtuosity.

Sacred music

While the old polyphonic style continued to be widely used in European church music during the first half of the 17th century, a new style called *concertato* style, contrasting multiple choirs and instrumentalists, developed in Venice and spread to Germany. In England, this new trend was reflected in the verse-anthem, in which "verses" for solo voices alternated with choral passages.

A virtuosic vespers

Monteverdi's *Vespers* was one of the first pieces of sacred music to exploit the rich possibilities of seconda pratica, but the composer did not forget the advantages of prima pratica and set the texts that are strictly liturgical in traditional plainsong. The usual musical sequence for the vespers service consisted of eight movements, starting with an opening "versicle" that began with the words *"Deus in adjutorium meum intende"* ("God make speed to save us"). The original 1610 edition of *Vespers* contains 13 movements, and includes a version of the Magnificat for six voices and organ. In addition to music for vespers itself, the volume includes an *a cappella* ("in the chapel," or unaccompanied) Mass setting—*Missa in Illo Tempore*—based upon a motet of the same name by the Renaissance composer Nicolas Gombert. (Mass and vespers were the two services of the Roman Catholic liturgy most elaborately set in late 16th- and early 17th-century Italy.)

Within the 13 movements of *Vespers*, Monteverdi sets five psalms that honor the Virgin Mary, together with *Ave Maris Stella* (Hail Star of the Sea), an eighth-century hymn to Mary that precedes the Magnificat in the official set of daily prayers, and the Magnificat itself. Monteverdi »

Claudio Monteverdi

Born in Cremona in 1567, Monteverdi began composing music while still a teenager, producing a collection of three-part motets and a book of madrigals. These achievements enabled him to leave Cremona to become a string player at the court of Duke Vincenzo Gonzaga in Mantua, where he was influenced by the court's *maestro di cappella* (music director), Giaches de Wert, and started writing operas. In 1607, his first opera, *L'Orfeo* was performed in Mantua, followed by *L'Arianna* in 1608.

After Gonzaga's death in 1612, Monteverdi went to Rome, where he presented his *Vespers* to the Pope. The following year he became maestro di cappella at St. Mark's, Venice. His final opera *L'incoronazione di Poppea* was performed in 1642, the year before he died.

Other key works

1605 Fifth Book of Madrigals
1607 *L'Orfeo*
1640–1641 *Selva morale e spirituale*
1642 *L'incoronazione di Poppea*

uses plainsong (single line unaccompanied Latin chants, associated today with monks and monasteries) as the basis of the seven sections. The repeated return to plainsong provides a compositional thread that connects the very different Renaissance and early Baroque styles. It also helped ensure that his work would not alienate the Church.

Sacred concertos

In addition to Monteverdi's five psalm settings, the *Ave Maris Stella* setting, and the Magnificat, he set four antiphons—short sentences sung or recited before or after a psalm or canticle. The first two (non-liturgical—not part of the service) antiphons come from the Old Testament's Song of Solomon. They are *Nigra Sum, sed Formosa* (I am Black but Comely) and *Pulchra Es* (Thou Art Fair), sung by two sopranos whose lines interweave as if in a love duet.

In the third antiphon, *Duo Seraphim*, two angels call across the heavens, and in the fourth, *Audi Coelum* (Hear, O Heaven), the endings of the words sung by one tenor are echoed by another,

Monteverdi dedicated and presented his *Vespers* to Pope Paul V, a member of the powerful Borghese family, possibly in the hope of commissions.

creating an other-worldly effect. For example, the first singer's *"gaudio"* (joy) is echoed as *"audio"* (I hear). Devices such as repeated phrases for emphasis might have appeared in an opera.

The vesper settings are completed by the *Sonata sopra Sancta Maria* ("Sonata on [the plainsong] Holy Mary, Pray for Us"). Together, the four antiphons and the Sonata were described by Monteverdi as "sacred concertos." "Sonata" and "concerto" are terms that date from the 18th century,

when they had slightly different meanings and usage from today. Until around 1650, "sonata" was used interchangeably with "canzona," an instrumental composition employing repetition, while "concerto" simply meant an ensemble piece for voices and instruments.

Monteverdi's intentions

It is not known whether Monteverdi expected to hear the *Vespers* sung as a complete work. There is little evidence that any of the 1610 publication was actually performed during his lifetime and it is not known whether the vesper movements were ever performed together. Some scholars have suggested that *Vespers* is simply a collection of religious settings honoring the Virgin Mary, which were published together for convenience. The publication may have been intended by the composer as two works—Vespers and Mass—complete in their own right, and also as a compendium of sacred music from which to draw movements for different occasions when expert singers and instrumentalists were

The Family in Concert, c.1752, by the Venetian artist Pietro Longhi, who specialized in contemporary domestic scenes.

Music in Venice

Few other cities in Europe have a longer or more glorious musical tradition than Venice. In the Baroque age, it was a major center of the arts and a powerful trading hub, with a great tradition of church and state ceremonies requiring music. The fame of Venetian composers, such as Andrea and Giovanni Gabrieli, Monteverdi, and Vivaldi, rivals that of the city's artists—Bellini, Titian, Veronese, Tintoretto, and Tiepolo. Opera first found a mass following in the city, with the

opening of the world's first opera house, the Teatro di San Cassiana, in 1637.

In the 19th century, Rossini saw some of his greatest triumphs in Venice, while Wagner, a regular visitor who later died in the city, composed *Tristan und Isolde* here, and Verdi premiered *Rigoletto* (1851) and *La traviata* (1853) at Teatro La Fenice, the chief opera house from 1792. In the 20th century, Stravinsky's *The Rake's Progress* (1951) and Benjamin Britten's *The Turn of the Screw* (1953) were also premiered here.

> I would rather be
> moderately praised for
> the new style than
> greatly praised for
> the ordinary.
> **Claudio Monteverdi**

available, such as at a court like Mantua, St. Peter's in Rome, or St. Mark's in Venice. A minimum of ten voices is required to perform *Vespers*, and instrumental and vocal parts require enormous dexterity. For the more "choral" sections, such as *Laudate Pueri*, *Dixit Dominus*, and the closing movement of the Magnificat,

A page from a manuscript shows Monteverdi's handwritten notation for *L'incoronazione di Poppea* ("The Coronation of Poppea") of 1642, his last work before his death in 1643.

some performances contrast large choirs with smaller ensembles using the *cori spezzati* (separated choirs) technique to create a "stereo" effect. Instruments are only specified for certain sections of the work: the opening fanfare borrowed from Monteverdi's opera *Orfeo* of 1607; the Sonata; and sections of the Magnificat.

Voices and instruments

Contemporaries were sometimes critical of Monteverdi's change in style from the traditional prima pratica to the more operatic seconda pratica technique he used in the sacred concertos and also in his madrigals. They may have found this sort of writing too ostentatious for religious music.

One writer, Giovanni Artusi, attacked the Baroque style, quoting madrigals by Monteverdi in support of his arguments. He found the use of dissonance, unorthodox key changes, and irregular cadences objectionable. However, Monteverdi did not see the two techniques as radically different: they were both ways of setting a text expressively and of being faithful to it. ■

From the Renaissance to the Baroque

The Monteverdi *Vespers* builds on traditional **Gregorian plainchant** structure.

It adds **virtuoso music** for solo singers, creating a more emphatic, expressive effect.

This freer expression is supplemented by **improvisational flourishes** and dramatic devices.

A greater **emphasis on harmony** leads to a freer compositional technique.

The ultimate effect is a **grand public sound** …

… that builds upon traditional structures to create a new choral style.

LULLY MERITS WITH GOOD REASON THE TITLE OF PRINCE OF FRENCH MUSICIANS
LE BOURGEOIS GENTILHOMME (1670), JEAN-BAPTISTE LULLY

IN CONTEXT

FOCUS
French Baroque

BEFORE
1626 Les vingt-quatre violons du roi, the King's orchestra, is founded—an ensemble in which Lully later performs.

1647 The premiere is held of Luigi Rossi's opera *Orpheus*, the first opera commissioned by the French court.

AFTER
1691 Henry Purcell composes his opera *King Arthur*, with "shivering" effects in the violins, allegedly influenced by Lully's opera *Isis*.

1693 Marc-Antoine Charpentier's opera *Médée* is indebted to Lully's style.

1733 Jean-Philippe Rameau's *Hippolyte et Aricie* is the first French opera to depart from Lully's style and the first piece of music to be described as "Baroque."

The 1670 *comédie-ballet Le bourgeois gentilhomme*, devised by the French composer Jean-Baptiste Lully and the playwright and actor Molière, represents the high point of this specifically French genre. It was the culmination of a series of comedy-ballets by the two men who were known as *Les deux Baptistes* (Molière's real name being Jean Baptiste Poquelin). The *comédie-ballet* genre mixed spoken drama with music and dance, ballet having long been enjoyed at the court of King Louis XIV.

The story of *Le bourgeois gentilhomme*, the foolish Monsieur Jourdain, who has delusions of grandeur, is told through a mixture of spoken dialogue written by Molière, interspersed with lively orchestral interludes and dances by Lully. The choruses and solo arias were the work of both men.

Dramatic skill
Lully was a skilled musician, dancer, and actor, and this is evident in his compositions. Instead of merely accompanying the singers, Lully's orchestra enhances the drama of his works, commenting on the actions of the characters and creating a sense of place and occasion. His earlier *Ballet des Muses* (1666) anticipated the rise of the concerto, by pitting solo instrumental passages against alternating orchestral responses.

Examples of virtuosity and complexity are often evident in *Le bourgeois gentilhomme*, particularly in the quickfire exchanges between characters, in the whirling violin and flute ornamentations of the Spanish tunes, and in the stately flourishes of the overture. Over the course of five acts, Lully uses every tool at his disposal, from popular dance forms, such as jigs and minuets, to drinking songs and even a

I do not believe there is any sweeter music under the heaven than Lully's.
Madame de Sévigné
French aristocrat (1626–1696)

See also: *Le jeu de Robin et de Marion* 32–35 ▪ *Euridice* 62–63 ▪ *Hippolyte et Aricie* 107 ▪ *Orfeo ed Euridice* 118–119 ▪ *The Magic Flute* 134–137 ▪ *The Barber of Seville* 148 ▪ *Der Freischütz* 149 ▪ *La traviata* 174–175 ▪ *Tosca* 194–197

A skilled violinist, Lully performed in his own works. He is thought to be the man holding the violin in François Puget's painting of 1688.

grandiose "Turkish" march with lively percussion. Although Lully was not the innovator of musical "orientalism," he is widely credited with spreading its influence in the 18th century. His use of a scene-setting *overture*—an orchestral, marchlike introduction usually to allow for royal pageantry and homage to be paid—became a standard musical feature for almost all subsequent operas.

Enter the conductor

Lully's increased instrumentation, with five-part strings, woodwind, and percussion, meant that *Le bourgeois gentilhomme* was one of the earliest pieces of music to require a conductor to coordinate the timing of both singers and orchestra. Indeed, there is an etching of Lully's later opera, *Alceste*, premiered in 1674, that shows a man "beating time" on the floor with a staff. Unfortunately for Lully, it was this vigorous method of musical direction that precipitated his untimely demise. In March 1687, he died from a gangrenous wound that developed after a blow to his toe while beating time as he conducted his own *Te Deum*. ▪

Jean-Baptiste Lully

Born into a family of Florentine millers in 1632, Giovanni Battista Lulli began his rise through French society when he gained a position as a servant at the French court at the age of 14. He attracted the attention of Louis XIV, with whom he later danced in courtly spectacles. By 1661, he had been placed in charge of court music, at which point he gallicized his name. Lully's monopoly on French opera enabled him to produce multiple works of his own creation. His prolific output before his early death in 1687 also included chamber music and sacred works.

Other key works

1663 *Miserere mei Deus*
1674 *Alceste*
1677 *Te Deum*
1686 *Armide*

HE HAD A PECULIAR GENIUS TO EXPRESS THE ENERGY OF ENGLISH WORDS

DIDO AND AENEAS (c.1683–1689), HENRY PURCELL

IN CONTEXT

FOCUS
Baroque opera in England

BEFORE
1617 *Lovers Made Men*, a masque by Ben Jonson, is set to music by Nicholas Lanier in the Italian recitative style.

1656 *The Siege of Rhodes*, by five composers, is considered the first English opera, but is called "recitative music" to avoid the Puritan ban on plays.

c.1683 John Blow's *Venus and Adonis* is premiered at Charles II's court.

1685 *Albion and Albanius,* with a libretto by John Dryden set to music by Louis Grabu, is the earliest full-length English opera to survive in its entirety.

AFTER
1705 Jakob Greber's *Gli amori d'Ergasto* is the first Italian opera produced in London.

1711 Handel premieres the Italian opera *Rinaldo*, his first work for the London stage.

Dido and Aeneas is one of the most original expressions of genius in all opera.
Gustav Holst

Puritans show disdain for the flamboyantly dressed Cavaliers in a 17th-century tavern scene. Cromwell closed many inns and theatres, which he called bastions of "lascivious mirth."

The greatness of *Dido and Aeneas* by Henry Purcell (1659–1695) lies in the perfection of its characterization and musical depth. Although conceived on a miniature scale, it is the most significant early English opera and a masterpiece of the entire Baroque musical era.

In the late 17th century, when *Dido and Aeneas* was composed, opera was still in its infancy in England. It had evolved in Florence in the 1590s from a form of private entertainment organized by groups of artists and musicians known as "academies" (see pp.62–63). From there, it had spread throughout Italy with performances in one or other of the many small courts. Only in 1637, with the opening of the Teatro di San Cassiano in Venice, was opera performed for a wider public. The new genre had reached Germany by this time and France by the 1640s, quickly taking root in both countries.

In England, opera advanced more slowly, partly because of a prejudice against sung drama in a country where spoken drama was dominant. England also lacked a royal court around which operatic tradition could develop, due to the exile of the future King Charles II following the defeat of the Cavaliers (Royalists) in the English Civil War (1642–1651) and the establishment of a Protectorate under the rule of the Puritan Oliver Cromwell. During this period, English composers were often not exposed to foreign influences and their music tended to retain a strong national identity. Forms such as the verse anthem, in which solo voices and choir sang alternate verses, were favored in Anglican liturgy. Secular music included "catches"—simple, often bawdy rounds or canons, usually sung in taverns—which had no direct continental equivalents.

A mysterious genesis

The Restoration of the monarchy under Charles II in 1660 brought England closer to Europe and its musical repertoire. This would have influenced Purcell as he developed his skills composing masterly

anthems and songs from the age of 16. Many of these early works show the depth of imagination that would later make *Dido and Aeneas* such a powerful work.

Surprisingly little is known about the creation of *Dido and Aeneas*. The earliest surviving manuscripts date from several decades after Purcell's death, and some material, such as music for his librettist Nahum Tate's prologue, has been lost. There is also a mystery about when and where the work was first performed. Although it was staged at Josias Priest's Boarding School for Young Ladies in Chelsea in the late 1680s,

Dido entertains Aeneas in a scene by an unknown 18th-century Italian artist. While based on Virgil's epic poem, Purcell's opera used witches, rather than gods, to separate the lovers.

some suggest that it was commissioned originally for the court of Charles II. There is, however, no evidence of any performance in the proposed period (1683–1684). Priest himself was a choreographer and dancing master who knew Purcell from stage productions on which they had both worked. John Blow's *Venus and Adonis,* the model for *Dido and Aeneas* and also an opera with a prologue and three acts, had been revived by Priest and his pupils and premiered at court around 1683.

The continental influence

While Purcell drew on the style of his English predecessors and contemporaries such as Matthew Locke and Blow, European musical models are evident in *Dido and Aeneas* and other works. During his years in exile, Charles II had »

Henry Purcell

Born in 1659, when court life was about to be restored with the accession of Charles II, Purcell was a thoroughly trained musician. In his relatively brief career, he acquired the range of skills needed to succeed in every available genre. He was a boy chorister in the Chapel Royal, and, as an adult, held a series of court appointments, writing music for state occasions in addition to works for church and chamber, songs, and harpsichord suites. As the organist of Westminster Abbey from 1680, he worked close to London's West End and wrote incidental music for dozens of plays. He also collaborated on a series of dramatic or semi-operas with substantial musical content, including *King Arthur* and *The Fairy Queen.* He died in 1695 during the composition of *The Indian Queen,* leaving his brother to complete the work.

Other key works

1691 *King Arthur*
1692 *The Fairy Queen*
1694 *Come, Ye Sons of Art*
1695 Funeral music for Queen Mary

As a child, Purcell served as a chorister of the Chapel Royal at Hampton Court, England, a training ground for young musicians.

A musical revival

The creative foundations for England's music and drama were in a poor state when Charles II came to the throne in 1660. The Puritans had closed London's theatres from around 1642 and, abhorring music in places of worship, had even disbanded cathedral choirs. Charles's interest in the arts and his subsequent support for them was part of a wider policy of encouraging entertainment.

This influenced music in several ways. Charles created a royal string orchestra modeled on the Vingt-quatre violons du roy ("The king's 24 violins") at the court of Louis XIV. It played for church services and court occasions, performing birthday odes by Purcell and others. The post of "Master of the King's Musick" was reinstated with the reappointment of Nicholas Lanier. Foundations such as the Chapel Royal, which trained professional musicians, were also renewed. New theatres were opened and thrived, producing what is now called Restoration drama—often bawdy comedies—for which songs and incidental music were required, frequently supplied by Purcell himself.

acquired a taste for French and Italian music. Such preferences influenced aspiring musicians eager for royal patronage.

French influences are noticeable from the start of *Dido and Aeneas*. Act One starts with a typical French overture, its slow, stately introduction based on intense dotted rhythms (which divide the beat between a long note and a short one). The second part of the overture is fast, using imitative

As poetry is the harmony of words, so music is that of notes; and as poetry is a rise above prose ... so is music the exaltation of poetry.
Henry Purcell

counterpoint, as well as a structural device by which sections are repeatedly built up from a short aria, followed by a chorus, and then a dance. The opera included several dances, a feature common for French and English operas of the time. Such dances would no doubt have pleased the dancing master, Priest, when the opera was staged at his school.

Equally noticeable is the impact of Italian opera—and specifically of *Didone*, another opera about Dido and Aeneas by Francesco Cavalli. Both operas employ a ground bass or *passacaglia*, in which the bass line is repeated throughout with changing melodies and harmonies above it. Purcell uses this to great dramatic effect for two of Dido's arias, including her lament, which comes close to the end of the score and provides a natural climax to the whole drama.

Dramatic effects

As it has survived, *Dido and Aeneas* consists of three short acts telling the story of the arrival in ancient Carthage of Aeneas, the classical hero of Virgil's epic poem, the *Aeneid*. Having escaped from the burning city of Troy at the end of the Trojan War, he had sailed with his followers to North Africa. There he woos the Carthaginian queen Dido—a wary widow who finally submits to his advances. Wicked witches plot against her, however, sending an imp in the likeness of Mercury to call Aeneas away to his glorious destiny as the founder of Rome. In despair at his departure, Dido commits suicide.

Purcell masterfully employs stirring motifs and deft word-painting to express the fluctuating moods that shape the action. Throughout the opera's varied movements, Purcell's text and music work together in perfect synergy to evoke the necessary emotions of sadness, joy, or the evil intent of the witches—music and poetry "walking hand in hand support each other," an ideal Purcell expressed in the dedication of his semi-opera *Dioclesian* (1690). His use of melismas—setting one syllable on several notes—is striking, enhancing the effect of

descriptions of "valor," "torment," and Dido "languishing" in grief in her recitative "Whence could so much virtue spring." Purcell also intentionally creates dissonance (disharmony between notes) in the string parts during Dido's lament, to express the queen's extreme anguish in one of the most moving musical statements of grief ever composed. The last death scene is remarkable, too, in an era when operatic heroes or heroines seldom perished. In Cavalli's *Didone*, Dido is saved from herself and marries someone else.

A lasting legacy

Little is known about performances of *Dido and Aeneas* in Purcell's lifetime. It was revived on the London stage in 1700 and again in 1704, yet these productions seem to have been the last until the late 19th century. Increasingly performed ever since, it is now regularly presented by schools and amateurs as well as in the world's great opera houses.

The accession of William III to the throne in 1689 diminished court patronage, although Purcell wrote fine odes for William's consort

Compositional devices in Dido's Lament

A five-bar bass repeated throughout suggests **inevitability**.

"Remember me" motif lends a **sense of yearning**.

Appoggiatura (short "leaning" note) suggests sobbing.

Falling phrases and dissonance to indicate **anguish**.

Queen Mary until 1694. Theatre work dominated Purcell's last years. Here the chief form was that of dramatic or semi-opera. This very English type of entertainment comprised a play with interludes of songs, dances, and choruses at the ends of acts; these had little direct connection to the play and were performed by a separate company of singers and dancers. The best known examples are *King Arthur* (1691), to a text by the poet John Dryden, and *The Fairy Queen* (1692), whose spoken text is an adaptation by the actor-manager Thomas Betterton of Shakespeare's *A Midsummer Night's Dream*.

Purcell's other works ranged from church and chamber music to songs and formal odes. His *Dido*

and *Aeneas* suggests, however, that, but for his early death at the age of 36, Purcell could have laid the ground for an English operatic tradition. That space would eventually be filled by the German-born George Frideric Handel, who would compose his own operas in London between 1711 and 1741. ∎

Music is yet but in its nonage, a forward child, which gives hope of what it may be hereafter in England, when the masters of it shall find more encouragement.
Henry Purcell

The score of Dido and Aeneas uses a simple bass line which may have been provided by cello, bassoon, double bass—or bass viol, as shown here by Dutch artist Caspar Netscher (1639–84).

THE OBJECT OF CHURCHES IS NOT THE BAWLING OF CHORISTERS
CHORALE PRELUDE, *EIN FESTE BURG IST UNSER GOTT* (1690), DIETERICH BUXTEHUDE

IN CONTEXT

FOCUS
Lutheran hymn tunes

BEFORE
1529 Martin Luther composes the hymn *Ein feste Burg*.

1624 Samuel Scheidt publishes his *Tablatura nova*, a collection of keyboard music containing eight sets of chorale variations.

AFTER
1705–1706 J.S. Bach walks from Arnstadt to Lübeck—a distance of 235 miles (378 km) to meet and hear Buxtehude.

1726 J.S. Bach completes the final chorales in his *Orgelbüchlein* ("Little Organ Book"), his largest collection of chorale preludes.

1830 Felix Mendelssohn bases the *finale* of his "Reformation" Symphony (No. 5) on Luther's *Ein feste Burg*.

When, in 1517, Martin Luther penned the 95 theses that would trigger the Reformation, his main objections had little to do with music: they rather concerned the selling of indulgences and the question of papal authority. As the Reformation got underway, however, church music was to be profoundly affected. For centuries, singing in church had been the preserve of monks and trained singers and, being in Latin, it was incomprehensible to the average person in the congregation.

Luther placed particular emphasis on congregational participation and on the use of the vernacular, so that everyone could understand what they were hearing and singing. The chorale—a congregational hymn—was key to this. Luther himself composed many of the earliest chorales, of which perhaps the most famous is his *Ein feste Burg*, based on Psalm 46—"A mighty fortress is our God, a tower of strength never failing."

By the Baroque period, chorale melodies formed the basis for many different genres of music in the Lutheran church. One of these was the chorale prelude, a short organ piece to introduce the melody of the chorale so that people would know what tune to sing.

Signature trait
The chief pioneer of the chorale prelude was Dieterich Buxtehude. His practice was to present the chorale melody in an ornamented version in one single upper voice, projected by the right hand on a separate manual (organ keyboard), while the left hand and pedals provided an accompaniment, normally on softer-sounding stops. Buxtehude drew some influence from the works of earlier composers, such as the keyboard variations of the Dutch organist Jan Pieterszoon

[I wanted] to comprehend one thing and another about his art.
J.S. Bach

See also: Plainchant 22–23 ▪ *Magnus liber organi* 28–31 ▪ *Great Service* 52–53 ▪ *Pièces de clavecin* 82–83 ▪ *St. Matthew Passion* 98–105 ▪ *The Art of Fugue* 108–111 ▪ *Elijah* 170–173

An Allegory of Friendship by Dutch artist Johannes Voorhout shows Buxtehude leaning on his elbow. Among the other musicians is the harpsichordist Johann Adam Reincken.

Sweelinck (1562–1621) and his pupil Samuel Scheidt (1587–1654), but while Scheidt often presented the tune of the chorale in slower, unornamented notes and wove the variations around it, Buxtehude made the chorale melody itself the clearest and most ornamented line, with the variations being simpler.

Buxtehude's prelude on *Ein feste Burg ist unser Gott*, composed around 1690, is a perfect example of this approach. The right hand presents a spontaneous-sounding solo melody that follows the contour of the chorale tune. The chorale itself is made clearer by the fact that each of its notes is either held for longer than the decorative, improvisatory notes that connect

them, or is presented as the first (and "strongest-sounding") of a collection of four notes.

The accompaniment in the left hand and pedals is generally in two- or three-part harmony, sometimes using motifs from the chorale melody and interweaving

them imitatively, while at other times opting for a chordal approach. In this manner the tune is presented once from beginning to end. This particular style of setting influenced J.S. Bach, who followed a similar model in his Chorale Preludes. ■

Dieterich Buxtehude

It is uncertain exactly when and where Dieterich Buxtehude was born, but by his early childhood, his family was living in Helsingborg (in modern-day Sweden), from where they later moved to Helsingør in Denmark. It was there that Buxtehude learned his musical craft from his organist father.

After working at his father's former church in Helsingborg and then at St. Mary's church in Helsingør, in 1668 Buxtehude accepted the prestigious

position of organist at St. Mary's in Lübeck. Tradition held that new organists should marry a daughter of their predecessor, an obligation that Buxtehude fulfilled within weeks of taking up office. He retained his role as organist of Lübeck until his death in 1707.

Other key works

1680 *Membra Jesu Nostri*
c.1680 Praeludium in C major
1694 Trio Sonatas, Op. 1

THE NEW ORPHEUS OF OUR TIMES
CONCERTI GROSSI, OP. 6 (1714), ARCANGELO CORELLI

IN CONTEXT

FOCUS
The concerto grosso

BEFORE
1610 The publication of Giovanni Cima's *Sonate a Tre* for violin, cornet, and continuo—an early example of secular Italian chamber music for three instruments.

1675 The first performance of Alessandro Stradella's *Sonata di Viole* No. 25, which contrasts a soloist with an ensemble. Corelli is likely to have heard this during his time in Rome.

AFTER
1721 J.S. Bach puts together his *Brandenburg Concertos*, several of which experiment with the instrumentation of both solo and ensemble groups.

1741 Handel's Twelve *Concerti Grossi*, Op. 6, are published, in direct homage to Corelli's *Concerti Grossi*.

The Italian term "concerto" was initially used to describe any music for voices and added instruments, with a distinction evolving in the early 17th century between *concerti ecclesiastici* (church music) and *concerti di camera* (chamber music). By the late 18th century it had evolved into the much grander showcase for virtuosity that is familiar today, but its roots lie in the modest setup of a small group of soloists and a string ensemble with continuo (bass line), as developed by the Italian composer Arcangelo Corelli around the turn of the 18th century.

Corelli's early Concerti Grossi were premiered in Rome's Palazzo Pamphilj, a dazzling example of Italian Baroque architecture that reflected the order and playfulness of the music.

See also: *The Four Seasons* 92–97 ▪ *Musique de table* 106 ▪ Saint-Saëns' Piano Concerto No. 2 in G minor 179

> It is wonderful to observe what a scratching of Corelli there is everywhere—nothing will relish but Corelli.
> **Roger North**
> *Writer and musician*
> *(1653–1734)*

Corelli's masterful Op. 6, *Concerti Grossi,* published posthumously as a set of 12, epitomize the form.

Each of Corelli's concerti consists of four to six movements, played by a *trio concertino*—three soloists comprising two violins and a cello continuo—and the *ripieno,* a larger string ensemble with harpsichord accompaniment. Confusingly, Corelli often expanded the concertino section to four musicians. The *basso continuo* (cello and harpsichord) provided a continuous musical framework, or foundation, over which the melody and harmony of both the soloists and the accompanying group, or ripieno, were constructed.

Dynamic expression
By employing these contrasting instrumental forces, Corelli explored the possibilities for dynamic expression, enlivening the exchanges between the sections through dramatic juxtapositions—often enhanced when the concertino ensemble joins in with the ripieno sections.

The music ranges from serene adagios (in slow time) wrought with exquisite suspensions, to allegros (fast time), peppered with quickfire exchanges between the large and small ensembles. Corelli's use of harmony in these concerti was in keeping with a more general shift in Italian Baroque music away from the myriad lines of Renaissance polyphony toward the use of chord sequences and cadences to create a stable tonal center.

Corelli's work immediately attracted the admiration of patrons and fellow musicians. Among the Op. 6 concerti, No. 8 in G minor, subtitled *"Fatto per la Notte di Natale,"* was commissioned by his patron of the 1690s, Cardinal Pietro Ottoboni. Known as the Christmas Concerto, the work has enjoyed long-lasting popularity.

Harmony and balance
Although Corelli had previously written for the *concertino* combination of instruments in his 48 trio sonatas, it is impossible to dismiss the *Concerti Grossi* as a mere inflation of these small-scale chamber works. Some performances involved as many as 80 musicians—a huge number, especially in Corelli's day, when orchestras more usually numbered around 20 musicians.

In 1789, more than 70 years after Corelli's death, the English musician, composer, and music historian Dr. Charles Burney wrote of the *Concerti Grossi:* "The effect of the whole … [is] so majestic, solemn, and sublime that they preclude all criticism." Even today, their melodies continue to resonate. ▪

Arcangelo Corelli

Born into a prosperous family in the small Italian town of Fusignano, in 1653, Corelli was accepted into Bologna's Accademia Filarmonica orchestra at the age of 17. His mastery of the violin, combined with the rigor of his teaching methods and his many pupils, who included Antonio Vivaldi and Francesco Geminiani, caused his reputation to grow.

In the mid-1670s, Corelli moved to Rome, where he entered the service of Queen Christina of Sweden, who had a home in Rome, and later served as Music Director to Cardinal Pamphili. His last patron was Cardinal Pietro Ottoboni, who was himself a musician and librettist.

Corelli died in 1713. Despite his relatively modest output, his most active composing years coincided with a boom in music publishing at the turn of the 18th century. As a result, his influence spread across Europe, even during his lifetime.

Other key works

1694 12 Trio Sonatas, Op. 4
1700 12 Violin Sonatas, Op. 5

THE UNITING OF THE FRENCH AND ITALIAN STYLES MUST CREATE THE PERFECTION OF MUSIC

PIÈCES DE CLAVECIN (1713), FRANÇOIS COUPERIN

IN CONTEXT

FOCUS
French Baroque harpsichord music

BEFORE
1670 Jacques Champion de Chambonnières publishes *Les pièces de clavessin* ("Pieces for Harpsichord"), the first major French work on harpsichords.

1677 Nicholas-Antoine Lebègue writes *Les pièces de clavessin*, the first dance suites published in France.

AFTER
1725 J.S. Bach includes *Les bergeries* (from *Sixième Ordre* 1717) in his *Notebook for Anna Magdalena* under the title of *Rondeau*.

1753 C.P.E. Bach pens volume 1 of *Versuch über die wahre Art das Clavier zu spielen*, a treatise influenced by Couperin's *L'art de toucher le clavecin* ("The Art of Playing the Harpsichord").

ntil François Couperin's *Ordres*, or suites, French keyboard music had largely taken the form of Baroque popular dances, such as the allemande, courante, and sarabande. However, in part due to his connections at the French court, Couperin was also familiar with Italian music, including the sonata, a piece in several movements for a small group of instruments, which involved no dancing or singing.

Sonatas of this period usually had a two-part structure, with each half repeated. As seen in the more than 500 sonatas of Domenico Scarlatti, they tended to focus on

I like better what touches me than what surprises me.
François Couperin
Pièces de clavecin (1713)

technical virtuosity and the formal modulation of melodies, rather than changes of mood and feeling.

Ornamental flourishes
Although he used the sonata structure in his music, Couperin concentrated on grace and gesture, swayed by the prevailing French view of music as a sophisticated, elegant, and even frivolous pastime. Many of his works have descriptive titles, which he claimed were ideas that occurred to him as he was writing. The careful balance he struck between the lighthearted French sensibility and the more formal, structured Italian approach gave his work wide appeal.

The keyboard works were written entirely for harpsichord or spinet. On these instruments, the player has no control of volume. Couperin incorporated subtle embellishments into his music to control its flow and intensity and, unusually for the period, expected performers not to add to, or improvise around, what he had written. Furthermore, he published detailed instructions for these "ornaments," marking the notes precisely as they should be played, thereby codifying such signs for

See also: *Micrologus* 24–25 ▪ Scarlatti's Sonata in D minor 90–91 ▪ *Musique de table* 106 ▪ Clementi's Piano Sonata in F-sharp minor 132–133

later generations. His style was not to everyone's taste—while J.S. Bach arranged some of Couperin's works, he is said to have found them overly fussy.

Such reliance on ornamentation tends to mean that Couperin's music translates less well onto the modern piano, which, with its fuller and more sustained sound, makes the decoration too prominent. This, coupled with his dislike of overt virtuosity and harmonic daring (such as sudden key changes or clashing notes), may explain why his music has been eclipsed by Scarlatti's in the concert hall.

Although not the first treatise on keyboard playing, Couperin's *L'art de toucher le clavecin* was one of the most important, offering not a complete course, but advice for the player on body postures and technical issues. It included a series of eight preludes for study and fingerings for some of Couperin's published pieces.

Particularly forward-looking are his suggestions that children should master a few pieces before learning to read music and that practice should be supervised. These ideas anticipated some modern approaches to music education, such as the Suzuki method in the mid-20th century. ∎

A young girl learns to play the harpsichord in *The Music Lesson* by Jean-Honoré Fragonard. François Couperin taught music to Louis XIV's children at Versailles.

François Couperin

Even within the dynasty of great musicians into which he was born in 1668, François Couperin was extraordinary. Appointed on the death of his father, Charles, to take over the role of organist at St. Gervais Church in Paris at the tender age of 11, he went on to become one of the most sought-after performers and teachers in France. In 1693, Couperin was appointed by Louis XIV as organist at the Royal Chapel. He became court harpsichordist to Louis XV in 1717 and composed works for the royal family. He died in Paris in 1733.

Couperin's series of *Ordres* for keyboard are considered some of the most significant contributions to Baroque harpsichord music. Players of the instrument today still study *L'art de toucher le clavecin* in order to inform their performances.

Other key works

1713–1730 24 *Ordres* (in four books)
1714–1715 *Les concerts royaux* (The Royal Concerts)
1724–1725 *Apothéoses*

WHAT THE ENGLISH LIKE IS SOMETHING THEY CAN BEAT TIME TO

WATER MUSIC, HWV 348–350 (1717), GEORGE FRIDERIC HANDEL

IN CONTEXT

FOCUS
An international style

BEFORE
1660s Following the restoration of the monarchy in England, Charles II reinstates music to the English court. He favors the French style and particularly promotes dancing, a passion he acquired during his exile in France.

1670s A group of professional musicians called the Music Meeting open a concert hall near Charing Cross, London.

AFTER
1727 Handel composes the anthem *Zadok the Priest* for George II's coronation.

1800s Composers turn away from an international style to highlight the individuality of nations, finding inspiration in folk dance rhythms and nationalist themes.

Until the late 19th century, England was often known as the land without music. Even though London had a thriving concert life, with the earliest tradition of public concerts in Europe, the fashion was to promote foreign composers and performers rather than native musicians. Both Handel and Johann Christian Bach (known as the English Bach) moved to London to make the most of its opportunities, and composers such as Mozart and Haydn often visited the city as well-paid and feted musicians.

Music as pleasure

When Handel arrived in London in 1711, he already had a distinctive style that was rooted in his North German upbringing and influenced by his time in Italy. He had met Arcangelo Corelli and Domenico Scarlatti in Italy and achieved success with Italian operas and religious works there. He was also familiar with the work of Jean-Baptiste Lully, who dominated French music, and England's Henry Purcell. This cosmopolitanism appealed to London concert-goers, who welcomed Handel's avoidance

Handel is the greatest composer that ever lived ... I would uncover my head and kneel down on his tomb.
Ludwig van Beethoven

of some of the florid excesses of High Baroque counterpoint that were favored by Bach.

Handel was soon appointed director of music to the Duke of Chandos, who introduced him to other members of the English aristocracy. While employed by the duke, Handel honed a new, more forthright style, which can be heard in his Chandos Anthems and the masque *Acis and Galatea*. It was also at this time that he wrote *Esther*, the first of his English oratorios, a genre for which he would become renowned.

George Frideric Handel

Born in Halle, in northeastern Germany, in 1685, Handel received his earliest musical training from a local organist. While still a teenager, he moved to Hamburg to work as a composer and from there went to Italy. He developed his dramatic talent in the comic operas *Rodrigo* (1707) and *Agrippina* (1709) and the psalm setting *Dixit Dominus* (1707).

Returning to Hanover in 1710, Handel became *Kapellmeister* (music director) to the Elector of Hanover (later George I of Great Britain and Ireland). He relocated to London a year later and lived there for the rest of his life. He later found fame with his oratorios, especially *Messiah*, and set a seal on his career with the *Music for the Royal Fireworks* in 1749. Handel died a wealthy man and was buried with the great and the good in London's Westminster Abbey.

Other key works

1725 *Rodelinda*, HWV 19
1742 *Messiah*, HWV 56
1749 *The Music for the Royal Fireworks*, HWV 351
1751 *Jephtha*, HWV 70

See also: Gabrieli's *Sonata pian' e forte* 55 ▪ *Euridice* 62–63 ▪ *The Four Seasons* 92–97 ▪ *The Magic Flute* 134–137 ▪ *Elijah* 170–173 ▪ *La traviata* 174–175 ▪ *The Ring Cycle* 180–187 ▪ *Tosca* 194–197

Handel presents *Water Music* to George I in a painting by the Belgian artist Edouard Hamman. According to newspaper reports, the whole river was filled with small boats and barges.

In 1717, George I asked Handel to compose the music for a barge trip down the Thames. The music needed to be sensational: the King wanted to make a big public statement to draw attention away from his son, the Prince of Wales, who was forming an opposing political faction. Handel had to balance a desire for novelty with the need for broad popular appeal. While a concert in a barge with some 50 performers was a novelty in itself, Handel added to the occasion by importing Bohemian horn players, whose elegant fanfares would have sounded very different from the hunting horns familiar to English audiences. Along with bassoons and trumpets, these helped the music carry in the open air.

Essentially, *Water Music* is a blend of popular European styles. It starts with an overture in the uneven rhythms of the French style, incorporates dances that were fashionable across Europe at the time, and includes the most English of music—the hornpipe—which became the signature tune of the work.

Opera in London

In 1719, the Duke of Chandos and his friends, taking advantage of the growing interest in opera in England, inaugurated the Royal Academy of Music (unrelated to the conservatoire of the same name founded a century later) under a charter from the King. It was a commercial venture, formed as a joint-stock corporation, with the aim of commissioning and performing new Italian operas in Britain. Handel was one of its three composers as well as its musical »

I should be sorry if I only entertained them. I wish to make them better.
George Frideric Handel

Public music and concert-going

London was the first city to establish public concerts with paying audiences. The trend began around 1672, when the violinist and composer John Banister organized a paying concert in his own house. By the time Handel arrived in London, there were purpose-built venues for chamber music concerts. In addition, theatres in Drury Lane and the Haymarket offered Italian and, later, English opera to London's beau monde.

From around 1740, pleasure gardens sprang up across the capital, most famously in Vauxhall. Here visitors would stroll, dine, and be entertained by live music from wind bands and orchestras. A rehearsal of Handel's *Music for the Royal Fireworks* in Vauxhall Gardens, in 1749, attracted some 12,000 people, each paying two shillings and sixpence, and causing a three-hour traffic jam on London Bridge.

The band plays music from an illuminated bandstand in London's Vauxhall Gardens, UK, while visitors stroll and dance in the open air.

director. He traveled to Europe to engage the finest orchestral musicians and the most celebrated singers, including the Italian castrato Senesino, and the soprano Francesca Cuzzoni.

Handel understood the audience's continual hunger for novelty. When London audiences became used to these artists, he brought in another soprano, Faustina Bordoni, who built a rival fan base among the audience, reinvigorating interest in the opera for a few more seasons. The high fees paid to such luminaries may have been part of the reason that the company went out of business in 1728 with debts of around £20,000 (over $5.5 million today).

Master of stagecraft

Handel wrote a series of 13 operas for the Royal Academy of Music, which had 235 performances in his lifetime. Masterpieces in the Italian style, they included *Giulio Cesare in Egitto* ("Julius Caesar in Egypt", 1724) and *Alcina* (1735). Although he used the operatic conventions of the day—recitatives and arias—to unfold the narrative, he gave the operas a dramatic structure that

Handel understands effect better than any of us—when he chooses, he strikes like a thunderbolt.
Wolfgang Amadeus Mozart

He saw men and women where others have seen only historical-mythical busts.
Paul Henry Lang
Music critic

was unusual at the time. He also understood the importance of spectacle, and a number of his operas required elaborate stage machinery. In *Alcina*, which was written for the new opera house at Covent Garden, the stage directions include "with lightning and thunder, the mountain crumbles, revealing Alcina's delightful palace." Such stage effects attracted audiences just as much as the music.

A new direction

When Italian opera went out of fashion in London after the extraordinary success in 1728 of John Gay's *The Beggar's Opera*, which satirized the form, Handel used his skills to create and popularize oratorios in English. Starting with *Deborah* (1733), these thrillingly dramatic works for solo singers, chorus, and orchestra told biblical stories with English-language librettos, but were performed unstaged in theatres. To some extent influenced by operatic traditions, and even Greek tragedy, Handel developed a directness of style and a new kind of robustness that appealed to British audiences. The public flocked to hear works such as *Messiah* (1742), *Samson*

Some of the dances in *Water Music*

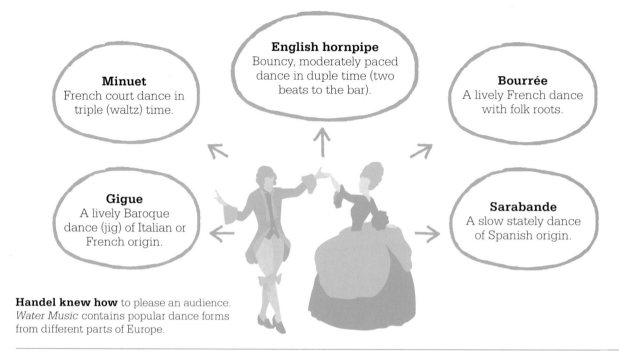

Minuet
French court dance in triple (waltz) time.

English hornpipe
Bouncy, moderately paced dance in duple time (two beats to the bar).

Bourrée
A lively French dance with folk roots.

Gigue
A lively Baroque dance (jig) of Italian or French origin.

Sarabande
A slow stately dance of Spanish origin.

Handel knew how to please an audience. *Water Music* contains popular dance forms from different parts of Europe.

(1743), and *Belshazzar* (1745). *Messiah* was so popular that men were asked to attend performances without their swords to create more room for the audience.

Handel often presented these works himself, renting theatres and hiring performers, and often netting a good profit. When a rival company provided stiff competition, Handel wrote a number of organ concertos which he performed as interludes during the performances. Unusual as this was, it provided a rare opportunity to hear his great keyboard virtuosity in public and was therefore something of a marketing masterstroke.

The Handelian oratorio became so popular that Handel wrote secular works in the same style. He designated *Semele* (1744), which was based on classical mythology, as a musical drama "after the manner of an oratorio" and even presented it during the Lenten period, when its depiction of adultery caused consternation. Works such as this were essentially operas in English and are usually performed as such today.

National yet international
During a period when music was considered ephemeral and works were seldom heard in the years after their first performances, Handel was considered a major composer in his lifetime. He was probably the first composer whose work did not suffer a fall in popularity after his death. In England, he helped to broaden interest in music beyond the confines of the aristocracy and created a national musical identity in an international style that lasted until Edward Elgar in the late 19th century. His anthem *Zadok the Priest*, composed for the coronation of George II, is still used in the crowning of British monarchs today. ∎

GEORGE FREDERICK HANDEL, Efqʳ
born February XXIII MDCLXXXIV.
died April XIV MDCCLIX. *L.F.Roubiliac. inv.ᵗ et sc.*

Louis François Roubiliac's memorial to Handel stands above his tomb in Westminster Abbey, UK. Just three days before his death, Handel said that he wished to be buried there.

DO NOT EXPECT ANY PROFOUND INTENTION, BUT RATHER AN INGENIOUS JESTING WITH ART

SONATA IN D MINOR, K. 9 "PASTORALE" (1738), DOMENICO SCARLATTI

IN CONTEXT

FOCUS
Italian Baroque sonata

BEFORE
1701 Baroque composer Arcangelo Corelli publishes his *Violin Sonatas,* Op. 5—an early example of solo instrumental writing.

1709 Antonio Vivaldi publishes *Twelve Sonatas for Violin and Basso Continuo,* Op. 2, again showcasing the virtuosic abilities of a solo instrument.

AFTER
1784 Mozart publishes Piano Sonata No. 1, K279, following in Scarlatti's footsteps with his focus on solo keyboard writing.

1795 Beethoven publishes Piano Sonata No. 1, Op. 2, continuing Scarlatti's experimentation with the genre.

The Italian virtuoso harpsichord player and composer Domenico Scarlatti published his first edition of *Essercizi per gravicembalo* ("Exercises for Harpsichord") in 1738. As the title of the collection suggests, the 30 sonatas were intended to be *études* (studies) for students of the harpsichord—although by Scarlatti's own admission, the originality of their content belies their seemingly mundane and practical purpose.

A contemporary of both J.S. Bach and George Frideric Handel, Scarlatti's dazzling skills on the

A family poses with their harpsichord in a 1739 work by Cornelis Troost. The instrument's popularity would soon wane in favor of the piano.

See also: *Pièces de clavecin* 82–83 ▪ *Musique de table* 106 ▪ Clementi's Piano Sonata in F-sharp minor, Op. 25, No. 5 132–133 ▪ "Eroica" Symphony 138–141

> For bold playing of the harpsichord … [s]how yourself more human than critical, and thus increase your own pleasure. … LIVE HAPPILY.
> **Domenico Scarlatti**

keyboard were legendary, his dancing fingers described by one astonished British observer as resembling "a thousand devils." Scarlatti allegedly once had a public contest of keyboard skills with Handel, a musical duel that, by all accounts, ended in a draw. Scarlatti put his talents to use at the highest level of royal service, tutoring Maria Barbara when she was both princess of Portugal and later queen of Spain. It was her aptitude for the instrument and her continuous employment of Scarlatti that provided the conditions for his groundbreaking *Essercizi*.

Scarlatti's sonata style

The term "sonata" derives from the Italian verb *suonare,* meaning "to sound," and generally denotes solo instrumental music—that is, music which is "sounded" as opposed to sung (or "cantata"). In the early 18th century, Italian composers such as Arcangelo Corelli, Antonio Vivaldi, and Tomaso Albinoni had written widely for solo instruments—the violin being a particularly popular choice—but

their sonatas tended to consist of three to four movements of contrasting moods. However, Scarlatti's sonatas for the solo harpsichord—at that point, a relatively neglected instrument—typically follow a two-part, single-movement structure, often pivoting around a central "crux," or pause, and tending to be of shorter proportions, lasting only around three to four minutes in total.

The Pastorale

Although he was influenced by the *sarabandes* and *courantes* (both courtly dances) of his contemporaries, Scarlatti's music of this era is unique in its use of folk idioms taken from his Iberian surroundings. The Sonata K9 in D minor is nicknamed the *Pastorale* (Pastoral). This is in part due to the deceptive simplicity of its melody but also owing to the traditional music it evoked, including elements of Spanish folk dance music such as the strumming, percussive effects of Spanish guitar. This addition of country stylings to the formal courtly influences was to continue to define Scarlatti's music. He broke down the expectations of Baroque chamber music convention, experimenting with dissonance and syncopation in his later sonatas.

It is such playful "jesting with art" that places Scarlatti as a master of both Baroque music and the evolving classical style. Scarlatti helped pave the way for the still more radical sonata experiments of Mozart and Beethoven that followed and that further emphasized the importance of freestyle, expressive melody lines over the more formal structure of Baroque music. ∎

Domenico Scarlatti

The son of the prolific opera composer, Alessandro Scarlatti, Domenico Scarlatti was born in Naples in 1685. A talented musician himself, he followed his father into a musical career of wide-ranging commissions and royal patronage. At 16 he became composer and organist to the royal chapel in Naples before going on to serve the exiled Polish queen, Maria Casimira, in Rome. He later became *maestro di cappella* (music director) at St. Peter's.

In 1721, Scarlatti joined the Portuguese court in Lisbon, where he gave music lessons to Princess Maria Barbara. When the princess married Fernando VI of Spain, she summoned Scarlatti to be her music tutor. He served the queen until his death in Madrid in 1757. Scarlatti is mainly known for his 555 keyboard sonatas, although he also produced a huge quantity of chamber and sacred vocal music.

Other key works

1724 *Stabat Mater* for 10 voices
1757 *Salve Regina*

SPRING

HAS COME, AND WITH IT GAIETY

THE FOUR SEASONS (1725),
ANTONIO VIVALDI

IN CONTEXT

FOCUS
**Italian Baroque solo
concerto**

BEFORE
1692 Giuseppe Torelli, based
in Bologna, publishes the first
of three collections of concertos
that give a new prominence to
the solo violinist.

1707 Concertos published by
the Venetian Tomaso Albinoni
use the three-movement
(fast–slow–fast) structure that
will become the standard.

1721 J.S. Bach's six
Brandenburg Concertos use
the structure and principles
standardized by Vivaldi in
his concertos.

AFTER
1773 Mozart composes his
first violin concerto using the
three-movement structure.

I n Italy, in the 1720s, Vivaldi
was best known as a composer
of operas, but in northern
Europe—as well as after the
composer's death—his fame
rested on his concertos, a form he
shaped, developed, and made his
own, perhaps most famously in
Le quattro stagioni (*The Four
Seasons*) of 1725.

Since Vivaldi's day, the word
"concerto" has found a clear
meaning as a piece for one or
more instrumental soloists and
an orchestra: a solo concerto
showcases one musician; a
concerto grosso ("big concerto")
has two or more. Before Vivaldi,
however, the term was used more
fluidly to describe works written
for combined ensembles, whether
of voices and instruments or
comprising different groups of
instruments. In Rome, for example,
Arcangelo Corelli wrote concerti
grossi for an ensemble of two
violins and keyboard. These
instruments could be joined by a
larger string ensemble, the role of
which was more to augment than
to stand in musical contrast to the
smaller group.

The concerto develops

It was in Northern Italy, and Venice
in particular, that the concerto
started to take the form that Vivaldi
would come to use. In Bologna,

The Ospedale della Pietà, a
foundling hospital on the Grand Canal
in Venice, where Vivaldi became violin
master in 1703. The *ospedale* had an
all-female choir and orchestra.

violinist and composer Giuseppe
Torelli wrote works for solo violin
and a larger instrumental ensemble,
while in Venice, wealthy amateur
Tomaso Albinoni composed
beautiful oboe concertos. Written
for one or two oboes and a larger
ensemble, they were among the
first notable solo works written
for the instrument.

In the works of both Torelli and
Albinoni, a contrast was starting to
emerge between the solo sections

See also: C.P.E. Bach's Flute Concerto in A major 120–121 ▪ Saint-Saëns' Piano Concerto No. 2 in G minor 179 ▪ Ravel's Piano Concerto in D for the Left Hand 266–267

and the parts played by the larger ensemble, as if two voices were being heard simultaneously within the same piece. These were the foundations upon which Vivaldi built his body of work.

Slightly younger than Albinoni, his fellow Venetian, Vivaldi wrote his first known concertos when he was in his mid-20s. Overall, during the next 40 or so years, he would write around 500 concertos, many of which were published in collections such as *Il cimento dell'armonia e dell'inventione*. Others were sold in manuscript—a form that the commercially minded Vivaldi found was more profitable. Of these concertos, more than 200 were for solo violin; Vivaldi himself was a renowned and flamboyant violinist. Others were for solo bassoon, cello, flute, oboe, mandolin, and recorder.

Vivali wrote nearly 50 double concertos (composed for two solo instruments), along with other variations, including one concerto that included solo parts for 16 different instruments. Through his astonishing oeuvre, Vivaldi

helped to change the course of musical history. Yet he was never a revolutionary. Instead, he took existing trends and modified them, creating a new musical language that exhilarated both musicians and contemporary audiences. Many of his borrowings were from opera, another genre that found new life in the Baroque period and with which Vivaldi was heavily involved as a composer. Following in Albinoni's footsteps, he took the basic fast-slow-fast structure of the operatic overture and transformed it into the standard three-movement structure of the concerto: a fast first movement, filled with musical action as solo and ensemble sections alternate with one another, followed by a slow, more meditative middle movement, succeeded by a renewed burst of activity in the final movement.

The ritornello

Within the fast movements, Vivaldi borrowed the key structuring device from opera—he used the ritornello ("little return"), a refrain

He can compose a concerto more quickly than a copyist can write.
Charles de Brosses
French scholar and politician

or musical idea played, repeated, and modified over the course of the movement by the orchestra.

Typically in Vivaldi's work, a fast movement starts with the orchestra making a full statement of the ritornello. This gives way to a solo section, in which the musician merely receives background accompaniment from the orchestra. The full orchestra then returns, restating part of the ritornello in a new key. Ritornello and solo sections then alternate, typically **»**

Antonio Vivaldi

Vivaldi was born in 1678, the son of a violinist in the orchestra of St. Mark's in Venice. He initially trained for the priesthood and was ordained in 1703, but he soon ceased to practice as a priest. His break as a musician came when he was appointed violin master at Venice's Ospedale della Pietà.

Vivaldi's first published collection of concertos, *L'estro armonico* ("Harmonic Inspiration"), printed in 1711, made his name internationally known, especially in Germany, where the young J.S. Bach was one of its admirers. He went on to compose hundreds of

other concertos, as well as some 50 operas and numerous religious vocal works, sonatas, and cantatas. His popularity had declined by the late 1730s. He died in Vienna in 1741, while trying to restore his fortunes, and was buried in a pauper's grave.

Other key works

1711 *L'estro armonico*, Op. 3
1714 *La stravaganza*, Op. 4
1725 *Il cimento dell'armonia e dell'inventione*, Op. 8
1727 *La cetra*, Op. 9

The concerto

The main attraction of the concerto for composers and musicians is the sheer dramatic potential of the form, as soloist and orchestra alternately compete and collaborate with one another. Many composers have been inspired to write concertos by the talents of particular performers, such as the cellist Antonín Kraft, for whom Haydn wrote his Cello Concerto No. 2 in D and Beethoven his Triple Concerto. Mozart wrote his famous Horn Concertos for the horn player Joseph Leutgeb. Concertos soon became a showcase for virtuoso performers, such as the violinist Paganini and the pianists Liszt and Chopin. Around the turn of the 20th century, Rachmaninov wrote his piano concertos—and Dvorak and Elgar their much-loved cello concertos. Later, fans of the concerto grosso included Michael Tippett in his *Fantasia Concertante on a Theme of Corelli*.

Violinist Nigel Kennedy records *The Four Seasons* with the English Chamber Orchestra in 1989. The recording sold more than two million copies.

four to six times, culminating in a final orchestral restatement of the ritornello.

The solo sections, meanwhile, can also be seen in opera. Baroque operas gave new prominence to the aria, which allowed singers to show off the power, range, and expressive nature of their voices. Similarly, the solo sections of concertos allowed instrumental soloists to display their virtuoso skills. In an age characterized by theatricality, Vivaldi brought a dose of dramatic virtuosity to the concerto.

Four Seasons

Vivaldi allowed his theatricality free rein in *The Four Seasons*, first published in Amsterdam in 1725. Earlier versions of the pieces had been circulating for a number of years in manuscript form, and were already widely known and admired.

Le quattro stagioni represented the first four in a collection of 12 violin concertos entitled *Il cimento dell'armonia e dell'inventione* ("The Contest of Harmony and Invention"), all written between 1723 and 1725. Many of Vivaldi's concertos sought to evoke or describe particular

The score of "Spring" from *The Four Seasons*, part of *L'estro armonico* (Harmonic Inspiration), a collection of 12 concertos whose lively flamboyance transformed the stately form.

moods and states of mind, as their titles made clear—for example, *Il piacere* (Pleasure), *L'inquietudine* (Anxiety), *L'amoroso* (The Lover), and *Il riposo* (Rest). *Le quattro stagioni*, however, along with a cycle of three concertos called *La Notte* (Night), took this a step further, and used the music to relate a simple musical narrative known as a "programme," a form that was taken up by many composers in the Romantic era.

In the published version, Vivaldi made the programme explicit by including four sonnets of unknown authorship, often theorized to have been written by Vivaldi himself. These sonnets each tell the story of one of the four seasons. The sonnet for spring, for example, starts by describing how birds salute the new season "with joyous song" and how brooks fanned by soft breezes flow "with sweet murmurings." All this Vivaldi

describes musically in the first movement of the "Spring" concerto, where the opening ritornello is a dance representing the celebratory joy of returning spring, succeeded by three solo violins conveying birdsong and other characteristics of the season.

High praise

In Italy, Vivaldi's popularity had waned by the end of his life due to rising interest in a new Neapolitan style of opera. North of the Alps, however, Vivaldi's concertos, and *Le quattro stagioni* in particular, made him one of the most famous composers of the day. Vivaldi's patrons included the Bohemian nobleman Count Wenzel von Morzin, to whom Vivaldi dedicated *Il cimento dell'armonia e dell'inventione*, the collection that contained *Le quattro stagioni*. "I beg you not to be surprised," he wrote, "if among these few and feeble concertos Your Illustrious Grace should find the Four Seasons which, with your noble bounty, Your Illustrious Grace has so long regarded with indulgence."

Another illustrious endorsement came from King Louis XV of France, who in November 1730

Vivaldi played a splendid solo … Such playing has not been heard before and can never be equalled.
J.F.A. von Uffenbach
German traveler
(1687–1769)

Painting pictures with music

Spring
Three solo violins mimic chirruping birds and babbling brooks. An upbeat third movement suggests a spring festival with dancing.

Summer
Tranquil sounds speak of summer heat, with buzzing insects, a cuckoo, and a lark. Minor chords and dramatic undertones convey a summer storm.

Autumn
The fast first movement captures the drama of a harvest festival. The orchestra is interrupted by a solo violin representing a "swaying drunkard."

Winter
Fast violins convey chattering teeth and stamping feet, and rapid scales and dissonance suggest winter chills and gales.

commanded a performance of the "Spring" concerto, played by an orchestra assembled entirely of musically gifted nobles and courtiers. Another lover of the "Spring" concerto was philosopher Jean-Jacques Rousseau, who in 1775 arranged the piece for unaccompanied flute.

Influence on composers

Most remarkable, however, was the legacy of Vivaldi's concertos to his fellow musicians. One notable devotee was J.S. Bach. His patron, the Duke of Saxe-Weimar, returned from a trip to the Netherlands with a copy of Vivaldi's first concerto collection, the *L'estro armonico* ("Harmonic Inspiration"), published in Amsterdam. Bach transcribed six of the concertos for solo harpsichord, and according

to his earliest biographer, Johann Nikolaus Forkel, it was this experience that taught him the importance of "order, coherence, and proportion" in music.

According to modern scholars, Forkel's assessment may be an exaggeration, but Vivaldi's influence on Bach is clearly evident in, for example, Bach's use of the ritornello form. Equally evident is the fact that Vivaldi gave the three-movement (fast-slow-fast) concerto a place among the most important music forms, inspiring countless future composers from Bach, Haydn, and Mozart to Beethoven onward. Moreover, the concerto was a major influence on another emerging form, one that soon became the supreme form of instrumental expression for composers—the symphony. ∎

THE END AND FINAL AIM OF ALL

MUSIC

SHOULD BE NONE OTHER THAN THE

GLORY OF GOD

ST. MATTHEW PASSION (1727),
JOHANN SEBASTIAN BACH

IN CONTEXT

FOCUS
**High Baroque religious
choral music**

BEFORE
1471 The Flemish composer
Jacob Obrecht writes a *Passio
secundum Matthaeum*
(Matthew Passion).

1620s In Rome, Giacomo
Carissimi produces oratorios
on Old Testament subjects to
satisfy the demand for operatic
entertainment during Lent.

1718 Handel composes
the first version of *Esther*,
about the Old Testament
queen. Eventually, in 1732,
this piece would be revised
into the first English oratorio.

AFTER
1829 Felix Mendelssohn
conducts the Berlin premier
of the *St. Matthew Passion*—a
key moment in the revival of
interest in Bach's music.

1846 Mendelssohn premieres
his oratorio *Elijah*, depicting
the life of the Prophet Elijah.

1850 The Bach–Gesellschaft
is formed in Leipzig by Moritz
Hauptmann (Cantor of the
Thomaskirche), Otto Jahn
(a biographer of Mozart),
and the composer Robert
Schumann, in order to publish
the complete works of Bach.

1963–1966 Polish composer
Krzysztof Penderecki writes
the *St. Luke Passion*, an atonal
orchestral-choral setting of the
Passion story.

T the final development of the
Baroque aesthetic known
as the High Baroque was
underway by around 1680. The new
tonal system, in which music was
built from notes forming major and
minor scales, was fixed by this
time, and High Baroque composers
such as Johann Sebastian Bach

The Crucifixion, often depicted in
Renaissance art, as here by the German
painter Lucas Cranach the Elder,
became a subject for composers, too,
as music grew ever more descriptive.

used it to control the flow of their
work by modulating between
different keys. Increasingly complex
counterpoint, combining distinct
melodic lines, one of the defining
characteristics of Baroque music,
was employed to create vivid
dramatic effects; coupled with
incisive rhythmic features, the
music achieved an unprecedented
emotional power.

In earlier periods, vocal art
music had been preeminent; now
increasing interest in instrumental
music offered composers another

See also: *Ein feste Burg ist unser Gott* 78–79 ▪ *The Art of Fugue* 108–111 ▪ *Elijah* 170–173 ▪ *The Dream of Gerontius* 218–219

dramatic resource. Breaking the bounds of pure accompaniment, the ever-more prominent orchestra could play a far more varied and expressive role, which helped to fuel the popularity of Baroque opera. This tended to flourish in mercantile centers, where wealthy individuals joined the nobility to enjoy the spectacle, offering rich opportunities for composers such as George Frideric Handel. Most citizens, however, experienced the new musical developments during church services.

Dramatizing church music

Composers soon realized that the operatic techniques and music that infused classical myths with contemporary relevance could serve liturgical purposes equally, bringing life to the biblical texts, which many in the congregation could not themselves read. Since operas were not permitted to be staged during the six weeks of Lent, composers would present performances of oratorios on biblical themes instead.

Not "brook" [in German: *Bach*], but "sea" should he be called because of his infinite, inexhaustible richness in tone combinations and harmonies.
Ludwig van Beethoven

Many of the genres heard in choral music of this time are the same as those found in secular music. As church composers were required to write music for more than 60 services a year, it was not unusual for them to remodel secular pieces, as Johann Sebastian Bach did (1685–1750) when writing his *Christmas Oratorio* (1734–1735).

Evolving choral genres

During the High Baroque period, the form of the Mass in north Germany evolved from the *prima pratica* ("first practice"), characterized by a polyphonic setting of the most important parts of the church service (Kyrie, Gloria, Credo, Sanctus, Agnus Dei) with a choir and an instrumental accompaniment, into a much grander entity. This was due partly to the influence of Italian traditions, which, after 1712, Bach encountered through the music of Antonio Vivaldi. The orchestra grew in size and, especially with *obbligato* (essential, fully written) accompaniments, made a much greater musical contribution. Solo voices were also more common.

Bach wrote five Masses, but the B minor Mass (1749) stands apart as one of the most important works in the Western music canon. It was written at the end of his life and unperformed before his death. Unusually for the Lutheran tradition, it presents a complete setting of the Latin Ordinary in 25 separate movements over some two hours.

Although on the wane by this period, the motet (sacred verses set to music) was still an important choral genre, particularly in France, where two distinct styles had been established. The *petits* »

Johann Sebastian Bach

Born in Eisenach, Germany, in 1685, Bach was the most prominent of a long line of musicians. Taught music first by his father, then his brother, Bach was appointed as a court musician in Weimar on leaving school in 1703. His reputation as an outstanding keyboard player quickly spread. He had soon written the first of more than 200 cantatas.

In 1717, Bach moved to Köthen to take up a postion as *Kapellmeister* and wrote many instrumental works, including the Brandenburg Concertos. In 1723, he took up his last post as cantor of St. Thomas Church in Leipzig, where he remained until his death in 1750 at the age of 65. During this period, he became the preeminent composer of High Baroque music, with a skill for counterpoint that has arguably never been equalled.

Other key works

1723–1732 Six Motets, BWV 225–231
1733 *Magnificat*, BWV 243
1749 Mass in B minor, BWV 232

Oratorio

Oratorio versus Opera

Opera

Takes **religious text** as its subject matter.

Plots are inspired by **stirring myths**, history, and literature.

Performed as a **concert piece** without props.

Performed as **musical theatre**, with sets, scenery, and costumes.

Uses a **singing narrator** to **advance** the plot.

In later operas, **characters advance** the plot.

Singers are static and characters do **not interact**.

Characters move and **interact**.

motets were accompanied only by continuo, whereas the grands motets, such as those of Jean-Baptist Lully, included soloists and an increasing number of instruments. They were less common in Germany; the best-known examples today are by Heinrich Schütz and Bach. Bach's motets, which strongly influenced Wolfgang Amadeus Mozart (1756–1791), were virtually the only works of his to be regularly performed after his death until the Bach revival in the early 19th century. Each was arranged for different sized choirs, and it is unclear how they were used within church services, although some were written for funerals.

Other choral forms of the High Baroque period include the anthem, the Magnificat, and the madrigal.

The anthem was prevalent in England, as a sectional dramatic work placing instrumental sections with solo passages, recitatives, and full choruses. Purcell was a gifted exponent of the form, and Handel took it to even greater heights. His four ceremonial anthems include the renowned Zadok the Priest, written for the coronation of King George II in 1727.

The Magnificat, sung at vespers and evensong, is the canticle (hymn) of the Virgin Mary from Luke's Gospel, first set in the Renaissance. Monteverdi and Vivaldi produced important Baroque settings, but Bach's Magnificat for five parts and orchestra is probably the best known today.

Although the madrigal is more usually associated with earlier periods, this secular form for voices

and accompaniment continued to be popular in the Baroque period. The subtle word-painting that the madrigal engendered influenced other genres and is found in many sacred choral works of the period.

St. Matthew Passion

For a musician such as Bach who was principally concerned with church music, the Passion, which set the biblical events from the Last Supper up to the Crucifixion, was an opportunity to use the dramatic techniques of opera within a religious setting. Bach wrote at least three such works (only two have survived); for its mastery of emotion, imagination, and power of expression make the St. Matthew Passion a towering monument of human creativity. It was written to be performed either side of the

sermon at the Good Friday service (in either 1727 or 1729). Bach also collaborated with the Leipzig poet Picander to create a libretto, which both presented the biblical drama and offered contemplations upon the content. The St. Thomas Church for which it was written added an extra layer of drama to proceedings; by using its two organ lofts, Bach was able to distribute his forces as a double choir across the venue. Although he had employed such techniques in other works, such as the motets, its use here with the addition of two orchestras and organists allowed for the widest variety of dramatic textures.

In addition to the original material, Bach also inserted a number of Lutheran chorales. When Martin Luther had started translating services into German, new melodies had been required. These formed well-known hymns that became the mainstay of congregational worship. Bach harmonized many hundreds of such melodies, regularly using them as the basis of cantatas or chorale preludes. In the *St. Matthew Passion*, the chorale melodies date from between 1525 and 1656, and would therefore have been familiar to his audience. Most are presented

> One who has completely forgotten Christianity truly hears it here as Gospel.
> **Friedrich Nietzsche**

Cantatas and oratorios

The oratorio had traditionally been a concert piece for orchestra, choir, and soloists, depicting a biblical episode or the life of a saint. It differed from opera only in being unstaged and lacking interaction between characters. The cantata often used similar forces but was performed in church before and after the sermon and was a series of reflections on the service's biblical texts. Both genres used operatic elements such as recitatives, arias, and choruses, but the cantata tends to use them more subtly in order to imply the drama.

By the High Baroque period, it is difficult to differentiate the cantata from the oratorio. Bach's *Christmas Oratorio*, for example, is actually a cantata. Bach, whose cantatas are considered to be some of the most sublime religious music ever written, also wrote secular works in the genre, such as the *Coffee Cantata*, which is essentially a short comic opera.

in four-part harmony, but three are referenced as accompanying elements in other movements. In this way, Bach was able to mix the known with the new—essential for a congregation first experiencing such an intense, large-scale work.

Musical characterization

Rather like an opera, the key roles in the *St. Matthew Passion* are taken by soloists, but in the absence of physical drama and costumes, Bach often gives them distinct musical characterizations. The tenor Evangelist, the narrator, always uses recitative *secco* with continuo (speechlike solo singing with a sparse bass accompaniment) to deliver the Gospel texts. This allows the narrative to be strong, clear, and unambiguous. The words of Jesus, however, are recitatives accompanied by the strings from the first orchestra. In playing sustained notes and highlighting key words, they add an unworldly sound to the Vox Christi (voice of Christ)—often likened to a halo. Such characterization is perhaps most strongly heard when, almost operatically, Jesus utters his last words without the accompaniment of strings, resulting in the truly

devastating pathos of abandonment. However, in the hands of Bach, this same absence of strings in the soprano aria *"Aus Liebe will mein Heiland sterben"* ("Out of Love My Saviour Is Willing to Die") suggests a different, almost plaintive mood.

Throughout the work, Bach is clearly aware of the need to use the orchestra to ensure that his congregation receives the full »

Bach played the organ and taught for 27 years at the St Thomas School in Leipzig, as shown here in an 1882 engraving. He and his pupils supplied music for the city's four main churches.

impact of the text. This attention to orchestration, which was far more prevalent in stage works of the time (which were often of similar length to the Passion), can be seen in the use of the oboes da caccia (a low oboe similar to the cor anglais) to underpin the eerie description of Golgotha in *"Ach Golgotha."* No less vivid is the moment in *"Buss und Reu"* ("Guilt and Pain") where the alto describes his tears to the sound of flutes playing staccato notes.

A large, varied cast

The piece also has parts for Judas, Peter, two priests, Pontius Pilate and his wife, two witnesses, and

The St. Thomas Boys Choir, Leipzig, still flourishing today, dates back more than 800 years to 1212. With Bach as Cantor (1723–1750), the church and city became the center of Protestant music.

two maids, although they are not usually all taken by different soloists. In many performances the minor soloists are also members of the choirs. With such a diverse cast and discursive text, it was also possible for Bach to break from the oratorio tradition of avoiding interaction between soloists; he included duets and crowd scenes with passages that simulate simultaneous and interjecting speakers. So, in *"Weissage uns, Christie"* ("Prophesy Christ") the two choruses alternate in a style known as *cori spezzati*, which was first developed at St. Mark's in Venice, while in *"Herr, wir haben gedacht"* ("Lord, We Thought") they sing simultaneously to represent the power-hungry Pharisees.

The real glory of the choruses is in the contrapuntal writing, notably when, after singing in excruciating dissonance as they call for the

> He demands that singers should be able to do with their throats whatever he can play on the keyboard.
> **Johann Scheibe**
> *Critic and composer (1708–1776)*

freedom of the prisoner Barrabas, they then embark on a series of complex musical structures notoriously difficult to perform. An earlier, particularly poignant moment follows Jesus's capture in the garden, where after a sighing orchestral introduction, the soprano

and alto bemoan Jesus's fate in resigned tones. In contrast, the chorus demands his release, creating an extraordinary tension between the two moods. While the resignation continues, the chorus, which may depict the disciples or the congregation, gets more agitated, and the orchestra drives the music forward to a breathless conclusion. The ending of this section in the major key might seem surprising, underpinning as it does the words "murderous blood." It is suggested, however, that the music might be reminding the listener that while the story is one of suffering, without the capture of Jesus, his Crucifixion—and thereby salvation—is not possible.

Elsewhere, many of the more contemplative texts, such as the chorale *"Ich bin's ich sollte büssen"* ("It is I who should suffer") or the bass aria *"Mache dich, mein Herze, rein"* ("Make thyself clean my heart"), encourage listeners to feel the emotion and identify with the drama. The most striking example is perhaps the aria *"Erbarme dich, mein Gott"* ("Have mercy Lord, my God"). The simplicity of the lilting rhythm, accompanied by a lamenting violin, underpins and emphasizes the intensity of Peter's sense of horror and guilt at his

Bach and three of his sons pose for a portrait (1730) by Balthasar Denner. Bach had 20 children, and from the early 1500s to the late 1700s, his family produced more than 70 musicians.

The most beautiful piece of music ever written for the violin.
Yehudi Menhuin
Describing "Erbarme dich, mein Gott"

betrayal of Jesus, as he repeats the 17 words of the text with increasing anguish.

The *St. Matthew Passion* received only a handful of performances in Bach's lifetime. The newer Classical style had begun to revolutionize musical composition and enjoyment, and the composer was considered to be behind the times in writing contrapuntal music of this kind.

Bach's legacy
By the end of Bach's life, his music was called "learned" in the most pejorative sense; the music of his son Carl Philipp Emanuel Bach was better known. Very little of Bach's music was printed, although the keyboard works were sometimes studied; Ludwig van Beethoven (1770–1827) often performed fugues and preludes from Bach's *The Well-Tempered Clavier*. However, major works such as the *St. Matthew Passion* existed only in hand-copied examples within a very small circle of admirers, some of whom had been his students.

It was through such a group that Mendelssohn came to study Bach's works in the early 19th century and put on a performance of the *St. Matthew Passion* in 1829. This performance, although a landmark in the revival of Bach's music, was neither complete nor authentic, but it did help to raise awareness of Bach's work. It was not long before societies were created to publish and perform his work. Today, the *St. Matthew Passion* is frequently presented as a staged work; with its similarities to opera, it can have a powerful effect on audiences. ■

TELEMANN IS ABOVE ALL PRAISE

MUSIQUE DE TABLE (1733), GEORG PHILIPP TELEMANN

IN CONTEXT

FOCUS
Tafelmusik

BEFORE
1650 Joachim von Sandrart's painting *Das Friedensmahl* ("The peace meal") depicts musicians performing Tafelmusik at a banquet for a diplomatic conference.

1680s Printed collections of Tafelmusik, mostly by German composers of the day, become more common.

AFTER
1770s The genre of Tafelmusik is gradually replaced by other types of "light" musical entertainment such as the *divertimento* and serenade.

1820 An engraving by Johann Wunder depicts a performance of Tafelmusik at a municipal banquet in "Krähwinkel"—an invented place name intended to suggest old-fashioned, small-town parochialism.

The demand for *Tafelmusik* (table music)—background music for banquets—grew steadily from the mid-16th century onward. *Musique de table*, a collection of such music by Georg Philipp Telemann, a prolific German composer who relished the assimilation and mastery of different musical styles, draws together a range of chamber genres that lent themselves to Tafelmusik. Telemann marketed the collection as a prestige product that could be purchased by subscription.

Telemann's collection divides into three "productions," each one containing an orchestral dance suite, a concerto, a quartet, a trio sonata, and solo sonata, finishing with an orchestral "conclusion." Apart from the dance suites, considerable use is made of the slow-fast-slow-fast four-movement pattern of the traditional *Sonata da Chiesa* (a genre of instrumental chamber or orchestral music sometimes performed at church services). Each "production" provides enough music for an evening's entertainment and contains meticulously crafted music that is always memorably melodious—even evoking popular folk songs at times.

Handel, who was among the collection's 206 subscribers, appears to have borrowed some of its musical ideas. Themes in his oratorio *The Arrival of the Queen of Sheba* bear resemblance to material from the Concerto in the second "production" of *Musique de table*. ∎

He [Telemann] could write a church piece in eight parts with the same expedition another would write a letter.
George Frideric Handel

See also: Corelli's *Concerti Grossi* 80–81 ▪ *Water Music* 84–89 ▪ *The Four Seasons* 92–97 ▪ C.P.E. Bach's Flute Concerto in A major 120–121

HIS WHOLE HEART AND SOUL WERE IN HIS HARPSICHORD

HIPPOLYTE ET ARICIE (1733), JEAN-PHILIPPE RAMEAU

Galant music was born out of opposition to the perceived complexity of Baroque music. While the latter was often characterized by seriousness and grandeur, the *style galante* was elegant, light, and immediate.

One of the most lauded advocates of this style was the French composer Jean-Philippe Rameau, whose first opera, *Hippolyte et Aricie*, premiered in Paris in 1733. Rameau cast his opera in the conventional five-act form of a *tragédie en musique* that was established by Jean-Baptiste Lully. In every other way, however, he broke Lully's mold, using daring dissonances, longer phrase structures, and an ornate approach to melodic writing that came to typify the style galante.

War of words

Hippolyte et Aricie drew harsh criticism from so-called "Lullistes," who feared that Rameau's Italianate music threatened the iconic status of Lully's operas in French culture.

US mezzo-soprano Jennifer Holloway plays Diane during a rehearsal of Rameau's *Hippolyte et Aricie* in the Théâtre du Capitole, Toulouse, in 2009.

The debate between Lullistes and Ramistes raged for several years, during which Rameau released a further four operas. In time, however, his music became more accepted, and by the time of the *Querelle des Bouffons* in 1752, a two-year dispute about the relative merits of French and Italian opera, Rameau's music was considered typically French. ∎

See also: *Le bourgeois gentilhomme* 70–71 ▪ *Orfeo ed Euridice* 118–119 ▪ *The Magic Flute* 134–137 ▪ *The Barber of Seville* 148 ▪ *La traviata* 174–175

BACH IS LIKE AN ASTRONOMER WHO ... FINDS THE MOST WONDERFUL STARS

THE ART OF FUGUE (1751),
JOHANN SEBASTIAN BACH

IN CONTEXT

FOCUS
Baroque counterpoint

BEFORE
c.1606–1621 Sweelinck composes the *Fantasia chromatica*, one of the first works to demonstrate contrapuntal development of a single subject.

1725 Fux publishes *Gradus ad Parnassum* ("Steps to Parnassus"), which includes exercises in how to write fugues. Mozart later studied this work.

AFTER
1837 Mendelssohn publishes Six Preludes and Fugues, Op. 35, demonstrating the fugue as a viable Romantic genre.

1910 Busoni publishes the *Fantasia contrappuntistica*, a homage to *The Art of Fugue* which includes a postmodern completion of its last fugue.

I n contrast to later music that frequently depended on a single melody line over a series of harmonies, Baroque music was often constructed by combining a number of independent and interlacing melody lines, or voices. This technique, known as counterpoint, allowed composers to create works of overwhelming complexity and drama, reflecting the richness of other contemporary art forms. However, it also required consummate skill to compose long spans of music with sufficient variety and interest.

The rise of the Classical style, and its emphasis on simplicity and preference for more slowly changing

See also: *Missa l'homme armé* 42 ▪ *Ein feste Burg ist unser Gott* 78–79 ▪ *St. Matthew Passion* 98–105 ▪ *Elijah* 170–173 ▪ *Fauré's Requiem* 210–211 ▪ *The Dream of Gerontius* 218–219

The second fugue of Bach's *The Well-tempered Clavier* is in C minor. Both sets of 24 preludes and fugues are arranged in the 12 major and minor keys between C and the B above it.

harmony, reduced the need for musicians to master such complex techniques. However, Bach, the preeminent practitioner of counterpoint in the Baroque period, considered the skill to be so vital that he attempted toward the end of his life to organize and display the results of his knowledge in works such as *The Art of Fugue*, a cycle of some 20 fugues.

Principles of counterpoint

Much earlier, Bach had published didactic works to teach keyboard players counterpoint. These included two collections of special significance—the *15 Inventions in two parts* and the *15 Sinfonias in three parts*. In each of the pieces, a simple opening melody is presented unaccompanied and

then transferred to the other parts (or "voices" as they are known, even in instrumental music) while the first part continues with a complementary melody.

For the performer, the difficulty of such works is not just to be able to play the often swiftly flowing parts with ease but also to be able to balance the relative importance of the voices, so that the listener can appreciate the interplay and

experience a satisfying musical performance. While these works abide by the strict Baroque rules that govern dissonance when it is permitted (for instance, on passing notes on weak beats), their structure is relatively free.

Building a fugue

Bach was best known for his fugues, which follow the same principles but organize them »

Preludes, fugues, and well-tempered tuning

Bach's two books entitled *The Well-Tempered Clavier* each contained 24 preludes and fugues in all the major and minor keys. These provided models that keyboard players could use to develop their proficiency and also celebrated the range of keys that could be employed using the tuning methods of his time.

Tuning, or "temperament," was always a tricky issue. A note one octave apart from another sounds similar because the sound frequency can be reduced to a simple 2:1 ratio.

Frequency ratios between other notes are more complex, so tuning to a C major scale, keeping all the intervals pure, would make other scales sound out of tune to slightly different degrees. The mean-tone system, used from c.1570 and based on a pure third interval, worked well only for 10–15 of 24 keys. The well-tempered system was a compromise, tuning to intervals sufficiently equidistant to allow for performances in all keys. The modern equal temperament system divides the octave into equal, mostly impure intervals.

When tuning a piano, such as this Schimmel concert instrument from Germany, the tuner uses a tuning fork or an electronic device to adjust the strings to the required pitch.

Structure: The fugue													
	EXPOSITION			EPISODE	MIDDLE SECTION					EPISODE	FINAL SECTION		CODA
Soprano			S	FP	FP	A	FP	S	CS	FP	CS	FP	FP
Alto		A	CS	FP	S	CS	FP	FP	FP	FP	S	FP	FP
Bass	S	CS	FP	FP	FP	FP	FP	FP	A	FP	FP	S	TP

In a fugue, a word derived from the Latin for "flight," each of three or more voices enter one after the other, imitating and modifying the initial theme. The structure illustrated here has many other possible variants.

Key

S = *Subject*—The principal theme of the fugue.
A = *Answer*—The subject, repeated a fifth (5 notes) higher.
CS = *Counter-Subject*—A contrasting secondary theme.
FP = *Free Part*—Material based on the first theme.
TP = *Tonic Pedal*—Sustained final bass note.

within far more rigorous structures, which allow for very rich listening experiences. The basic structure of a fugue requires a melody known as the "subject" to be presented by the first voice in the home key. The next voice then presents the same melody but starting on the fifth note of the scale being used, and this is known as the "answer." When replying to this, the original voice plays a "counter-subject," which may be very contrasting. The third voice then enters with the "subject" again, starting on the

Ceaseless work, analysis, reflection, writing much, endless self-correction, that is my secret.
Johann Sebastian Bach

same note in a different octave, while the second voice now performs the counter-subject and the first voice will usually play free material derived from the subject. This continues in the same way until all the voices have entered, creating an exposition that moves rapidly from simplicity to complexity, while using limited musical material.

The fugue will then progress by adding mood-changing "episodes," again often derived from the opening material. The middle section, in turn, presents the subject in different keys and formats until the work returns to the opening key. However, further variants heighten this journey, such as the "stretto," where subjects and answers enter before the previous ones have been resolved.

Teaching tools

In writing the 48 fugues of *The Well-Tempered Clavier*, Bach offered a compendium of techniques to be studied by both keyboard players and composers. These were designed as teaching tools, and

although they are often performed in concert halls, they are not as powerful as his organ fugues or those found in his sacred music. However, they had a considerable influence on later composers, who dubbed them the "Old Testament" of music (the Beethoven sonatas were the New Testament) and paid tribute to them; Shostakovich, for instance, composed *24 Preludes and Fugues*. Even now, pianists study Bach's *The Well-Tempered Clavier* as part of their training.

Bach's fascination with counterpoint did not merely focus on the fugue. His suites of dance movements rely on an understanding of counterpoint for their inner energy; even when the music is for solo violin or cello, it often hints at what the other voices would play if there were more instruments by injecting notes and phrases in different registers.

Bach was similarly attracted to canons, where one voice follows the exact melodic contour of the other but slightly later (the round, "London's Burning" is an example of this). His use of this technique is

particularly evident in the *Goldberg Variations*, a set of 30 keyboard variations published in 1741, which were, he said, for "connoisseurs to refresh their spirits."

Based on a repeating base line, Bach composed every third variation as a canon, but with one extra dimension. The first canon begins with both voices starting on the same note. In the next canon, however, although the second voice is playing the same tune as the first, it plays it one note higher; here incredible skill is required to create melodic material that works and sounds pleasing to the listener's ear. The next canon presents the second voice two notes higher, and this continues until, in the last canon, the voices are nine notes apart. Apparently not content with this plethora of canons, Bach had 14 more sketched out in his copy of *Goldberg Variations*, built on the first eight notes of the bass line.

In *The Musical Offering*, his last major keyboard work, written for the newly invented piano, Bach wrote a collection of 14 canons and fugues based on a theme purportedly composed by the King of Prussia, Frederick II. Rather than always writing out the music in full, here Bach presents some musical conundrums that have come to be called "riddle fugues." In these, he writes out only the main melody, sometimes as an acrostic, and then, in Latin, briefly states what kind of canon it should be and in how many voices. The performer has to work out how to play the piece. He even includes a so-called "crab canon" where the theme is played backward and forward at the same time. Interestingly, the six-part fugue from this work, known as the "Ricercar a 6" is written on six staves—one staff per voice—rather than in an arrangement for two hands. Bach

> It's the most difficult thing I've ever approached. You've got to keep it going; how do you do that? … There's never been anything more beautiful in all of music.
> **Glenn Gould**
> *Pianist (1932–1982)*

presented *The Art of Fugue* in the same way, perhaps to suggest that it was pure music without being tied to any particular instrument.

Unfinished legacy

The Art of Fugue is the culmination of Bach's contrapuntal interests. Written as 14 fugues and four canons, each one uses the same principal theme in some way to generate music of extraordinary subtlety and variety. The last fugue, or "contrapunctus" as he calls them, presents a series of three different subjects, each worked out in four voices before moving to the next. The final one presents one of the most poignant moments in the history of music. Bach introduces a four-note theme that spells out his name (in German notation B = B-flat and H = B, so BACH = B-flat A C B), but before he finishes working it out, the manuscript trails off. ∎

Glenn Gould, a brilliant 20th-century Canadian pianist, seen here recording Bach's keyboard music, was noted for his skill in clearly articulating the texture of the preludes and fugues.

CLASSI

1750–1820

CAL

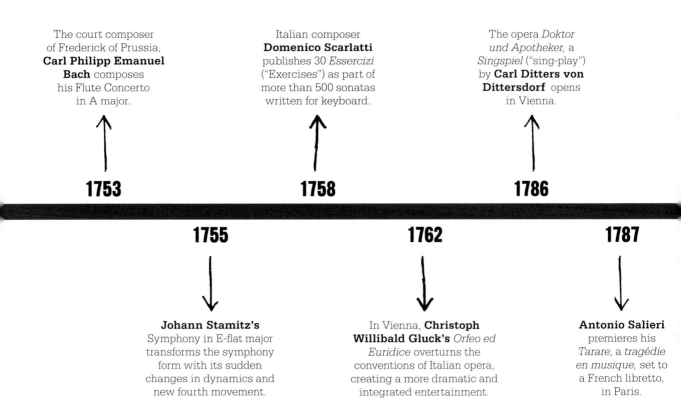

The court composer of Frederick of Prussia, **Carl Philipp Emanuel Bach** composes his Flute Concerto in A major.

Italian composer **Domenico Scarlatti** publishes 30 *Essercizi* ("Exercises") as part of more than 500 sonatas written for keyboard.

The opera *Doktor und Apotheker,* a *Singspiel* ("sing-play") by **Carl Ditters von Dittersdorf** opens in Vienna.

1753

1758

1786

1755

1762

1787

Johann Stamitz's Symphony in E-flat major transforms the symphony form with its sudden changes in dynamics and new fourth movement.

In Vienna, **Christoph Willibald Gluck's** *Orfeo ed Euridice* overturns the conventions of Italian opera, creating a more dramatic and integrated entertainment.

Antonio Salieri premieres his *Tarare,* a *tragédie en musique,* set to a French libretto, in Paris.

T he 18th century was the "Age of Enlightenment" in Europe, a time when the old political order was giving way to a new, more inclusive society. The aristocratic courts continued to provide patronage for the arts, but the rise of an urban middle class created a new concert- and operagoing audience with different tastes. The music of the period also reflected Enlightenment values of rationalism and humanism that looked to the aesthetic ideals of Ancient Greece, rejecting the extravagant counterpoint of the Baroque era in favor of a more detached style that emphasized elegance and proportion.

The Classical period in music history began around 1750. It lasted not much more than 50 years yet was so influential that the term "classical music" is widely used to refer to long-established musical traditions in general. Among the first to adopt the new style were two of J.S. Bach's sons: Carl Philipp Emmanuel, a court musician who bridged the gap between Baroque and Classical styles of music, and his brother Johann Christian, who made his name in London, staging public concerts and popularizing the newly invented piano. Some of the most exciting developments, however, were happening in Mannheim, Germany, where the court orchestra enabled composers such as Johann Stamitz to explore new musical forms, including the symphony and concerto.

Opera was undergoing a similar transformation. Christoph Willibald Gluck, dissatisfied with the stilted, artificial nature of Baroque opera, began a series of "reform operas," simplifying the music and aiming for a more realistic drama.

The Viennese scene
As the Classical style became established, composers and performers tended to gravitate toward Vienna, which was becoming the cultural as well as geographical center of Europe, with a prosperous population eager to hear new music. Three composers stood out from the others: Joseph Haydn, Wolfgang Amadeus Mozart, and Ludwig van Beethoven.

Haydn, although a central figure in the formation of this Viennese musical scene, was not initially a part of it. He took a conventional job as *Kapellmeister* (musical

Inventor of the string quartet, **Joseph Haydn** composes his Opus 54, three string quartets whose originality transforms chamber music.

Muzio Clementi publishes his Piano Sonata in F-Sharp minor, Op. 25, No. 5, introducing innovations to the sonata form.

In London, the Czech piano virtuoso and composer **Jan Ladislav Dussek** publishes an influential treatise on piano playing.

1788

1790

1793

1788

1791

1803

Wolfgang Amadeus Mozart composes Symphony No. 40 in G minor, the high point of the symphony in the Classical period.

Singspiel reaches its zenith with the highly successful premiere of **Mozart's** *The Magic Flute* in Vienna.

Beethoven releases his "Eroica" Symphony to widespread acclaim, paving the way for the music of the Romantic period.

director) at the Esterházy family's rural estate in Hungary, producing music for twice-weekly concerts. Isolated from the wider musical world, Haydn developed his own particular style. He had a staff of talented musicians (who referred to him as "Papa Haydn") and was able to both hone his skills and refine musical forms, such as the symphony, string quartet, sonata, and solo concerto. Despite the remoteness of the Esterházy estate, news of his music spread to Vienna and beyond, once it was published.

As Haydn was starting his career as a court musician, a young musical prodigy from Salzburg was being paraded around the courts and concert halls by his ambitious father. A precocious genius, Wolfgang Amadeus Mozart learned the elements of the new Classical

style as he toured Europe. Realizing he was not suited to life as a court musician, he decided to try to earn a living as a freelance composer—one of the first to do so—in Vienna. Here he met Haydn on one of his trips to the capital from Esterházy, and the two became friends. Mozart was inspired to develop his symphonies and string quartets along the same lines as Haydn had, but he also made a living—and a reputation— as a composer and performer of piano music. He later became known as the foremost opera composer of the period.

Enter Beethoven
While Haydn and Mozart were at the height of their fame in the 1770s, another ambitious father had aspirations for his gifted son. Although Ludwig van Beethoven

did not make it as a child prodigy, at the age of 13 he got a job as a court musician in Bonn and then became a freelance composer, performer, and teacher in Vienna. He settled there in 1792, too late to meet his hero, Mozart, who had died the year before, but he took lessons in composition from Haydn.

Beethoven's early compositions, symphonies, piano sonatas, and chamber music were in the style established by Haydn and Mozart but showed signs of a more passionate temperament that differed from the Classicism of his elders. In 1803, Beethoven's Third Symphony, the "Eroica," extended the form of the symphony, developing and expanding expressive musical language and heralding the beginning of a new period of musical history. ■

ITS FORTE IS LIKE THUNDER, ITS CRESCENDO A CATARACT

SYMPHONY IN E FLAT MAJOR, OP. 11, NO. 3, (1754–1755), JOHANN STAMITZ

IN CONTEXT

FOCUS
Expanding the scope of the orchestra

BEFORE
1720s Composers of Neapolitan operas, such as Leonardo Vinci, write "sinfonie" (symphonies) in three movements as preludes to their dramatic works.

1732 Italian composer Giovanni Battista Sammartini begins to write a series of three-movement symphonies.

AFTER
1766 In Paris, Mozart befriends the Mannheim composer and conductor Christian Cannabich, a pupil and follower of Stamitz.

1772 Haydn, in his *Sturm und Drang* ("Storm and Stress") symphonies, further explores the emotive style of orchestral music pioneered by the Mannheim composers.

Stamitz's musical home Mannheim, seen here in an engraving of 1788 showing the Elector's castle, court church (Hofkirche), and armoury became a center of music innovation.

I n 1741, the composer Johann Stamitz moved from his home in Bohemia (now the Czech Republic) to Mannheim, capital of the Electoral Palatinate, a German territory. There he became court violinist and, in 1745, was appointed concertmaster of the orchestra. Stamitz raised the standards of orchestral playing, hiring talented musicians, some of whom were also composers in their own right, and extended the orchestra by adding wind instruments, such as oboes and horns. He directed this diverse group, not from the keyboard, as had previously been the norm, but from his desk at the head of the violin section, using his bow to signal the start of the piece and to indicate rhythm and tempo. Under Stamitz, the Mannheim orchestra became renowned for the superb quality and precision of its playing and for the new soundscape that it created.

See also: Mozart's Symphony No. 40 in G minor 128–131 ▪ *Symphonie fantastique* 162–163 ▪ Schumann's Symphony No. 1 166–169 ▪ *Faust Symphony* 176–177

The wind instruments could not be used to better advantage; they lift and carry, they reinforce and give life to the storm of the violins.
C.F.D. Schubart
Poet, organist, and composer

Many of the works played by Stamitz's Mannheim orchestra were symphonies, a form that had originated in Italy as the prelude, or overture, to operas but had now become part of the Baroque concert repertoire. These works usually consisted of three movements: one slow between two fast.

The symphony reinvented

In the Symphony in E-flat, and other works, Stamitz took hold of the symphony form and transformed it, creating many of the features that distinguish its musical style. He added an extra movement: a minuet with a contrasting section, called a "trio" because it was originally meant to be played by three musicians. He also adopted the sonata form, used in the opening movement of the E-flat symphony, in which the first theme, played in the home key (E-flat) by the full orchestra is contrasted with a second theme, here played by the oboes, in the dominant key (B-flat). This is followed by a development section,

with the first movement concluding on a recapitulation of the second theme, this time in the home key. This sonata form (usually with a recapitulation of the first theme) became the template for symphonic writing in the Classical period, particularly in first movements.

Musical fireworks

An even more striking feature of Stamitz's symphonies, including the E-flat—and of the Mannheim school in general—was the use of strong, dynamic contrasts. Sometimes a sudden fortissimo appears in a passage of soft music, sometimes a dramatic crescendo, in which the orchestra's sound gets gradually louder and louder, to exhilarating effect. Another favorite mannerism was the "Mannheim rocket," a rapidly rising melody or phrase accompanied by a crescendo. Combined with the Mannheim orchestra's varied instrumental palette of strings and wind instruments, symphonies like those of Stamitz thrilled audiences and pointed the way to a more dramatic, emotional music.

The E-flat symphony was one of Stamitz's last orchestral works, but his legacy lived on through his two composer sons, Carl and Anton. They and others, such as Christian Cannabich (1731–1798), who led the Mannheim orchestra after Stamitz's death, developed his style, and soon court composers all over Europe were writing new symphonies to entertain their employers. The Mannheim composers impressed the young Mozart, who admired their orchestra and adopted some of Stamitz's compositional techniques in his own music. ▪

Johann Stamitz

Born in Německý Brod (now Havlíčkův Brod), Bohemia, in 1717, Stamitz learned music from his father, an organist and choirmaster, before attending a Jesuit school in Jihlava and university in Prague. He probably worked as a violinist before arriving in Mannheim in the early 1740s, rising rapidly to the court post of director of orchestral music in 1750.

Stamitz lived most of his working life in Mannheim, although he also spent a year in Paris, in 1754–1755, where he was already celebrated as a composer and performed in a series of successful concerts. Stamitz wrote church music and many chamber works, but he is best remembered for his orchestral pieces, which include violin concertos and many symphonies, of which 58 survive. He returned from Paris to Mannheim in 1755 and died there in 1757.

Other key works

c.1745 *Three Mannheim Symphonies* (in G major, A major, and B-flat major)
c.1750 Mass in D major
1754 Flute concerto in C major

THE MOST MOVING ACT IN ALL OF OPERA

ORFEO ED EURIDICE (1762), CHRISTOPH WILLIBALD GLUCK

IN CONTEXT

FOCUS
Classical *opera seria*

BEFORE
1690 Composers such as Alessandro Scarlatti create a new style of opera derived from Baroque vocal works—the Neapolitan School—rapidly popularizing the genre.

1748 Gluck's fame is enhanced when his opera *La Semiramide riconosciuta* ("Semiramis Revealed") is performed in Vienna for the birthday of Habsburg empress Maria Theresa.

1752 Gluck and librettist Pietro Metastasio produce the highly successful opera, *La clemenza di Tito* (*The Clemency of Titus*).

AFTER
1781 Mozart's opera *Idomeneo* premieres. It shows the influence of Gluck, particularly in the accompanied recitatives.

The opera *Orfeo ed Euridice* by Christoph Willibald Gluck was first performed in Vienna in 1762. It is based on a familiar tale from classical mythology, the story of Orpheus's journey to the underworld to rescue his wife, Eurydice. Unlike the original myth, but in line with contemporary taste, Gluck's opera has a happy ending.

Even if the opera's story was largely familiar, Gluck's style was quite new. He transformed opera to integrate the music and drama more fully than before, streamlining distracting elements that slowed up the action, making the work more

There is no musical rule that I have not willingly sacrificed to dramatic effect.
Christoph W. Gluck

involving and more real. He also humanized his characters and their arias by making them express emotions more directly.

Opera seria

In the mid-18th century, the most fashionable type of opera was what is now called *opera seria* (serious opera). This type of opera features recitative—passages sung in the rhythm of speech with many syllables on the same note that are usually accompanied only by continuo instruments (typically harpsichord and cello alone), playing an improvised added bass line—and arias, accompanied by full orchestra. The arias have a distinct structure, called *da capo* ("from the top"), with three sections, the third being a repeat of the first, with ornamentation to show off the singer's ability. In between, the second section introduces a new melody or develops the initial tune. Meanwhile, features such as rich and varied stage sets and elaborate ballets, often enliven the event.

Gluck believed that the lavish spectacles and the long showy arias tended to get in the way of the drama and that the difference in musical texture between the

See also: *Euridice* 62–63 ▪ *St. Matthew Passion* 98–105 ▪ *The Magic Flute* 134–137 ▪ *Der Freischütz* 149

arias and recitatives interrupted the flow. Gluck and his librettist, Ranieri de' Calzabigi, wanted to reform opera by putting the drama center stage, sweeping away absurdities of plot and making the music serve the action. Musically this meant doing away with the repeats in the da capo arias and developing a simpler, clearer style. A good example is Orfeo's Act III aria *"Che farò senza Euridice"* ("What shall I do without Eurydice"), an aria in rondo form in which the opening theme returns at the end but without the direct da capo repetition. Gluck also integrated the arias and recitatives, using the whole orchestra to accompany the latter as well as the former.

Gluck's opera *Il Parnasso confuso* premiered in 1765 at the marriage of Emperor Joseph II. Johann Franz Greipel's painting shows Archduke Leopold on the harpsichord.

This improved the flow and made the music more expressive of character and emotion. In the Act One aria in which Orfeo sings of his grief, the composer inserts moving recitatives before each verse, further integrating the elements.

Outcomes and effects

The effect of these changes was to make operas more focused on character and action—in other words, if not fully realistic, more real and more emotionally moving. The plots tended to be more coherent and the characters and situations—even when drawn from mythology—more credible. At the same time, there were fewer opportunities for singers to make the sort of virtuosic displays that could interrupt the action. Later composers, especially Mozart, further developed these ideas to produce operatic masterpieces. ■

Christoph Willibald Gluck

The son of a forester, Gluck was born in Erasbach, Bavaria, in 1714. Largely self-taught, he traveled widely, learning the organ and cello in Prague. He studied with the composer Giuseppe Sammartini in Milan, before heading to London in the 1740s, where he composed operas for the King's Theatre. There, he met Handel, who famously stated that his own cook (bass singer Gustavus Waltz) knew more about counterpoint than Gluck.

Gluck eventually settled in Vienna, where he worked with librettist Ranieri de' Calzabigi. The pair aimed to "reform" opera by integrating the music and the action. They made operas inspired by classical mythology, including *Orfeo ed Euridice* (1762) and *Alceste* (1767). Gluck's fame grew with further works, including French versions of *Orfeo* and some of his other operas. He retired after suffering a stroke in 1779 and died in 1787.

Other key works

1767 *Alceste*
1777 *Armide*
1779 *Iphigénie en Tauride*

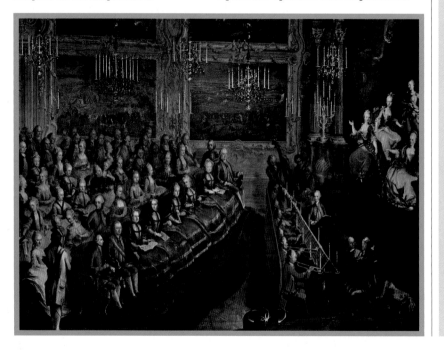

WE MUST PLAY FROM THE SOUL, NOT LIKE TRAINED BIRDS

FLUTE CONCERTO IN A MAJOR, WQ 168 (1753), CARL PHILIPP EMANUEL BACH

IN CONTEXT

FOCUS
A new freedom of expression

BEFORE
1750 C.P.E. Bach writes a setting of the Magnificat in a style like that of J.S. Bach, possibly in a bid to secure his father's former job as cantor of the Thomasschule in Leipzig.

AFTER
1772 Joseph Haydn writes his Symphony No. 44, the "Trauer" (Mourning) symphony, a masterpiece of the portrayal of emotion in orchestral music.

1777 Johann Christian Bach, Emanuel's younger brother, publishes his Op. 13 Keyboard Concertos, almost the musical opposite of Emanuel's dramatic, emotional music.

1779 C.P.E. Bach begins to publish his series of rondos and other solo keyboard works that mark the high point of his "emotional" musical style.

I n 1738, the young C.P.E., or Emanuel, Bach was appointed court harpsichordist in the household of the Crown Prince Frederick of Prussia. Two years later the prince acceded to the throne and became known as Frederick the Great as his power increased.

Emanuel, as Bach was known, traveled with the court to Berlin, where he lived as a court musician for 28 years. The best keyboard player of his generation, he attracted widespread admiration but never felt truly valued. Court musicians of the time had the status of servants, and had to write and play music that suited their employer's tastes.

The king calls the tune

Frederick was an accomplished flautist. Emanuel was therefore junior to the much better paid court flautist Johann Joachim Quantz and had the task of accompanying the king in court concerts. He was also expected to compose music for Frederick to play—pieces such as his Flute Concerto in A major. To save time, Emanuel took concertos that he had written for another

Carl Philipp Emanuel Bach

The second surviving son of Johann Sebastian Bach, Emanuel was born in Weimar, Germany, in 1714. His father nurtured his son's gift for the harpsichord.

Emanuel studied law before devoting all his time to music. In the service of Frederick the Great from 1740, he composed works for the court musicians and wrote a treatise on playing keyboard instruments. He is, however, best known for the symphonies and concertos in a highly personal and emotional style that were written later in his career. Emanuel died in Hamburg in 1788, aged 74.

Other key works

1749 Magnificat in D, Wq 215
1775–1776 Symphonies, Wq 183
1783–1787 Keyboard Sonatas, Fantasias and Rondos, Wq 58, 59, 61

See also: *Great Service* 52–53 ▪ *Water Music* 84–89 ▪ *Musique de table* 106 ▪ *Hippolyte et Aricie* 107 ▪
The Art of Fugue 108–111 ▪ Beethoven's String Quartet No. 14 in C-sharp minor 156–161

Patronage during the 18th century

Grand Prince Ferdinando de' Medici (1663–1713)		**The Esterházy family of Hungary (from 1761)**		**Habsburg ruler Emperor Joseph II (1741–1790)**		**Diplomat Baron Gottfried van Swieten (1733–1803)**	
Invites Domenico Scarlatti to his court in Florence in 1702	Commissions Handel 's opera Rodrigo (1707)	Employs Haydn for life from 1761	Commissions Beethoven's Opus 1 Piano trios (1795)	Helps Salieri become director of the Italian opera in 1774	Sponsors Mozart's Die Entführung aus dem Serail (1788)	Commissions C.P.E. Bach's six symphonies for string orchestra (1773)	Employs Mozart on various musical projects (1782–1790)

A small circle of noble patrons supported composers in
the 1700s. As music became more popular, musicians gained
a greater independence, but patronage still played a crucial role.

instrument and transcribed them for the flute—like others, the A major concerto began life as a harpsichord concerto.

Although Emanuel Bach studied composition with his father, Johann Sebastian, their styles are very different. The father's music was based on counterpoint, while his son was interested in conveying emotion. In this he was following a fashion known as *Empfindsamkeit* (sensibility) that was a reaction against the rationalism of Enlightenment philosophy. In his bid to create expressive music, Emanuel developed a distinctive style that featured sudden, dramatic changes in harmony, dynamics, and rhythm, giving his works (especially in the fast movements) a spontaneous quality; he also created affecting, melodic slow movements. Some strong rhythmic and dynamic contrasts appear in the outer movements of the A major Flute Concerto, and Emanuel would no doubt have heightened the drama had he not had to consider what Frederick would want to play.

Seeking independence
The king did not like Emanuel's more dramatic, unpredictable pieces; he preferred simpler works. In 1768, Emanuel left to become music director of Hamburg's five principal churches. He still had to write to order, but he had time to compose the music he wanted to write, either to perform himself or for patrons who were willing to give full rein to his emotional style. Later composers such as Mozart and Beethoven worked increasingly in this freelance way, carving out a role that was less like that of servant and creating music that was more personal. ■

> Keyboardists whose chief asset is mere technique … overwhelm our hearing without satisfying it and stun the mind without moving it.
> **C.P.E. Bach**

> A musician … must feel all the emotions that he hopes to arouse in his audience.
> **C.P.E. Bach**

I WAS FORCED TO BECOME ORIGINAL

STRING QUARTET IN C MAJOR, OP. 54 NO. 2, HOBOKEN III:57 (1788–1790), JOSEPH HAYDN

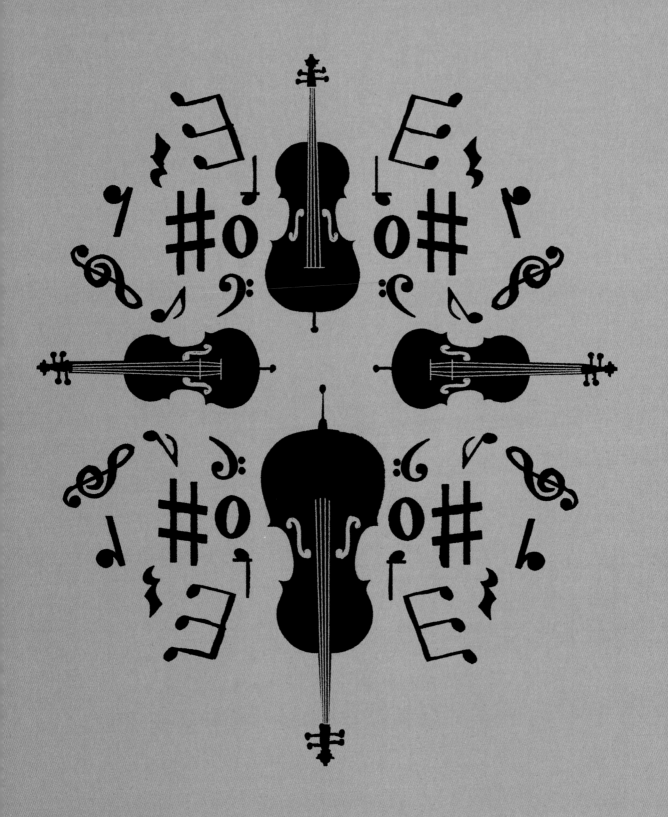

Joseph Haydn invented the
string quartet. Why he
settled on the combination
of two violins, viola, and cello is not
certain, but it may be that their
individual pitch registers closely
reflect the voices in a choir. The
instruments, and the musicians to
play them, would also have been
readily available at the Hungarian
court of the Esterházy family, where
Haydn was composer-in-residence.

The standard chamber music
grouping before Haydn was the
trio sonata, in which a keyboard
instrument was joined by two high-
melody instruments (violin or flute),
with a continuo instrument, such
as a cello, doubling the bass line of
the keyboard. Haydn's inspired use
of four instruments of the string
family effectively modernized an
older tradition that Henry Purcell
had developed a century earlier
with his String Fantasias for up to
six voices, performed on viols.

Enhanced sound
Haydn benefited from the great
strides that had been made in
instrument-making, epitomized
in Italy by the Amati family,
Antonio Stradivari, Francesco
Rugeri, and the Guarneri family.
More responsive violins, violas,
and cellos were exciting both to
composers and players. Haydn was
also interested in the advances in
bow-making. Earlier bows had to
stay close to the string, releasing
sounds in a sustained manner; by
"bouncing" the new bow off the
string, a quick, almost percussive
sound could be produced, as Haydn
shows in the finale of his Op. 33, C
major quartet (1781).

The sound-carrying qualities
of these new instruments and
techniques eventually spurred the
composition of chamber music that
could be performed in large concert
halls and not just in private salons.

Original, emotive works
The emotional expressiveness of
Haydn's mature work links it to the
German *Sturm und Drang* (Storm
and Stress) artistic movement.
For Haydn, the string quartet was
the perfect vehicle for extreme
emotional contrasts designed to
shock the audience. His early
accomplished quartets include
Op. 9, which he later declared
was the true starting point of
his quartet compositions, and

Joseph Haydn

Spanning the Baroque and
Classical periods, Joseph
Haydn was a key figure in
the development of the Classical
style. Born in Lower Austria in
1732 to parents of modest means,
he was a musically gifted child
and attended a cathedral choir
school in Vienna from the age of
eight. His early music, including
some string quartets, was first
published in Paris in 1764.

Haydn's employment from
1761 to 1790 at Esterházy
Palace, in Hungary, cemented
his reputation as a composer. He
later traveled to many musical
capitals, most notably to London
where his compositions were in
great demand. After the London
Symphonies (93–104), Haydn
wrote only six Masses and two
oratorios. In his last public
appearance, he conducted *The
Seven Last Words* in December
1803. He died quietly at home
in Vienna in 1809.

Other key works

1768 Symphony No. 49
1795 Piano trio No. 24 in D major
1797–1798 *The Creation*
1798 *Nelson Mass*

See also: Corelli's *Concerti Grossi* 80–81 ▪ C.P.E. Bach's Flute Concerto in A major 120–121 ▪ Clementi's Piano Sonata in F-sharp minor 132–133 ▪ *Die schöne Müllerin* 150–155 ▪ Beethoven's String Quartet No. 14 in C-sharp minor 156–161

Op. 20, in which the gradual liberation of the four parts into solo voices within the quartet framework marked a new development of the genre.

Op. 20, No. 2 is particularly interesting, as it reverses the more usual form of a quartet, in which the first violin dominates, by casting the cello as top voice, the second violin and viola below it, while the first violin is initially silent. The minuet third movement of Op. 20, No. 4, is also innovative. The standard pulse for minuets is three, but here accents make it sound as though it is in the rhythm of two. Likewise, in three of the finales (Op. 20, Nos. 2, 5, and 6), Haydn uses a well-established form, a fugue, to develop new ideas, such as interrupting long stretches of *sotto voce* (very soft) playing by sudden bursts of *forte* (loud).

European acclaim

Haydn is thought to have first met Mozart in the early 1780s, and they became close friends. With Haydn on second violin, Mozart on viola,

the Austrian Carl Ditters von Dittersdorf on first violin, and the Czech Johann Baptist Vanhal on cello, the four composers would often play quartets together and experiment with each other's compositions. This led Mozart to dedicate his first six mature string quartets to Haydn.

As the demand for Haydn's music spread through Europe, his quartets were performed in concert halls as well as in private salons, and he adjusted their style accordingly. By making the first violin parts ever more brilliant, with higher notes and displays of virtuosity, he naturally made the lower three voices more athletic, too. The performers also had to learn to project their sound.

A memorable, daring work

Haydn's Op. 54, No. 2 in C major, composed in 1788, is one of his many exceptionally inventive

At the Esterházy Palace, shown here in an 18th-century image, Haydn had a secure but onerous post—not only composing, but also managing musicians, manuscripts, and events.

quartets. He experimented with almost all possible tonalities (changes in pitch, and major and minor modes), as well as Classical forms (sonata, fugue, variations, minuet, scherzo, and rondo). There are quartets that are more consistently virtuosic and more brilliantly projected, and there are also earlier compositions, such as the slow movement of his Op. 20, No. 1, that perhaps better convey the perfect intimate sound of a quartet, but the extreme contrasts between the movements of Op. 54, No. 2, as well as Haydn's inspired and brave decision to end with a slow movement, single this out as a truly memorable piece of music. »

When we invoke the name Haydn, we mean one of our greatest men … Every harmonic artifice is at his command.
Ernst Ludwig Gerber
Organist and composer
(1746–1819)

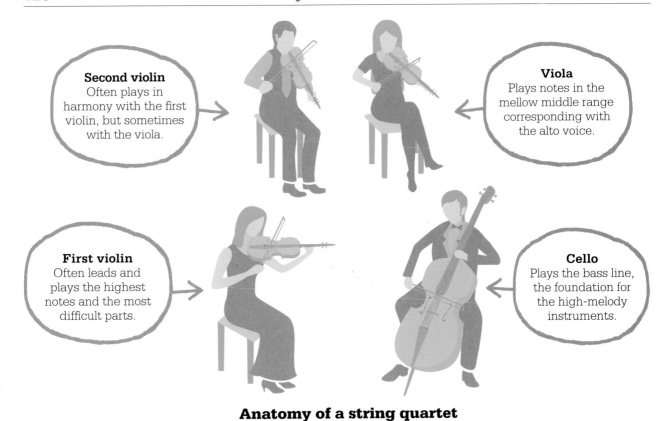

Second violin
Often plays in harmony with the first violin, but sometimes with the viola.

Viola
Plays notes in the mellow middle range corresponding with the alto voice.

First violin
Often leads and plays the highest notes and the most difficult parts.

Cello
Plays the bass line, the foundation for the high-melody instruments.

Anatomy of a string quartet

The Op. 54, No. 2 quartet was among those that Johann Tost, a violinist much admired by Haydn and a wily merchant, took to Paris to promote and sell. Its brilliantly soloistic writing for first violin was aimed at a musical audience that preferred the *quatuor concertant*, a string quartet genre fashionable in the French capital from around 1775 to the French Revolution of 1789. It must also have suited Tost's talent for playing in very high registers.

An exuberant opening
The key of C major that Haydn chose for the quartet is traditionally an indication of happy, optimistic music. The piece begins with bright and brilliant opening bars and a fast and vivaciously improvised melody in celebratory mood. Each instrument leads in

turn in the development section, while the recapitulation is marked by the cello's exuberant arpeggio and interjections from the first violin. When the movement should head to its conclusion, Haydn—like other great Classical composers, such as Mozart, Beethoven, and Schubert—ignores compositional conventions by ending with a huge climax. With both violins at their loudest, the viola and cello join in before the movement ends almost reflectively but for its final two upright chords.

Surprising contrasts
The ensuing adagio (slow) in C minor is highly introspective in mood. A sad gypsy melody is pitched in the lowest registers of all four instruments. The miracle of this movement is the imperceptible

creation of what appears to be a quintet, when the lower three play on with occasional double stops, freeing up the first violin to present a lament that sounds as if it is totally improvised. The freedom of Haydn's notation gives every violinist an opportunity to present an individual and uninhibited interpretation of this passage, which Brahms emulates in the slow movement of his Clarinet Quintet Op. 115.

The sadness of the ending—on a quiet chord—is deliberately unresolved. Instead of the normal break (and even the tuning of instruments between movements that often occurred), the piece moves straight on into the minuet, which starts hesitatingly and then gradually emulates the optimism of the first movement. In the

contrasting trio sections, this all changes as a dissonant A-flat note is repeatedly accented on a weak beat, sounding like screams of anguish. The conventional repeat of the minuet plays a critical role in restoring an optimistic mood.

The finale, however, produces the biggest surprise. Instead of the conventional fast movement, Haydn presents an adagio with a calm and reassuring melody. Yet even here the cello behaves unusually, climbing into the pitch of the first violin. After a fast interlude, the quartet ends peacefully.

Haydn's legacy

It is not known how well the quartet was received, and indeed, the much less imaginative works of a fellow Austrian, Ignace Joseph Pleyel, were more popular in Paris at the time. However, less than 20 years later, when Beethoven produced his Op. 18 quartets in 1800, a revival of Haydn's quartets occurred. The style of Haydn's 83 quartets had revolutionized chamber music. Schumann studied them before embarking on his three Op. 41 quartets, and all future composers of quartets would take inspiration from Haydn. ∎

Haydn often visited Vienna as part of Prince Esterházy's retinue. In this 19th-century painting, he is shown (in light blue) directing a quartet from his preferred second violin position.

Chamber groups

In the 18th century, as education widened and the middle class expanded, appreciation of music spread beyond the court and church. The number of amateur musicians with money and leisure time rapidly increased, and musical friends would get together in a "chamber," or room, to make music at home. This created a market for musical compositions suited to an intimate setting, especially for strings, which blended harmoniously and were more affordable and widely available, following improvements in the manufacture of instruments.

While string quartets were the most popular form of chamber ensemble during the Classical and Romantic periods, composers also wrote for quintets, with an extra viola, cello, or the addition of a double bass, and eventually works featuring other "fifth" instruments, such as the clarinet, creating a richer sound. Work for woodwind quintets (flute, oboe, clarinet, bassoon, and horn) also appeared.

As many middle-class households acquired a piano in the late 18th century, composers produced chamber music for the piano—the piano trio (piano, violin, and cello), quartet (piano trio and viola), and quintet (string quartet with piano). The piano duet for two players at one instrument also became popular for domestic and concert performances, and a number of composers wrote works for four hands, including Mozart and Schubert.

THE MOST TREMENDOUS GENIUS RAISED MOZART ABOVE ALL MASTERS

SYMPHONY NO. 40 IN G MINOR, K. 550 (1788), WOLFGANG AMADEUS MOZART

IN CONTEXT

FOCUS
Innovation in the Classical symphony

BEFORE
1759–1795 Joseph Haydn composes more than 100 symphonies in the four-movement format.

1764 Aged eight, Wolfgang Amadeus Mozart composes his First Symphony in E-flat major, K.16.

AFTER
1803 Ludwig van Beethoven completes his stormy, political "Eroica" symphony.

1824 Beethoven finishes his symphonic project with the Ninth Symphony, including a final movement featuring vocal soloists and chorus.

B y the beginning of the 1780s, Mozart had written more than 30 symphonies. These works were influenced by both musical and extra-musical factors, including his work in the archbishop's court in his home city of Salzburg, his tours of Italy's musical centers, his search for employment in Munich and Paris, and his visits to Mannheim, the capital of the symphony during the 18th century.

Classical zenith
After he settled in Vienna in 1781, Mozart wrote relatively few symphonies, focusing instead on piano concertos, chamber music, and works for the theatre. Yet in the summer of 1788, he wrote his

See also: Stamitz's Symphony in E-flat major 116–117 ▪ *The Magic Flute* 134–137 ▪ "Eroica" Symphony 138–141 ▪ *Der Freischütz* 149 ▪ *The Ring Cycle* 180–187

final three symphonies, Nos. 39–41, including the Symphony No. 40 in G minor, K.550, possibly composed for a projected concert series in a central Viennese casino. These works represent the culmination of the symphonic genre during the Classical period—though they also look ahead to the music of the 19th century, with its emphasis on a broad range of harmonies, along with concert programs ascribing distinct narratives and themes to musical pieces.

Expressive forces

As a young man, Mozart had been influenced by the *Sturm und Drang* ("storm and stress") movement that emphasized emotion and creative individuality. This style, which took its lead from contemporary literature, is also evident in works by the pioneering and prolific "father of the symphony," Joseph Haydn. In music, Sturm und Drang found expression in the use of minor keys, syncopated rhythms, melodic leaps, and other flourishes, all of which characterize Mozart's "Little" G minor symphony (No. 25, K. 183/173dB), completed in 1773.

This moody music often went hand in hand with the virtuoso playing associated with the city of Mannheim in Germany, which Mozart visited in both 1763, when he was seven years old, and again in 1777–1778, at age 21. Mannheim's instrumentalists were famous for creating dynamic shifts and thrilling crescendoes. But it was not just the style of the Mannheim symphony that was new. Its structure also differed from its counterparts, consisting of four rather than three movements. The symphony's previously dancing »

Mozart often composed music in segments before fleshing them out as finished manuscripts, such as the one below of his Symphony No. 40 in G minor.

Wolfgang Amadeus Mozart

Born in Salzburg, then part of the Holy Roman Empire, in 1756, Mozart followed in the footsteps of his father, Leopold, a musician and composer in the archbishop's court. Yet Mozart's brilliance as a violinist, pianist, and composer meant that Salzburg often seemed stifling, even provincial, and he tried to find employment elsewhere.

In 1781, he settled in the city of Vienna, the seat of Habsburg pomp and power. Working as a freelance composer, he perfected genres such as the symphony, the concerto, and the string quartet, and wrote a handful of highly successful operas. Mozart died of mysterious causes in late 1791, at the age of 35, leaving behind some 600 musical works and an extraordinary legacy for the generation that followed.

Other key works

1773 Symphony No. 25 in G minor
1779 *Krönungsmesse*
1786 *The Marriage of Figaro*
1790 *Così fan tutte*
1791 *Requiem* (incomplete)

(and somewhat frivolous) finales were also given greater weight by these court composers, further revolutionizing the genre.

The 40th symphony

While several of Mozart's early works flaunt these Mannheim-influenced, dramatic musical characteristics—for example, juxtaposing the woodwind and string sections to powerful effect—his later "Great" Symphony, No. 40 in G minor is characterized by a more integrated instrumental palette. This style is typical of works from Vienna, which along with Mannheim was the city most strongly associated with the symphony as a genre in the 18th century. While ostensibly more subdued, harmonic color and melodic drama are in plentiful supply here as well.

Beginning with a sighing figure in the strings, Symphony No. 40 in G minor features a number of bold, stormy passages, as well as virtuoso writing for the entire orchestra. Indeed, the whole work has the feeling of an unspoken, tragic drama and often echoes Mozart's music for the stage. All

of this was designed to impress the worldly Viennese, as were the audacious tonal choices that Mozart made across all four movements. These often require feats of musical ingenuity across the scale, particularly at the beginning of the development section of the energetic finale. Here, Mozart uses 11 out of the 12 notes of the chromatic scale (leaving out only G, the tonic—or central note—of the symphony), creating a complex and sometimes dissonant sound. It is little wonder that Arnold Schoenberg, known for employing all 12 notes in a scale, would later be drawn to this work in particular.

The home key, G minor, is also an important component of the work. It was, for Mozart, the musical channel through which he frequently expressed pain or tragedy, not just in complete works but also in arias such as Pamina's *"Ach, ich fühl's"* ("Oh, I feel it") in *The Magic Flute*. In addition to Symphony No. 40's harmonic twists and turns, its feeling of emotional unpredictability stems from the varying lengths of its musical phrases, as at the beginning of the

Mozart created a second version of Symphony No. 40 that included clarinets, which had only recently been invented. These were created by the 18th-century craftsman Jacob Denner.

first movement, which starts as if in mid-flow. Equally complex—and sometimes quite confrontational—is the orchestral texture. Although it never breaks out into a full fugue, as in the final movement of Mozart's "Jupiter" Symphony

A musical hub

As capital of the Habsburg Empire, Vienna was the center of European music for two centuries. It was home to many of the great Classical composers, including Mozart, Haydn, and Beethoven. They converged on the city in search of patronage and audiences, the first in a long list of composers, including

The Burgtheater on Michaelerplatz, Vienna, was operated by the Habsburg court. A number of Mozart's operas were premiered here.

Schubert (who was born in Vienna), the Strauss family, Brahms, Bruckner, Mahler, Schoenberg, and Webern.

As the public interest in music expanded, new theatres and concert halls were built to cater for them. Empress Maria Theresa built the Burgtheater close to the royal palace in 1741, and in 1833, the composer and conductor Franz Lachner founded the Künstlerverein, the forerunner of the Vienna Philharmonic Orchestra, rival to the Berlin Philharmonic for the title of world's top orchestra.

in C major (No. 41) that followed, counterpoint—alternate melodic lines played above or below the main melody—is apparent throughout. Even the minuet and trio of the symphony's third movement, normally an exercise in pleasant repetition, prove rather heated, more in the manner of a quarrel than a courtly dance.

Together, the symphony's four movements move us far beyond the balance and poise of Mozart's earlier works—as well as those of his contemporaries. They look ahead to the more turbulent music of the Romantic period.

Mozart's legacy
It is not clear if Symphony No. 40 was premiered during Mozart's lifetime, and many commentators claimed that it was not written for Vienna at all, but for posterity. However, the presence of a second version of the score, including parts for two clarinets, probably written for Mozart's friends, the clarinetists and basset horn players Anton and Johann Stadler, indicates that Mozart must have heard at least one performance before he died in 1791.

Mozart's music is so pure and beautiful that I see it as a reflection of the inner workings of the universe.
Albert Einstein

After Mozart's death, his final three symphonies, a magnificent triptych with the G minor at its heart, were repeatedly held up as the pinnacle of the Classical symphony. These works—along with Haydn's own great body of symphonies—no doubt provided the benchmark for the young Ludwig van Beethoven. Born in Bonn, Beethoven arrived in Vienna the year after Mozart's death and became one of Haydn's pupils, initially emulating the music of both his teacher and his idol Mozart. Eventually, however, Beethoven would break their

mold with radically different works, such as "Eroica" in 1804, and the Ninth Symphony of 1824.

Romantic developments
The tonally (and expressively) diverse music of Beethoven's contemporary Franz Schubert also found its model in Mozart's final works. Those who followed these Viennese masters, such as Hector Berlioz and Franz Liszt, continued to adapt the Classical symphony to their own Romantic ends, introducing new dramatic effects and elements, such as program notes to help the audience interpret the music, as in Berlioz's *Symphonie fantastique* and Liszt's symphonic poems.

Collectively, these gave the symphony an even greater sense of theater and formed the basis for Richard Wagner's "symphonic" operas, with their emphasis on recurrent motifs and the changing role of the orchestra—Wagner was the first to place the orchestra out of sight of the audience, focusing attention on the stage. The roots of such bold innovations are found in the symphonic works Mozart wrote toward the end of his short life. ■

The first movement of a symphony presents several themes and develops the sections in different keys, ending in the main key, usually in a fast-pace sonata-allegro form.

The second movement presents lyrical melodies. It usually has a ternary form, with three sections, the third repeating the first.

Two brisk minuets separated by a contrasting trio section in ternary form make up the **third movement**.

The fourth movement is fairly fast and often in a rondo form, in which the first section is repeated and there is a different new section between each repetition.

THE OBJECT OF THE PIANO IS TO SUBSTITUTE ONE PERFORMER FOR A WHOLE ORCHESTRA
PIANO SONATA IN F-SHARP MINOR, OP. 25, NO. 5 (1790), MUZIO CLEMENTI

IN CONTEXT

FOCUS
The instrumental sonata

BEFORE
1758 Domenico Scarlatti publishes his 30 *Essercizi per Gravicembalo,* which form part of his more than 500 sonatas for keyboard.

1771 Joseph Haydn specifically names a piano piece a "sonata" rather than a *divertimento*.

AFTER
1818 Beethoven completes his *Hammerklavier Sonata*, Op. 106, which takes the sonata to new heights of complexity and virtuosity.

1853 Franz Liszt writes his piano Sonata in B minor and redefines the genre for the Romantic age.

The development of the instrumental sonata mirrored a change in the function of music in the Classical period. Music was no longer an accompaniment to dance or prayer but a focus in its own right, and composers thus worked to find new ways to engage the audience. With the rise in popularity of the newly invented piano, one way of achieving this was through the drama of juxtaposing loud and soft passages, which had not been possible on the harpsichord. This became commonplace. Composers also began structuring their music into large-scale arcs called sonatas, which allowed the audience to experience a more varied musical journey. Anglo-Italian composer Muzio Clementi was an important innovator in this evolving structure, his Sonata in F-sharp minor being a prime example of the form.

A Clementi & Co. square piano
from London, where Clementi's piano manufacturing company flourished in the early 18th century.

See also: Scarlatti's Sonata in D minor 90–91 ▪ Haydn's String Quartet in C major, Op. 5, No. 2 122–127 ▪ "Eroica" Symphony 138–141 ▪ *Préludes* 164–165

Generally, sonatas were formed of three or four movements, the first of which was structured according to what is now called the Sonata Principle. This was usually the longest and most dramatic of the movements and the one in which the composer was expected to demonstrate his dexterity in musical discourse to move and grip the audience. Usually a fast, driving movement, the first movement of Clementi's Sonata in F-sharp minor is unusual in that it portrayed a slower, more meditative mood of considerable pathos, distinguishing it from other works of the time.

A sonata's second movement was usually slower, giving the composer a chance to demonstrate his finer sensibilities, and often had songlike sections. In his F-sharp minor sonata, Clementi goes one step further: sometimes the treble has a single line, resembling a singer's aria, accompanied by the light repeated chords found in operatic string writing. By using such a technique, Clementi was perhaps attempting to steal a little limelight from the opera—the most public forum for music at the time.

Minuet/trio and finale

In four-movement sonatas, it was then traditional to include a minuet and trio as a throwback to the Baroque dance suites, and this provided a kind of respite amid the stronger movements—although Beethoven would soon exchange this respite for a vigorous "scherzo" (Italian for "to joke"), whose mood might range from irony to terror.

The finale was usually lighter in substance but far more brilliant in terms of technical display, thus allowing a satisfying ending for an

The Sonata Principle

Exposition
Two themes are presented in two different keys. The first theme is in the tonic key.

⬇

Development
The themes are **manipulated**, fragmented, extended, and **transformed**.

⬇

Recapitulation
Both themes are replayed, now both in the tonic **key**.

⬇

Coda
Rounds off the movement.

⬇

The sonata principle creates a musical argument that creates tension and resolution.

audience and often great acclaim for the performers. In this sonata, Clementi enjoyed showing off his technique of playing two passages a third apart with one hand—a skill for which he was famous. This was beyond the ability of amateurs (and most performers), thereby setting a seal on this work as a piece worthy of the concert hall. ∎

Muzio Clementi

Born in Rome in 1752, Muzio Clementi came to the notice of the English patron, Sir Peter Beckford, at the age of 14. Taking Clementi to his estate in Dorset, England, Beckford sponsored Clementi's musical education for the next seven years. At his debut, Clementi was possibly the most accomplished keyboard player in the world, and he was the first true piano virtuoso.

In 1780, Clementi began a two-year tour of Europe, during which he met Mozart in Vienna. (While Clementi was impressed by Mozart's "spirit and grace," Mozart in turn called him a "charlatan.") Back in London, Clementi became a celebrated composer and teacher. He was also a very successful publisher and piano manufacturer, and he helped to found the Royal Philharmonic Society. He died in 1832 and is buried in Westminster Abbey.

Other key works

Before 1781 Piano Sonata in B-flat minor, Op. 24 No. 2.
1800 12 Waltzes for Piano, Triangle, and Tambourine
1826 *Gradus ad Parnassum*

WE WALK, BY THE POWER OF MUSIC, IN JOY THROUGH DEATH'S DARK NIGHT

THE MAGIC FLUTE (1791), WOLFGANG AMADEUS MOZART

IN CONTEXT

FOCUS
Opera in German

BEFORE
1770 Johann Adam Hiller's comic opera *Die Jagd* ("The Hunt"), one of the most popular 18th-century *singspiels* opens.

1789 The premiere of *Oberon, König der Elfen* (*Oberon, King of the Elves*) by Czech Paul Wranitzky sets a trend for *Zauberoper* ("magic opera").

AFTER
1805 Beethoven's only opera, *Fidelio,* a singspiel, has its first performance in Vienna.

1816 E.T.A. Hoffmann's *Undine,* a Zauberoper about a water spirit, opens in Berlin.

1821 Carl Maria von Weber's *Der Freischütz* ("The Marksman"), a Romantic singspiel with a supernatural theme, premieres in Berlin.

Mozart's *The Magic Flute,* a two-act opera first performed in Vienna in September 1791, marked the peak of the development of *singspiel* ("sing-play"), a uniquely German opera genre that combined music with spoken word.

Based on a libretto by Mozart's friend Emanuel Schikaneder, the opera is set in ancient Egypt and tells the story of a prince, Tamino, who strays into the realm of the mysterious Queen of the Night where he is attacked by a serpent. Rescued by the queen's three ladies-in-waiting, he falls in love with a portrait they show him of the queen's daughter, Pamina, who

See also: *Orfeo ed Euridice* 118–119 ▪ C.P.E. Bach's Flute Concerto in A major 120–121 ▪ Mozart's Symphony No. 40 in G minor 128–131 ▪ *The Barber of Seville* 148 ▪ *Der Freischütz* 149 ▪ *Tosca* 194–197

Mozart's *The Magic Flute* remains hugely popular. The opera drew more than 400,000 spectators at Austria's Bregenz Festival during a two-year run in 2013 and 2014.

has been abducted by Sarastro, high priest of the gods Isis and Osiris. Tamino vows to rescue Pamina. He, his comic companion, Papageno (the queen's bird-catcher), and Pamina undergo a series of ordeals, armed only with a magic flute and magic chimes. Light eventually triumphs over darkness, bringing a happy ending.

Popular appeal

Mozart wrote 20 operas in all, in three genres: *opera seria, opera buffa* (both sung throughout), and singspiel. Opera seria, the grandest form of opera—a style that includes Mozart's *Idomeneo* (1781) and *La clemenza di Tito* (1791)—often drew its stories from the mythology and history of ancient Greece and Rome. *Opera buffa* was comic, with Mozart's *The Marriage of Figaro* (1786) an outstanding example of the genre.

Singspiel had its roots in early 18th-century Vienna, where the imposing Theater am Kärntnertor specialized in popular musical dramas. Unlike the Italian operas performed for the court and nobility, these entertainments were for Viennese of all social backgrounds. From Vienna, singspiels spread to Germany, where in the mid-century they gained in popularity due to the influence of French *opéra comique* and English ballad opera. Both these genres mingled spoken dialogue, often satirical, with songs. John Gay's *The Beggar's Opera* (1728) was the most famous ballad opera, but it was Gay's Irish contemporary Charles Coffey who had the greatest impact in 18th-century Germany. His ballad »

I've just got back from the opera; it was as full as ever … you can see [it] continuing to rise in people's estimation.
Wolfgang Amadeus Mozart

Freemasons swear in a new member in a colored copper engraving of c.1750. Mozart was similarly initiated into Vienna's "Beneficence" lodge in 1784.

Mozart and Freemasonry

On December 14, 1784, Mozart was admitted to one of Vienna's eight Freemason lodges. The city at that time had more than 700 Masons, including "brethren"—then, as now, only men could be Masons—drawn from the highest nobility, officialdom, and even clergy, but also from the ranks of the middle classes: doctors, merchants, booksellers, and musicians, including Mozart's librettist for *The Magic Flute,* Emanuel Schikaneder. For men like Mozart, Freemasonry had many attractions—it offered a free-thinking and enlightened approach to religion; espoused the virtue of justice, which for many Masons meant active opposition to abuses of state and clerical power; and provided a place where men of different status could mix on terms of relative equality. Mozart remained a devoted Mason the rest of his life and wrote several pieces for performance at Masonic occasions, notably 1785's *Masonic Funeral Music in C Minor* in memory of two of his recently passed brethren.

opera *The Devil to Pay,* a huge success in Britain, became a success in translation in Berlin, in the 1740s. Two adaptations of other operas by Coffey inspired the Leipzig-based Johann Adam Hiller, regarded as the father of singspiel, to begin his career in the 1760s.

National genre

In the hands of composers such as Hiller, Georg Anton Benda, Karl Ditters von Dittersdorf, and Ignaz Umlauf, singspiels were no longer simply spoken dramas with musical numbers added for atmosphere and to convey character. In works such as Hiller's *Die Jagd* ("The Hunt") (1770) and Benda's *Walder* (1776) and *Romeo und Julie* (1776), the singing parts became the dramatic core of the piece. Official recognition of such works as examples of a popular and distinctively German genre, to be encouraged in the face of the all-dominant Italian opera, came when Habsburg Emperor Joseph II, a lover and patron of the arts, established a short-lived National-Singspiel company at Vienna's Burgtheater in 1778. One of its biggest successes was Mozart's *The Abduction from the Seraglio* (1782).

In the spring of 1791, Emanuel Schikaneder commissioned Mozart to write another singspiel—this time for the Theatre auf der Wieden in Vienna, where Schikaneder was the director. *Oberon, the King of the Elves,* with music by Mozart's friend Paul Wranitzky, was a recent hit for Schikaneder's company and an example of a new breed of singspiel, sometimes called

The Magic Flute's characters expressed through music

The Queen of the Night
Soprano, whose vocal dexterity culminates in a staccato aria that represents instability, greed, and duplicity.

Papageno (bird-catcher)
Baritone, who sings upbeat and bouncy folk melodies with prominent use of pan pipes, suggesting his happy-go-lucky nature.

Tamino and Pamina
Tenor and soprano, respectively, whose romantic and deeply felt arias represent enlightened principles of light and joy.

Sarastro (high priest)
Bass, whose slow and dignified performance, with speechlike delivery in parts and heightened by grand orchestral flourishes, suggests justice and wisdom.

Zauberoper ("magic opera"), which mingled comedy with supernatural elements and impressive spectacle. Keen to repeat the success of Wranitzky's work, Schikaneder himself wrote the libretto for the new opera, although it is likely that Mozart collaborated as well. The two men took a fairy tale by August Jacob Liebeskind, *Lulu, oder die Zauberflöte* (*Lulu, or The Magic Flute*), as their starting point but transformed it almost beyond recognition. Among other things, they added Masonic elements (Wranitzky, Schikaneder, and Mozart were Freemasons), such as in the initiatory ordeals that the protagonists endure.

The Magic Flute

Mozart died in 1791, just two months after *The Magic Flute* premiered. It was not only his last major completed work but also one of his most sublime. In all Mozart's operas, he showed an unsurpassed gift for creating the right music to fit each character, situation, or emotion. In *The Magic Flute*, this ranges from the deep solemnity of the priest Sarastro's songs and two powerful arias of the Queen of the

Salieri listened and watched with total attentiveness … there wasn't a number that didn't call forth from him a "bravo" or a "bello."
Wolfgang Amadeus Mozart

Opera-goers in London watch from a box in a 1796 painting by an unknown artist. Opera became fashionable in the early 18th century, with new operas commissioned for each season.

Night to the touching comedy of the duet, "Pa-pa-pa-Papagena," in which Papageno and his mate Papagena imagine a blissful future together. Only such a perfect command of musical expression enabled Mozart to hold together convincingly the often unsettling ambivalences and reversals of the opera, such as the point when the Queen of the Night unexpectedly turns from grieving mother to spite-filled ally of her daughter's worst enemy, Monostatos.

The opera's premiere on September 30, 1791, started badly but ended well. During the first act, the audience was muted in its response. Perhaps, despite the recent success of *Oberon, King of the Elves*, they were baffled by the Zauberoper's strangely magical qualities. In the second act, however, the audience came alive and at the end called Mozart onto the stage to applaud him. *The Magic Flute* has remained perennially popular ever since.

The Magic Flute's influence on the development of singspiel and German Romantic opera was fundamental. It carried singspiel into the 19th century, when the genre developed in two directions. One strand led to Beethoven's opera *Fidelio* (1805), and—more formatively—to further "magic operas," such as E.T.A. Hoffmann's *Undine* (1816) and Carl Maria von Weber's *Der Freischütz* (1821) and *Oberon* (1826). These were the precursors of full-blown German Romantic opera, best exemplified in the works of Richard Wagner. The other strand of singspiel stayed true to its lighter-hearted origins, leading to the Viennese operettas of Johann Strauss the younger (*Die Fledermaus*) and Franz Lehár (*The Merry Widow*). ∎

I LIVE ONLY IN MY NOTES

SYMPHONY NO. 3 IN E-FLAT MAJOR, "EROICA," OP. 55 (1804), LUDWIG VAN BEETHOVEN

IN CONTEXT

FOCUS
Breaking the mold of the classical sonata

BEFORE
1759 Joseph Haydn writes his First Symphony—in three movements.

1793 The German theorist Heinrich Christoph Koch is the first to describe how the sonata form works.

1800 Beethoven completes his First Symphony.

AFTER
1810 Critic E.T.A. Hoffmann describes Beethoven as "a purely romantic composer" in a review of Symphony No. 5.

1824 Beethoven's Symphony No. 9 amazes audiences by adding voices to a previously purely instrumental genre.

Beethoven's "Eroica" broke boundaries and audience expectations on its public premiere in 1805, representing a radical reworking of what was understood by a "symphony." The composer's daring expansion of sonata form, his rebalancing of musical structure, and even his ordering of the work's movements, met with puzzlement and outrage.

The seeds of the symphony were sown, surprisingly, with a dance. In March 1801, a new ballet, *Die Geschöpfe des Prometheus* (*The Creatures of Prometheus*) had its first performance at the Vienna Burgtheater. Beethoven provided the music, which ended with a jolly theme in E-flat major. The melody

See also: Stamitz's Symphony in E-flat major 116–117 ▪ Mozart's Symphony No. 40 in G minor 128–131 ▪ *Symphonie fantastique* 162–163 ▪ Schumann's Symphony No. 1 166–169 ▪ Dvořák's Symphony No. 9 212–215

> I'll give another kreuzer if the thing will only stop!
> **Audience member**
> *Public premiere of the "Eroica" (1805)*

obviously appealed to him, as around the same time he included it in a collection of 12 orchestral *Contredanses* (country dances) and Fifteen Variations and Fugue for solo piano, which would later form the basis of the "Eroica" finale.

A symphony takes shape

Beethoven began to plan his Third Symphony in autumn 1802, had a complete piano score by October 1803, and had an orchestrated version by early summer 1804. The work was first performed privately at the home of Prince Franz Joseph von Lobkowitz, one of Beethoven's patrons and sponsors, and then given its public premiere at the Theater an der Wien, in Vienna.

The composer had intended to dedicate his work to Napoleon Bonaparte. But when the general declared himself the Emperor of France, Beethoven crossed his name from the manuscript. Removing the dedication made political sense: once Napoleon's invasion plans became clear, it would have been career suicide to celebrate him in a new symphony. The work was eventually printed

with a dedication to Prince Franz Joseph (who paid Beethoven handsomely for it) and given the subtitle "composed to celebrate the memory of a great man." The most likely candidate for the "great man," and the source of the title "Eroica" (Italian for "heroic"), is Louis Ferdinand, Prince of Prussia, who was killed in battle against the French in 1806 and to whom Beethoven had dedicated his Third Piano Concerto, Op. 37, in 1803.

Tearing up the rule book

Symphony No. 3 begins with a movement that was stretched and expanded far beyond anything that Viennese audiences had heard before. Instead of the carefully balanced proportions of the classical sonata form, where an "exposition" and "recapitulation" match each other around a short "development" section, with a brief "coda" ("tail" in Italian) to »

The heroic deeds of Napoleon Bonaparte, depicted in *Napoleon Crossing the Alps* by Jacques-Louis David (1748–1825), inspired Beethoven to write the "Eroica" symphony.

Ludwig van Beethoven

The son of an obscure court musician, Beethoven was born in Bonn in 1770. He moved to Vienna in 1792 and studied briefly with Haydn and Antonio Salieri. A prodigiously talented pianist, he made his name first as a virtuoso and acquired a number of wealthy noble admirers, who aided his establishment as a composer.

In every musical genre he explored, Beethoven was a radical innovator, constantly surprising audiences. After Haydn's death in 1809, he was the preeminent composer of his generation and a leading figure in the new Romantic age. In a cruel twist of fate, Beethoven started to lose his hearing in his late 20s, and by 1818 he was nearly completely deaf. Nevertheless, after this date, until his death in Vienna in 1827, Beethoven wrote some of his most inventive and radical works.

Other key works

1808 Symphonies No. 5 and No. 6, Op. 67 and Op. 68
1818 Piano Sonata in B-flat, *Hammerklavier*, Op. 106
1824 Symphony No. 9 in D minor, Op. 125

The Lobkowitz Palace, in Vienna, in a colored etching by Vincenz Reim (1796–1858), was the site of the first performance of Beethoven's Symphony No. 3 in August 1804.

The third movement is lighter—a lively scherzo (Italian for "joke"). Like most scherzo symphony movements, it includes a trio middle section based on three instruments. Beethoven innovated here by using French horns more prominently in a symphony than ever before. These instruments had no valves in the early 1800s, so they could play arpeggios only in a single key, which made them sound especially martial, like a battle call.

The main theme of the scherzo starts in an unexpected key. The music has already changed key, from E-flat to B-flat, before the oboe finally begins the theme. Once again, Beethoven was deliberately catching his audience by surprise.

The end and beyond
The finale of "Eroica" is a set of variations on a theme. Although this was not the first symphony to

round off the movement, Beethoven composed a hugely extended development, falling between a long exposition and recapitulation, and ending with a coda of more than 100 measures.

Not only was the extreme duration and balance of the first movement unusual, but Beethoven also introduced an entirely new theme after the exposition (where all themes were traditionally first stated) had ended. This new theme was in E major, a key very far from the home key of the piece.

The shape of the opening theme of the "Eroica" is also atypical. It includes a C-sharp, a rogue note that does not belong in the key of E-flat major, and so pulls the music away from its home key and unsettles it. As a result, Beethoven had to rewrite this subject in the recapitulation to get rid of the C-sharp and create a satisfactory resolution. This defied the rules of sonata form, in which the recapitulation is meant to contain the work's musical ideas in the same form as they appeared in the exposition.

Beyond the thematic manipulation, the music of the first movement is full of syncopations that distort the listener's sense of the rhythm. Also, strong dissonances—ugly to listeners in the early 1800s— leap out, where major and minor seconds (notes two semitones and one semitone apart, respectively) grate against each other.

Constant surprises
Beethoven followed the huge structure of the first movement, with its surprising tonal twists and turns, with a slow movement, cast as a *Marcia funebre*, or funeral march. It is an intensely dramatic piece, with the minor-key opening theme eventually giving way to a blazing, more hopeful C major, before the opening theme returns and is presented as a fugato—a short fuguelike piece, where the theme is imitated simultaneously by different instruments as if they are chasing each other. To have such rich and intricate musical textures woven so extensively into more than one movement was groundbreaking.

This strange and thundering work, the most extensive and richly artistic piece of all those created by Beethoven's original and wondrous spirit.
Opening of a review
Allgemeine musikalische Zeitung
(February 18, 1807)

Expressive grandeur in Beethoven's "Eroica"

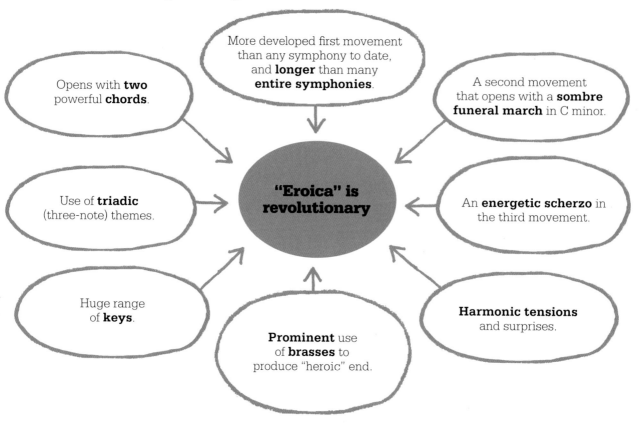

Opens with **two** powerful **chords**.

More developed first movement than any symphony to date, and **longer** than many **entire symphonies**.

A second movement that opens with a **sombre funeral march** in C minor.

Use of **triadic** (three-note) themes.

"Eroica" is revolutionary

An **energetic scherzo** in the third movement.

Huge range of **keys**.

Prominent use of **brasses** to produce "heroic" end.

Harmonic tensions and surprises.

use a theme-and-variation form as its closing movement, Beethoven broke with tradition by failing to start with the theme itself. Instead, the movement begins with a bass line, from which Beethoven builds the orchestral texture until we finally reach the theme melody. He was turning the form on its head by effectively writing variations before he had even got to the theme. Also, rather than the variations being based on a single melody, the whole orchestra is involved in exchanging and developing interweaving lines of material, ending in an elaborate fugato that brings the music firmly and finally to the home key.

Beethoven had created a four-movement journey through keys, themes, and ideas, cleverly and subtly interlinked. He was to venture even further in his later symphonies, and by the time he reached the Ninth, in 1824, what had once been four separate units linked only by a common title, had become a musical narrative brilliantly interwoven across the old sonata structure.

Those who witnessed the early performances of the "Eroica" found it a difficult work to understand—it was simply too far from their idea of how a symphony *should* work, both in terms of its length and its structure. But it was soon accepted as a work of profound genius and was to exert a huge influence on later generations of symphonists, from Schumann and Brahms to Bruckner and Mahler. ∎

Symphony No. 3 was already known as the "Eroica" by the time it was published, as this frontispiece of the first edition shows.

ROMA
1810–1920

NTIC

Niccolò Paganini composes the first of his 24 Caprices for Solo Violin, which are among the most difficult violin pieces of all time.

Franz Schubert's song cycle *Die schöne Müllerin* marks the high point in the German *Lied* (song) form.

In Paris, **Hector Berlioz** premieres *Symphonie fantastique*, one of the most influential works in the programmatic genre.

Intended to convey a longing for springtime, **Robert Schumann** writes his Symphony No. 1 over four days in January.

1805   **1824**   **1830**   **1841**

1821   **1826**   **1839**   **1846**

Based on a German folk legend, **Carl Maria von Weber's** opera *Der Freischütz* explores German national identity.

Epitomizing **Beethoven's** late style, his String Quartet No. 14, Op. 131 abandons the quartet's traditional form and development.

Frédéric Chopin's cycle of 24 preludes, covering all major and minor keys, defies conventional thematic structure.

The colorful orchestration of **Felix Mendelssohn's** *Elijah* breathes new life into the oratorio, a Baroque genre.

The Romantic movement arose largely as a reaction to the rationalization and urbanization of European society following the Industrial Revolution. From the end of the 18th century, writers, artists, and composers turned away from the formal elegance of the Classical period in favor of personal expression and a fascination with nature. In music, this manifested itself in a gradual expansion of the harmonic and instrumental palette to appeal to the emotions rather than the intellects of the audience.

The new style

Beethoven fulfilled the stereotype of the Romantic musician, as did the violinist Niccolò Paganini and some other virtuoso performer-composers. Long unkempt hair and bohemian clothes replaced the wigs and formal costumes of the Classical period, and the lifestyles of the Romantic composers were often as colorful as their music.

Beethoven developed a more personal style of music from 1803. In what is regarded as his "middle period," he produced groundbreaking piano sonatas, string quartets, other forms of chamber music, and, above all, symphonies. In his "late period," a final burst of creativity, when he was isolated from the world by profound deafness, he produced work of extraordinary intensity, such as his last piano sonatas, string quartets, and the Ninth Symphony, with its innovative choral finale.

Not every composer joined the Romantic tide. The instrumental works of Franz Schubert, for example, are in a more Classical style. Yet Schubert was inspired by the subjects of German Romantic poetry in the songs, or *Lieder*, for which he is best known. This aspect of Romanticism, especially the love of nature, later inspired the work of Robert Schumann, whose symphonies and piano pieces were often programmatic (painting a picture or telling a story in music), a genre begun by Beethoven's "Pastoral" Sixth Symphony, which depicts a series of rural scenes.

Hector Berlioz relished the possibilities offered by a larger orchestra and extended harmonic language. His operas, orchestral, and choral works, all on a grand scale with large orchestras, were expressive and highly personal. He continued the drift away from the abstract to the programmatic in his

The premiere of **Giuseppe Verdi's** *La traviata* in Venice shocks audiences by taking a fallen woman as its subject matter.

Johann Strauss II writes *The Blue Danube*, a waltz with a rich symphonic sound that takes Europe by storm.

Johannes Brahms's First Symphony premieres in Karlsruhe, Germany, recalling the Classical style of Beethoven.

The brutal plot of **Giacomo Puccini's** opera *Tosca* typifies *verismo* ("realism"), a form of opera popular in Italy and France.

 1853

1867

 1876

 1900

1857

1876

1896

1908

Franz Liszt's *Faust Symphony*, inspired by Johann Wolfgang von Goethe's play of the same name, premieres in Weimar, Germany.

The fourth part of **Richard Wagner's** *Ring Cycle* opens in Bayreuth, marking the end of his "total artwork," composed over 26 years.

Inspired by Nietzsche's novel, **Richard Strauss** composes *Also sprach Zarathustra*, a symphonic poem that rejects Romantic conventions.

Gustav Mahler writes *Das Lied von der Erde*, a contemplation on the inevitability of death.

symphonies, a trend that was taken up later by many composers, especially Franz Liszt, who developed a form known as the symphonic poem, or tone poem.

Liszt was also famous as a young man for his virtuosity when performing his own piano pieces, and he gained a large and devoted following. These solo piano recitals were popular entertainment of the period, especially when given by Romantic characters such as Liszt or Frédéric Chopin, whose more delicate and lyrical style of composition appealed particularly to French audiences.

Exceptions to the rule

Despite the popularity of Romantic music, some composers missed the elegance of Classicism. In fashionable Vienna, for example,

Johann Strauss I and II, father and son, played on this nostalgia with their waltzes, but other composers also felt the lack of discipline in Romantic music. Foremost among them was Johannes Brahms, who moderated expression within stricter Classical forms. Another was Felix Mendelssohn, whose oratorios harked back to the Baroque period, reviving German and English choral traditions laid down by Handel and Bach.

Romantic opera

Opera, with its combination of literature and music, was ideally suited to portraying Romantic themes and ideas. Carl Maria von Weber established the template for Romantic opera by choosing German folklore rather than Classical mythology as his subject

matter and aiming for a more convincing form of dramatic representation. Others followed his lead: Bizet in France, the giants of Italian opera, Verdi and Puccini, who pursued a new kind of realism in opera, and in Germany, Richard Wagner, whose operas were on the grandest of scales and stretched musical language. With his innovatory harmonies, Wagner challenged the idea of tonality, which had been the foundation of musical form since the end of the Renaissance.

Wagner inspired what is now known as the late Romantic style, exemplified by composers such as Anton Bruckner, Gustav Mahler, and Richard Strauss. This heralded the beginning of modern music in which the old rules of harmony no longer applied. ∎

THE VIOLINIST IS THAT PECULIARLY HUMAN PHENOMENON ... HALF TIGER, HALF POET

24 CAPRICES FOR SOLO VIOLIN, OP. 1 (1824), NICCOLÒ PAGANINI

IN CONTEXT

FOCUS
The rise of the virtuoso

BEFORE
1733 Pietro Locatelli publishes
L'arte del violino, which inspires
Paganini's own *Caprices*.

1740 The violinist Giuseppe
Tartini, known for his fast and
exciting playing, epitomized by
his violin sonata *Devil's Trill*,
makes a concert tour of Italy.

AFTER
1834 Hector Berlioz completes
Harold en Italie, a symphony
featuring a solo viola part
composed for Paganini.

1838 Franz Liszt publishes
an early form of his technically
demanding *Études d'exécution
transcendante d'après
Paganini* ("Transcendental
studies after Paganini"), in
which he transcribed six of
Paganini's violin caprices for
solo piano.

iolinist-composer Niccolò
Paganini's career as an
international performer
lasted just six years, from 1828 to
1834, but his influence on music
was immense. Setting out to
entertain, he introduced new
playing techniques and raised
the expectations of audiences,
performing feats no one had
achieved before him. He owned
numerous violins, including a
handful by perhaps the greatest
maker of all, Antonio Stradivarius.

Chronic illness, thought to be
Marfan syndrome, left Paganini
looking gaunt. This led to rumors

Easter Sunday; in the
evening I heard Paganini.
What ecstasy! In his hands
the driest exercises flame up
like bithium pronouncements.
Robert Schumann

that he had struck a deal with
the devil in return for his gifts.
His greatest triumphs were
in Paris, which was in thrall to
grand spectacle, new technology,
and brilliance in every field.

Technical innovations
Paganini had studied and honed
his art in Italy. It is thought that
he started composing his *24
Caprices* in the early 1800s, even
though he did not publish them
until 1820. In these showpiece
works, and numerous others, he
challenged every aspect of existing
violin technique and introduced
new ideas designed to showcase
the performer's skills. The pieces
are peppered with breakneck
passage work, double- or even
triple-stopping (bowing two or
three strings at the same time), as
well as new tricks such as left-hand
pizzicato (using the fingers of the
left hand to pluck the strings) and
ricochet (bouncing bowing).

Inspired by Paganini
As a 19-year-old, in 1831, the
Hungarian composer Franz Liszt
heard Paganini in Paris and was
inspired to achieve the same level
of virtuosity on the piano and to

See also: *The Four Seasons* 92–97 ▪ *Faust Symphony* 176–177

cultivate an equally dramatic persona. His career coincided with technical advances in piano manufacturing that made the instrument reliable, versatile, and loud enough to fill the large concert halls that catered for the growing middle classes. Liszt was the most highly gifted of a new breed of composer-pianists who competed for prominence—sometimes in piano-playing duels. His celebrity status helped establish the piano recital in its present form, thereby benefiting other composers.

The First Triumph of Paganini, by Annibale Gatti, c.1890, possibly depicts a performance at the court at Lucca, where Paganini built his reputation during the early 1800s.

Paganini's and Liszt's talent pushed the boundaries of existing techniques for both violin and piano. The concerto became a stage for soloists to excel on these instruments, while the theme and variations form, in which a simple, often well-known melody would be submitted to increasingly impressive reworkings, became popular among concert-goers and composers. The theme of Paganini's Caprice No. 24 inspired works by Liszt, Johannes Brahms, and Sergei Rachmaninoff.

Later virtuosos included the Belgian composer-violinist Henri Vieuxtemps and composer-pianists Louis Moreau Gottschalk in the US, Leopold Godowsky in Poland, and Rachmaninoff in Russia. ▪

Niccolò Paganini

Born in the Italian port town of Genoa in October 1782, Paganini learned the violin and guitar from his father, who was an outstanding amateur musician. The young Paganini supplemented his training with a strict regimen of practice, later claiming he became a virtuoso after hearing a performance by the Polish-born French violinist August Duranowski.

In 1809, Paganini left a court appointment in Lucca to pursue a solo career. He traveled in Italy, composing and performing works that displayed his skills. Health problems, including syphilis, delayed him until 1828, after which he went first to Austria, Bohemia, and Germany and then, in 1831, to Paris, where his 10 concerts at the *Opéra* caused a sensation. In 1834, continuing ill health forced him into semi-retirement in Italy, where he died in 1840.

Other key works

1813 *Le Streghe* (*The Witches*)
1816 Violin Concerto No. 1
1819 Sonata "a Preghiera"
1826 Violin Concerto No. 2 in B minor

GIVE ME A LAUNDRY LIST, AND I WILL SET IT TO MUSIC

THE BARBER OF SEVILLE (1816), GIOACHINO ROSSINI

IN CONTEXT

FOCUS
Italian *opera buffa*

BEFORE
1782 An earlier operatic version of *Il barbiere di Siviglia* (*The Barber of Seville*) by the Italian composer Giovanni Paisiello is performed for the first time in St. Petersburg.

1786 Mozart's *The Marriage of Figaro* receives its first performance in Vienna.

AFTER
1843 Gaetano Donizetti's comic opera *Don Pasquale* is performed for the first time at the Théâtre Italien in Paris.

1850 *Crispino e la comare* ("The cobbler and the fairy") by the brothers Luigi and Federico Ricci is one of the last examples of true *opera buffa*.

Surviving a disastrous first night in Rome in 1816, *Il barbiere di Siviglia* (*The Barber of Seville*) by Gioachino Rossini quickly won universal acclaim. Rossini had already written 16 operas, but this was his first *opera buffa* ("comic opera") as opposed to an *opera seria* ("serious opera"). It relates the attempts of the Count Almaviva to win the beautiful Rosina, ward of the much older Dr. Bartolo, who intends to marry her himself. Central to the plot is the barber Figaro, a "fixer" in Seville. Its songs include Figaros's *"Largo al factotum della città"* ("Make way for the factotum of the city") and Rosina's *"Una voce poco fa"* ("A voice has just").

Operatic realism

The low-life settings and street language of the opera buffa brought fresh realism to musical drama, and its popularity spread throughout Europe. Mozart's *The Marriage of Figaro* and *Così fan tutte* are other examples of the comic opera genre.

Beethoven admired *The Barber of Seville*, as did Verdi and Wagner. Yet, apart from a one-act farce, Rossini wrote no other comedies. In the 1820s, he became director of the Théâtre Italien, in Paris, where he wrote five more operas, culminating in *Guillaume Tell* (*William Tell*) in 1829. After this, his output declined. One of his few large-scale pieces in the last three decades of his life was his *Petite messe solennelle* ("small solemn mass") of 1863. ∎

Dear God, here it is finished, this poor little Mass. Is this sacred music … or music of the devil? I was born for opera buffa, as you well know.
Gioachino Rossini

See also: *Le bourgeois gentilhomme* 70–71 ▪ *The Magic Flute* 134–137 ▪ *La traviata* 174–175 ▪ *Tosca* 194–197

MUSIC IS TRULY LOVE ITSELF
DER FREISCHÜTZ (1821), CARL MARIA VON WEBER

IN CONTEXT

FOCUS
German Romantic opera

BEFORE
1791 Mozart's *The Magic Flute*, the supreme example of the *Singspiel* tradition, is performed in Vienna.

1816 The premiere of E.T.A. Hoffmann's Romantic opera *Undine*, about a water spirit who marries a human, takes place in Berlin.

AFTER
1833 Heinrich Marschner's opera *Hans Heiling*, like his earlier success *Der Vampyr*, contrasts the real and supernatural worlds.

1834 Richard Wagner completes his opera *Die Feen* (*The Fairies*), which is heavily influenced by Weber's *Der Freischütz*.

The magic bullets used in the shooting contest in *Der Freischütz* are fired in the spooky Wolf's Glen, depicted here in an aquatint of the opera scene.

A n example of a Viennese Singspiel ("play in song"), which links songs with spoken dialogue, Carl Maria von Weber's *Der Freischütz* (*The Freeshooter*) tells the story of Max, a young huntsman from Bohemia who is persuaded by the wicked Caspar to take part in a shooting contest that will win Max the hand of Agathe. To ensure victory, Caspar gives him magic bullets forged in the Wolf's Glen.

Premiered in Berlin in 1821, *Der Freischütz* propelled its composer to stardom. Its success was partly because it was grounded firmly in German culture, using easily recognizable characters, settings, folklore, and folk music. Weber had envisaged a great new German opera tradition.

The combination of national pride, emotional content, and the depiction of the supernatural impressed the young Richard Wagner, who saw *Der Freischütz* at the age of nine. At the same time, Weber's innovative orchestration, especially the evocative use of woodwinds and horns, influenced Berlioz, Mahler, and Debussy.

Weber wrote two more operas. He was in London to conduct the premiere of his last work, *Oberon*, in 1826, when he died of tuberculosis, aged 39. ∎

See also: *The Magic Flute* 134–137 ▪ *The Barber of Seville* 148 ▪ *La traviata* 174–175 ▪ *The Ring Cycle* 180–187 ▪ *Tosca* 194–197

NO ONE FEELS ANOTHER'S GRIEF, NO ONE UNDERSTANDS ANOTHER'S JOY

DIE SCHÖNE MÜLLERIN (1824), FRANZ SCHUBERT

The composer Franz Schubert is most often linked to the German art song (or *Lied;* plural, *Lieder*). He did not invent the genre. Several major composers had written songs before him, such as Beethoven, Mozart, and Haydn, as well as lesser-known figures. It is not even true to say that Schubert produced the first "song cycle," the term used later for a set of songs with an overarching narrative or theme. Beethoven's *An die ferne Geliebte*, composed in 1816, was the first important work to fit such a description.

Schubert, however, transformed the genre. Before Schubert, Lieder were predominantly naïve or straightforwardly lyrical. The form tended to be strophic, the same melody repeated for each verse of the poem; the music engaged with the text only as far as capturing its general mood, and the keyboard accompaniment was often formulaic, functional, and without expression. Haydn and Beethoven were introduced to the medium when commissioned to produce arrangements of folk songs, while the songs of Mozart, who reserved his most sophisticated word setting for opera, are small-scale and modest in their scope. Writing songs was a sideline rather than a central part of any of these composers' activities.

Piano and song
Schubert came of age in a world of increased poetic sensibility, of emphasis on subjective experience. The piano, still a relatively recent invention, had grown both in technical capacity and availability. Domestic performances were on the rise, especially in Vienna, whose middle class, held back in many ways by a strictly controlled society, sought private outlets

Schubert's art songs, or Lieder, were usually played in the private homes of his friends. Large-scale public concerts were typically reserved for more sweeping orchestral works.

See also: *Symphonie fantastique* 162–163 ▪ Schumann's Symphony No. 1 166–169 ▪
Faust Symphony 176–177 ▪ *Also sprach Zarathustra* 192–193

> My compositions spring
> from my sorrows. Those
> that give the world
> the greatest delight were
> born of my deepest griefs.
> **Franz Schubert**

for their artistic impulses. This amateur form of music making, away from the formal courts and concert societies, was reaching new levels of sophistication.

In his all too brief life, Schubert composed some 600 songs. The first to be published, "Erlkönig" and "Gretchen am Spinnrade" ("Gretchen at the spinning wheel"), composed when Schubert was just 17, remain among his most popular. Set to texts by Johann Wolfgang von Goethe, they offered a new sort of song: both are "through-composed" (without strictly repeated verses) and present powerful miniature dramas moving inexorably toward their climaxes.

"Erlkönig" features a narrating voice as well as the voices of a father, his son, and the titular Erlking—a malevolent goblinlike creature who inhabits the dark forest of the Romantic imagination. Gretchen, meanwhile, is the tragic heroine of Goethe's masterpiece, *Faust*. In 1816, Schubert composed "Der Wanderer," one of many songs focusing on another quintessential figure of German Romanticism,

whose dilemma is summed up in the song's final line: "There, where you are not, is happiness!"

Schubert would also compose songs that espoused folkish simplicity, and throughout his short but intensely creative life, he would alternate between complex and more straightforward forms. His output for voice is remarkable for the variety and richness of his melodic inspiration, but the role of the piano accompaniment also developed greatly in Schubert's hands. It grew from offering straightforward support to include sophisticated reflections of, and reactions to, the content of the poem he was setting.

Song cycles
The complete array of Schubert's art is evident in his first song cycle, *Die schöne Müllerin* ("The beautiful miller's maid"), published in 1824. For the cycle's 20 songs, Schubert selected poems from a collection by Wilhelm Müller, a contemporary poet whose verses Schubert also used for *Winterreise* ("Winter journey"), his second song cycle, three years later. *Die schöne Müllerin* loosely follows the story of a young miller boy's infatuation with the beautiful daughter of a mill owner, from his early obsession, through jealousy and resignation to, listeners are left to assume, suicide.

The narrative is presented largely through suggestion, with the poems giving snapshots in time, presented primarily in the voice of the miller boy himself. Together the songs encapsulate many of the quintessential themes of Romantic poetry, not least the solitude of the outsider and the »

Franz Schubert

Born in a poor district of Vienna in 1797, Schubert was the son of a well-known schoolmaster and music teacher who taught him to play the piano and violin. He composed from an early age and soon found favor with prominent figures in Vienna, such as Antonio Salieri. Despite this, success in large-scale "public" composition eluded him.

Schubert managed to make a respectable living with works aimed at the amateur market, such as compositions and songs for piano. Although a few of his chamber pieces were performed in public, many of his best works—piano sonatas and symphonies among them—were only rediscovered years after his death in 1828, at 31. This led to a reappraisal that cemented his reputation as a master composer of instrumental music as well as song.

Other key works

1822 Symphony in B minor ("Unfinished"), D759
1822 Mass No. 2 in G major, D167
1828 String Quintet in C, D956

Lied and Song Cycles

Written for voice and piano for performance in homes or concert halls, sometimes as a cycle of three or more songs linked by a story or theme.

↓

They appear in three major forms

↓   ↓   ↓

Strophic:
all verses are sung to the same music, as in Schubert's "Der Fischer" and "Heidenröslein."

Modified strophic:
the music varies in some verses, such as "Der Lindenbaum" in Schubert's *Winterreise*.

Through-composed:
each verse has different music to match the words. Schubert's "Erlkönig" is through-composed.

desire, in the face of rejection, to find solace in nature. These ideas would be explored with an even greater level of intensity in *Winterreise,* in which the poems chart the progress of a lovelorn, solitary wanderer through a bleak wintry landscape. The songs of *Schwanengesang* ("Swan song"), published together after Schubert's death but never conceived as a cycle, push the genre even further and can be shocking in their expressionistic power.

Private to public

The songs of *Die schöne Müllerin* were, like so much of the music by Schubert that was disseminated during his lifetime, originally designed primarily for private performances, such as those Schubert would give with his friends, known as *Schubertiads*, and they were not initially published together as a cycle. The first public performance of the cycle as a whole was not until 1856. As the 20th century approached, the Lied also became an increasingly public form, even if many composers continued to use it for some of their most personal works.

Romantic vehicle

Schubert's influence, in terms of the later development of the Lied, is difficult to overestimate. What had been a peripheral activity for earlier composers became a major area of activity for several composers who came after him. The genre's unique mix of music and poetry proved particularly attractive to the

Schubert set several of Goethe's poems to music, including his tragic 1778 work "An den Mond" ("To the moon"). This handwritten manuscript of Schubert's dates from 1815.

French Romantic chanson

The story of the art song in France was largely colored by the cultural landscape in Paris, where song—*mélodie* or *chanson*—designed primarily for performance in private salons, existed in the shadows of opera. French song faced an additional problem: the irregular emphases and rhythms of the language made it difficult to set words to music with naturalness.

Nevertheless, the genre in France became more ambitious and sophisticated toward the end of the 19th century,

following works by composers such as Hector Berlioz, whose *Les Nuits d'été* (Summer Nights, 1841), a setting for six poems by Théophile Gautier, count among the first songs for voice and orchestra in the repertoire, although they were written for piano accompaniment originally. While subsequently influenced by German composer Richard Wagner, a uniquely French branch of art song developed in the hands of Gabriel Fauré, Claude Debussy, and Francis Poulenc.

and beyond. The songs of such composers as Antonín Dvořák and Modest Mussorgsky often have a nationalistic coloring.

At the turn of the 20th century, Gustav Mahler firmly put the genre in the public sphere, not least because he was one of the first composers to orchestrate his songs himself, as would Richard Strauss. Several of Mahler's songs also found their way into his early symphonies, either complete or reworked as instrumental movements. Strauss, meanwhile, composed songs throughout his long life and wrote his valedictory masterpiece, *The Four Last Songs,* for soprano voice and orchestra, in 1948.

The art song also flourished in France, Great Britain, and the United States, especially in the 20th century, with such composers as Ralph Vaughan Williams, Gerald Finzi, Charles Ives, and Benjamin Britten, who, as a fine pianist, made a speciality of performing Schubert's song cycles. ∎

Romantics. Subsequent song cycles often represented attempts to build on Schubert's legacy.

Robert Schumann was greatly influenced by Schubert. His own song cycles, many of them composed in a burst of inspiration in 1840, the year of his marriage to pianist and composer Clara Wieck, tend to be on a smaller scale, offering a series of poetic impressions or, in the case of *Frauenliebe und Leben* ("A woman's love and life"), a broad picture of a relationship. Schumann often wrote short piano preludes to set

the scene for his songs, as well as postludes to summarize the mood. Although Johannes Brahms wrote two song cycles, both he and the Austrian composer Hugo Wolf concentrated on grouping their songs into combinations that were suitable for publication, which did not necessarily imply that they should be performed together. Wolf, in particular, was remarkable for composing Lieder almost exclusively. In his works, he successfully incorporated Wagnerian harmonic complexity and psychological insight into the form on the most intimate scale.

Song legacy

Schubert's wider influence was enormous, too, and a greater desire to raise song to a higher artistic plane coincided, in the second half of the 19th century, with attempts to assert and define nationhood, both in the German-speaking world

There is no song of Schubert's from which one cannot learn something.
Johannes Brahms

Hugo Wolf wrote several hundred art songs, often with deeply romantic and personal themes, as captured on this postcard depicting a song from his *Spanish Songbook* of 1891.

MUSIC IS LIKE A DREAM. ONE THAT I CANNOT HEAR

STRING QUARTET NO. 14 IN C-SHARP MINOR, OP. 131 (1826), BEETHOVEN

Beethoven's music divides
into three stylistic periods:
the early (up to 1802), the
middle (1803–1813), and the late
(1817–1827). He was born in 1770,
and by the age of 27, he had written
a variety of works. However, for
much of this period, he avoided the
territory dominated by Haydn and
Mozart—the string quartet. It was
not until the end of the 1790s, by
which time he was no longer being
compared to Mozart, that Beethoven
wrote his first quartets, the Op. 18.
These six works show such energy
and technical mastery that had
his life been cut short at this point,
he would still be placed among
the world's great composers. The
shadow of Mozart mixes with the
spirit of Haydn through his first five
quartets, but in the sixth Beethoven
sowed the seeds of his later work.

No composer before
Beethoven ever disregarded
the capacities of both his
performers and his audience
with such ruthlessness.
Charles Rosen

Increasing deafness from the age
of 30 led Beethoven to commission
hearing devices from Johann Nepomuk
Maelzel, inventor of the metronome,
including this "ear trumpet."

Beethoven's middle period included
his "Heroic Phase" of 1803–1808,
during which he wrote the "Eroica"
Symphony for and about Napoleon
Bonaparte. The middle period was
a time of energy and positive
commitment to Beethoven's
humanistic and political beliefs.
The period is often considered to
have begun in the wake of his
"Heiligenstadt Testament" of 1802—
a letter he had written to his two
brothers describing his despair
at his profound loss of hearing.
Only his music, Beethoven wrote,
held him back from suicide.

Beethoven's violin concerto
(Op. 61) is an outstanding example
of the productive middle period, in
which he began to turn away from
classical conventions—developing
a bolder individual style and
producing many of his most famous
compositions. The beginnings of
Romantic music can be found in
the slow movements of Beethoven's
middle quartets. These five quartets
stretched the boundaries of the
form, first by extending the length,
in his Op. 59 and Op. 74, and then
by compressing it in the concise
Quartetto Serioso, Op. 95. In all five,
four players evolve into soloists,
each with virtuoso passages

See also: Haydn's String Quartet in C major, Op. 54 122–125 ▪ "Eroica" Symphony 138–141 ▪ Brahms's Symphony No. 1 188–189 ▪ *Pierrot lunaire* 240–245 ▪ Shostakovich's Fifth Symphony 274–279

worthy of a concerto, while Op. 74, known as the "Harp" quartet, has movements in both the heroic and classical moods.

The late period

Between 1813–1816, Beethoven experienced major emotional upheavals, from financial troubles to the struggle to gain custody of his nephew. These years saw a decline in his production, with those works Beethoven did produce showing him to be struggling to develop his style further. However, he emerged from these years of refinement with unparalleled ability to imagine melodies, forms, and harmonies that would serve him well during his late period.

Beethoven's indifference to contemporary social conventions and his passionate belief in his own ideas created a unique set of circumstances that would lead to the composition of his five late quartets. He was determined to push the boundaries of composition to new limits; having successfully extended the length and developed the structure of the conventional

Variations on a theme in the fourth movement

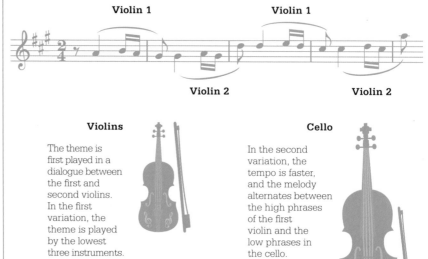

Violin 1   Violin 1

Violin 2   Violin 2

Violins

The theme is first played in a dialogue between the first and second violins. In the first variation, the theme is played by the lowest three instruments.

Cello

In the second variation, the tempo is faster, and the melody alternates between the high phrases of the first violin and the low phrases in the cello.

Subsequent variations share the developing theme between the different instruments, in varying time signatures.

forms in concerti, symphonies, sonatas, and chamber works, he was ready to experiment further.

Opus 131 (1826) is the most unorthodox of Beethoven's five late quartets, all written in 1825–1826. Its seven movements, ranging from

14 minutes to less than one minute, totaling around 40 minutes and performed without a break, are in an unconventional sequence that at the time seemed unlikely to succeed as a major work.

Conventional quartets follow a four-movement formula: they begin with an allegro in sonata form, in the tonic key; they slow down in the second movement; they employ a minuet and trio as the third movement; and they end in rondo form. In Op. 131, however, the first movement—a sombre, extended fugue (a piece in which a melody is strictly imitated by the other voices)—is followed by a very short dance in the second movement. The third movement (just 11 measures) concludes with a florid solo harking back to an earlier musical period, while the fourth presents a powerful theme and »

Music as self-expression

The cultural and literary world of Germany and the small states that surrounded it at the time of Beethoven's birth were strongly influenced by the *Sturm und Drang* (Storm and Stress) movement. Led by the poet and philosopher Johann Gottfried von Herder, it was expounded by writers and artists, such as Johann Wolfgang von Goethe and Friedrich Schiller. The movement emphasized national identities, language, and arts,

and placed a high value on personal freedom and heroic resistance to oppressors. It advocated a synthesis of Romantic, Classical, and Enlightenment ideas.

Like literature and art, the musical world began to reflect these ideals, giving them expression in symphonies and vocal music, with Beethoven himself later setting Schiller's poem *An die Freude* ("Ode to Joy") in his Ninth Symphony.

Differences between the Classical quartet and Beethoven's Op. 131

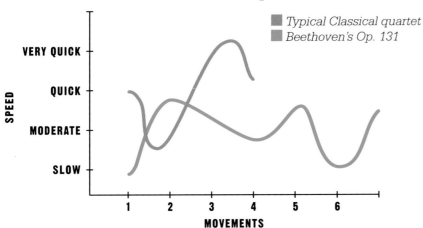

Typical Classical quartet
Beethoven's Op. 131

Classical quartets generally had four movements. After Beethoven, some Romantic quartets had more (or fewer) movements and abandoned the usual pattern of development.

variations. The fifth jumps in with an extensive scherzo (a fast dance). A 28-measure adagio (leisurely) sixth movement leads to an intense and energetic seventh movement of the kind that is generally placed first in more conventional works.

Building a structure with such unconventional foundations was a challenge that Beethoven set for himself. Some consider Op. 131 to be the greatest composition of

[Beethoven's quartets] stand ... on the extreme boundary of all that has hitherto been attained by human art and imagination.
Robert Schumann

Beethoven's output; it cemented his great legacy and ensured praise for his late quartets.

Natural variations

A good example of Beethoven's structural ingenuity can be seen in his handling of the theme and variations in the fourth movement (which builds on techniques developed in his Diabelli variations, Op. 120). The traditional problem faced by composers in this form was how to create a feeling of natural continuity instead of the formulaic repetition of a set theme. Beethoven's approach is to allow constant evolution of the music, even from the very outset of the theme. It begins at the top of the texture, as a dialogue between the first and second violin; it is then doubled in 10ths, before moving down toward the middle of the texture. When the first variation begins with the theme in the three lower strings, it feels like a natural continuation of this development, but by the end of this variation,

the theme has undergone several transformations of rhythm as well as texture. The second variation begins as a gentle dance in which melodic eighth-note phrases pass from one instrument to another, accompanied by detached chords, but as the variation progresses, the running eighth notes take over and build to a climax with all four instruments playing in octaves— a different sound world altogether from the variation's opening. The variations continue, punctuated by a couple of cadenzalike first violin flourishes recalling the "archaic" third movement.

Thematic development also takes place on a large scale. As in many of Beethoven's works (most famously the Fifth Symphony of 1807–1808), the quartet begins with a short four-note motif, which also preoccupied Beethoven in his Op. 132 quartet, although the pitches are presented here in a slightly different order, to unsettling effect. This motif forms the first half of the opening fugue subject, which, in turn, provides many of the motivic ideas from which the other movements are developed.

Rousing ending

The fifth movement's key of E major is the optimistic sister to the sad home key of C-sharp minor, and, following convention, a light-hearted scherzo alternates with a contrasting trio. Unusually, however, Beethoven not only extends the conventional "A-B-A" form with a further repeat of the trio and scherzo (as he does in several other works) but finishes with a curtailed repeat of each theme.

This repetition allows him to explore various moods and techniques, not least in a passage played sul ponticello (with the bow near the bridge of the instrument), creating a glassy, delicate sound.

A powerful crescendo then leads to two sets of three chords, each followed by a dramatic silence heralding the sixth movement. In this short adagio, led by the viola, the four-note motif from the first movement is transformed by denying the use of its fourth and most expressive note. An optimistic upward motion is always repelled by a sad, descending answer.

In the seventh movement, the previous ideas come to a satisfying musical conclusion. As the music progresses, fragments of the first movement begin to surface until the four-note motif reappears. Many dark and menacing sounds follow

A statue of Beethoven was erected, in 1880, on the Beethovenplatz in Vienna, Austria. The figures sitting below the composer are allegorical representations of his symphonies.

before one of Beethoven's most Romantic themes appears, free in its pacing and encompassing expressive leaps. After the theme reaches its culmination, a "ghost" appears, recalling the melody first heard at the very start of the work.

After this, the music begins to reflect the drained physical state of the players after continuous playing for almost 40 minutes. The music dissipates as the tempo gets slower, yet the expected soft ending to the piece does not appear. In one last, defiant gesture, the energies of the players are revived for a last push to end on three affirmative chords.

Lasting influence
Beethoven's late quartets—which start and end with four movement structures (Op. 127 and Op. 135) but experiment with five, six, and seven movements (Op. 130–132)—

To play a wrong note is insignificant. To play without passion is inexcusable.
Ludwig van Beethoven

were his final gift to the world before his death in 1827. With them, Beethoven transformed the string quartet—influencing Schumann, Mendelssohn, Brahms, Bartók, Schoenberg, Shostakovich, and Tippett—and became an imposing mentor and inspiration to all those who came after. ∎

INSTRUMENTATION IS AT THE HEAD OF THE MARCH

SYMPHONIE FANTASTIQUE (1830), HECTOR BERLIOZ

IN CONTEXT

FOCUS
The programmatic symphony

BEFORE
1808 Beethoven premieres his Sixth Symphony, the "Pastoral," which the composer insists is "more expression of feeling than tone-painting."

1824 Beethoven's Ninth Symphony ends with a choral setting of a text taken from German poet Friedrich Schiller's "Ode to Joy."

AFTER
1848–1849 Liszt composes *Ce qu'on entend sur la montagne*, the first symphonic poem, based on a poem by Victor Hugo.

1857 First performance of Liszt's *Faust Symphony*, which he dedicated to Berlioz.

Throughout his career, French composer Hector Berlioz explored the format of the programmatic symphony—a mood-evoking work influenced by subjects outside of music, such as literature and art. It was his *Symphonie fantastique*, however, composed early in his career, that proved to be his most successful and enduring work in the genre.

Berlioz's inspiraton

In 1827, as a 23-year-old music student, Berlioz went to see a performance in Paris of

No one who hears this symphony here in Paris, played by Berlioz's orchestra, can help believing that he is hearing a marvel without precedent.
Richard Wagner

Shakespeare's *Romeo and Juliet* starring the Irish actress Harriet Smithson as Juliet. It proved to be a fateful encounter, because Berlioz fell in love with Smithson and would expend much energy over the next few years pursuing her.

During the course of this infatuation, he felt compelled to write a piece that would describe his heightened passion and its attendant joys and sorrows. He intended its performance to launch his career with a bold stroke and at the same time dazzle Smithson. The resulting piece *Symphonie fantastique* premiered at the Paris Conservatoire on December 5, 1830, and a printed synopsis of the "plot" was supplied.

Love and death

The title suggests a symphony of the imagination, while its subtitle—"Episode in the life of an artist"—hints at the work's autobiographical element, although its descriptive program (which Berlioz provided to audiences) focuses more on fantasy than reality. In the first movement, a young musician awakens to find love in the shape of an unknown beautiful woman. Her image

See also: *The Four Seasons* 92–97 ▪ *Faust Symphony* 176–177 ▪ *The Ring Cycle* 180–187 ▪ *Also sprach Zarathustra* 192–193 ▪ *Das Lied von der Erde* 198–201

(represented by a recurring melody Berlioz called the *idée fixe*) imposes itself upon his vision everywhere he goes, such as at a ball and even in the country, where the sound of thunder seems to symbolize his gloomy state of mind.

Determined to poison himself with opium, he finds instead that the dose merely induces nightmares. In the first of these, he imagines he has been condemned to death for murdering his beloved: at the end of the "March to the Scaffold," he is executed. In the second nightmare, he dreams that he is at a Witches' Sabbath and sees his beloved joining in the grisly spectacle.

Lasting influence

Other composers emulated Berlioz's combination of music and story-telling, notably Franz Liszt in *A Faust Symphony* and 12 symphonic poems (one-movement pieces in the programmatic genre), including *Mazeppa* and *Hamlet*. Although some major composers, including Bruckner and Brahms, avoided the form, others such as Tchaikovsky, César Franck, Elgar, and Richard Strauss mined its possibilities inventively and exhaustively. ∎

Hector Berlioz conducts a deafening orchestra in a caricature published by the French newspaper *L'Illustration*, in 1845. Behind him, members of the audience hold their ears.

Hector Berlioz

The son of a doctor, Berlioz was born at La Côte-Saint-André, in southeastern France, in 1803. At 12, he began studying music, and at 17, he moved to Paris to study at the Conservatoire.

In 1833, on his fifth attempt, Berlioz won the Prix de Rome (a prestigious scholarship). By then, he had produced his *Symphonie fantastique* to impress the actress Harriet Smithson, whom he later married. In Paris, he enjoyed limited success as a composer and so also worked as a journalist. From 1842, he toured abroad, finding audiences in Russia, England, and Germany more receptive. He longed for success in the opera house, but his opera *Benvenuto Cellini* (1838) failed, and his masterpiece *Les Troyens* (1858) had only a partial production during his lifetime. Suffering from Crohn's disease and depression, he died in 1869.

Other key works

1837 *Grande Messe des morts* (*Requiem*)
1839 *Roméo et Juliette*
1856–1858 *Les Troyens*

SIMPLICITY IS THE FINAL ACHIEVEMENT

PRÉLUDES (1839), FRÉDÉRIC CHOPIN

IN CONTEXT

FOCUS
Solo piano music

BEFORE
1812 John Field, an Irish composer based in St. Petersburg, publishes the first Romantic piano piece to be called a "nocturne."

1833 In Paris, Chopin's Nocturnes, Op. 9, are the composer's first nocturnes to be published.

1834–1835 Robert Schumann composes *Carnaval*, a collection of 21 piano movements, one of which is titled *Chopin*.

AFTER
1892–1893 Brahms publishes four collections of small piano pieces, including intermezzos, fantasias, and capriccios.

1910–1913 Debussy, who described Chopin as "the greatest of us all," writes his two books of *Préludes*.

While Chopin was one of the supreme composers of the early Romantic period, he was in some respects untypical of the age he has come to embody. Unlike fellow musicians Robert Schumann and Franz Liszt, Chopin had little interest in using music to express narratives inspired by Romantic art and literature, or in producing grandiose works with huge orchestras in the manner of Hector Berlioz. Instead, Chopin perfected his art within circumscribed confines, tending toward brevity and the evocation of moods. Every one of his compositions includes the piano, and the vast majority are for piano alone, yet within this precisely defined area the breadth of his musical thought is vast.

Chopin created an unparalleled intensity of melody, harmony, and expression. Writing in a style that seemed to represent the soul of

Chopin plays for Prince Radziwiłł during a trip to Berlin, in 1829. The same year, he composed the *Polonaise brillante* for the prince (a cellist) and his daughter (a pianist) to practice.

See also: *Pièces de clavecin* 82–83 ▪ *Die schöne Müllerin* 150–155 ▪ *Prélude à l'après-midi d'un faune* 228–231 ▪ Ravel's Piano Concerto in D for the left hand 266–267

Preludes, nocturnes, and études

Preludes	Short introductory movement often preceding a larger piece.
Nocturnes	Expressive and tranquil compositions inspired by the night, following no set form.
Études	Pieces designed for practice, to perfect musical skills.

the instrument itself, Chopin had a profound effect on piano technique and helped push the instrument to the forefront of 19th-century music. Preferring to compose in miniature rather than on a large scale, he produced three four-movement piano sonatas and many short "character" pieces, especially preludes, nocturnes, études, and dances, such as the mazurka, polonaise, and waltz.

Mood and style
Between 1835 and 1839, Chopin composed a set of 24 preludes—one in each of the major and minor keys—using J.S. Bach's Preludes from the *Well-Tempered Clavier* (1722) as his model. For Chopin, the prelude was essentially an abstract form, although some of his pieces were prescribed titles by his publishers that suggested specific influences. The "Raindrop" Prelude, for example, earned its (inauthentic) nickname from the French novelist George Sand's account of incessant

rain at Valldemossa, on the island of Majorca, where she and Chopin, who was then her lover, spent the winter of 1838–1839 together.

Polish dance
Chopin's interest in dance was partly a conscious homage to his Polish heritage. The polonaise (meaning "Polish" in French) was used by many composers across Europe, and Chopin wrote more than a dozen examples, his first when he was just seven years old. Like the polonaise, the mazurka was a traditional dance form to which Chopin returned regularly on no fewer than 50 occasions.

Chopin mainly used the waltz dance form for lighter salon music. The so-called "Minute Waltz" and the Waltz in E-flat, Op. 18 (*Grande valse brillante*) are rapid pieces. In contrast to the showy waltzes, Chopin's 20 nocturnes are predominantly intimate and introverted in mood, slow and dreamy, as their title suggests. The nocturnes enjoy an enduring legacy as some of the most popular solo works ever written for piano. The term "nocturne" and its style were the invention of the Irish composer and celebrated pianist John Field, whose work Chopin knew and admired.

Like Field, Chopin was a virtuoso pianist, and his interest in the extension of piano technique is demonstrated in his 27 études ("studies"), which he began writing in his teens. In these pieces, Chopin managed to combine technical advances with great expressive and musical quality. They have remained both a challenge and a joy to pianists ever since. ∎

Frédéric Chopin

Born near Warsaw in 1810, Chopin studied the piano in the Polish capital and performed at musical soirées in its greatest houses. He visited Paris at the age of 20 and settled there, making a living by teaching, publishing his music, and appearing at salons. Chopin disliked concerts, and performed in few, yet his influence was huge, founded on works that embraced the folk music of his native land, as well as other, more conceptual forms that lifted piano technique to new levels. Initially composing in a style that favored virtuosity in the tradition of composers Johann Nepomuk Hummel, Friedrich Kalkbrenner, and Carl Maria von Weber, he later absorbed within his piano textures the influence of Bach. His most durable personal relationship, with the novelist George Sand, ended in 1847. He died of tuberculosis two years later in Paris.

Other key works

1830 Piano Concerto No. 1
1835 Ballade No. 1 in G minor
1844 Sonata No. 3 in B minor
1846 Barcarolle in F-sharp

MY SYMPHONIES WOULD HAVE REACHED OPUS 100 IF I HAD WRITTEN THEM DOWN

SYMPHONY NO. 1, THE "SPRING" SYMPHONY (1841), ROBERT SCHUMANN

IN CONTEXT

FOCUS
The Romantic symphony

BEFORE
1824 First performance of Beethoven's Symphony No. 9 in Vienna.

1838 Schumann "discovers" Schubert's "Great" C major Symphony in Vienna.

AFTER
1876 Premiere of Brahms's Symphony No. 1, which Hans von Bulow dubs "Beethoven's Tenth."

1889 Mahler's Symphony No. 1 premieres in Budapest. It marks the beginning of a cycle that redefines the symphony as a form.

At the end of the Classical age, Beethoven's Ninth Symphony, with its revolutionary message, inclusion of a choir and soloists, and many narrative musical features, offered a bold new vision of what a symphony might be. Yet many other Romantic composers, such as Chopin and Wagner, felt that Beethoven had taken the symphony to such heights with his Ninth that they could go no further with developing its form, and they turned to other genres instead. This led to a dearth of symphonic writing until the second half of the 19th century.

Nonetheless, the symphonies that were produced by the most successful Romantic composers were among the greatest music written in the 19th century. These

See also: "Eroica" Symphony 136–139 ▪ *Die schöne Müllerin* 148–153 ▪ *Symphonie fantastique* 162–163 ▪ *Faust Symphony* 176–177

> Nothing right in art can
> be accomplished
> without enthusiasm.
> **Robert Schumann**

works include Hector Berlioz's *Symphonie fantastique*, Franz Liszt's *Faust Symphony*, and Robert Schumann's Symphony No. 1, known as the "Spring" Symphony.

Schubert's influence

At the same time that Beethoven was writing his last symphony, Schubert was also working on his mature works in the genre. In 1822, he started on his Ninth Symphony, now known as the "Great C Major" Symphony. Unperformed in his lifetime, it was discovered by Schubert's friend Schumann, on

a visit to Vienna after Schubert's death. Schumann took a copy of the manuscript back to Leipzig, where Felix Mendelssohn conducted its premiere in 1839.

While Beethoven's works focused on an intense musical argument and inner drive, Schubert approached the form as a more gentle and discursive structure, reminiscent of the romantic novels of the period. In Schubert's Ninth Symphony, unexpected and nontraditional keys are used to produce a greater range of moods. Taking some 55 minutes to perform, a long work for the period, the piece extends many traditional features of the symphony, such as the introduction to the first movement (almost a complete sonata in itself) and the numerous thematic elements in the last.

Taking up the baton

It was only after hearing Schubert's Ninth Symphony that Robert Schumann was inspired to begin working on his own first symphony, in 1841. Until then, he had mainly been known as a composer of piano pieces. For the most part eschewing large-scale works, he had concentrated on collections or cycles of smaller pieces, cementing his reputation as a miniaturist. As such, writing a symphony was a new challenge for Schumann. Extraordinarily, he sketched the whole work in just four days. Five weeks later, the fully orchestrated work premiered in »

Schumann's wife, Clara, was the daughter of his first piano instructor, Friedrich Wieck. Both Clara and her father were celebrated for their skills on the keyboard.

Robert Schumann

Born in the Saxon city of Zwickau (now part of Germany) in 1810, Schumann began composing music as a young boy. No less interested in literature, he wrote a number of youthful novels before heading to Leipzig to study law. Schumann gave up his studies in order to become a concert pianist, but a hand injury prevented him from achieving his goal. Instead, he focused on composition and musical criticism, becoming editor of the *New Journal for Music*, through which he introduced the world to the music of Chopin and Brahms. His novel piano works, often inspired by literature, quickly became popular. After marrying Clara Wieck, a famous pianist herself, he began to concentrate on other musical genres. His last years were plagued with mental illness, and he died in an asylum in 1856.

Other key works

1838 *Kreisleriana*, Op. 16
1840 *Dichterliebe*, Op. 48
1845 Piano Concerto in A minor, Op. 54
1850 Symphony No. 3, Op. 97

New era, new aesthetics

Classical   **Romantic**

Inspired by the **Enlightenment** and the **Age of Reason**.

Emphasis is on **elegance** and **structure**.

Era of the **symphony**, **instrumental sonata**, and **string quartet**.

Music is largely the preserve of the **court** and the **wealthy**.

Inspired by **nature**, **poetry**, and **myth**.

Emphasis is on **emotional expression**.

New styles of **melody**, **harmony**, and **rhythm** emerge.

Growing audiences expand to include the **middle classes**.

Leipzig, with Mendelssohn as its conductor, and was well recieved by its audience.

A Romantic symphony

The title of the "Spring" Symphony was taken from a poem by Adolf Böttger that ends with the lines, "Oh turn and turn and change your course, In the valley Spring blooms forth," which inspired the opening of the symphony. The poem is about a melancholy lover whose pain is heightened by the arrival of spring, but Schumann claimed that a longing for spring in general inspired the work. In a letter to the conductor William Taubert in 1843, he wrote, "I should like the very first trumpet call to sound as though proceeding from on high and like a summons to awaken. … It might be possible to feel the world turning green; perhaps … a butterfly fluttering." In Schumann's first score for the symphony, he gave each of his movements titles: "Beginning of Spring," "Evening," "Jolly Playmates," and "Spring Replete." However, by the time the symphony was published, he had removed them.

It is clear from the opening brass fanfare, with its intense feeling of expectation, that this is

To send light into the darkness of men's hearts—such is the duty of the artist.
Robert Schumann

a symphony of the Romantic period. Full of contrast and surprise, its quickly shifting moods keep listeners in suspense. Avoiding both the musical arguments of Beethoven and the discursive approach of Schubert, Schumann found a way to direct the music's energy through juxtaposition and repetition, while still conveying subtle emotions. He also avoids using traditional key structures so that the second subject—or melodic theme—is in a minor key, adding a note of melancholy.

The symphony's second movement often seems as if it were originally written for the piano—a criticism frequently leveled at Schumann's orchestral works—but this brings an original, almost improvisatory quality to the piece that marked a departure from classical strictures. Meanwhile, in choosing to write the third

> I feel so entirely in my element with a full orchestra; even if my mortal enemies were … before me, I could lead them, master them, surround them, or repulse them.
> **Robert Schumann**

movement as a scherzo and trio, Schumann was influenced by Beethoven, who had created this structure out of the older minuet and trio, but here, too, Schumann's composition contains further innovation: there are two trios instead of the usual one, and they are in different time signatures. The last movement of the "Spring" Symphony is traditional in its structure but full of a humor that seems to anticipate Tchaikovsky in his lighter moments. Toward the end, Schumann has one last surprise in store—a theme from his piano piece *Kreisleriana* suddenly appears in a slightly altered form. Although it is not known why he did this, such self-quotation was not unusual for Schumann.

New approach
Almost entirely self-taught as a composer, Schumann brought an originality and freshness to the symphony that earned him

The German city of Leipzig became Schumann's home from 1828. He wrote many works at the house he shared with his wife, Clara Wieck. Situated on Inselstrasse 18, this is now a museum.

considerable acclaim. In using programmatic titles and literary references, as well as in the very sounds of the music he produced, Schumann helped to define the early Romantic ethos.

The early Romantic symphony paid more attention to orchestration than the classical symphony had; it used a wider palette of orchestral timbres and combined instrumental forces in new ways. Instruments that had previously been less popular—such as the harp, tuba, and trombone, as well as a number of percussion instruments—also became standard features.

Composers of this period seldom thought of themselves as markedly different from their classical forebears and were essentially trying to bring the new "Romantic" spirit of revolutionary politics to life, using quite traditional means. However, as the wider Romantic movement gained traction, some innovative composers—such as Berlioz and Liszt—experimented, not always successfully, with new approaches to harmony, rhythm, and structure. It was this spirit of experimentation that paved the way for late Romanticism. ∎

Form gives way to expression

The music composed by the Romantic generation strove to reflect the importance of the individual. Taking their cue in part from Beethoven—whose Ninth Symphony had broken the mold—composers sought to create music free from well-established structures, such as the minuet and trio and the rondo, and develop other forms, such as the sonata principle and fugue.

Their innovations gave the music of the Romantic composers an immediacy that enabled it to be more easily understood by middle-class audiences, who were generally untrained in music but wished to enjoy it as entertainment. In the same vein, Romantic works were often given titles to help new listeners grasp the mood and story of the music. Some musicians, such as Berlioz and Liszt, would even provide a written program to explain the intended narrative of the music to their audience.

THE LAST NOTE WAS DROWNED ... IN A UNANIMOUS VOLLEY OF PLAUDITS

ELIJAH (1846), FELIX MENDELSSOHN

IN CONTEXT

FOCUS
19th-century sacred choral music

BEFORE
1741 Handel composes his oratorio, *Messiah.*

1829 Felix Mendelssohn conducts Bach's *St. Matthew Passion* for the first time since the composer's death in 1750.

AFTER
1857 The Handel Festival at the Crystal Palace in London includes a performance of *Messiah* with a choir of 2,000 people and an orchestra of 500, creating a vogue for very large choral performances in England.

1900 Edward Elgar composes *The Dream of Gerontius*—a setting of an 1866 poem by Cardinal Newman—for the Birmingham Music Festival.

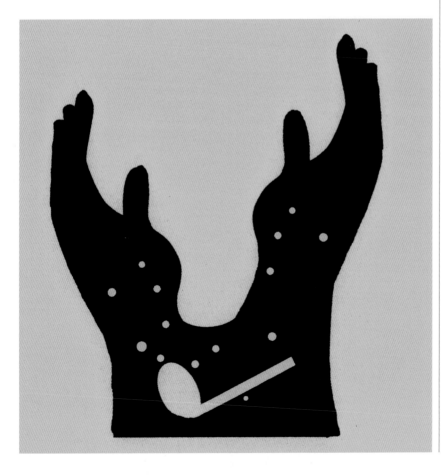

C horal music had started to wane in popularity by the 19th century. The Classical period had heralded a new philosophy that deemed music to be at its purest when it was self-contained and referenced nothing outside itself. Instrumental music—especially the symphony— had become the most important genre. While church musicians kept the choral tradition alive to some extent, they were increasingly amateurs. Secular choirs began to flourish, but because they were not professional musicians, the prestige of choral music suffered, compared to other types of music. In the absence of a market for choral

See also: *Magnus Liber organi* 28–31 ▪ *Canticum Canticorum* 46–51 ▪ Monteverdi's *Vespers* 64–69 ▪ *St. Matthew Passion* 98–105

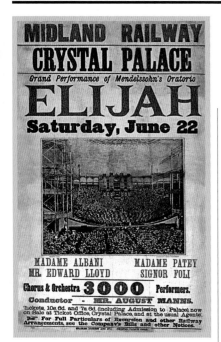

Oratorios, such as *Elijah*, were regularly performed with huge choirs and crowd-drawing soloists at the Crystal Palace, London, and elsewhere in England during the Victorian era.

sacred music, there was also little incentive for composers to write new choral works. As a result, the choral music performed tended to draw on works from the past.

An appetite for oratorios

In England, regular renditions of Handel's oratorios in the late 1700s marked the start of a trend that continued through the 19th century. Among the first works to be revived after the composer's death, they were often updated for large, grandiose performances. At later music events, such as the Three Choirs Festival (instituted by the cathedrals of Hereford, Worcester, and Gloucester), choirs could number more than a thousand singers—a far cry from the composer's original intentions.

The Berlin *Singakademie* was one of the first choral societies to be established, with amateurs paying a regular subscription to engage a professional conductor and defray concert expenses. It started as an educational venture for wealthy ladies, then went on to include men in 1791, and thereafter gave regular concerts. It was here that the young Felix Mendelssohn, whose father was a member of the choir, first came across the works of J.S. Bach and was inspired to conduct a performance of the *St. Matthew Passion*, which helped to establish the Bach revival in Germany. Further choral societies sprang up throughout Europe and America, and publishing choral music became a lucrative concern, as some choirs needed in excess of 300 copies of a vocal score for a single performance.

It was almost certainly through attending performances of Handel's oratorios in London in the 1790s that Haydn was inspired to create a similar work in the Classical style. *The Creation*, based on the Book of Genesis, was published in 1800, and curiously in a bilingual edition in both German and English— probably because Haydn had an eye on the British market, in which he was very successful. *The Creation* was an instant success and was performed throughout the Western world in Haydn's lifetime. Even as his other music dropped out of the standard repertoire, this oratorio remained one of the core works for choral societies and festivals.

It was within this cultural climate that Mendelssohn composed his oratorio *St. Paul* in »

Felix Mendelssohn

Born into a wealthy German-Jewish family in 1809, the young Mendelssohn was a child prodigy. He excelled not only at the piano, violin, conducting, and composition but also at painting, fencing, and riding. At the age of 20, he conducted a performance of the *St. Matthew Passion*— the first since Bach's death.

Mendelssohn's visit to England in 1829 was well received and made a great impression on him, resulting in nine further extended trips and invitations to Buckingham Palace. As well as composing and performing, Mendelssohn conducted the Leipzig Gewandhaus Orchestra and also founded the Leipzig Conservatoire. Following ill-health, possibly due to overwork and the death of his beloved sister, he suffered a series of strokes and died in 1847, at the age of 38.

Other key works

1826 Overture "A Midsummer Night's Dream," Op. 21
1833 Symphony No. 4 in A major ("Italian"), Op. 90
1844 Violin Concerto in E minor, Op. 64

1836. Its subsequent performance (in an English translation) in Liverpool, England, and later in the US gained him a reputation as a composer who was sympathetic to the possibilities of amateurs performing his works.

Mendelssohn had conducted *St. Paul* for the Birmingham Triennial Music Festival in 1837, and its organizers requested a new oratorio for 1846, the year before he died. The composer at first declined the invitation but was persuaded to write *Elijah* when told that the festival could provide as many performers as he requested. Its premiere featured an orchestra of 125 players and a chorus of 271 singers. The organizers even tried to engage the famous Swedish opera singer Jenny Lind, for whom Mendelssohn had tailored the soprano part. However, because this would have been her British debut, she declined, preferring an opera to showcase her vocal skills.

> Never before was anything like this season … I got through more music in two months than in all the rest of the year.
> **Felix Mendelssohn**

Eventually, she sang the soprano role of *Elijah* in London in 1848, after Mendelssohn's death, in a charity concert that funded the Mendelssohn Scholarship, which still exists today.

Elijah itself has a curious hybrid quality. Although clearly influenced by the Baroque and modeled on the oratorios of Bach and Handel,

it still reflects the Early Romantic period in its colorful orchestration and subtle lyricism. The chorales mark structural divisions in the music, as found in the Bach Passions. Also, unlike other works of the period, a surprisingly wide variety of styles and textures can be heard, which is reminiscent of Handel. However, Mendelssohn also uses innovative forms, such as including the choir in certain recitatives for dramatic effect, and he attempts to bring a sense of unity to the whole work by linking movements and using recurring motifs, both of which were musical devices of his own era. Of special interest are the fugues in the overture and finale, which clearly demonstrated to the Romantic generation that this Baroque form could be revived to great effect.

Elijah was immediately successful, especially in its English version, and became a mainstay of choral concerts throughout the 19th century. Later commentators, however, often found it too conventional and considered it a product of mid-Victorian values.

Grand sacred works

While many composers of the period were not very interested in choral music, Hector Berlioz created two of the grandest choral works in the repertoire. With their extraordinarily large forces, his *Requiem* of 1837 and his *Te Deum*, first performed in 1855, are vivid examples of the excesses of High Romanticism; the *Requiem* requires four off-stage brass ensembles while the score of

The prophet summons the Israelites in the bass recitative "Draw near all ye people" from the oratorio *Elijah*. This page, handwritten by Mendelssohn, is from an original 1846 score of the work.

Elijah's curse

Four strong chords introduce drama and foreboding.

Somber woodwind and brass are used. The brighter strings are silent.

Descending tritones, signaling **danger**, are capped by a trombone **blast**.

A **final drum roll** imparts a sense of doom.

Mendelssohn's *Elijah* begins with the prophet's curse on King Ahab and the Israelites. Their punishment for corrupt governance and the worship of false idols will be a terrible drought.

the *Te Deum* specifies 12 harps. As a result, performances were—and still are—rare and impractical, and so this music had little opportunity to affect the genre. Composers such as Rossini wrote a number of cantatas, but these tended to be overshadowed by their more popular operas and are seldom heard. It was Verdi's *Requiem* that managed to bridge the gap between secular operatic and sacred choral works. Verdi composed it in the operatic style, with immense drama, especially in the powerful "Dies Irae," and wrote parts for female voices at a time when the Catholic Church used only men in its choirs. The Requiem's first performance was at St. Mark's in Milan, but its second was at La Scala. Ever

since, opinion has been divided as to whether it is a religious work or an outpouring of rather more drama than sacrament.

A "human" requiem

Brahms's *German Requiem* was perhaps the most singular sacred choral work of the period. It was his first major composition and brought him international acclaim. He avoided the traditional requiem Mass text, instead creating his own from the Lutheran Bible. There is a focus in the work on comforting the living, no reference to the Day of Judgment, and no mention of Jesus. Brahms thought of it as a "human requiem" rather than belonging to any particular theological outlook, which is perhaps why it is still so frequently performed. Written in seven large sections, the musical material is tightly organized around the opening notes sung to *Selig sind* ("Blessed are"). This creates a very unified whole, in which Brahms seems to have avoided using any previous models. A work of subtle majesty, the *German Requiem* stands in sharp relief to most choral music of the 19th century. ■

Music in Victorian Britain

Between industrial innovation and empire building, the arts—especially music—were rather marginalized in early Victorian Britain. Although there was a thriving concert culture, it was predominated by foreign artists. Yet, with a rapidly expanding, wealthy middle class, there were many amateurs—young women especially—who needed socially acceptable music to play. In this climate, *Songs Without Words* by Mendelssohn, a "respectable" composer from a wealthy background, and even feted by the Queen, became ubiquitous. Meanwhile, the brass band movement in northern England and music halls in the cities were both thriving musical outlets for the working classes.

Later in the century, the search for a cultural identity inspired British classical musicians, which also led to the creation of British conservatoires. Figures as diverse as Sullivan and Elgar emerged from this new, so-called "English Musical Renaissance."

Prince Albert plays the organ for Mendelssohn as Queen Victoria looks on. The composer enjoyed several visits to Buckingham Palace in 1842.

I LOVE ITALIAN OPERA—IT'S SO RECKLESS
LA TRAVIATA (1853), GIUSEPPE VERDI

IN CONTEXT

IN CONTEXT

FOCUS
Italian opera

BEFORE
1829 Rossini shocks the musical world by retiring from opera after his final stage work, *William Tell*, premieres in Paris.

1848 Composer Gaetano Donizetti dies, 13 years after his compatriot Vincenzo Bellini, leaving Verdi as the leading light of Italian opera.

AFTER
1887 Milan hosts the premiere of Verdi's *Otello*, his first opera since *Aida* in 1871.

1890 Italian composer Pietro Mascagni's masterpiece *Cavalleria rusticana* premieres in Rome and ushers in the naturalistic, melodramatic "verismo" style of opera.

It was usual in the first decades of the 19th century for Italian opera to be concerned with the tragedies of the great and noble. Giuseppe Verdi challenged this and produced operas about ordinary people as well.

Verdi enjoyed notable early successes, such as *Nabucco* (1842), based on the biblical story of Nebuchadnezzar II. Its chorus "Va pensiero," in which the Hebrew slaves lament the loss of their homeland, would later become an anthem for Italian independence.

Italian tenor Francesco Meli performs as Violetta's lover, Alfredo, in the *brindisi* drinking song in a 2016 production of *La traviata*. His love for Violetta brings shame upon his family.

However, it wasn't until well into Verdi's creative life that he fulfilled his democratic ambitions with three masterpieces composed in quick succession—*Rigoletto* (1851), *Il trovatore* (1853), and *La traviata* (1853). *Rigoletto* focuses on the eponymous character—a hunchback who, in trying to protect his

See also: *The Magic Flute* 134–137 ▪ *The Barber of Seville* 148 ▪ *Der Freischütz* 149 ▪ *Tosca* 194–197 ▪ *The Wreckers* 232–239 ▪ *Peter Grimes* 288–293

daughter, unwittingly brings about her undoing; *Il trovatore* tells the melodramatic tale of the beautiful Leonora who is caught between two men and a gypsy woman's vengeance; and in *La traviata* ("The fallen woman"), a courtesan named Violetta sacrifices her love and, ultimately, herself, for the sake of the patriarchal society that seeks to control her. These three operas confirmed Verdi's break away from what he described as his galley years: time spent producing works to order for the "opera industry."

Bending the rules

Verdi managed to manipulate and subvert operatic conventions to achieve a synthesis of tradition and innovation. With *La traviata*, he took a subject drawn from a well-known novel, *La Dame aux camélias* (*The Lady of the Camellias*) by Alexandre Dumas, and, in a step unprecedented then, set the drama at the time of composition. Ultimately, the portrayal of a fallen woman in modern society was rejected as too risqué by the Italian censors, so the opera was set in the 1700s for the premiere. *La traviata* was nonetheless unique as it boldly confronted society's hypocritical treatment of women.

Although some of *La traviata*'s most famous numbers—especially the *brindisi* drinking song in Act One—feature crowd scenes, *La traviata* is an opera remarkable for its moments of intimacy. Verdi draws us into the world of his heroine, and this groundbreaking focus on a female protagonist paved the way for others, such as the gypsy heroine of Georges Bizet's *Carmen* (1875)—a character from French opera, who is similarly drawn from the literary world (from a story by Prosper Mérimée) and similarly exposed the hypocrisy of 19th-century sexual mores.

Final masterpieces

Verdi's many subsequent works saw the composer tackle the different conventions of *grand opéra* in such masterpieces as *Don Carlos*, composed for the Paris opera in 1867. However, *Aida*,

To copy the truth can be a good thing, but to invent the truth is better, much better.
Giuseppe Verdi

written for the opening of the new opera house in Cairo in 1871, marked a break for Verdi, who was unhappy with the importation of French and German opera to Italy. Verdi began to focus on other aspects of his life and composed little after the *Missa da Requiem* of 1874, written in memory of the nationalist poet, Alessandro Manzoni, until his final two pieces, which were both based on works by his beloved Shakespeare: *Otello* (1887) and *Falstaff* (1893). ▪

Giuseppe Verdi

Verdi was born in Busseto, northern Italy, in 1813. His father, an innkeeper of modest social standing, encouraged his son's early education, and a wealthy merchant in the town, Antonio Barezzi, paid for the young Verdi to study in Milan.

In 1836, Verdi married Barezzi's daughter, but both she and their two young children died four years later. In spite of this tragedy, Verdi's career began to take off. His breakthrough came with *Nabucco* in 1841. Over the following decade, he produced 13 operas. The 1850s saw him become the most successful opera composer of his day, and from the 1850s his music was embraced by the nationalist *Risorgimento* movement.

In 1859, Verdi married the operatic soprano Giuseppina Strepponi, staying with her until her death in 1897. Verdi himself died four years later, in 1901.

Other key works

1842 *Nabucco*
1867 *Don Carlos*
1874 *Missa da Requiem*
1887 *Otello*

WHO HOLDS THE DEVIL, LET HIM HOLD HIM WELL

FAUST SYMPHONY (1854–1857), FRANZ LISZT

IN CONTEXT

FOCUS
The Faust legend and German Romanticism

BEFORE
1830 The premiere of Berlioz's *Symphonie fantastique*, with the young Liszt in the Paris audience, sees the debut of the Romantic symphony orchestra, much more colorful than those that came before.

1846 Berlioz conducts the first performances of *The Damnation of Faust*, based on Goethe's *Faust* Part I.

AFTER
1861 Liszt arranges a piano version of his *Mephisto-Waltz No. 1*, which was originally written for orchestra.

1906 Mahler composes his Eighth Symphony; its main movement is a huge setting of the closing "Chorus mysticus" scene of Goethe's *Faust* Part II.

Mephistopheles holds a mirror up to Faust in a poster created by Richard Roland Holst for a 1918 Dutch National Theatre production of Goethe's play.

The central myths of European art can often be traced back to sources thousands of years old. Unusually, the Faust legend is a more recent phenomenon, based on a real person. The original Johann Faustus was a late 15th-century magician-illusionist, who claimed to be in league with the devil. His dubious career traveling through the southeast German region of Thuringia even secured him a doctorate from Heidelberg University. The Faust story had already become part of folklore when the literary doyen of the German Romantic movement, Johann Wolfgang von Goethe, began to explore the character in the 1770s.

Powerful appeal

Romanticism had multiple roots in the political and social upheavals of its time. With industrialism came the rise of a middle-class less beholden to the Church and the aristocracy, and in this more liberated climate, Goethe's verse-play *Faust* developed a potent appeal. *Faust* concerns the corruption of a secular, rational mind. Goethe's hero is a brilliant

See also: Stamitz's Symphony in E-flat major 116–117 ▪ Mozart's Symphony No. 40 in G minor 128–131 ▪ "Eroica" 138–141 ▪ *Symphonie fantastique* 162–163 ▪ Schumann's Symphony No. 1 166–169 ▪ Brahms's Symphony No. 1 188–189

agnostic philosopher, whose intellectual disillusionment leads him to be waylaid by the demon Mephistopheles's offer of a world of sensual and sexual satisfaction.

In the poem's first part (published in 1808), Faust is introduced to the trusting young Gretchen, whom he seduces, impregnates, and abandons to madness and death. The second part (completed in 1831) finds the remorseful Faust applying his powers to the cause of human good; as Faust's death approaches, Gretchen's soul intercedes for him, and angels carry Faust aloft to a higher world. The legend was taken up in Charles Gounod's grand opera *Faust*, Robert Schumann's oratorio *Scenes from Goethe's Faust*, and by Wagner in his *Faust Overture*. The most significant musical version, however, is the one by Hungarian virtuoso Franz Lizst.

Liszt's Faust

The young Liszt was introduced to *Faust Part I* (in Gérard de Nerval's French translation) by his friend

Berlioz. Enthralled, he sketched out some ideas first for an opera, then a symphony, but the idea remained on hold until he had settled in Goethe's adopted hometown of Weimar. In 1854, over a period of two months, he composed and orchestrated the first three movements of his *Faust Symphony*. Dedicating the work to Berlioz, he

A frontispiece of sheet music for Lizst's *Faust Symphony*, published in Leipzig, Germany, lists the main characters of the symphony and the type of orchestral arrangement.

added the finale, with its tenor soloist and male-voice choir, for the first performance three years later.

Rather than following Goethe's complex narrative, each of the symphony's first three movements presents a portrait of one of the main characters. The long first movement portrays the multiple layers of Faust's restless nature in a complex, chromatic musical language (based on all 12 semitones in an octave). While Gretchen's movement is Faust's opposite in its sweet winsomeness, Mephistopheles has a diabolic Scherzo, in which each theme is a distortion of one already used to portray Faust. The finale is a radiant choral setting of the poem's concluding "Chorus mysticus," as Gretchen's theme leads Faust's soul, much like in Goethe's version, into a transfigured musical world. ▪

Franz Liszt

Born in Raiding, eastern Austria, in 1811, Liszt showed early talent as a pianist. He studied in Vienna, where he played to an amazed Beethoven, and his subsequent teenage years in Paris consolidated his standing as the supreme pianist of his time. At 24 years old, he eloped to Switzerland with Countess Marie d'Agoult; later, in Italy, they had three children but drifted apart as Liszt pursued a relentless concert schedule throughout Europe.

In 1848, Liszt moved with the Ukrainian Princess Carolyne Sayn-Wittgenstein to Weimar, where he composed principal works of the Romantic era. Later, he took minor Catholic orders in Rome. In 1886, Liszt died of pneumonia in Bayreuth, Germany.

Other key works

1842 *Années de pèlerinage* (Years of Pilgrimage)
1853 Piano Sonata in B minor
1856 *Dante Symphony* (choir and orchestra)
1868 *Christus* (choral oratorio)

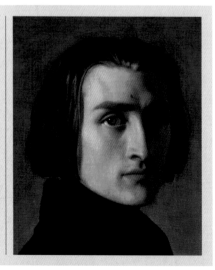

AND THE DANCERS WHIRL AROUND GAILY IN THE WALTZ'S GIDDY MAZES

THE BLUE DANUBE (1867), JOHANN STRAUSS II

IN CONTEXT

FOCUS
19th-century waltz music

BEFORE
1819 Carl Maria von Weber's *Invitation to the Dance* is the first waltz written for concert performance rather than dancing.

1823 Schubert writes *Valses sentimentales*, a collection of 34 waltzes for solo piano.

1834 Chopin's *Grande valse brillante* is the first of his solo piano waltzes to be published.

AFTER
1877 Tchaikovsky's *Swan Lake* is one of many late 19th-century ballets and operas that feature waltzes.

1911 Maurice Ravel publishes a suite of waltzes, *Valses nobles et sentimentales*.

1919–1920 Ravel composes *La valse*, about the rise and fall of the waltz as a musical genre.

One of the most instantly recognizable waltzes ever written, *An der schönen, blauen Donau* (*By the Beautiful Blue Danube*) was first performed in Vienna in February 1867 as a choral piece, conducted by its Austrian composer, Johann Strauss II. Comprising five interlinked waltz themes, it was designed to lift the spirit of the Austrian nation after its defeat by Prussia in the Seven Weeks' War. It was, however, the purely orchestral version, premiered in Paris later that year, that took off. The lilting beauty of Strauss's melodies made the piece beloved the world over.

Waltzes have their roots in the country dances of southern Germany, Bohemia, and Austria. From the mid-1700s, more refined versions, with a distinctive triple beat, started to become popular in Europe's ballrooms. Couples held one another face to face as they twirled around the floor, in contrast to the stately minuets and other French-style court dances that the waltz was starting to replace. By the early 1800s, the waltz had spread throughout Europe, with Vienna as its capital. Invigorated first by Johann Strauss I, then his son, it became the signature dance of the 19th century. ∎

A statue of "The Waltz King" playing the violin stands in Stadtpark, Vienna. As a child, Strauss practiced the violin secretly, as his musician father wanted him to become a banker.

See also: *Le bourgeois gentilhomme* 70–71 ▪ *Water Music* 84–89 ▪ *Symphonie fantastique* 162–163 ▪ *The Nutcracker* 190–191

I LIVE IN MUSIC LIKE A FISH IN WATER

PIANO CONCERTO NO. 2 IN G MINOR (1868), CAMILLE SAINT-SAËNS

IN CONTEXT

FOCUS
19th-century solo concertos

BEFORE
1830 Chopin's Piano Concerto No. 1 in E minor is premiered in Warsaw, Poland.

1836 Clara Schumann writes her Piano Concerto in A minor, nine years before her husband, Robert Schumann, writes his Piano Concerto in A minor.

1849 Liszt completes the final version of his Piano Concerto No. 1 in E-flat major.

AFTER
1868 Grieg composes one of the most popular piano concertos ever written, his Piano Concerto in A minor.

1881 Johannes Brahms completes his Piano Concerto No. 2 in B-flat major.

The French composer Camille Saint-Saëns' Piano Concerto No. 2 premiered in Paris in May 1868. It had taken him 17 days of flat-out labor to finish it in time for the concert, which his friend, the Russian musician Anton Rubinstein, conducted. Saint-Saëns played the solo part.

Exploring the form

Solo concertos had evolved over the course of the 19th century. Dazzling displays by virtuoso performer-composers, notably violinist Paganini and pianists Chopin and Liszt, dominated the years after 1810, with the orchestra providing little more than a backdrop. Later figures, such as Robert Schumann, called for a better balance.

Most major composers of the time, including Mendelssohn, Brahms, Grieg, and Dvořák, wrote concertos and experimented widely with the form. In his Piano Concerto No. 2, Saint-Saëns ignored convention by opening not with the orchestra but with a solo piano prelude in the style of Bach, and he replaced the usual fast-slow-fast sequence of movements with a slow-fast-faster progression, giving rise to the quip that it "begins with Bach and ends with Offenbach."

Lack of rehearsal time resulted in a disappointing premiere, but the concerto won admirers and remains a staple of the concert repertoire. Saint-Saëns wrote another three concertos for the piano, three for the violin, and two for the cello. ∎

He who does not get absolute pleasure from a simple series of well-constructed chords, beautiful only in their arrangement, is not really fond of music.
Camille Saint-Saëns

See also: *Pièces de clavecin* 82–83 ▪ Scarlatti's Sonata in D minor, K.9, "Pastorale" 90–91 ▪ Clementi's Piano Sonata in F-sharp minor 132–133

OPERA MUST MAKE PEOPLE WEEP, FEEL HORRIFIED, DIE

THE RING CYCLE (1848–1874),
RICHARD WAGNER

IN CONTEXT

FOCUS
Complete art work

BEFORE
1821 Weber's *Der Freischütz*, considered to be the first German Romantic opera, premieres in Berlin.

1824 Beethoven completes his Ninth Symphony. In a form that was traditionally wordless, Beethoven's use of words in the symphony's finale greatly influenced Wagner.

1849 After being forced into exile, Wagner begins a series of essays setting out a plan for reforming opera. The first step later becomes *The Ring*.

1862 Wagner conducts Beethoven's Ninth Symphony in Bayreuth to celebrate the laying of the corner stone of the *Festspielhaus*.

AFTER
1883 Wagner's widow Cosima takes over the running of the Bayreuth Festival, exercising iron control until her death in 1930.

1933 Hitler comes to power in Germany and, as an ardent Wagnerian, involves himself intimately with the running of the festival.

1976 Bayreuth's centenary staging of *The Ring*, later widely televised, presents the work as a critique of 19th-century industrialization.

The valkyrie Brünnhilde meets the lovers Siegmund and Sieglinde to warn Siegmund of his imminent death. This scene from Wagner's *Die Walküre* was painted by Gaston Bussière (1893).

wo things changed beyond recognition in Wagner's lifetime: German opera and Germany itself. The country that he grew up in was little more than a group of loosely linked principalities and kingdoms, while German opera before Wagner was fighting a losing battle against imports from France and Italy—apart from a few notable exceptions. Beethoven's *Fidelio*, Mozart's *Don Giovanni* (performed in German in the German-speaking lands), and the Romantic operas of Carl Maria von Weber represented the only resistance against the prevailing taste for foreign operatic imports, often poorly performed in the various court theatres that were dotted around Germany.

By the time of Wagner's death in 1883, Germany was a nation-state. German opera—or, more correctly, Wagnerian opera—had conquered France, Italy, and beyond. Other composers rushed to emulate his harmonic adventurousness and his richly symphonic style and longed for even a fraction of the quasi-religious devotion that Wagner's vast musical dramas inspired.

The road to Revolution

More than any other composer before him, Wagner's own life and art were intertwined with the developments—political, historical, and philosophical—of the world around him. From an early age, he was fascinated with how to combine drama and music, and increasingly, with how a new sort of opera could help revitalize the art form in Germany, as well as inspire and unite the country itself. He was unusual among opera composers in that he always wrote his own librettos (the words that were set to music) and did so even in his early operas. His first opera, *Die Feen*

("The fairies," 1834) delved deep into Romanticism, while his second, *Das Liebesverbot* ("The ban on love," 1836), loosely based on Shakespeare's *Measure for Measure*, was closer to Italian comic opera.

A largely unsuccessful period in Paris in the late 1830s exposed the young composer to the *bel canto* of Vincenzo Bellini (whom he much admired) as well as to *grand opéra*, a local genre whose extravagant scenic features would broaden his theatrical horizons. The German-born composer Giacomo Meyerbeer was among the most successful exponents of this type of operatic spectacle. Wagner's next work, *Rienzi* (1840), was modeled closely on Meyerbeer's style and proved to be his first breakthrough, leading to Wagner's appointment as *Kapellmeister* (director of music) at the Dresden Court Theatre.

Wagner's subsequent works in the 1840s, *Der fliegende Holländer* (*The Flying Dutchman*), *Tannhäuser,* and *Lohengrin*, are the earliest operas included in the canon of works performed at the festival that Wagner founded at Bayreuth. They show the composer increasingly breaking down the traditional structures of opera—blurring the lines between individual arias, duets, and choruses, and focusing on the psychological development of characters of unprecedented complexity. The operas addressed subjects that would concern him for the rest of his creative life: redemption, the nature of desire, and, in *Tannhäuser*, how religion can and should temper this desire.

Theory and practice

Wagner's involvement in the uprising in Dresden in 1849—part of a series of republican revolts that swept through Germany and other parts of Europe—led to a warrant being issued for his arrest, forcing him into exile in Switzerland. During the first five years in exile, he did not compose a single note of music, concentrating instead on setting out the foundations for his operatic reforms in a series of long essays. It was during this period that Wagner

> With one bound I became a revolutionist, and acquired the conviction that every decently active being ought to occupy himself with politics exclusively.
> **Richard Wagner**

came up with the idea of the *Gesamtkunstwerk* (literally "complete art work"), which would combine all the elements of stage performance in one. His new works would amalgamate the genius of Beethoven and Shakespeare and be modeled on ancient Greek drama, which, as far as Wagner understood it, not only combined all the arts but did so in a way that was essential for uniting a »

Richard Wagner

Wagner was born in Leipzig in 1813 and was drawn to the theatre at an early age, also developing an obsession with music—particularly Beethoven. His early years were dominated by instability, exacerbated by his irresponsible attitude toward money. His operas began to see success in the 1840s, and a job as Kapellmeister in Dresden followed, but both were jeopardized by his political activism.

Forced into exile in Switzerland in the 1850s, he set about a wholesale reform of opera: first in theoretical essays, then in practice, most ambitiously in *The Ring*. In the 1860s, his fortunes improved thanks to the financial aid of King Ludwig II of Bavaria, which gave him new artistic freedom. Wagner died in Venice in 1883, the year after *Parsifal* premiered in Bayreuth.

Other key works

1841 *The Flying Dutchman*
1848 *Lohengrin*
1859 *Tristan und Isolde*
1867 *Die Meistersinger von Nürnberg*
1882 *Parsifal*

population. Wagner sought to create an artistic experience with religious, social, and ethical aspects.

Such an artwork would gain yet further resonance with its audience, he argued, by being based on subjects rooted deep in their unconscious, ideally myth. In his new "music dramas," as his works became known, he would be able to harness the power of music to explore the inner workings of his characters. Unlike with the predominant forms of opera, in which musical concerns and, in the worst cases, the vanity of singers, were primary considerations, here it would be the drama that would define the form of the music.

Composing the world

The work that came closest to this aim was a cycle of operas, *Der Ring des Nibelungen* ("The ring of the Nibelung"), based on a mixture of Norse and Germanic mythology. It was not initially conceived as a tetralogy (a cycle of four works), but Wagner's inability to progress with the subject as a single opera,

originally called *Siegfrieds Tod* ("Siegfried's death"), led to him expanding it backward, adding more and more prehistory in each additional work.

This process also necessitated the development of "leitmotif"—a technique latent in his works of the 1840s but raised in *The Ring* to a level of extraordinary complexity and sophistication. This method allowed Wagner to weave together continuous acts over large spans but also meant that the orchestra could begin to offer "commentary" on the action, much as the chorus had done in ancient Greek drama.

Wagner finally completed his text for the cycle by 1852, and he began composing the music shortly afterward, without any realistic prospect of the works ever being performed. *Das Rheingold*, which Wagner called a "preliminary evening" to the main drama, came first and was the nearest Wagner came to realizing the theoretical ideal laid out in his essays. The opera's cast of Norse gods, dwarves, and giants communicate

I shall never write an Opera more. As I have no wish to invent an arbitrary title for my works, I will call them Dramas.
Richard Wagner

with conversation-like directness (using punchy alliterative verse called *Stabreim*), while the orchestra provides commentary.

For the "first day" of the cycle, *Die Walküre* ("The Valkyrie," 1856), Wagner created music of far greater sensuality and warmth, in part because this installment added humans into the tale, specifically the long-lost twins Siegmund and Sieglinde, who fall in love during the course of the first act. (The

Timeline for the production of *The Ring*

The Ring was made up of four operas, which Wagner worked on in two distinct phases during his lifetime, beginning and ending with *Götterdämmerung*.

Key
■ Text written   ▨ *Tristan und Isolde*   ▨ First performance
■ Music composed   ▨ *Die Meistersinger*

Das Rheingold		Munich
Die Walküre		
Siegfried		Bayreuth
Götterdämmerung		

1845   1850   1855   1860   1865   1870   1875   1880   1885

Wagner's style was not popular with everyone, as seen in this American cartoon (1877), which criticized the dense noise of *Götterdämmerung*, the last opera of the Ring Cycle.

Tristan and its chord

Inspired by his discovery of Arthur Schopenhauer's philosophies and a romantic obsession with Mathilde von Wesendonck—the wife of his Swiss patron—Wagner began composing *Tristan und Isolde* in 1857, finishing it less than two years later. The work, which explores the adulterous romance and subsequent death of the legendary lovers, arguably laid the foundations for the breakdown of tonality. In it, Wagner creates a disorientating, intoxicating world built on harmonic tension that—reflecting the drama's obsession with the impossibility of perfect love—remains unresolved until the very end. Emblematic of this work is the so-called "Tristan chord"—the first chord in the Prelude—whose apparently unrelated notes of F, B, D-sharp, and G-sharp form the basis for the work's harmonic instability. The Tristan chord, as used by Wagner, was hugely influential on composers seeking to push—and break—the boundaries of harmony.

Tristan und Isolde (1859) first premiered in Munich in 1865, starring Ludwig Schnorr von Carolsfeld and his wife Malwina Garrigues as the doomed lovers.

promotion of incest was just one of many sins the composer would be accused of during his career.) By 1856, however, Wagner had also discovered the philosopher Arthur Schopenhauer, who would prove to be a powerful influence on his creative output. Not only did Schopenhauer present a philosophy of pessimism incompatible with the revolutionary zeal that inspired *The Ring*, but he viewed music as the most profoundly expressive of any of the arts—turning Wagner's drama-first conviction on its head.

Breaking the cycle

In practical terms, Wagner's discovery of Schopenhauer brought about a break in his composition »

of *The Ring*: he stopped composing *Siegfried* (the "second day" of the cycle) after completing a draft score of the second act in 1857. He did not return to it for seven years.

During the interim, Wagner completed two very different works, both of which were deeply inspired by Schopenhauer's philosophy—specifically, its idea that relative fulfillment could be achieved only through renunciation. The first of these new works was *Tristan und Isolde* (completed in 1859, though not performed in its entirety until 1865), an overtly philosophical and sensuous work in which Wagner pushed traditional harmony to its limits. The second work, *Die Meistersinger von Nürnberg* ("The master-singers of Nuremberg," 1867), was a comedy of unprecedented dimensions—the final act alone is more than two hours long when staged—that dealt with profound issues, such as the place of art within society, art's relationship with national identity, and the balance to be struck between rule-based tradition and innovation.

When Wagner finally returned to his composition of *The Ring*, he immediately applied the musical and philosophical lessons learned from his interim projects to the

cycle, bringing an even greater harmonic richness to the third act of *Siegfried* and to the fourth opera, *Götterdämmerung* ("The twilight of the Gods")—in which the Ring is finally returned to the Rhine Maidens, and Valhalla, home of the gods, collapses. Wagner completed his final installment in November 1874, 25 years after first starting work on the project.

Festival theatre
Upon completion of *The Ring*, Wagner decided that no existing theatre would do to stage it and set about raising funds for a new *Festspielhaus* (festival theatre).

The English National Opera performs "The Ride of the Valkyries" at Glastonbury Festival in 2004. The well-known piece comes at the start of Act Three of *Die Walküre*.

The theatre that Wagner built in the Franconian town of Bayreuth to stage *The Ring* in 1876 is in many ways as revolutionary as the works it was built to stage. It has a broad auditorium, with long rows of seats laid out to resemble an ancient amphitheatre. The orchestra and conductor are not visible to the audience, as their pit is sunk beneath the stage. In an unprecedented step for the

I laid my plans on so important a scale, that it would be impossible to produce this opera … at any lesser theatre.
Richard Wagner

Leitmotif

The leitmotif (or "leading motif") technique is related to Berlioz's *idée fixe*, a fixed idea or theme in a work, which he used in his *Symphonie fantastique*. It is also related to other earlier forms of "reminiscence motif," a recurring set of notes signifying a character or their memories. Motifs were utilized to a greater extent, and with unprecedented sophistication, in Wagner's *The Ring*, however, where the whole musical fabric—specifically in the orchestra—of the work was built from melodic fragments that become associated with different characters, ideas, or states of mind. From the very first performances of *The Ring*, attempts were made to "decode" these leitmotifs and to interpret the orchestral writing as a commentary on the drama. The technique went on to be widely adopted—including, in the 20th century, by film composers.

time, the lights in the auditorium would be extinguished during the performance, and comings and goings were forbidden.

Operatic pilgrimage

From the very first festival in 1876, the great and the good flocked to Bayreuth, and with Wagner's final opera, *Parsifal* (1882), the unmistakable allure of the festival only grew. Things were not straightforward, however, and the unprecedented scenic demands of *The Ring* were only imperfectly met at its first production. One of Wagner's most vocal critics, Eduard Hanslick, said that the rainbow bridge that leads to Valhalla at the end of *Das Rheingold* resembled a "seven-colored sausage"; Wagner's

wife, Cosima, famously complained that the costumes, painstakingly researched, made everyone look like Native American chiefs. The dragon Wagner had ordered from Manchester, UK, for *Siegfried*, never arrived in full—the neck section, the story goes, ended up not in Bayreuth but Beirut.

A new beginning

The legacy of *The Ring*, Wagner's Bayreuth project, and the composer himself cannot be overestimated. *Wagnérisme* was fashionable in Paris at the end of the 19th century as artists were inspired by the heady mix of religion and sex in *Parsifal*. Meanwhile, in Vienna, debate raged between those who supported Brahms and his more

conventional symphonies and those who were fully under the Wagnerian spell.

Leitmotif became a standard technique for a generation of younger composers, many of whom attempted, after Wagner's death, to create earnest facsimiles of his operatic works. Italy, traditionally the home of opera, had a crisis of musical identity, torn between embracing Wagner's innovations and preserving its own revered traditions. Thanks to Wagner, opera—which he once criticized for being too susceptible to frivolousness—was now an art form that dealt with the grandest philosophical questions and demanded a new revolutionary sort of music to do so. ∎

Bayreuth Festspielhaus

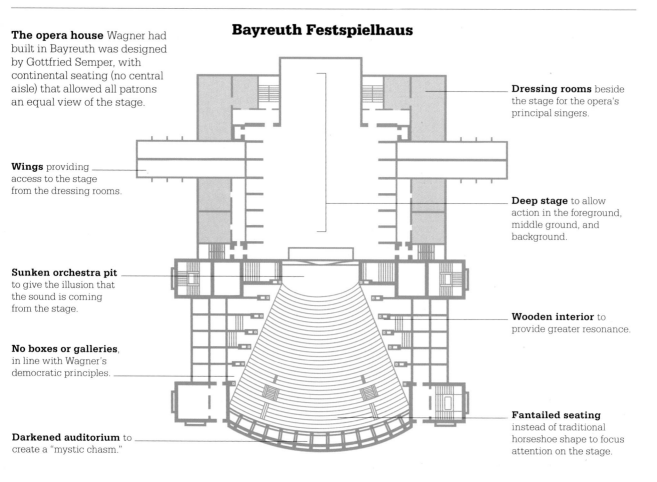

The opera house Wagner had built in Bayreuth was designed by Gottfried Semper, with continental seating (no central aisle) that allowed all patrons an equal view of the stage.

Wings providing access to the stage from the dressing rooms.

Sunken orchestra pit to give the illusion that the sound is coming from the stage.

No boxes or galleries, in line with Wagner's democratic principles.

Darkened auditorium to create a "mystic chasm."

Dressing rooms beside the stage for the opera's principal singers.

Deep stage to allow action in the foreground, middle ground, and background.

Wooden interior to provide greater resonance.

Fantailed seating instead of traditional horseshoe shape to focus attention on the stage.

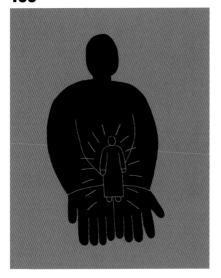

HE ... COMES AS IF SENT STRAIGHT FROM GOD

SYMPHONY NO. 1 (1876), JOHANNES BRAHMS

I n the first decades of the 19th century, Beethoven took the symphony to new heights, making it the most important genre in the Austro-German tradition. In the wake of his death, a handful of composers stepped in to assume Beethoven's mantle. Among them was German composer Johannes Brahms, who deplored program music—music that sought to follow or describe a narrative line—and openly criticized the New German School represented by Richard Wagner and Franz Liszt. Brahms believed in producing "pure" music, which was abstract, rather than associated with a plot line.

In 1853, Brahms met Robert Schumann and his pianist wife, Clara. Schumann, who was the composer of four symphonies, hailed Brahms as the great hope

Brahms and Adele Strauss, wife of Johann Strauss II, sit down to breakfast in his villa in the summer of 1894. Brahms often visited their villa in Bad Ischl, Austria.

See also: Mozart's Symphony No. 40 128–131 ▪ "Eroica" Symphony 138–141 ▪ *Symphonie fantastique* 162–163 ▪
Schumann's Symphony No. 1 166–169 ▪ *Faust Symphony* 176–177 ▪ Dvořák's Symphony No. 9 212–215

Johannes Brahms

The son of a struggling musician, Brahms was born in Hamburg, northern Germany, in 1833. He received his first music lessons from his father, and as a teenager he helped support his family by playing piano in the inns of Hamburg, before finding work as a choral conductor.

In 1863, Brahms settled in Vienna, marking the start of a highly successful period in which he composed *A German Requiem*, the First Symphony, and his *Hungarian Dances*. In the years following Robert Schumann's death in 1856, Brahms became particularly close to his widow, Clara, and would be a friend of hers for life.

In later life, Brahms focused on instrumental music, but in 1896, the year before his death, he wrote *Vier ernste Gesänge* ("Four Serious Songs"), reflecting on the transience of life.

Other key works

1853 Piano Sonata No. 3 in F minor, Op. 5
1868 *A German Requiem*
1869 *Hungarian Dances* (for piano duet)

of German music, describing the 20-year-old composer as a "man of destiny," placing on Brahms the weight of public expectation.

First Symphony

Brahms started sketching his First Symphony soon after Schumann's endorsement but did not complete it until the mid-1870s—more than 20 years later. In the interim, Brahms tried his hand at other symphonies, but none reached fruition. Meanwhile, he composed many orchestral and chamber works, including sonatas for violin, cello, and piano. He destroyed the works he was unhappy with, but parts of his attempts at symphonic writing were recast in other pieces, such as the opening of his First Piano Concerto.

The intensely self-critical composer published his first string quartets—another Beethovenian genre par excellence—only in 1873, and they, as well as two other important works rooted in different traditions, arguably paved the way for the symphonic breakthrough. In

A German Requiem (1868), Brahms set Lutheran texts in a manner that looked back to the earliest German choral music, while his so-called *Haydn Variations* (1873) explored an array of compositional devices old and new in an orchestral context.

This synthesis of tradition and innovation distinguished the First Symphony, whose themes fused folk song and chorale, as well as allusions to Bach and to Beethoven's Ninth Symphony.

[Brahms is] someone destined to give ideal presentment to the highest expression of the times.
Robert Schumann

Brahms's First Symphony, like Beethoven's Ninth, moves from darkness to light, with a stormy opening from bass and timpani that subsides into a dreamy Andante before bringing in urgent pizzicato strings. The third movement, the Allegretto, captures a joyful atmosphere while at the same time showcasing Brahms's close attention to symmetry.

Further works

Following the success of his First Symphony, Brahms composed three more, choosing to conclude his Fourth Symphony (1885) with a thrilling *passacaglia*—a Baroque form that develops its material over a constantly repeating bass line. Brahms's symphonies may seem conservative in comparison to those who succeeded him—such as Gustav Mahler, whose First Symphony heralded a new direction when it burst onto the scene in 1889—but Brahms's development of earlier forms and processes would prove influential for a whole generation of modernists. ▪

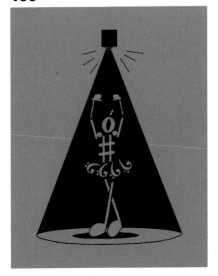

THE NOTES DANCE UP THERE ON THE STAGE

THE NUTCRACKER (1892)
PYOTR ILYICH TCHAIKOVSKY

IN CONTEXT

FOCUS
Ballet music

BEFORE
1832 *La Sylphide,* the first Romantic ballet, opens in Paris, choreographed by Filippo Taglioni to music composed by Jean-Madeleine Schneitzhoeffer.

1870 Léo Delibes's ballet *Coppélia,* about a dancing doll that comes to life, is staged at the Paris Opéra.

1876 Delibes's ballet *Sylvia* opens in Paris. Tchaikovsky praises his score for *Sylvia* above Wagner's *Ring Cycle.*

AFTER
1911 Stravinsky's ballet *Petrushka* premieres in Paris.

1920 The Paris Opéra stages the premiere of Stravinsky's *Pulcinella,* with choreography by Leonid Massine. The libretto is inspired by a folk tale.

The 19th century brought a revolution in the world of ballet. Earlier ballet music had been largely made up of well-known opera songs linked by melodies written by a theatre musician. Few original scores for ballet were composed before 1820.

At this time, light Romantic ballets began to appear, dominated in Europe by dancers such as Marie Taglioni, whose father Filippo choreographed *La Sylphide* to showcase her skills. Its central themes of enchantment and an ethereal female lead were a vehicle for dancers to explore "floating motion" and *pointe* work (dancing on tiptoe), with ever-shorter dresses to allow the dancers' feet and legs to be seen. The music for these earlier ballets was very much at the service of the dance, and usually written by "specialists"— composers prepared to produce light, rhythmic music that would not upstage the dance.

Ballet moves east

From about 1850, ballet's center began to shift from Paris to Russia, where tsarist patronage facilitated lavish productions. Tchaikovsky received the commission for his first ballet, *Swan Lake,* in 1875. Approaching the commission with symphonic ambition, he created melodies associated with characters in the story. The critics, however, were not ready for a ballet score worthy of the concert hall, and in spite of a warm audience reception, critical incomprehension saw the work shelved.

While the choreographer on *Swan Lake,* Julius Reisinger, had allowed Tchaikovsky quite a lot of freedom, the choreographer Marius Petipa was more specific about what he required of the music when

The heart of the classical repertory is the Tchaikovsky–Petipa *Sleeping Beauty,* and no ballet is harder to get right.
Robert Gottlieb
American writer and dance critic

See also: *Le bourgeois gentilhomme* 70–71 ▪ *The Magic Flute* 134–137 ▪ *Le Sacre du printemps* 246–251 ▪ *Romeo and Juliet* 272 ▪ *Appalachian Spring* 286–287

he collaborated with Tchaikovsky on *Sleeping Beauty* (1890). The work was well received by the critics, and the two men joined forces again for *The Nutcracker* two years later, although illness compelled Petipa to delegate much of the work to his assistant Lev Ivanov.

Fairytale ending

Composition of *The Nutcracker* had a difficult start. Tchaikovsky felt constrained by the unimaginative libretto Petipa had created from Alexandre Dumas's adaptation of German author E.T.A. Hoffman's darker tale. The composer finally found inspiration in the death of his sister, his childhood playmate. He poured his memories of her into the music, particularly into the central character, the young girl Clara, who creeps down on Christmas Eve to play with her favorite gift, a nutcracker figure, which magically comes to life. After she helps it to defeat a vicious Mouse King, the Nutcracker turns into a prince, who takes her to the Land of Sweets, ruled by the Sugar Plum Fairy.

The charm of Tchaikovsky's score is in large part due to his creative use of the orchestra, from the sinuous woodwind of the Arabian Dance and the trilling flutes' and piccolos' contrast with the low bassoons in the Chinese Dance, to the novelty of the celesta, a newly invented keyboard instrument with bars like a glockenspiel, to introduce the Sugar Plum Fairy. While the music gave Petipa and his dancers the lead they required, Tchaikovsky's unique sonority raises the music far above the old music of the "specialists." ▪

Columbine and Harlequin evoke *The Nutcracker*'s fantasy world in costumes designed by Denmark's Queen Margrethe II for a production in Copenhagen in 2016.

Pyotr Ilyich Tchaikovsky

Born in Votkinsk, Russia, in 1840, Tchaikovsky received piano lessons from an early age. He enrolled at the newly opened St. Petersburg Conservatory in 1861 and wrote his First Symphony in 1866. His *Romeo and Juliet* overture (1869) was his first international success.

Despite recognizing his own homosexuality, Tchaikovsky entered a doomed marriage in 1877. A year earlier, the wealthy widow and arts lover Nadezhda von Meck had become his patroness, enabling him to devote his time to composing. Von Meck declared herself bankrupt in 1890, causing a rift with Tchaikovsky. The fatalism that often tinged his music is clearly present in last works, such as his Sixth Symphony ("Pathétique," 1893). He died nine days after its premiere.

Other key works

1876 *Swan Lake*
1878 *Eugene Onegin*
1889 *Sleeping Beauty*
1893 Symphony No. 6 ("Pathétique")

A SYMPHONY MUST BE LIKE THE WORLD. IT MUST CONTAIN EVERYTHING
ALSO SPRACH ZARATHUSTRA (1896)
RICHARD STRAUSS

IN CONTEXT

FOCUS
**From Romanticism
to modernism**

BEFORE
1849 Franz Liszt completes
his first tone poem, *Ce qu'on
entend sur la montagne*
("What one hears on the
mountain"), after the poem
by Victor Hugo.

1865 Richard Strauss's father,
Franz, plays the horn in the
premiere of Wagner's *Tristan
und Isolde* in Munich.

AFTER
1903 Gustav Mahler conducts
the first full performance of his
100-minute Third Symphony,
which he completed in 1896.

1917 The premiere is held of
Alexander von Zemlinsky's
A Florentine Tragedy, an opera
based, like Strauss's *Salome*,
on a work by Oscar Wilde.

The period after Richard Wagner's death in 1883 was a time of uncertainty for German music. Some composers sought to emulate Wagner in their own operas; others avoided opera altogether and applied Wagner's innovations to music composed for the concert hall. Anton Bruckner, for example, brought Wagnerian grandeur, dimensions, and harmonic adventurousness to the traditional symphonic form. Gustav Mahler expanded the form even further, employing an orchestra of unprecedented size in symphonies that incorporated programmatic elements and vocal parts.

New forms
Richard Strauss, Mahler's great contemporary, took a different route with the tone poem—a musical form that seeks to capture the story or atmosphere of a nonmusical work, such as a poem or painting. The genre was pioneered by Franz Liszt and formed the basis for Strauss's early reputation as a firebrand.

Strauss's breakthrough was the daringly erotic *Don Juan* (1888), and in the next decade he produced a series of works that combined his virtuosity as an orchestrator with formal innovation—eschewing, for example, the need for a piece to end in the key it begins in. Controversial at the time, Strauss's works were not written to be

The prophet Zarathustra's
(or Zoroaster's) writings about Ahura Mazda (god) form the basis of the Zoroastrian faith. This portrait of him hangs at a fire temple in Yazd, Iran.

See also: *The Four Seasons* 92–97 ▪ *Faust Symphony* 176–177 ▪ *The Ring Cycle* 180–187 ▪ *Symphonie fantastique* 162–163 ▪ *Das Lied von der Erde* 198–201

I would only believe
in a God that knows
how to dance.
Friedrich Nietzsche
Also sprach Zarathustra **(1883–1891)**

edifying or morally empowering, as demanded by 19th-century musical aesthetics. This aligned him with other "modernist" composers, whose defining feature was their emphasis on innovation and progress—redefining composition by challenging formal conventions.

Role of the artist

Also sprach Zarathustra ("Thus spake Zarathustra," 1896) was arguably Strauss's boldest tone poem. The 35-minute work took its title from the book by Friedrich Nietzsche, in which the philosopher used the character of the ancient Persian prophet to present his philosophy. In Strauss's own words, he set out "to convey in music an idea of the evolution of the human race from its origin, through the various phases of development … up to Nietzsche's idea of the *Übermensch*" through his tone poem. This idea of the *Übermensch* (superman), a figure unburdened by conventional morality or religion, resonated well with Strauss's own vision of the role of the independent artist at the dawn of the 20th century. It also helped to pave

the way for his brand of amoral modernism, epitomized in his scandalous breakthrough opera *Salome* (1905)—based on a play by Oscar Wilde that featured incest, necrophilia, and blasphemy.

Age of uncertainty

Strauss's *Also sprach Zarathustra* depicts a conflict between nature, which is represented by the trumpet's simple opening C-G-C motif, and humanity, whose complex passions and intellectual struggles are conveyed by more harmonically adventurous writing. The tone poem includes nine sections, named from Nietzsche's book, with music that includes a mocking fugue and a light-hearted waltz. Man and nature remain unreconciled at the work's daring conclusion, which vacillates uncertainly between the keys of C major and B major. ∎

Also sprach Zarathustra was completed in 1896. This frontispiece from that year, printed in Munich by Joseph Aibl, prefaced the original orchestral score.

Richard Georg Strauss

The son of a famous horn player, Richard Strauss was born in Munich in 1864. After early success with his tone poems and songs (many composed for his wife), he finally found the operatic success he longed for with *Salome* (1905), followed by *Elektra* (1909). The latter marked the start of a 20-year collaboration with the writer and librettist Hugo von Hofmannsthal—one of the greatest partnerships in operatic history.

Strauss's prestige suffered in the 1920s and especially in the 1930s, as his relations with the Nazi Party tarnished his reputation in the English-speaking world. In the 1940s, however, the elderly Strauss, heartbroken by the national catastrophe, produced a series of late works, including the *Four Last Songs*, composed just months before his death in Garmisch-Partenkirchen, Germany, in 1949.

Other key works

1888 *Don Juan*
1905 *Salome*
1911 *Der Rosenkavalier*
1949 *Four Last Songs*

EMOTIONAL ART IS A KIND OF ILLNESS

TOSCA (1900), GIACOMO PUCCINI

IN CONTEXT

FOCUS
Verismo

BEFORE
1890 Winner of a competition for a new one-act opera, Pietro Mascagni's *Cavalleria rusticana* launches the "verismo" (realism) music movement in Rome.

1892 Modeled on *Cavalleria*, Ruggero Leoncavallo's opera *Pagliacci* is a hit in Milan, consolidating verismo style.

AFTER
1904 Puccini suffers a setback when *Madama Butterfly* is booed at its premiere in Milan, although it bounces back three months later in Brescia.

1926 Two years after Puccini's death, his *Turandot*, completed by his younger colleague Franco Alfano, is premiered at La Scala in Milan.

With the first performance of *Cavalleria rusticana* in 1890, a new kind of opera was born. Rather than being based on romanticized historical or legendary subjects, it strove for realism (or *verismo*, in Italian), embracing down-to-earth, sometimes sordid events, lived by believably ordinary people in often contemporary settings.

At this time, Puccini, a former flatmate of *Cavalleria*'s composer Pietro Mascagni, was six years into an opera career. This had begun in 1884 with *Le villi*, a picturesque *leggenda drammatica* (dramatic legend) based on the same story of dead spirits as the romantic ballet

See also: *Orfeo ed Euridice* 118–119 ▪ *The Barber of Seville* 148 ▪
Der Freischütz 149 ▪ *La traviata* 174 ▪ *The Wreckers* 232–239 ▪
Peter Grimes 288–293

Giselle (1841). It was followed five years later by *Edgar* (1889), an opera set in a 14th-century world of medieval knights. Although not the strictest follower of verismo, Puccini, once the new style became established, took its passionate, heartrending, and cruel elements and clothed them in daring music that reached a breathtaking climax in the tragic opera *Tosca*.

Embracing the realistic

Puccini's first response to verismo was the opera *Manon Lescaut* (1893), based on an 18th-century French novel by the Abbé Prévost. This had already been turned into several operas, notably *Manon* (1884) by the opera specialist, Jules Massenet. He was one of a number of French composers whose operas had been gaining ground in Italian theatres. These included *Faust* (1859) by Charles Gounod and *Carmen* (1875), the final masterpiece of Georges Bizet, which shocked critics of the time with its earthy realism and amoral heroine.

Although *Manon Lescaut* was not truly a "realist" work, it contained two scenes in particular that sat squarely in the new style. In Act III, the poignant spectacle of the embarkation of the prostitutes condemned to transportation and, in Act IV, the heroine's lengthy death scene in an American desert both provided a focus for some of the most emotionally powerful writing in the score, delivered in a style that epitomized the essence of musical verismo.

Puccini's next opera, *La Bohème* (1896), set among down-at-the-heels artists and their girlfriends in Paris around 1830, was closer to the true subject matter of verismo. It also crystallized the intense sentiment, characterization, and craftsmanship of the musical language of verismo that was »

Carmen talks to the smuggler Le Dancaïre in a scene from *Carmen* by Georges Bizet. The opera, with its themes of passion, jealousy, and violence, was an influence on verismo.

Giacomo Puccini

Born into a family of church musicians in Lucca in 1858, Puccini claimed to have decided on an operatic career after watching a performance of Verdi's *Aida* in Pisa in 1876. After studying at the Milan Conservatory, he entered his one-act opera-ballet *Le Villi* in a competition. Although it was rejected for being illegible, it was staged by the publisher Giulio Ricordi.

Puccini's breakthrough came in 1893 with *Manon Lescaut*, which put him at the forefront of Italian composers. Thereafter, he produced his three greatest successes—*La Bohème*, *Tosca*, and *Madama Butterfly*. His productivity slowed in later years, but the operas *La fanciulla del West* (1910), *La rondine* (1917), *Il trittico* (1918), and the posthumously produced *Turandot* displayed increasing refinement. He died of a heart attack in Brussels in 1924 following an operation for throat cancer.

Other key works

1896 *La Bohème*
1904 *Madama Butterfly*
1918 *Il trittico*

widely apparent in Puccini's work. This he handled with a greater degree of flexibility and far more technical variety and finesse than most of his contemporaries. There was also in Puccini's scores a persistent interest in new musical developments from beyond Italy's (or even opera's) borders, which added heightened expressive color and richness to his music. He made use of the harmonies, rhythms, and orchestral effects displayed in the

At the premiere of *Tosca*, the lead role was played by the Romanian-born 39-year-old soprano Hariclea Darclée, seen here in Act II holding the knife she will use to kill Scarpia.

works of fellow composers, such as Debussy, Strauss, Stravinsky, and even Schoenberg, but also made modernist musical initiatives of his own, many of which came to the fore in *Tosca*.

Using music for menace

Puccini premiered *Tosca*, his fifth opera, in Rome in 1900, a time of great uncertainty and instability in Italian politics. Though clothed in the theatrical dress of a period 100 years prior to its opening, the opera dealt with issues and characters that seemed contemporary to its first audience but would become even more starkly relevant as the 20th century progressed. In particular, the figure of Scarpia, the sadistic police chief, who is a presence in the opera musically from its opening bars right through to the final act (although dead

News of Napoleon's victory at Marengo, pictured here by the French artist Louis-François Lejeune (1775–1848), reaches Rome in Act II of *Tosca*, three days after the battle.

by this time), seems to prefigure innumerable individuals who, over the next century, served cruel, dictatorial regimes, including Fascist Italy.

Scarpia is introduced in the concise motif of two chords on lower woodwind, brass, and strings, followed by an unrelated and clashing third chord by the higher strings and woodwind, and a lurid gleam from the cymbals. Every note in this chord sequence is accented and marked "*fff*" ("extremely loud"). Long before we see him, here stands Scarpia in all his power and brutality.

Musically, this tiny (yet sonically huge) motif also throws our expectations of standard harmonic progression out of kilter by landing not only in a key (E major) unrelated to the first chord (B-flat) but in a diminished

fifth (a semitone less than a fifth) below it, resulting in a tritone (an interval of three tones). Medieval musical theorists regarded this interval as highly disruptive and forbade its use, calling it *diabolus in musica* ("the devil in music"). Puccini, who came from a long line of distinguished church musicians, would certainly have been familiar with the nickname.

In a clear break with harmonic orthodoxies, Puccini not only uses the motif to characterize his secular devil-figure in the opera but also employs the theme throughout the opera as an emblem of Scarpia's influence on events that take place when he is not present, or even alive. The impact of this is to place harmonic instability at the center of the musical action.

Real drama

Immediately after the Scarpia theme, the curtain rises on the church of Sant'Andrea della Valle, and we see the fleeing figure of Cesare Angelotti, a political prisoner on the run. Beginning in another unrelated key (G minor), the harmonic movement here is much faster. The chord sequence,

which, at first, is loud, violent, and consistently moving off the beat. gradually diminishes into a downward slither that ends up, with a feeling of exhaustion, on another tritone. This image of disheveled flight and collapse serves as a second harbinger of what is to come in the opera.

The opera's action is based on the play *La Tosca* (1887) by the Frenchman Victorien Sardou, which was criticized at the time for its dizzying tempo of unrelenting action and reaction. Puccini's librettists despaired of making a viable libretto from it, but the composer was able to use daring harmonic instability not only to contain but also to hold together, and even magnify, the play's helter-skelter ride of swiftly changing events as part of his overall musical strategy.

Tosca's three central characters all begin the drama with their lives apparently secure, yet through an unpredictable and unstoppable sequence of cause and effect, all three are dead by the curtain, in less than 24 hours. Yet Puccini still manages to give all three of his chief characters their moments

of lyrical reflection, not simply as opportunities for aria or duet but to voice the hopes, desires, and memories that motivate them and drive the plot. The drama's final impression is of individuals hurtled along by events over which they have little control, and certainly far less than they believe they have. Its emotional and musical power helped to redefine the English tradition of choral music. ∎

Verismo

> Puccini's Verismo creates a **musical naturalism** that reflects real life.

↓

> He places the emphasis on **psychological reality**, with emotionally charged arias.

↓

> He uses atmospheric music to suggest a sense of character and **inner conflict**.

↓

> He uses **familiar sounds**, such as church bells, to mimic everyday reality.

↓

> **The ultimate effect is to make the music and drama more personal, immediate, and effective.**

Opera and the rise of the new reality

Verismo owed its philosophical basis to a literary movement begun in France by the novelists Émile Zola (1840–1902) and Honoré de Balzac (1799–1850). It was represented in Italy by the Sicilian Giovanni Verga, whose short story and play *Cavalleria rusticana* inspired Mascagni's opera of the same name. The premise of verismo lay in a scrutiny of the lives of "ordinary people"—usually urban or rural workers—in a local and everyday setting and often allied to a corresponding focus on the social evils of poverty, crime, and violence.

In opera, the new style's emotional extremities were realized in taxing vocal writing, which threw away the remnants of the display and niceties of *bel canto* ("beautiful singing") in favor of hard-hitting directness. Musical continuity was increased with the dissolution of the old divisions between recitative (speechlike singing), arias, and other set pieces.

IF A COMPOSER COULD SAY WHAT HE HAD TO SAY IN WORDS, HE WOULD NOT BOTHER SAYING IT IN MUSIC

DAS LIED VON DER ERDE (1908–1909), GUSTAV MAHLER

IN CONTEXT

FOCUS
Exotic worlds in music

BEFORE
1863 Set in Ceylon, *The Pearl Fishers*, by rising opera-composer Georges Bizet, is a success at its Paris premiere.

1882 Wagner's final opera, *Parsifal,* blending elements of Buddhist spirituality with Christian ideas and imagery, is first performed at Bayreuth's Festival Theatre.

AFTER
1926 Maurice Ravel composes *Chansons madécasses* (*Songs from Madagascar*), based on three prose-poems written in 1787 by Évariste de Parny.

1957 Benjamin Britten conducts the premiere of his ballet *The Prince of the Pagodas* in London. The score is influenced by Indonesian gamelan music, which Britten heard in Bali in 1956.

When Gustav Mahler began work on the six settings of Chinese poems that make up *Das Lied von der Erde* (*The Song of the Earth*), he was exploring what was for him new territory. But exotic oriental subject matter was already a familiar theme in European art and culture, reflecting the yearning of the popular imagination for more colorful and intriguing worlds.

This sense of longing had come into sharper focus in the 15th and 16th centuries, when long-distance sea voyages had led to the discovery

See also: *Prélude à l'après-midi d'un faune* 228–231 ▪ *Le Sacre du printemps* 246–251 ▪ *November Steps* 314–315 ▪ *L'Amour de loin* 325

Gustav Mahler

The second of 14 children of Jewish parents, Mahler was born in 1860 and spent his childhood in the Czech-speaking town of Iglau (now Jihlava). He gave his first piano recital at age 10 and five years later entered the Vienna Conservatory. His cantata *Das klagende Lied* (1880) showed amazing early self-awareness, exploring a spectral, folk-tale world in a vivid orchestral style. A stellar conducting career led to the composer's appointment in 1897 as artistic director of the Vienna Court Opera. Mahler wrote most of his music—largely song settings and symphonies—during summers among the Austrian lakes.

Departure from the Vienna Court Opera in 1907 was followed by conducting work in New York. Mahler died soon after returning to Europe from America, in 1911.

Other key works

1888–1894 Symphony No. 2 ("Resurrection")
1892–1901 *Des Knaben Wunderhorn* (*The Boy's Magic Horn*)
1908–1909 Symphony No. 9

of unknown regions. The decisive impetus for the cult of exoticism came in the 19th century, as European powers busily pursued global empire-building rivalries. At home, industrialization created rapid growth in towns and cities, with populations living and working in oppressive conditions that generated an inner need for psychological escape.

Selling the exotic

The world of literature latched onto the sales possibilities of exotic subject matter, as in the South Seas tales of Robert Louis Stevenson (1850–1894) or the romanticized Native American world depicted in *The Song of Hiawatha* by Henry Wadsworth Longfellow (1807–1882). Exoticism also flourished among painters. French artist Paul Gauguin (1848–1903) moved to the French Polynesian island of Tahiti in 1891, to explore new avenues of artistic expression, aware that the European vogue for the exotic would ensure sales of his work in Paris.

European classical music, too, was drawn to the imagined sounds of enticing worlds to the south and

Mahler wrote *Das Lied von der Erde* while staying at the Hotel Bellevue in the Italian town of Cortina. The peaks of the Dolomites provided a dramatic backdrop for his compositions.

east. Operas were set in alluringly foreign settings, such as Giuseppe Verdi's *Aida* (1871), a fictional story of ancient Egypt. In orchestral music, Russia's Nikolai Rimsky-Korsakov based his symphonic suite *Scheherazade* (1888) on stories from a collection of Middle Eastern folk tales that became known as *The Arabian Nights*. The French composer Claude Debussy found the piano especially suitable for suggesting images of remote worlds, using Javanese melodies in *Pagodes* (*Pagodas*), from his *Estampes* (*Engravings*) of 1903.

Life through new eyes

Before he composed *Das Lied von der Erde*, Mahler did not seem to be influenced by the growing European love of exoticism. His choice of texts for his songs and symphonies had come mostly from one particular area of Austro-German culture: the folk poetry, usually anonymous, »

Romantic themes and images in *Das Lied von der Erde*

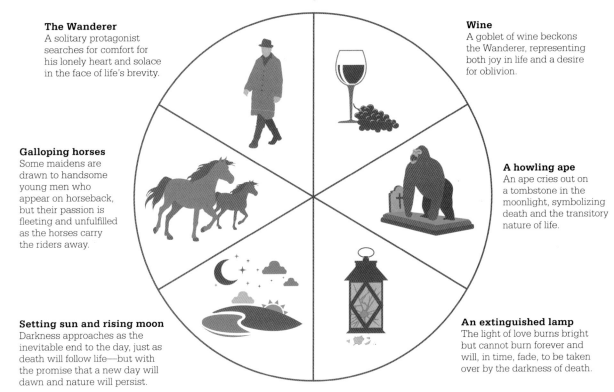

The Wanderer
A solitary protagonist searches for comfort for his lonely heart and solace in the face of life's brevity.

Wine
A goblet of wine beckons the Wanderer, representing both joy in life and a desire for oblivion.

Galloping horses
Some maidens are drawn to handsome young men who appear on horseback, but their passion is fleeting and unfulfilled as the horses carry the riders away.

A howling ape
An ape cries out on a tombstone in the moonlight, symbolizing death and the transitory nature of life.

Setting sun and rising moon
Darkness approaches as the inevitable end to the day, just as death will follow life—but with the promise that a new day will dawn and nature will persist.

An extinguished lamp
The light of love burns bright but cannot burn forever and will, in time, fade, to be taken over by the darkness of death.

assembled by Achim von Arnem and Clemens Brentano in their collection *Des Knaben Wunderhorn* (*The Boy's Magic Horn*), published in 1805 and 1808. For *Lieder eines fahrenden Gesellen* (*Songs of a Wayfarer*, 1885–1886), Mahler had written his own texts in a similar folk style, with a wide range of emotional moods projected against the surrounding, vividly perceived world of nature.

East meets West

Mahler did not, however, ignore eastern culture. The song cycle *Kindertotenlieder* (*Songs on the Death of Children*) composed in 1901–1904 was based on poems by Friedrich Rückert (1788–1866), a German professor of eastern languages. Rückert's writings were influenced by the eastern concept

of serene acceptance of life and death, rather than the keenness for turbulent self-dramatization of both displayed in western Romanticism.

When Mahler read a copy of *Die chinesische Flöte* (*The Chinese Flute*)—a collection of Chinese poems adapted by German poet Hans Bethge—in autumn 1907, the composer was already familiar with the artistic world within its pages. Mahler's life was also in a turbulent state, coloring his view of life and death. The devastating death of his four-year-old daughter in the summer of 1907 was followed by the onset of a heart condition that required Mahler to slow down. In a letter to the conductor Bruno Walter, his former assistant at the Vienna Court Opera, Mahler wrote: "I have always known that I must die … but all at once I have lost the

serenity and clarity which I had acquired. I have to start a new life as a complete beginner."

Bethge's adaptation of the original Chinese texts was not particularly faithful. He knew no Chinese and used a German translation of a French translation of the original. In effect, Bethge's poems were beautifully written paraphrases, evoking an emotional world that was by turns anguished, poignant, idyllic, resigned, drunken, or quietly radiant, all reflected in exquisitely drawn scenes from nature. This approach connected more to the world of German lyric poetry that was familiar to Mahler than to the 9th-century Chinese originals, with their ultra-concentrated diction. Still, Mahler alluded to exotic influences by using the oriental

Is it at all bearable? Will it drive people to do away with themselves?
Gustav Mahler

five-note "pentatonic" scale (distinct from the Western seven-note scale), providing an element of local color that his European audiences would easily recognize.

Large ambitions

In *Das Lied von der Erde*, Mahler managed to combine his two principal musical concerns—song and the symphony—in a single large-scale work for the first time. In his Second, Third, and Fourth Symphonies, there had been a substantial overlapping of the two genres; in *Das Lied von der Erde* their fusion is so complete that neither can be separated out. A tenor and mezzosoprano alternate in the six song settings, and Mahler deploys a large orchestra with exceptional sensibility to mood and color, often with the finesse of a chamber group of solo instruments. The opening "Das Trinklied vom Jammer der Erde" ("Drinking-Song of the Earth's Sorrow"), music of wild and despairing fatalism, is followed by the desolate depiction of a mist-covered lake in "Der

Mahler's diverse influences are satirized in this caricature of him conducting his Symphony No. 1 in D major, from a November 1900 edition of *Illustriertes Wiener Extrablatt*.

Einsame im Herbst" ("The Lonely One in Autumn"). Then comes a group of three shorter settings, prominently colored by the pentatonic scale, recalling the innocent happiness of youth and the joys of springtime. The final setting, "Der Abschied" ("The Farewell"), is longer than the other five songs combined. Two different poems are here separated by an orchestral interlude and lead eventually to a conclusion with words added by Mahler himself: "Everywhere the dear earth blossoms forth in spring and grows green again! Everywhere and forever, distant horizons gleam blue: forever … forever …"

The music seems not so much to end as to dissolve into this vision, in which awareness of human mortality is transcended by the perception that life and the natural world will timelessly be renewed. The work as a whole relates more

Mahler's struggles are those of a psychic weakling, a complaining adolescent who enjoyed his misery, wanting the whole world to see how he was suffering.
Harold Schonberg
American critic

to Mahler's deepest creative and personal concerns than to a fashion for "exoticism for exoticism's sake," but, without that fashion and the inspiration Mahler found in Eastern culture, *Das Lied von der Erde* could not have existed. ∎

NATION
1830–1920

Bedřich Smetana
establishes Czech opera
with *The Bartered Bride*,
incorporating Czech
themes and written in
the Czech language.

Russian composer
Modest Mussorgsky
writes *Pictures at an
Exhibition*, inspired by the
death of the Russian artist
Viktor Hartmann.

Gabriel Fauré's
Requiem introduces
a new, more subtle
style to the form,
inspiring other
French composers.

Antonín Dvořák's
Symphony No. 9,
inspired by Native
American music and
African American
songs, premieres.

1863

1874

1887–1890

1893

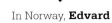

1869

1875

1890

Mily Balakirev
establishes the "Five,"
a group of Russian
composers who sought
to create music with a
Russian identity.

In Norway, **Edvard
Grieg** completes the
music for Henrik Ibsen's
Peer Gynt. Based on a
folk tale, the work
becomes a national epic.

One of Russia's "Five,"
Aleksandr Borodin
adapts the 12th-century
epic prose poem *The Lay
of Igor's Host* to develop
his opera *Prince Igor*.

As the 19th century
progressed, a growing
mood of nationalism
developed, and people sought
individual identities as nations
distinct from the old empires. The
dominant culture in Europe was
Germanic, and this was especially
true of the music being written for
the concert halls and opera houses.

A tradition of folk music thrived
almost everywhere, as regional and
local cultures of the many different
people asserted themselves. It was
this that provided the inspiration
for composers wishing to establish
a musical identity that matched the
nationalistic ideals of their people.
Opera was an obvious starting
point, as it could be based on
national history and legends, but
the same ideas were also expressed
in programmatic orchestral works.

Nationalism in music did not
confine itself to subject matter.
Composers incorporated folk songs
and dances into their music or
composed their own melodies
using elements of a particular
tradition of folk music, such as
its scales and rhythms.

Russia leads

The first signs of nationalism
in music came from Russia,
which had started to assert its
independence from European
culture at the beginning of the
Romantic period. Mikhail Glinka's
operas were based on Russian
stories, with Russian folk tunes
presented in the Romantic style,
inspiring more than a century of
distinctively Russian music. Quick
to take up the baton, Mily Balakirev
gathered together a group of

Russian composers who became
known as the "Five" or "Mighty
Handful" (Aleksandr Borodin,
César Cui, Modest Mussorgsky,
and Nikolai Rimsky-Korsakov),
whose work later influenced Pyotr
Ilyich Tchaikovsky, Alexander
Glazunov, and, in the 20th century,
Sergei Rachmaninoff.

The wave of nationalism gained
momentum in the mid-19th century,
especially as the Austro-Hungarian
Empire crumbled. Countries were
proud of their own folk culture, and
especially their music. Chopin
tinged much of his piano music
with inflections of folk melodies
from his native Poland, and wrote
several *polonaises*, while Liszt
incorporated Hungarian dance
styles into his work. More overtly
nationalistic was Bedřich Smetana,
who became a champion of Czech

The seven-scene opera *Sadko* by **Nikolai Rimsky-Korsakov** evokes a Russian epic poem about a merchant from Novgorod.

Jean Sibelius's *Finlandia* is composed as a form of protest against the actions of the Russian Empire in Finland.

Isaac Albéniz's *Iberia suite* conjures up the landscapes of Southern Spain and the Jewish quarter of Madrid.

1898

1900

1908

1896

1900

1919

American composer **Edward MacDowell**, a member of the Second New England School, publishes *Ten Woodland Sketches*.

In England, **Edward Elgar's** *The Dream of Gerontius* applies the dramatic devices of late Romantic opera to a choral work with great success.

Spanish composer **Manuel de Falla's** ballet *El sombrero de tres picos* premieres in London, with sets by Pablo Picasso.

nationalism with operas in his native language on Czech themes. Later Czech composers included Antonín Dvořák and Leoš Janáček.

Nationalism in music spread north into Scandinavia, too, with folk-inspired music from Edvard Grieg, Carl Nielsen, and Jean Sibelius, and south to Spain, where composers such as Isaac Albeniz and Manuel de Falla tapped into a particularly rich source of folk music.

American sounds

As Antonín Dvořák discovered when he visited the US at the end of the century, America had also developed its own musical voice, a mix of styles and traditions that reflected the diversity of its people. It was also a young culture, finding its way after centuries of following Europe's lead. Although Native

Americans had a long-established folk culture, the more recent settlers had yet to develop one. As a result, composers such as Louis Moreau Gottschalk borrowed from the songs and dances of slaves in the Southern States and the melting pot of sounds in places like New Orleans. These forms eventually evolved into ragtime and jazz.

The spirituals of the African slaves influenced popular song writers, such as Stephen Foster. Along with the hymn tunes sung by the early settlers, they formed the basis for an American classical tradition pioneered by Edward MacDowell and Charles Ives.

In Europe

Some countries did not feel the same need to flex their nationalist muscles. Italy and Germany were

in the process of unification, but their cultures—especially their musical cultures—needed little reinforcement. The same was true to a lesser extent of France, but composers such as Gabriel Fauré and Camille Saint-Saëns sought to distance themselves from the Germanic Romantic-style and wrote music that was lighter and more transparent.

In Britain, where composers generally accepted German domination of music, Edward Elgar embraced the richness of the orchestral sound and harmonies of German music but pursued a nationalistic intent, with evocations of the English landscape and themes. Later English composers, such as Ralph Vaughan Williams, came to use this style as a vehicle to carry folk tunes. ∎

MY FATHERLAND MEANS MORE TO ME THAN ANYTHING ELSE

THE BARTERED BRIDE (1866),
BEDŘICH SMETANA

IN CONTEXT

FOCUS
19th-century Czech opera

BEFORE
1826 František Škroup's
Drátenik (*The Tinker*), widely
regarded as the first Czech
opera, has its premiere.

1842–1845 Czech poet
and historian Karel Erben
publishes a pioneering
collection of Bohemian
folk songs.

1865 Karel Sebor's opera
Templari na Morave
(*The Templars in Moravia*) is
performed to local acclaim at
Prague's Provisional Theatre.

AFTER
1901 *Rusalka*, Antonín
Dvořák's most successful
opera, is premiered at Prague's
National Theatre.

1904 Leoš Janáček's opera
Jenůfa is performed for the first
time in the Czech city of Brno.

The second and best-loved of Czech composer Bedřich Smetana's operas, *The Bartered Bride* (*Prodaná nevesta*), is about two young lovers—Marenka and Jeniken—in a Bohemian village. They want to marry, but Marenka's parents, swayed by the village marriage broker, intend her to wed Vasek, the simple-minded son of a wealthy landlord. Jenik and Marenka are united in the end, and Jenik is revealed as the long-lost son of Vasek's rich father. The opera is a melding of French and Italian influences with inspiration from Czech folk settings and traditions, particularly dances such as the polka and the furiant.

A new Czech identity
During the 1860s and 1870s, Smetana almost single-handedly created Czech opera by writing operas in the Czech language. Czech culture had long been influenced by the Habsburg Empire. By the mid-19th century, however, nationalist aspirations were strong, and these grew in 1860 when the imperial authorities handed greater powers to the Czech parliament in Prague. Funds were raised to build a theatre for Czech drama and opera, and it was here that Smetana's first two operas were premiered. He completed six more operas, along with a cycle of symphonic poems called *Má vlast* (*My Fatherland*), celebrating Czech landscapes and culture. ∎

The Bartered Bride is only a toy and composing it was merely child's play! … At the time of writing, it was my opinion that not even Offenbach could compete with it!
Bedřich Smetana

See also: *The Magic Flute* 134–137 ▪ *The Barber of Seville* 148 ▪ *Der Freischütz* 149 ▪ *La traviata* 174–175 ▪ *The Ring Cycle* 180–187

MUSSORGSKY TYPIFIES THE GENIUS OF RUSSIA
PICTURES AT AN EXHIBITION (1874), MODEST PETROVICH MUSSORGSKY

IN CONTEXT

FOCUS
Nationalism in 19th-century Russian music

BEFORE
1815 In St. Petersburg, Venetian-born Catterino Cavos composes *Ivan Susanin*, the first opera about Russian characters, based on Russian history, and incorporating Russian folk music.

1836 Mikhail Glinka's *A Life for the Tsar* has its premiere in St. Petersburg. It is the first all-sung opera by a native Russian composer.

AFTER
1896 Nikolay Rimsky-Korsakov undertakes the first of his revisions of Mussorgsky's opera *Boris Godunov*. For decades, these remain the most-performed versions.

1922 French composer Maurice Ravel produces an orchestrated version of *Pictures at an Exhibition*.

The Russian composer Modest Mussorgsky's *Pictures at an Exhibition* is a piano suite in 10 movements. Each movement was inspired by the work of fellow Russian Viktor Hartmann, an architect and artist.

Mussorgsky belonged to a generation of composers who, in the 1860s, gave Russian music its first distinctive voice. He was part of a group nicknamed the "Five," also known as the "Mighty Handful," who sought to create music without being confined by western European conventions. Besides Mussorgsky, the "Five" were Mily Balakirev (1837–1910), the group's initial guiding spirit; Aleksandr Borodin (1833–1887), a scientist as well as a musician; César Cui, best known as a critic; and Nikolay Rimsky-Korsakov, who played a key role in mentoring a new generation of composers, including Aleksandr Scriabin and Sergei Rachmaninoff.

Pictures at an Exhibition was composed shortly after the premiere of Mussorgsky's opera *Boris Godunov* in January 1874, which marked the public high point of his career. The piano suite was not performed in the composer's lifetime, but its intensity and complexity, and distinctly Russian subject matter, helped to achieve the ultimate ambition of the "Five" to give Russian music its own unmistakable voice. ■

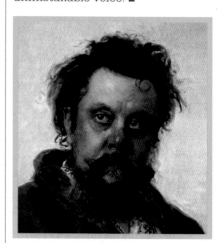

The early, alcohol-induced death of Mussorgsky, painted here by Ilya Repi in 1881, the year that he died, left Rimsky-Korsakov and other composers to finish or revise his work.

See also: Dvořák's Symphony No. 9 212–215 ▪ *Le Sacre du printemps* 246–251 ▪ *Romeo and Juliet* 272 ▪ Shostakovich's Fifth Symphony 274–279

208

I AM SURE MY MUSIC HAS A TASTE OF COD FISH IN IT
PEER GYNT (1875), EDVARD GRIEG

IN CONTEXT

FOCUS
Music for the theatre

BEFORE
1810 Beethoven writes the incidental music to Goethe's tragic play *Egmont*.

1843 Shakespeare's *A Midsummer Night's Dream* opens in Potsdam with Mendelssohn's music.

1872 Grieg composes music for Bjørnstjerne Bjørnson's *Sigurd Jorsalfar*, celebrating King Sigurd I of Norway.

AFTER
1908 *La Mort du duc de Guise,* a film with a score by Camille Saint-Saëns, opens in Paris.

1915 Edward Elgar writes the incidental music for *The Starlight Express,* a children's play by Violet Pearn.

I ncidental music has probably existed as long as theatre itself. It was intrinsic to Shakespeare's plays, which include cues for instrumental music as well as songs—some 100 in total—although no scores have survived.

By the late 1700s, Europe's major theatres would employ a substantial orchestra, and sometimes vocal soloists and a chorus, to accompany plays. Examples of incidental music of the 18th and early 19th century include Mozart's *Thamos, King of Egypt* (c.1773–1779), Beethoven's *Egmont* (1810), and Schubert's *Rosamunde* (1823), which were of sufficient quality to make it into the concert hall.

The music that Felix Mendelssohn composed for a German-language production of Shakespeare's *A Midsummer Night's Dream* was one of the most successful pieces to make such a transition. It was first staged in Potsdam, Germany, in 1843, including a masterful overture written when the composer was just 17. While under the patronage of Frederick IV, king of Prussia, Mendelssohn would go on to compose incidental music for

"The Dance of the Trolls" was illustrated in macabre style by the British artist Arthur Rackham for an edition of Ibsen's *Peer Gynt*.

productions of *Oedipus at Colonus* and Racine's *Athalie* in 1845. In 1849, Robert Schumann wrote music to accompany Byron's dramatic poem *Manfred*.

Norwegian collaboration
When Henrik Ibsen, Norway's most celebrated writer, completed *Peer Gynt*, based on a Norwegian folk hero, in 1867, he thought of it as a

See also: *The Bartered Bride* 206 ▪ *Pictures at an Exhibition* 207 ▪ Dvořák's Symphony No. 9 212–215 ▪ *Finlandia* 220–221 ▪ *Appalachian Spring* 286–287

> I have also written something for the scene in the hall of the mountain King ... it absolutely reeks of cow pies, exaggerated Norwegian provincialism, and trollish self-sufficiency.
> **Edvard Grieg**

poetic drama, to be read rather than staged. Seven years later when Ibsen adapted his work for a full-scale stage production, he invited another internationally renowned Norwegian artist— Edvard Grieg—to compose music for the first production. Grieg had already produced successful incidental music for Bjørnstjerne Bjørnson's play *Sigurd Jorsalfar*. The collaboration between Ibsen and Grieg would elevate *Peer Gynt* to the status of national epic.

Emotive music

Grieg eventually produced more than 20 individual pieces for the numerous cues in Ibsen's five-act drama, reflecting the emotional mood of each moment—from the uproar of the Hall of the Mountain King to the grief-filled death of Åse, Peer Gynt's mother. Grieg later assembled eight of the most substantial of these into two orchestral suites, which have become standard concert-hall works. They include movements

that reference the major characters and scenes in the drama: Åse; Anitra, a Bedouin chief's daughter whom Peer tries to seduce; Ingrid, the farmer's daughter he abducts on the eve of her wedding; the troll kingdom into which he stumbles; and Solveig, the faithful woman who waits patiently for his return.

Genre in decline

Later examples of incidental music that survive outside their original theatrical contexts include Fauré's and Sibelius's music for *Pelléas et Mélisande*, Debussy's *Le martyre de Saint Sébastien*, Elgar's *The Starlight Express*, and Sibelius's *The Tempest*. Incidental music is still commissioned for some theatrical productions but is generally performed with fewer musicians or even prerecorded. Modern examples include Michael Tippett's music for *The Tempest* and Harrison Birtwistle's *Oresteia*. Some characteristics of the genre have migrated to film, television, and even video games. ▪

> The more he saturated his mind with [*Peer Gynt*], the more clearly he saw that he was the right man for a work ... so permeated with the Norwegian spirit.
> **Nina Hagerup**
> *Grieg's wife*

Edvard Grieg

Grieg was taught to play the piano by his mother, a music teacher in the Norwegian town of Bergen, where he was born in 1843. As a teenager, Grieg met the internationally acclaimed violinist Ole Bull, who urged his parents to send him to study at the Leipzig Conservatoire. There, he was influenced by Schumann and Mendelssohn; it was only later, in Copenhagen, that Grieg became interested in the Norwegian folk tunes that inspired his music.

In 1867, Grieg married his cousin Nina Hagerup, for whom he composed many songs. The following year, he wrote his one piano concerto, which, like *Peer Gynt,* brought lasting fame. In later life, he devoted himself to smaller piano works, especially the 10 volumes of *Lyric Pieces,* some of which draw on folk idioms. Grieg died in Bergen in 1907.

Other key works

1868 Piano Concerto in A minor, Op. 16
1872 *Sigurd Jorsalfar*
1884 *Holberg Suite*
1902–1903 *Slåtter* (Norwegian Peasant Dances)

I WANTED TO DO SOMETHING DIFFERENT

REQUIEM (1887–1890), GABRIEL FAURÉ

IN CONTEXT

FOCUS
Requiem Mass

BEFORE
1837 Hector Berlioz composes his *Grande Messe des morts* (Requiem), for a large choir, enormous orchestra, and four offstage brass ensembles.

1874 Verdi's operatic Requiem, for four vocal soloists, double choir, and orchestra, has its first performance.

AFTER
1913 Fauré's opera *Pénélope* is premiered. While the influence of Wagner is more apparent than in earlier works, it still has an understated quality.

1948 Maurice Duruflé completes his Requiem, which, like Fauré's, includes the Pie Jesu, Libera me, and In paradisum sections.

It is unlikely that Fauré wrote his Requiem in direct response to the death of any individual, although the recent deaths of his parents may have focused his mind on the project. The composer stated that his main motivation was to produce an original requiem. He was familiar with the form having spent years as a choirmaster and organist, during which he had accompanied numerous funerals.

The differences began with the text. Fauré set a shortened version of the Latin Mass for the Dead, omitting, among other passages,

Fauré plays the piano at the home of the Catalan composer Isaac Albéniz (right). With them is the Belgian composer and conductor Léon Jehin and Albéniz's pupil Clara Sansoni.

the Sequence section, with its passage on the Dies Irae (Wrath of God), which so many previous composers had used as an opportunity to produce loud and dramatic music. This was replaced in Fauré's first version of the score by a setting of Pie Jesu, a prayer to Jesus for everlasting rest, at the end of which he also added an

See also: *Canticum Canticorum* 46–51 ▪ *Ein feste Burg ist unser Gott* 78–79 ▪ *St. Matthew Passion* 98–105 ▪ *Elijah* 170–173 ▪ *The Dream of Gerontius* 218–219

Fauré's setting for the Requiem Mass

The opening prayer, the **Introit et Kyrie**, is restful with sudden changes of dynamics.

The offering of the Eucharist, the **Offertory**, is reverent, calm, and peaceful.

Angelic strings and harp are broken by rich brasses in the **Sanctus**.

A prayer to Jesus, the **Pie Jesu**, is sung by a pure solo soprano voice.

A quiet melody sung by tenors switches to the intense **Agnus Dei**.

Libera Me is a pensive then fierce section dealing with judgment.

In the In paradisum, soprano voices bring a tranquil conclusion.

extra movement, In Paradisum, that comes not from the Mass but from the burial service.

The unusual selection of texts is matched with a distinctive choice of instruments to accompany the mixed choir and soloists—no violin section, but only violas, cellos, and double basses, a harp, trumpets, horns, trombones, organ, and timpani. In addition, a solo violin soars above the harp and lower strings in the Sanctus. Fauré clearly intended the work to be played by this unusual ensemble, but upon receiving the score in 1890, his publishers requested a version for full orchestra. An arrangement with added violins and woodwind instruments was published in 1900; many musicians, however, favor the earlier version.

Serenity and calm

The music of Fauré's Requiem is skilfully restrained, matching the themes of consolation and eternal rest in the text. It has relatively few loud passages, in contrast to requiems by composers such as Berlioz or Verdi. Fauré was seeking a style that differed both from the more dramatic, Romantic approach of composers such as Wagner in Germany, and the lyrical *bel canto* style of choral writing, then popular in France, with its emphasis on a singer's virtuosity. His is more carefully balanced, with subtle changes in harmony and dynamics.

Although the work was not immediately well received, Fauré opened new avenues for French music, paving the way for later French composers, such as Ravel and Debussy. Fauré's is now one of the most popular settings of the Requiem in the choral repertoire. ∎

Gabriel Fauré

Born in 1845 in Pamiers in southwest France, Gabriel Fauré showed an early musical talent and was sent to the École Niedermeyer de Paris. The school's focus was on church music, and when he left, Fauré worked in a succession of jobs as church organist in Brittany and then in Paris, in both places giving private music lessons to supplement his income.

In later life, Fauré became Professor of Composition at the Paris Conservatoire and finally its Director. Although his busy professional life left him little time for composing, Fauré produced many short piano pieces, notable chamber music, including two piano quartets and two piano quintets, two orchestral suites, many fine songs, and a string quartet completed in 1924, the year he died. By this time highly acclaimed, Fauré was given a state funeral.

Other key works

1879–1883 Piano Quartet No. 1 in C minor, Op. 15
1894 "La bonne chanson", Op. 61
1919 *Masques et bergamasques*, Op. 112

THE MUSIC OF THE PEOPLE IS LIKE A RARE AND LOVELY FLOWER

SYMPHONY NO. 9, "FROM THE NEW WORLD" (1893), ANTONÍN DVOŘÁK

IN CONTEXT

FOCUS
Nationalism and folk music

BEFORE
1723 Czech composer Dismas Zelenka writes his *Ouverture à 7 concertanti*.

1776 Czech-born Johann Baptist Vanhal publishes Six Symphonies, Op. 23, works that influenced Classical style.

1862 Bedřich Smetana composes the opera *The Brandenburgers in Bohemia*, which is a great success.

AFTER
1904 Leoš Janáček premieres his opera *Jenůfa*, which uses "speech tunes" based on a Moravian dialect of Czech.

1905–08 Béla Bartók and Zoltán Kodály visit Hungarian villages to research and record traditional songs and dances.

Bohemia, the largest and westernmost region of the Czech Republic today, was formerly part of the Austro-Hungarian Empire. For centuries, its capital Prague enjoyed a rich musical life, strongly influenced by German and Austrian composers. In the late 18th century, Mozart visited five times, wrote a "Prague" symphony (No. 38), and premiered his opera *Don Giovanni* in the city.

By the mid-1800s, however, fueled by a failed revolution in 1848, a nationalist movement was underway that would have a powerful impact on all the arts. In music, both Bedřich Smetana and Antonín Dvořák began to use

See also: *The Bartered Bride* 206 ▪ *Finlandia* 220–221 ▪ *The Lark Ascending* 252–253 ▪ Janáček's *Sinfonietta* 263 ▪ Bartók's *String Quartet No. 5* 270–271

The Bohemian polka, illustrated here by Herrman Koenig, is attributed to Anna Slezáková, who danced the steps to a folk song in 1834. Dvořák's earliest surviving composition was a polka.

classical European symphonic and chamber forms to produce works of a strongly patriotic nature that incorporated the spirit of regional folk songs and dances.

Two composers

Dvořák was an accomplished keyboard player and violinist, who had played in several Prague orchestras when he joined the one at the city's Provincial Theatre in 1866, conducted by Smetana. The older Smetana was already cultivating a reputation as a champion of a Czech style of music after spending most of his early creative years in Sweden.

Smetana's first language was German, and he had only recently begun to study Czech when he responded to a contest to compose a Czech opera. He submitted *The Brandenburgers in Bohemia*, which premiered in 1866, and went on to produce many celebrated works in Czech, such as *The Bartered Bride*, a set of symphonic poems called *Má vlast* (*My homeland*), and *Vlatava*, which paints the course of the river running through Prague.

Inspired by Smetana's Czech operas, Dvořák composed *Alfred* in 1870, but it was not performed in his lifetime. His next, *The King and the Charcoal Burner*, was at first rejected as unplayable, though eventually accepted after extensive rewrites. Dvořák gave up his »

Antonín Dvořák

The son of an innkeeper, Dvořák was born in a village north of Prague in 1841. He shared his father's passion for the violin, and from 1857 he also studied the organ in Prague, playing the instrument in several orchestras.

By the early 1870s, Dvořák had taken up composition full time and was married to Anna, with whom he would have nine children. Dvořák's career was aided by Johannes Brahms, who sat on a panel that awarded Dvořák a grant to pursue his music. He also recommended Dvořák to his publisher, who encouraged him to write a set of Slavonic dances. Their publication changed his fortunes; new commissions at home and from England soon followed. Dvořák directed the National Conservatory of Music in New York from 1892–1895, before returning to Prague to teach and write new works based on Bohemian folk tales. He died from a stroke in 1904.

Other key works

1878 Slavonic Dances, Book 1, Op. 46
1885 Symphony No. 7, Op. 70
1900 *Rusalka*, Op. 144

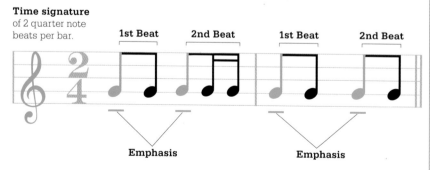

Time signature
of 2 quarter note beats per bar.

1st Beat   2nd Beat   1st Beat   2nd Beat

Emphasis   Emphasis

Originally a Bohemian peasant dance, the polka has two strong beats in each bar, inviting dancers to step in lively, bouncing fashion. It became a popular ballroom dance in the 1830s.

place in the theatre orchestra to concentrate on composition, and the critical success of his stirring hymn of Czech national pride *The Heirs of the White Mountain* (1873) marked the beginning of his recognition as a composer.

By 1880, Dvořák had cemented his reputation as the greatest of the Czech nationalist composers, particularly through his *Slavonic Dances* (1878; 1886), inspired by Brahms's *Hungarian Dances* (1869). However, Dvořák's approach to his orchestral dances was quite different from that used by Brahms. Whereas the Viennese composer made verbatim use of traditional tunes for his collection, Dvořák's lively dances did not borrow but were newly composed orchestral works imbued with national

Harry Burleigh was the first black composer to write down spirituals, influencing future American music. Dvořák greatly admired his fine baritone voice and the songs he sang.

character. His *Czech Suite* (1879), for example, has two movements completely modeled on Bohemian folk dances: the polka, in the second movement, and the slow "sousedská" in the fourth. Dvořák's seventh and eighth symphonies were also particularly Bohemian—the seventh has clear Slavonic influences, while the eighth sounds like a joyful folk celebration.

The New World

By the end of the century, Dvořák's fame was spreading beyond his homeland to England and the United States. In 1891, New York musical philanthropist Jeannette Thurber asked Dvořák to direct her National Conservatory of Music. Knowing that he had done much to establish Czech music, she wanted him to inspire her students to find a path toward an American national musical style. Dvořák, however, was reluctant to leave Prague for a long contract and initially turned down the offer, although he gave in

to pressure to accept, after his family heard that the salary he would earn per annum was equivalent to working 25 years at the Prague Conservatory.

Among the talented students that Thurber encouraged to apply to her conservatory, regardless of gender, ethnicity, or disability, was an African American singer, Henry (Harry) Thacker Burleigh, who enrolled in 1892, contributing to his fees by working as a handyman and cleaner in the building. His singing attracted the attention of Dvořák, and Burleigh later recalled singing old African American hymns to the composer: "I gave him what I knew of Negro songs."

Listening and responding

These "Negro spirituals," as they came to be known, were among the musical ideas that Dvořák drew on in his Symphony No. 9 ("From the New World"), in which he turned his attention from his native folk music to that of his adopted home. "From the New World" was inspired by both plantation songs and Native American chants; Dvořák felt strongly that this music of the poor of America could serve as the rootstock for a national musical

In the negro melodies of America I discover all that is needed for a great and noble school of music.
Antonín Dvořák

Structure of the Ninth Symphony

The **first movement**, *Adagio* (leisurely), is written in sonata form. This section builds to a **rousing climax**.

The **second movement**, *Largo* (slow, dignified), contains a **solo** that has become one of the most recognizable pieces of music ever composed.

The **third movement** is *Scherzo* (very lively). Its **bright tunes** and snappy rhythms are reminiscent of Czech folk dancing.

The **fourth movement**, *Allegro con fuoco* (fast and fiery), combines earlier themes of the piece with **marchlike** music.

For his voyage to a new world, the Apollo 11 mission to the moon in 1969, Neil Armstrong took a recording of Dvořák's Sympony No. 9 and is said to have listened to it as he stepped out.

style. While some people hear "Swing Low, Sweet Chariot" in the symphony's first movement, at its premiere, Dvořák denied using existing Native and African American songs. Dvořák believed there was a distinction between inspiration and imitation—whether singing under his breath in the orchestra pit or going straight from work to jot down ideas, his method was not to copy but rather to listen then respond in his own voice.

As well as these musical styles, Dvořák was inspired by Henry Wadsworth Longfellow's Ojibwe romance *The Song of Hiawatha* (1855) in writing his symphony. The third movement (Scherzo), for example, was suggested by the scene in *Hiawatha* at the feast where the Native Americans dance. For the second movement (Largo),

evoking Longfellow's description of the death of Minnehaha, Dvořák uses the stentorian chords of the low wind instruments to introduce the beautiful melody of the cor anglais. Here, he also drew on the old Eastern European tradition of funerary brass music, maintained in America by the trombone choirs of Moravian (Czech expatriate) communities, who would announce a death with the playing of trombones from the church belfry.

Lasting influence

In spring 1893, Dvořák's family joined him in the Moravian community of Spillville, Iowa, enjoying the company of their Czech compatriots as he completed his Symphony No. 9—the echoes of which would be heard in the music of American composers, such as Aaron Copland, George Gershwin, and Duke Ellington. Dvořák himself returned to Prague in 1895 and again took to composing works inspired by the dances, legends, and folklore of his homeland. ∎

MUSIC IS A LANGUAGE OF THE INTANGIBLE
WOODLAND SKETCHES (1896), EDWARD MACDOWELL

IN CONTEXT

FOCUS
American nationalism

BEFORE
1640 The *Bay Psalm Book* is published in Massachusetts.

1834 Anthony Heinrich composes *The Treaty of William Penn with the Indians*, a concerto grosso.

1848 Stephen Foster publishes the song "Oh! Susanna," which becomes an instant hit.

1863 Louis Moreau Gottschalk publishes *Battle Cry of Freedom*, based on an American Civil War song.

AFTER
1897 John Philip Sousa's march *The Stars and Stripes Forever* premieres.

A house of dreams untold, it looks out over the whispering treetops, and faces the setting sun.
Edward MacDowell

The first music published in North America were tunes in the *Bay Psalm Book*, a compilation selected from European psalters by the 17th-century emigrants who settled in the Massachusetts Bay Colony. By the late 18th century, however, American-born composers such as William Billings and Daniel Read, who formed part of the First New England School, began to publish music that marked a distinct departure from European models. These composers, who were usually self-taught, were writing new types of sacred music, such as the "fuguing tune," in which a choral melody is sung in unison and then in counterpoint but with scant regard for traditional Western standards of harmony.

America's first

The Bohemian-born Anthony Heinrich, who lived in the United States from 1810, is generally considered the first "professional" American composer. Inspired by different parts of the United States, he developed a more dissonant harmonic language than had been heard elsewhere and was the first American to write for a symphony orchestra. More famous, however, was the virtuoso pianist, Louis Moreau Gottschalk, who studied in Paris and was feted by Chopin and Liszt. Returning to America in 1853, he toured widely, performing his own works that would often reference the indigenous music and instruments of the New World.

As American tastes evolved, a new group of composers emerged—now known as the Second New England School. The strongest influence for these composers was the German Romantic tradition, and a number of them studied in Europe. The best remembered of this group is Edward MacDowell.

He was mentored by Liszt, who introduced the young composer to publishers in Leipzig during his time in Germany.

Country life

MacDowell published orchestral works, concertos, sonatas, and songs but is universally identified with miniature piano pieces, and most particularly the *Woodland Sketches* of 1896. Following on from a tradition started by Mendelssohn and Schumann—writing suites of short works aimed at the amateur domestic market—these could also be seen as a counterpart to Grieg's contemporaneous Lyric Pieces, due to their inherent nationalism and celebration of the countryside.

Woodland Sketches is an opus of ten pieces. Possibly inspired by MacDowell's move to the farm that later became the artist's colony bearing his name, they celebrate not only the landscape but also the everyday American experience. In parts such as "A Deserted Farm" and "At an Old Trysting Place," they also borrowed some melodic material from Native American songs. Tending toward starker textures than European Romantic piano music, and occasionally verging on impressionistic harmony, as in the more complex "By a Meadow Brook," these sketches contain elements that became a part of the American musical language of the 1920s and 1930s. ■

The MacDowell Colony in New Hampshire, pictured here in 1948, has supported thousands of artists since 1907. MacDowell's pianist wife, Marian, led the colony for almost 25 years.

Edward MacDowell

Born in New York in 1860, MacDowell studied the piano from early childhood and, at the age of 17, was offered a scholarship to the Paris Conservatoire. After his time in Paris, he went to Frankfurt to study composition with Joachim Raff. Raff introduced him to Franz Liszt, who arranged a performance of MacDowell's *First Modern Suite*, Op. 10 in Zurich.

In 1888, MacDowell returned to New York and premiered his Piano Concerto No. 2. He was then invited to create a department of music at Columbia University. Eight years later, he resigned in a dispute over courses. Amid the bad publicity, MacDowell suffered a nervous breakdown and further health problems. He never recovered. Just before his death in 1908, he and his wife established the MacDowell Colony, where artists of all kinds are supported in residence.

Other key works

1883 *First Modern Suite*, Op. 10
1890 Piano Concerto No. 2, Op. 23
1892 *Indian Suite*, Op. 48

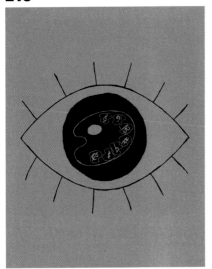

THE ART OF MUSIC ABOVE ALL THE OTHER ARTS IS EXPRESSION OF THE SOUL

THE DREAM OF GERONTIUS (1900), EDWARD ELGAR

IN CONTEXT

FOCUS
English choral tradition

BEFORE
1846 Mendelssohn's oratorio *Elijah* has its first performance in Birmingham, England.

1857 At the Handel Festival in London, England, choirs of up to 2,000 sing Handel's *Messiah* and other oratorios.

1882 Wagner's *Parsifal*, based on a 13th-century German epic poem, is his last and, for some, his greatest opera.

AFTER
1903 Elgar continues to develop large-scale choral works with *The Apostles*.

1939–1941 Michael Tippett composes his secular oratorio *A Child of Our Time*, which extends the oratorio still further with the inclusion of American spirituals in the score.

I n 1898, Edward Elgar was commissioned to write a new large-scale choral piece for the 1900 Birmingham Festival. Elgar, a Catholic, chose to set the poem *The Dream of Gerontius* by Cardinal John Henry Newman. In the poem, Gerontius, a devout old man, dreams of his death and the journey of his soul immediately after he dies. Elgar poured his own heart and soul into the work, inscribing it with a quote from the social thinker John Ruskin that began, "This is the best of me."

England had a strong tradition of amateur choral singing in the late 19th century, and many English

There is music in the air, music all around us, the world is full of it and you simply take as much as you require.
Edward Elgar

composers wrote oratorios—large-scale choral works on sacred themes. Few of these pieces stood the test of time, and Elgar decided to produce something different.

Oratorios, like the operas of Mozart, were usually made up of separate musical "numbers," such as arias and choruses. But with the work of late Romantic composers such as Richard Wagner, opera had evolved; Wagner's operas consist of music that flows continuously, without a break, enabling the composer to build huge climaxes and express deep emotions. Elgar used this technique for *The Dream of Gerontius,* rejecting the term "oratorio" due to this lack of breaks between pieces. Like Wagner, he employed a large orchestra with a substantial brass section and percussionists to reinforce the climaxes and underpin the most dramatic moments.

The soul's journey
The Dream of Gerontius is in two parts. Part One portrays the death of Gerontius. It includes the gentle prayers of his friends by his bedside, his passionate credo, "Sanctus fortis"—which expresses both his steadfast faith and his

See also: *Great Service* 52–53 ▪ *St. Matthew Passion* 98–105 ▪ *Elijah* 170–173 ▪ *The Ring Cycle* 180–187 ▪
A Child of Our Time 284–285

The Dream of Gerontius

As life drains from his body, Gerontius joins with his assistants in prayer.

Gerontius awakens in a place without time or space.

The guardian angel of Gerontius takes him to the judgment throne.

Gerontius encounters God and is judged.

Gerontius is lowered into the lake of Purgatory and promised that he will one day reawaken to **God's glory**.

anxieties—and the final swell of singers and orchestra in the chorus that exhorts Gerontius to "Go forth upon thy journey, Christian soul."

In Part Two, Gerontius's soul is guided by an angel past demons, who sing a sardonic fugal chorus, and a choir of angels, whose hymn "Praise to the Holiest in the Height" begins with a dramatic triple forte and ends in intricate eight-part harmony. This leads toward the climax, a deafening orchestral crescendo as the soul is finally led to judgment. Elgar rewrote this climactic passage at the insistence of his friend and publisher August Jaeger, who asked for something more dramatic than the composer's first attempt. The piece ends with the soul being taken in the arms of the angel and dipped into the soothing waters of Purgatory.

From disaster to success

Due to poorly prepared performers, *The Dream of Gerontius* had a disastrous premiere in Birmingham in 1900. However, after acclaimed performances in Germany, the work established itself as one of Elgar's masterpieces—a daring work for its time that develops late Romantic operatic style into a choral work, combines it with resourceful orchestral writing, and produces a setting of unusual power.

The Dream of Gerontius quickly transcended the question of doctrine that almost denied it an early performance in Worcester Cathedral, Cardinal Newman's words seeming too Catholic for the Anglican Church. Its emotional force and abiding themes of loss and hope in the face of death continue to exercise a universal appeal to audiences of every faith. ∎

Edward Elgar

Born in 1857 near Worcester, England, where his father owned a music shop, Elgar was largely a self-taught musician. As a young man, he played in orchestras and gave music lessons, marrying Alice Roberts, one of his pupils, in 1889. She encouraged him to move to London and spend more time on composition. His breakthrough work was *Enigma Variations* (1899), after which he wrote a series of large-scale compositions, including *The Apostles* (a choral piece), a violin concerto, and two symphonies, which brought him recognition in Britain and Europe.

Although depressed by World War I, in 1919 he wrote his String Quartet, Piano Quintet, and Cello Concerto. After Alice's death in 1920, Elgar composed little. He received many honors, but his music was out of fashion when he died in 1934.

Other key works

1899 *Enigma Variations*
1901–1930 *Pomp and Circumstance Marches*
1905 *Introduction and Allegro for Strings*
1919 *Cello Concerto in E minor*

I AM A SLAVE TO MY THEMES, AND SUBMIT TO THEIR DEMANDS
FINLANDIA (1900), JEAN SIBELIUS

IN CONTEXT

FOCUS
Finnish musical resistance to Russian political domination

BEFORE
1848 German-born Fredrik Pacius (1809–1891) composes the song *Vårt land* ("Our Country"), to Swedish words by Finnish poet Johan Ludvig Runeberg. After Finland's independence in 1917, a Finnish translation, *Maamme*, is adopted as the country's national anthem.

1892 Sibelius becomes a national celebrity when he first conducts his part-choral "symphonic poem" *Kullervo*, with texts from the Finnish national epic poem *Kalevala*.

AFTER
1917 Sibelius composes a *Jäger March* in support of the Finnish Jäger Batallion, trained in Germany to fight the Russian Empire in World War I.

O ut of all the musical nationalism that took shape during the 19th century in the four Nordic nations (Denmark, Finland, Norway, and Sweden), Finland's was perhaps the most powerful. In Jean Sibelius, Finland produced a composer who, even more than Norway's Edvard Grieg, Sweden's Franz Berwald, and Denmark's Carl Nielsen, captured the essence of his people and nation as they strove to throw off the shackles of foreign domination.

For nearly 700 years, up to the early 19th century, Finland had been part of the Swedish empire, and the language of the educated and governing classes was Swedish. When Sibelius was born into a Swedish-speaking family, Finland as a nation still did not exist. Since 1809, it had been a Grand Duchy of Imperial Russia, which imposed a

Sibelius captured the epic beauty of Finland's landscape, seen here in a view over the taiga forest, in the majestic string settings of *Finlandia*.

See also: *The Bartered Bride* 206 ▪ *Pictures at an Exhibition* 207 ▪ *Peer Gynt* 208–209 ▪ *Dvořák's Symphony No. 9* 212–215 ▪ *Appalachian Spring* 286–287

The development of Finnish motifs in *Finlandia*

Opening **brass fanfare** signifies the Russian menace.

Calm woodwind and fervent strings tell of **Finnish endurance** and hope for the future.

Loud and sudden emphasis (*fortissimo*) represents the turbulent anguish of the people.

Energetic and confident new melody asserts **pride and resistance**.

The building of the calming *Finlandia* tune, redolent of Finnish folk music, symbolizes **emerging clarity**.

Triumphant allegro climaxes in a rallying cry for the Finns.

resented autocratic rule. Against this uneasy backdrop, the Finnish language, spoken by urban and rural workers, became associated with a growing national resistance.

Sibelius had been to a Finnish-speaking school, so when his talent as a composer propelled him to the forefront of Finnish cultural life, he was ideally positioned to respond to the cultural interests of both linguistic communities. Besides mastery of powerful, large-scale symphonic forms, he had a flair for popular "light music" and sought out examples of Finnish folk music.

A Finnish fightback

In 1899, Russia proclaimed its "February Manifesto," which cracked down on Finnish autonomy and nationalism, including a ban on political rallies and the closure of a Finnish-language newspaper. An evening of "Press Celebrations" was organized in the capital, Helsinki, officially in support of the Press Pension Fund but was in reality a gathering of patriotic resistance. The evening included the display of specially painted tableaux, for which Sibelius was asked to compose the music. The last of these, "Finland Awakes," portrayed the region's proud achievements in culture and industry.

Sibelius then arranged some of the music for concert performance, revising "Finland Awakes" as *Finlandia*, its very title aimed at international recognition for a country known to every Finn as Suomi. Released in 1900, the work swept the musical world, and its popularity remains undiminished, with the central hymnlike tune widely seen as Finland's unofficial national anthem. ▪

Jean Sibelius

Johan Sibelius (he adopted the French version of his first name later) was born in the town of Hämeenlinna in 1865. At first, he wanted to be a virtuoso violinist, but his student years in Helsinki, Berlin, and Vienna led him to concentrate on composing. In 1892, after the success of his choral symphony *Kullervo*, he married Aino Järnefelt, with whom he went on to have six daughters.

Further success, including the symphonic poem (single-movement symphonic work) called *The Swan of Tuonela* of 1895, and then the first of seven symphonies, spread his name abroad. The onset of throat cancer in 1908, though successfully treated, brought a darker mood that influenced the austere Symphony No. 4 (1911). In the 30 years before his death, in 1957, troubled by self-criticism, alcoholism, and the pressures of fame, Sibelius released few works.

Other key works

1892 *Kullervo*
1902 Symphony No. 2
1924 Symphony No. 7
1926 *Tapiola*

SPANISH MUSIC WITH A UNIVERSAL ACCENT
IBERIA (1906–1908)
ISAAC ALBÉNIZ

IN CONTEXT

FOCUS
Nationalism in Spanish music

BEFORE
1874 Francisco Asenjo Barbieri's *El barberillo de Lavapiés* ("The little barber of Lavapiés") is his most successful *zarzuela* (traditional Spanish opera), a form he played a key role in reviving.

1890 Felipe Pedrell publishes *Por nuestra música* ("For our music"), in which he explores Spain's musical heritage.

AFTER
1915 Manuel de Falla's *Noches en los jardines de España* (*Nights in the Gardens of Spain*) mingles French modernism with inspiration from Spanish folk music.

1939 Joaquín Rodrigo's *Concierto de Aranjuez* evokes the history of the former royal summer palace of Aranjuez.

The piano suite *Iberia* by Isaac Albéniz is a collection of 12 solo pieces, published in four *cuadernos* (books). Influenced by his friend Claude Debussy and the Impressionist art movement, Albéniz called these solo pieces "impressions"—each seeks to evoke a different place or aspect of life in Spain. The pieces in the last two cuadernos are challenging to play, inspired by the virtuoso skills of Catalan pianist Joaquim Malats, for whom Albéniz wrote them. Nearly all of the pieces in *Iberia* are inspired by Andalusia, southern Spain, reflecting Albéniz's great love of the region. The single exception is "Lavapiés," which echoes the joyful buzz of the Jewish quarter of Madrid.

Historical influences

In the mid-19th century, Spanish music came alive after centuries of domination by foreign sounds. Romantic nationalism swept across Europe after the Napoleonic Wars; in Spain, this gave rise to figures such as Francisco Asenjo Barbieri—a composer and critic who helped to revive the native opera tradition, the zarzuela. Catalan composer Felipe Pedrell also renewed interest in Spain's musical heritage, both in classical and folk and dance music.

Inspired by Pedrell, Albéniz and his contemporaries drew on the rhythms of Spanish dances, such as the northern *jota* and the *fandango* and *zapateado* from the south, as well as Arabic-inspired melodies that evoked Spain's history as Al-Andalus, a Muslim land. ∎

[Albéniz represents] the reincorporation of Spain into the European musical world.
Joaquín Rodrigo
Virtuoso pianist (1901–1999)

See also: *The Bartered Bride* 206 ▪ *Pictures at an Exhibition* 207 ▪ *Finlandia* 220–221 ▪ *El sombrero de tres picos* 223 ▪ *Appalachian Spring* 286–287

A WONDERFUL MAZE OF RHYTHMICAL DEXTERITIES

EL SOMBRERO DE TRES PICOS (1919)
MANUEL DE FALLA

IN CONTEXT

FOCUS
20th-century Spanish music

BEFORE
1897 Ruperto Chapí's *La revoltosa* (*The Troublemaker*) is one of the most popular *zarzuelas* of the decades before World War I.

1911 In Barcelona, Enrique Granados premieres the first part of his piano suite *Goyescas*, inspired by the paintings of Francisco Goya.

AFTER
1920 Igor Stravinsky's ballet *Pulcinella* is premiered in Paris by Diaghilev's Ballets Russes, choreographed by Massine, with sets by Picasso.

1961 Catalan musician Eduard Toldrà conducts a concert version of de Falla's unfinished work *Atlántida* at the Liceu in Barcelona.

The ballet *El sombrero de tres picos* (*The Three-Cornered Hat*), with music by the composer Manuel de Falla, was first performed by Sergei Diaghilev's Ballets Russes in London's Alhambra Theatre. Based on a novella by Pedro Antonio de Alarcón, it is a comedy about the magistrate of a small Andalusian town, who falls in love with the wife of the local miller. The ballet was choreographed by the Russian Léonide Massine, who also danced the part of the miller, with sets and costumes by Pablo Picasso.

Falla grew up in the port city of Cádiz in Spain's far south but studied at the Madrid Conservatory where, like many composers of his generation, he was influenced by Felipe Pedrell's explorations of the country's traditional music. Falla made his name with an opera, *La vida breve* ("Life is short"), inspired by the *cante jondo* ("deep song") of his native Andalusia. In 1917, Falla and the impresarios María and Gregorio Martínez Sierra created an early, shorter version of *El sombrero*

Manuel de Falla composes at the piano in this 1925 portrait by Daniel Vázquez Díaz, who painted the most famous and influential Spanish figures of his time.

de tres picos. Its success in Madrid brought it to the attention of Sergei Diaghilev, who then commissioned de Falla to compose the music for an expanded version with full orchestra. Like *La vida breve*, it uses Andalusian melodies and also contains *cante jondo* songs. ∎

See also: *The Bartered Bride* 206 ▪ *Pictures at an Exhibition* 207 ▪ *Finlandia* 220–221 ▪ *Iberia* 222 ▪ *Appalachian Spring* 286–287

MODE
1900–1950

RN

French composer **Claude Debussy's** 10-minute symphonic poem *Prélude à l'après-midi d'un faune* premieres in Paris.

Arnold Schoenberg's *Pierrot lunaire* demonstrates his concept of serialism—using all 12 notes of the chromatic scale.

English composer **Ralph Vaughan Williams** composes *The Lark Ascending*, inspired by the English landscape and folk music.

George Gershwin writes *Rhapsody in Blue* for solo piano and jazz band, featuring large contrasts in musical texture and structure.

1894   **1912**   **1914**   **1924**

1906   **1913**   **1917**   **1927**

The Wreckers, an opera by British composer and suffragette **Ethel Smyth**, premieres in Germany to great success.

The premiere of **Igor Stravinsky's** avant-garde ballet *Le Sacre du printemps* is greeted by a riot in Paris.

French pianist **Erik Satie's** ballet *Parade* debuts, incorporating "noise-making" instruments such as a typewriter.

Charles Ives's Symphony No. 4, which incorporates hymns, gospel tunes, and band music, is performed for the first time.

As the 19th century drew to a close, composers began to realize that they were facing a crisis point. Wagner had undermined tonality, the system of major and minor keys that had been the cornerstone of Western music, and introduced a style that some found overemotional and lacking in clarity. The new generation reacted against Wagner's music in various ways, attempting to find a new musical language that better expressed modern times.

As a result, the first half of the new century was characterized by various "-isms": impressionism, expressionism, atonalism, serialism, neoclassicism, and more. There was one composer, however, who defied such classification, Erik Satie. He adopted a dry and witty style, with peculiarly static piano pieces that harked back to medieval and ancient music and at the same time made reference to popular Parisian café music.

French developments

Satie's lightness of touch was also noticeable in the music of his contemporary, Claude Debussy. Yet Debussy chose a different way of creating a new musical language. Rather than reacting against the lack of clarity that came with a weakened tonality, he embraced it, using exotic harmonies as an impressionist artist uses different shades of color. Although he disliked the term, he was a pioneer of musical impressionism, which was further refined by Maurice Ravel, and influenced the strikingly colorful compositions of Olivier Messiaen.

After World War I, a group of young French composers known as Les Six (Francis Poulenc, Darius Milhaud, Arthur Honegger, Georges Auric, Louis Durey, and Germaine Tailleferre) picked up on the simplicity and wit of Satie's music. Poulenc, in particular, cultivated an urbane style, unashamedly classical in its tonality, setting the style for neoclassicism, which was especially strong in France.

Twelve-tone serialism

Meanwhile, in turn-of-the-century Vienna, Arnold Schoenberg struggled to come to terms with the implications of the breakdown of tonality. After some early works in the Late Romantic style, he stretched tonality to its limits and beyond, creating a violently expressionistic style that was

Austrian composer
Anton Webern's
instrumental work
Symphonie further
develops Schoenberg's
ideas on serialism.

Edgard Varèse's
Ionisation premieres
as one of the first
concert hall pieces
written solely for a
percussion ensemble.

Olivier Messiaen stages
the first production of
Quartet for the End of Time
in the German prisoner
of war camp where he
is being held.

Aaron Copland
demonstrates American
nationalism with
Appalachian Spring,
Martha Graham's ballet
about young pioneers.

1928   **1933**   **1941**   **1944**

1930   **1937**   **1941**   **1945**

Commissioned by one-handed
pianist Paul Wittgenstein,
Maurice Ravel writes *Piano
Concerto in D for the Left Hand,*
infused with jazz-infuenced
rhythms and harmonies.

Having been denounced
by Stalin, **Dmitri
Shostakovich** writes
his *Fifth Symphony,*
which is acclaimed
by the Soviet regime.

British composer **Michael
Tippett** completes his
pacifistic oratorio *A Child of
Our Time,* influenced by events
from his life and Jungian
psychoanalysis.

**Benajamin
Britten** revives
British opera with
Peter Grimes, a
stirring drama about
a bullied outcast.

completely atonal, without reference
to any key. The difficulty of creating
a cohesive structure led him to
develop a system of composing in
which, instead of a having a "home
key," all 12 notes of the chromatic
scale are given equal importance
and arranged in a series. This
12-tone serialism became the
compositional method of choice
not only for Schoenberg but also
for his students Alban Berg and
Anton Webern (known as the
"Second Viennese School").

Shock of the new
In addition to these influential
French and Viennese composers,
there was a highly significant
Russian composer, Igor Stravinsky.
Stravinsky made his name writing
ballet music in the style of the
Russian nationalist composers, but

in 1913, he shocked audiences with
his discordant portrayal of Russian
folklore in *Le Sacre du printemps.*
The music was both primitive and
ultra-modern, and a world away
from the Romantic conception of
folk-inspired orchestral music.

Russian modernism was short-
lived: after the revolutions of 1917,
the Soviet authorities decried
anything that smacked of elitism.
Stravinsky, like several other
Russian composers, spent the
rest of his life abroad.

Nationalism was far from dead,
however, as the late works of Jean
Sibelius and Leoš Janáček show.
It had also taken root in England,
thanks to composers such as Ralph
Vaughan Williams, who toured the
country collecting folk tunes. The
distinctive nuances of English folk
music shaped the styles of

Benjamin Britten and Michael
Tippett in the next generation.
Another collector of folk music was
Béla Bartók, who, like Stravinsky,
did not integrate the songs and
dances of his native Hungary into
an existing style but used them
to create a new, modernist style.

Schoenberg, Stravinsky, and
Bartók all spent their final years
in the US, which had become a
center for new music. In the first
half of the 20th century, it had
given birth to ragtime and jazz and
popular tunes by masters of the
genre such as George Gershwin.
It had also seen a very American
tradition of experimentalism
emerge, starting with Charles Ives,
and attracting émigrés such as
Edgard Varèse, which would come
to shape the course of musical
development into the 21st century. ∎

I GO TO SEE THE SHADOW YOU HAVE BECOME

PRÉLUDE À L'APRÈS-MIDI D'UN FAUNE (1894), CLAUDE DEBUSSY

IN CONTEXT

FOCUS
Impressionism

BEFORE
1891 Gabriel Fauré's "Cinq mélodies 'de Venise'" uses subtle, elusive harmonic progressions, similar to the "impressionist" style.

1882–1892 Ernest Chausson's *Poème de l'amour et de la mer* contains passages and chord progressions, which more vividly prefigure the harmonic language of Debussy's *Prélude*.

AFTER
1912 In the ballet *Daphnis et Chloé*, Maurice Ravel uses fast-moving "dots" of sound, the musical equivalent of a pointillist painting.

1928–1929 The young Olivier Messiaen composes his *Préludes*, a collection of pieces heavily influenced by Debussy.

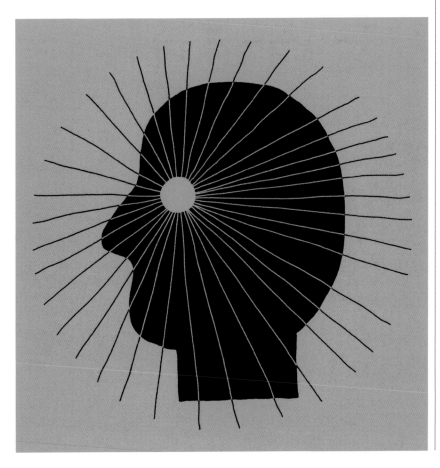

Composed between 1891–1894, and based on the poem by Stéphane Mallarmé, Claude Debussy's first published orchestral work *Prélude à l'après-midi d'un faune* (*Prelude to the Afternoon of a Faun*) has since been hailed as the first significant "impressionist" musical work. Later the composer Pierre Boulez even claimed that the work marked the very beginning of modern music.

Debussy's musical language was an ideal counterpart to Mallarmé's symbolist poetry. The composer described the work as "the general impression of the poem … it follows the ascending

See also: *The Ring Cycle* 180–187 ▪ *Das Lied von der Erde* 198–201 ▪ *Parade* 256 ▪ *Quartet for the End of Time* 282–283

> Its use of timbres seemed essentially new, of exceptional delicacy and assurance in touch.
> **Pierre Boulez**

shape of the poem, as well as the scenery so marvellously described in the text." In the poem, a faun awakens from an afternoon nap, recalling a moment of arousal at the sight of a pair of water nymphs. The faun tries to embrace the nymphs, but they disappear into nothingness. Mallarmé's poem is evocative, yet fundamentally ambiguous, focusing on the deep sensuality of the moment. Debussy's interpretation of the poem sought to replicate this sensuality, in an almost subversive upheaval of musical language.

Debussy and Wagner
This subversion is evident in Debussy's unmistakable references to the prelude from Wagner's *Tristan und Isolde*. That prelude opens with a yearning cello line (the "longing" motif) followed by a half-diminished chord (the famous "Tristan chord"). Debussy's *Prélude* also begins with a single line—a characterful flute flourish—before landing on a half-diminished chord. Wagner's Tristan chord then begins a chromatic progression ending in an unresolved imperfect cadence »

The Greek god Pan pursues the nymph Syrinx in François Boucher's work. The amorous faun Pan featured in many of Debussy's works, including "La Flûte de Pan" and "Syrinx."

Claude Debussy

Born in a Parisian suburb to a shop owner and his wife, in 1862, Debussy began music lessons at the age of seven, and at 10 he embarked on a decade of study at the Paris Conservatoire. By 1890, he had composed more than 50 songs, but fewer larger-scale pieces, of which many were not published and some never completed.

In the 1890s, he established the impressionist style for which he is best remembered. His *String Quartet* (1893) demonstrated many of the traits that were established in the *Prélude à l'après-midi d'un faune*, the culmination of which were his symphonic masterwork *La Mer* (1905) and his only published opera, *Pelléas et Melisande* (1902). In his later career, he focused on smaller-scale forms, composing many of his best-known piano works, including *L'isle joyeuse* (1904), and his two books of *Préludes*. Debussy died in Paris in 1918.

Other key works

1902 *Pelléas et Mélisande*
1903 *Estampes*
1903–1905 *La Mer*

The Afternoon of a Faun was adapted into a ballet by Vaslav Nijinsky in his first choreography for the Ballets Russes. It premiered at the Théâtre du Châtelet in Paris, in May 1912.

(above which an oboe plays the four chromatically rising notes of the "desire" motif). Debussy's chord, however—shimmering amidst a harp *glissando*—dissolves into a seemingly unrelated dominant seventh, colored by the horns with a major ninth and sharpened 11th. Unlike Wagner, Debussy's work contains little tension—each chord is to be appreciated for the sensuality of its sound.

The similarities to Wagner's work make Debussy's subversions all the more obvious. Like Wagner, Debussy also states his opening melody twice more—each time over increasingly lush harmony. This establishes E major as the tonic ("home") key of the piece, but the ambiguity of the chords used up to this point—which do not point clearly to a single key—means that the arrival at E major goes all but unnoticed in the moment. Despite this seeming ambiguity, under the surface,

Debussy follows a fairly traditional tonal structure that stops the piece from sounding incoherent.

Nine bars after the arrival of the tonic key, Debussy even quotes Wagner's "desire" motif in the clarinet, getting as far as the third note, which he distinctively accompanies with Wagner's own dominant-seventh harmony so it is unmistakable. Debussy strips the chord of Wagner's context, making it sound not tersely dissonant but lushly exotic. Turning the unfinished motif back and forth in descending and ascending chromatic scales, Debussy makes Wagner's profound utterance into his own plaything.

Technical experiments
The *Prélude* is notable for its use of "Debussian" added-note chords. While dominant sevenths, ninths, 11ths, or 13ths are easy to find in the works of Wagner and Liszt, Debussy strips them of any expectation that, for example, a dominant chord must always resolve to its tonic. Rather than working toward resolution, Debussy progresses chromatically in unexpected directions: often, chords are joined to each other by

one or two common pitches or by subtle semitonal shifts. Debussy manipulates his audience's listening experience by subverting their expectations of what will come next; unusual harmonies catch our attention, and we listen closely to their "color" and effect, hence, the reason why this sort of harmony is often called "coloristic."

The pulse of the Prélude is slow beneath the surface filigree. While mostly in triple meter, some of the passages are in duple time, which contain bars of two or four beats; likewise the subdivision of the beats varies between compound time (each beat of the pulse subdivided into three) and simple (divided into two). Triple and duple rhythms sometimes coexist; in the middle section, the accompaniment plays triplet cross-rhythms against the duple melody, moving attention away from any regularity of pulse toward the music's rich textural fabric. While impressionist music is

Sasha Waltz & Guests, a German dance troupe, reinterprets *L'Après-midi d'un faune* as a brightly colored and provocative beach scene at Sadler's Wells Theatre, London, in 2015.

Orchestra for *Prélude à l'après-midi d'un faune*

The original orchestra for Debussy's symphonic poem consisted of woodwinds, strings, harp, and horns, together creating a delicate, sensuous sound world.

Woodwind

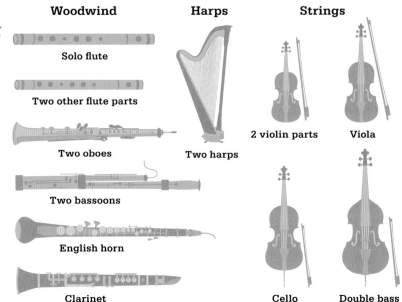

Solo flute

Two other flute parts

Two oboes

Two bassoons

English horn

Clarinet

Harps

Two harps

Strings

2 violin parts

Viola

Cello

Double bass

Percussion

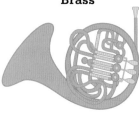

Antique Cymbals

Brass

Four horns

---

sometimes considered less technical than other genres, Debussy's experimentation with rhythmic techniques shows that atmosphere and technicality can coexist.

Staging the piece

Debussy's orchestra is moderately sized: its only brass instruments are four horns, and only two percussion "antique cymbals" color the latter part of the piece with their delicate, bell-like tone. The orchestra does, however, have two harps, which help to create a more luxuriant sound. Long sections use *divisi* in the strings, sometimes playing *sur la touche*—over the fingerboard, where the tone is more mellow.

Debussy's work premiered in Paris in December 1894, and Stéphane Mallarmé was invited to hear it. While he had initially opposed the composition of music based on his poem, Mallarmé came out full of praise, writing to Debussy that it went further "in nostalgia and light, with finesse, uneasiness, and richness" than his own work. ∎

I wasn't expecting anything like that! The music prolongs the emotion of my poem and conjures up the scenery more vividly than any color.
Stéphane Mallarmé

Debussy and impressionism

The word "impressionism" is controversial when applied to music. Debussy himself—its most iconic exponent—railed against it. "I'm attempting 'something different,'" he wrote in 1908, "[that] imbeciles call impressionism, just about the least appropriate term possible." Despite this, Debussy's work is as much a musical equivalent to Monet as to Mallarmé. His tonally ambiguous harmonies (which do not clearly suggest one particular resolution) could lead to numerous possible progressions, putting the focus on the sensual effect of each chord, while obscuring its role in the structure that underpins the piece—just as Monet's focus on colors and eschewal of lines communicates more about the sense than about the details of his subject. Both Debussy and Monet have been called "antirealist," but for Debussy, appealing to the very senses by which music is heard, was "more real" than realism.

I WANT WOMEN TO TURN THEIR MINDS TO BIG AND DIFFICULT JOBS

THE WRECKERS (1904), ETHEL SMYTH

IN CONTEXT

FOCUS
Female composers

BEFORE
1644 The Venetian composer and singer Barbara Strozzi publishes her first book of madrigals (*Il primo libro di madrigali*).

1850 In France, the premiere success of Louise Farrenc's *Nonet for wind and strings* allows her to negotiate equal pay as professor of piano at the Paris Conservatoire.

AFTER
1913 French composer Lili Boulanger is the first woman to receive the Prix de Rome for her cantata *Faust et Hélène*.

2000 Finnish composer Kaija Saariaho premieres her five-act opera *L'Amour de loin* (*Love From Afar*), based on the 12th-century troubadour Jaufré Rudel, at the Salzburg Festival.

W omen were writing opera from the form's first days. The earliest known opera by a woman, *La Liberazione di Ruggiero dall'isola d'Alcina* (*The Liberation of Ruggiero from the Island of Alcina*), by Francesca Caccini, was first performed in Caccini's native city of Florence in 1625. For Ethel Smyth, however, writing a three-act "grand opera"—serious in theme, with no spoken dialogue—at the turn of the 20th century was an ambitious undertaking, both because she was female and also because she was English, British opera having been almost extinct since Henry Purcell.

Life beyond the piano

For much of the 19th century, female composers were associated with piano and chamber music suited to the domestic sphere. Composers such as Louise Reichardt (1779–1826), Clara Schumann (1819–1896), and Fanny Mendelssohn (1805–1847) were known for "art songs," or *Lieder* (poems set to music for voice and piano). Toward the end of the century, female composers began

I feel awfully full of power—deadly sure of what I am doing—I love to see how I am getting to orchestrate better and better.
Ethel Smyth
Letter to librettist Henry Brewster

to spread their wings. Cécile Chaminade (1857–1944) and Augusta Holmès (1847–1903), both French and near contemporaries of Smyth, wrote major orchestral works, as did Amy Beach (1867–1944), who was the first American woman to write a symphony—the *Gaelic Symphony* (1896).

Some women also wrote opera. Thirty years older than Smyth, the French aristocrat Marie de Grandval (1828–1907) was a prolific composer whose works included a symphony (now lost), an oratorio (*Stabat Mater*), and seven operas, the last of which, *Mazeppa*, based on a poem by Byron, was staged with some success in Bordeaux in 1892. Three years later, Augusta Holmès's third and final opera, *La Montagne noire*, was produced at the Paris Opéra. Smyth was in the French capital at the time and saw the work. In common with many others, she was disappointed

The audience prepare to leave after watching an opera at the Royal Opera House, Covent Garden, London, in 1910—the year *The Wreckers* had its first performance at the venue.

See also: *La traviata* 174–175 ▪ *The Ring Cycle* 180–187 ▪ *Tosca* 194–197 ▪ *Peer Gynt* 208–209 ▪ *Peter Grimes* 288–293 ▪ *L'Amour de loin* 325 ▪ *blue cathedral* 326

by the opera but sympathized with the composer, writing later: "knowing what I do about the difficulties of opera composers, especially plus the handicap of sex, the astonishing fact about it was that it existed at all."

By then Smyth had embarked on her own career as an opera composer. Crucial encouragement had come from the German conductor and Wagner champion Hermann Levi, a friend for whom Smyth had played on the piano one of her earlier choral works, Mass in D (1891). Impressed by the drama of the music, Levi told her: "You must at once sit down and write an opera."

Taking up the challenge, in 1894 Smyth completed her first opera, a comedy called *Fantasio*, staged in Weimar in 1898. Her second, *Der Wald* (*The Forest*), was produced in Berlin and London in 1902 and a year later at the Metropolitan Opera in New York—the first opera by a woman to be performed there. By the time Smyth wrote *The Wreckers*, her third opera, she was winning wide recognition, though it was still difficult to get the work staged in her own country. For the British, opera was chiefly an upper-class entertainment put on by foreigners in London during the social season. When Smyth first submitted *The Wreckers* to the Royal Opera House in Covent Garden, the managing committee told her: "To announce a new work by a new composer is to secure an absolutely empty house, and in future no opera will be produced here that has not established its success abroad."

A Cornish tale

Completed in 1904 and first performed two years later in Leipzig, *The Wreckers* is set in a remote village on the coast of Cornwall in the late 18th century. The villagers are "wreckers," who make their living by luring ships onto the rocky shore and plundering them. The drama of the opera centers on two lovers, Thirza and Mark, who are opposed to this thievery. Thirza is the young wife of Pascoe, leader of the wreckers but also the village preacher—a dual role not at all incongruous to most of the villagers, who see no contradiction between their »

Two composer sisters, Nadia (left) and Lili Boulanger, pose together in 1913. Nadia was also an influential teacher, whose students included Aaron Copland and Philip Glass.

Ethel Smyth

The daughter of a French mother and a British major-general, Ethel Smyth was born in the English county of Kent in 1858. At the age of 19, she went to Germany to study music at Leipzig Conservatory, where her fellow students included Grieg, Dvořák, and Tchaikovsky. Back in England, she started to win recognition for musical composition in the 1890s, championed by such diverse figures as the exiled French Empress Eugénie (widow of Napoleon III) and the playwright George Bernard Shaw. In 1910, Smyth met the women's suffrage campaigner Emmeline Pankhurst (possibly a lover of the openly lesbian composer) and devoted the next two years to the Suffragette cause. In later years, she was hampered by deafness and so turned to writing instead of music. She was made a Dame of the British Empire in 1922 and died in 1944.

Other key works

1891 Mass in D
1894 *Fantasio*
1914 *The Boatswain's Mate*
1924 *Entente cordiale*

looting and their faith. Mark has been secretly lighting beacons to warn ships off the rocks.

When the villagers discover that a night of plundering has been sabotaged by Mark and Thirza, they condemn them to death as "adulterers and traitors," imprisoning them in a sea cave that fills with water at high tide.

Between whiles I would lie on the [Cornish] cliffs, buried in soft pink thrift, listening to the boom of the great Atlantic waves against those cruel rocks, and the wild treble cries of the seagulls.
Ethel Smyth

As the waves rise, the lovers sing their final duet, a bridal song: "Our last ecstasy thy embrace, O sea!"

Bringing the opera to life

Smyth's inspiration for the opera had been a walking holiday in Cornwall and the Isles of Scilly. Here, she had heard tales of the wreckers of old and of the religious revival in 18th-century Cornwall led by the founder of the Methodists, John Wesley. A sea cave called Piper's Hole in the Isles of Scilly had given her the idea for the cave in which the lovers Thirza and Mark meet their death. Her librettist, as with her two previous operas, was an old friend, Henry Brewster. The son of a Bostonian father and English mother, Brewster had been raised in France and was more at ease writing in French than in English, so they decided that the libretto would be in French, which Smyth also spoke and wrote fluently. The libretto was composed through correspondence between Brewster in Rome and Smyth in Surrey.

Wreckers seize cargo from a ship that has foundered on the Cornish coast, in an etching from the 1822 book *Scenes in England* by the Reverend Isaac Taylor.

The music, meanwhile, was firmly rooted in the German tradition. Trained in Leipzig, as a composer Smyth belonged to a lineage that passed from Beethoven through Brahms—whom Smyth, throughout her life an avid social networker, had known in Leipzig—to Mahler, just two years her junior. With such a clear Germanic background, the influence of Wagner (himself born in Leipzig) was inescapable, despite Smyth once protesting, "I never was, nor am I now, a Wagnerite in the extreme sense of the word." *The Wreckers* shows clear Wagnerian traces, such as the rich orchestration, evoking the coast and seascapes of Cornwall, and the use of "leitmotifs"—musical themes associated with particular individuals and emotions. At the same time, the drama has a marked

The sea in opera

Wagner, *The Flying Dutchman*, 1841
The atmosphere of the North Sea breathes throughout. The sea is there to be conquered but ultimately emerges victorious.

Bizet, *The Pearl Fishers*, 1863
The changing moods of the sea reflect the ups and downs of the relationship between two friends and their ultimate reconciliation.

Ethel Smyth, *The Wreckers*, 1904
The orchestration evokes Cornish seascapes. Powerful but impassive, the sea brings both prosperity and discord to the village.

Vaughan Williams, *Riders to the Sea*, 1932
The impressionistic music captures the power of wind and ocean in this lament for sons lost at sea set in an Irish fishing village.

Benjamin Britten, *Peter Grimes*, 1945
Four Interludes each represent a different mood of the sea. The sea is a metaphor for the struggle of the individual.

Benjamin Britten, *Billy Budd*, 1951
The sea represents an implacable backdrop to the turbulence of human affairs and a final, peaceful resting place.

The whole English attitude toward women in fields of art is ludicrous … There is no sex in art. How you play the violin, paint, or compose is what matters.
Ethel Smyth

British character in its setting and themes. The hymns and other choruses sung by the villagers, for instance, bear the clear imprint of the English oratorio tradition.

Derivative though the music is in many ways, Smyth had nonetheless achieved her objective with *The Wreckers*. She had written a viable British opera that could, for the first time, bear comparison with the works of the major continental opera composers of the late 19th and early 20th centuries. Although imperfectly worked out, the basic drama of the opera is compelling with strong characters and situations. It takes on serious themes of greed, love, moral conflict, and religious fanaticism. At its best, as in the prelude to the second act, "On the cliffs of Cornwall," the music is colorful and atmospheric. Although indebted to Wagner's *Siegfried*, the second-act duets between the lovers Thirza and Mark, torn between passion and moral responsibility, strike a new, raw note in British operatic music.

The premiere
Her work completed, it then took Smyth two years to get *The Wreckers* staged. The premiere, when it eventually came, was in Leipzig's Neues Theater, Brewster's libretto having been translated into German. To Smyth's fury the director had made cuts to the third act, although the first-night audience greeted the "mutilated" version with thunderous applause. After the director refused to reinstate his cuts for subsequent performances, an enraged Smyth stormed into the theatre early the next morning and removed all the scores she could find in the orchestra pit. There would be no more performances of *The Wreckers* in Leipzig.

Smyth then caught a train to Prague, where another performance was scheduled. This proved an even greater disaster, since the orchestra had not rehearsed properly, leading to damning reviews in the local press. The »

Female conductors

Only in the 20th century did women begin to conduct orchestras. When the role emerged in the 19th century, it was monopolized by male composers, with women confined to conducting choirs. In the 1930s, the Dutch-American Antonia Brico conducted the Berlin Philharmonic, and the French composer Nadia Boulanger became the first woman to conduct London's Royal Philharmonic. In the 1950s, Margaret Hollis achieved renown as a choral director, founding the Chicago Symphony Chorus in 1957, and, in 1976, Sarah Caldwell was the first female conductor at the Metropolitan Opera, New York.

It took another 30 years for a woman, Marin Alsop, to become chief conductor of a major American orchestra, the Baltimore Symphony Orchestra. In 2013, Alsop scored another first for a woman when she conducted the *Last Night of the Proms* in London's Albert Hall.

Marin Alsop conducts the Swedish Radio Symphony Orchestra in 2009. She has led orchestras in the UK, Brazil, and the US.

Dedicated to THE WOMEN'S SOCIAL AND POLITICAL UNION.

VOTES FOR WOMEN

W.S.P.U.

THE MARCH OF THE WOMEN
(Popular Edition in F...To be sung in Unison)
By **ETHEL SMYTH**, Mus.Doc.
Price: One Shilling & Sixpence net.
To be had of THE WOMAN'S PRESS, 156 Charing Cross R! London W.C. and BREITKOPF & HÄRTEL, 54 G! Marlborough S! London W.

composer had better luck at the next location, Vienna, where Mahler was director of the opera house. He expressed an interest in seeing Smyth, but the person she actually met was his second-in-command, the conductor Bruno Walter. He was impressed but could not promise a production.

Back in London, Smyth's experiences were similarly checkered. In 1908, a concert version of the first two acts was well received by many critics but overshadowed by personal sadness. Brewster, who was in the final stages of liver cancer, had traveled from Rome for the performance. He died less than a month later. The next year, *The Wreckers*—now translated by Smyth into English—was successfully staged at His Majesty's Theatre, London, conducted by the young Thomas Beecham. The conductor also included it in his first season at the Royal Opera House the year after, although it suffered by comparison with a new work being performed at Covent Garden that season: Richard Strauss's *Elektra*.

In 1911, Smyth wrote "The March of the Women" as a Suffragette rallying cry. An active protester, she was sentenced to two months in Holloway Prison, in 1912, for smashing a window.

Many contemporaries were generous in their praise of *The Wreckers*. Writing in 1910 in the second edition of *The New Grove Dictionary of Music and Musicians*, the British music critic John Fuller Maitland observed: "It is difficult to point to a work of any nationality since Wagner that has a more direct appeal to the emotions, or that is more skilfully planned and carried out." The novelist Virginia Woolf was more ambivalent. In 1931, she, her husband, Leonard, and her lover, Vita Sackville-West, accompanied Smyth to see *The Wreckers* at the Sadler's Wells Theatre, London. She noted in her diary that the opera was "vigorous & even beautiful; & active & absurd & extreme; & youthful: as if some song in her had tried to issue & been choked." Beecham in his memoirs, published in 1944, was a whole-hearted enthusiast, judging *The Wreckers* "one of the three or four English operas of real musical merit and vitality written during the past forty years."

Blazing a trail

While Woolf's judgment is perhaps the one most modern critics would come closest to, Smyth's role in opening up a path for later female composers is beyond doubt. In *The Wreckers*, she took on one of the most ambitious forms of composition. Through her talent, perseverance, and sheer drive, Smyth established herself as a serious composer. She went on to write three further smaller-scale operas—two one-act comedies and *Fête galante* (1922), a "dance-

drama" based on a short story of the same name by Smyth's friend Maurice Baring.

Where Smyth led the way, many others have followed. In Britain alone, a generation of female composers born in the decade that *The Wreckers* was composed and first performed included Elisabeth Lutyens, Elizabeth Maconchy, and Imogen Holst. The work of Lutyens included nearly 200 scores for film and radio, as well as the operas *The Numbered* (1965) and *Isis and Osiris* (1969). Best known for her 13 string quartets (1933–1984), Maconchy also wrote five operas, including *The Sofa* (1957) and *The Departure* (1961). Holst, only child of Gustav Holst, while a less prolific composer, proved a tireless assistant to Benjamin Britten. In the late 20th century, the work of two Scottish composers won world acclaim. The 10 operas of Thea

Dressed in red, the title character of Judith Weir's opera *Miss Fortune* takes center state at the United Kingdom premiere of the work at the Royal Opera House, Covent Garden, in 2012.

> Miss Smyth is one of the few women composers one can seriously consider to be achieving something valuable in the field of musical composition.
> **Pyotr Ilyich Tchaikovsky**

Musgrave include *Mary, Queen of Scots* (1976), and *Simón Bolívar* (1995), while the successes of Judith Weir include *A Night at the Chinese Opera* (1987), *The Vanishing Bridegroom* (1990), and *Blond Eckbert* (1994).

Male heirs

It is not only female composers who were influenced by Smyth. Surprisingly, Benjamin Britten seems not to have known *The*

Wreckers, at least at first hand. Yet his first opera, *Peter Grimes*, premiered in 1945, has almost uncanny parallels with Smyth's work. Both operas are set in remote coastal areas, where a pair of protagonists find themselves at odds with the rest of the community, which is in the grip of evangelical religion and set on violence against them. Both employ the device of the protagonists singing onstage while a chorus of villagers perform a hymn offstage. And both include powerful orchestral evocations of the sea, endowing it with a personal presence and force so great that the watery element becomes a key presence in the work.

Whether Britten was aware of *The Wreckers* or not, Smyth's work clearly played some role in revitalizing a distinctively British tradition of opera, both in terms of music and subject matter. In this sense, major male composers of the 20th century, such as Britten and Michael Tippett, can be counted among the inheritors of Smyth's musical mantle. ∎

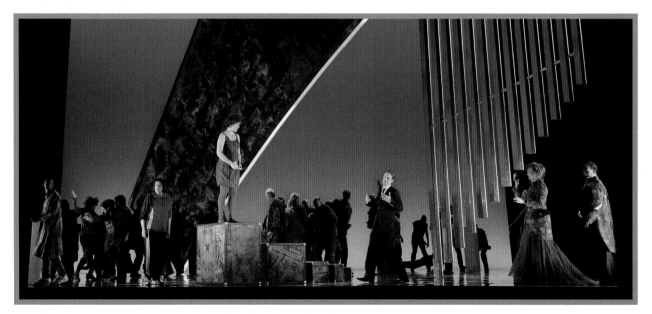

AN AUDIENCE SHOULDN'T LISTEN WITH COMPLACENCY

PIERROT LUNAIRE, OP. 21 (1912), ARNOLD SCHOENBERG

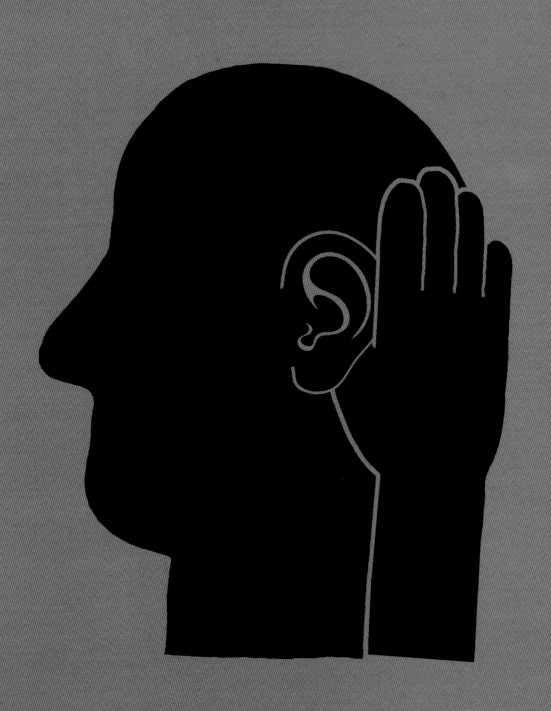

IN CONTEXT

FOCUS
Atonality

BEFORE
1865 Richard Wagner's opera *Tristan und Isolde* is first performed—a turning point in the move away from tonality.

1894 French composer Claude Debussy uses ambiguous harmonies and fluid harmonic progressions in his *Prélude à l'après-midi d'un faune*.

1899 Schoenberg stretches the bounds of tonality to its limits in his string sextet *Verklärte Nacht*, Op. 4.

AFTER
1917–1922 In his *Five Sacred Songs*, Op. 15, Austrian composer Anton Webern uses a similar small ensemble to that of *Pierrot lunaire* and develops many of the same compositional techniques.

1921–1923 *The Suite for Piano*, Op. 25, is the first of Schoenberg's works to use his 12-tone serial method of composition throughout.

1922 French composer Edgard Varèse's *Offrandes* for soprano and chamber orchestra has its premiere in New York.

1965 An ensemble, the Pierrot Players, later known as the Fires of London, is founded to perform *Pierrot lunaire* and other new works.

Until the end of the 19th century, music had been largely dictated by a tonal system, in which keys, chords, and scales complemented each other to create melody and harmony that were pleasing to the ear. Even where dissonant, or unsettling, passages were used in a piece of music, it was still resolved onto a consonant, or harmonious, chord.

The seeds for the unraveling of this tonal tradition were sown by Richard Wagner. In his operas, especially *Tristan und Isolde* (1859), Wagner undermined the concept of music written in one key by moving through a range of different, often unrelated, keys, without settling on any one, and introducing dissonant chords for dramatic effect. A few decades later, Arnold Schoenberg

Arnold Schoenberg poses with his second wife, Gertrud, and their children, in 1950. Gertrud wrote the libretto for Schoenberg's one-act opera *Von heute auf morgen* (1928–1930).

and other composers, including Alexander Scriabin and Béla Bartók, started to experiment further, escaping from traditional harmony, and chords and melodies based on diatonic (major and minor) scales, instead exploring more dissonant 12-note chromatic scales. The Austrian composer and critic Joseph Marx coined the term "atonality" for this music, which had no recognizable tonality, or key. Schoenberg gave it full rein in the works of his middle period (roughly 1908–1921), of which *Pierrot lunaire* is arguably the most influential.

Tonality taken to the limit

The use of chromatic scales to create new harmonies had become the norm among composers at the end of the 19th century, especially in Austria and Germany. But in the early years of the new century, Schoenberg came to realize that tonality, the system of major and minor scales that had formed the basis of Western music since

See also: *The Ring Cycle* 180–187 ▪ *Prélude à l'après-midi d'un faune* 228–231 ▪ *Le Sacre du printemps* 246–251 ▪ Webern's *Symphonie*, Op. 21 264–265 ▪ *Ionisation* 268–269 ▪ *Gruppen* 306–307

> The expression, "atonal music" is most unfortunate— it is on a par with calling swimming "the art of not drowning."
> **Arnold Schoenberg**

the 17th century, was being stretched to its limits. In 1908, he also faced a personal crisis when his wife, Mathilde, had an affair with the artist Richard Gerstl, who then committed suicide. Schoenberg's resulting sense of despair was reflected in a more chaotic, free chromatic style, with little tonal structure, first in a setting of *"Du lehnest wider eine Silberweide"* by the German symbolist poet Stefan George, and more dramatically in his String Quartet No. 2, which moves in and out of keys, seemingly at random, and adds the surprise of a soprano voice to its third and fourth movements.

Soon, Schoenberg recognized a drawback to his new compositional technique: while free chromaticism allowed a more varied harmonic range for emotional expression, it lacked the structural discipline of classical forms, such as the sonata, which are based mainly on relationships between keys. Schoenberg therefore set about finding a way to reconcile atonality with classical structure and romantic expression—the opposing

legacies of Haydn and Mozart, and Wagner. He was not alone in trying to find a new way of approaching these legacies. In France, for example, Erik Satie was producing coolly detached and often static music, and Claude Debussy was developing his free-flowing style using the less dissonant of the chromatic harmonies.

Embracing dissonance

In his early forays into atonality, Schoenberg used chromatic chords to create an ethereal atmosphere through an unexpected but still harmonious combination of notes. However, his interest in the new expressionist movement of writers and artists in Vienna led him to develop a starker musical language. Above all, he saw his task as the "emancipation of dissonance," allowing a dissonant chord to stand by itself as a harmony, not as a "subsidiary" chord requiring resolution onto a consonance. This was similar to Debussy's use of chromatic chords, but Schoenberg did not confine himself to mild dissonance; he also boldly used harsh and jarring dissonances. »

> It is the organization of a piece which helps the listener to keep the idea in mind, to follow its development.
> **Arnold Schoenberg**

Arnold Schoenberg

Born in 1874 in Vienna to a Jewish family, Schoenberg was primarily self-taught in music but took theory lessons with the composer Alexander Zemlinsky, whose sister, Mathilde, Schoenberg married. In 1898, he converted to Christianity, hoping for greater acceptance in Viennese cultural life. His first compositions, in a late Romantic style, were well received. In the 1920s, after his "middle period" rejection of traditional tonality, he invented a new method of composition, systematically using all 12 notes of the chromatic scale.

With the rise of Nazism, Schoenberg felt increasingly vulnerable in Europe, and in 1933 he moved to the US, having reverted to Judaism during a short stay in Paris. He became a US citizen in 1941 and spent the rest of his life in California, where he died in 1951.

Other key works

1899 *Verklärte Nacht*, Op. 4
1909 *Erwartung*, Op. 17
1926–1928 Variations for Orchestra, Op. 31
1930–1932 *Moses und Aron*

> With a grotesque giant bow, Pierrot scratches on his viola. Like the stork on one leg, He bleakly plucks a pizzicato.
> **Albert Giraud**

The resulting music chimed well with expressionism and had a disturbing, often nightmarish effect. Where Wagner's unresolved harmonies evoked anticipation, yearning, or unrequited love, Schoenberg's created anxiety and apprehension. Rather than express emotions, his atonality dealt with psychological states. Schoenberg would have been aware of the research being carried out in Vienna at the time by the founder of psychoanalysis, Sigmund Freud.

The unsettling nature of the free chromaticism employed by Schoenberg is due largely to its lack of formal structure; without some kind of organization or sense of progression, it is unpredictable and offers little relief or resolution. Schoenberg, nevertheless, felt the need to harness this freedom to avoid a musical anarchy that could limit his expressive range. He turned to some pre-classical formal structures in which the emphasis was more on counterpoint than harmony. These included imitative devices, such as canons and fugues, as well as simple forms, such as the rondo and passacaglia (a style using the repetition of a theme or sequence of chords over which there are certain variations). Within these structures, Schoenberg used as his building blocks small fragments or motifs that consisted of a handful of notes

Pierrot and Columbine, played by Alexander Zaitsev and Mara Galeazzi, look to the moon in a production of *Pierrot lunaire* at the Royal Opera House, London, in 2007.

with a distinctive structure of tone intervals, which could then be subjected to freer atonal treatment.

A new music takes shape
In 1912, the Viennese actress Albertine Zehme commissioned Schoenberg to write a song cycle, setting verses from *Pierrot lunaire: rondels bergamasques* by Belgian symbolist poet Albert Giraud. Schoenberg chose 21 of Giraud's 50 poems for his *Pierrot lunaire*, using the German translation by Otto Erich Hartleben. He saw the work, though, not as a collection of songs sung in sequence but as a melodrama. It was to be a dramatic recitation accompanied by a small ensemble of instruments, in a "light, ironical, satirical tone," with echoes of both the Italian comedy form *commedia dell'arte*, from which the Pierrot character originated, and contemporary cabaret performances.

The poems present surreal and often grotesque glimpses of the world of the commedia dell'arte. Their mystical quality is matched by Schoenberg's settings. Without tonality, the music creates an

> To call any relation of tones atonal is as little justified as to designate a relation of colors aspectral or acomplementary. Such an antithesis does not exist.
> **Arnold Schoenberg**

Audience and orchestra fight in a 1913 cartoon from the newspaper *Die Zeit* titled "The upcoming Schoenberg concert," satirizing the anger that the composer's new music could provoke.

unsettling atmosphere, and the dissonance of the harmonies suits the strange and sometimes violent imagery. Like the poems, the music is highly structured. Hartleben's translation is in a German rondel form: each poem has 13 lines split into three stanzas. Line one is repeated at lines seven and 13, and line two is repeated at line eight. Schoenberg's settings employ a variety of similarly strict formal techniques. Schoenberg uses small motif "cells" of notes as the basis for forms such as passacaglias and canons, presenting them in various guises: transposed up or down, in retrograde (played backward), and inversion (upside down).

The piece is written for a quintet playing seven instruments: piano, violin (also playing viola), cello, clarinet, and flute (also playing piccolo). The combination of this pared-down ensemble and Schoenberg's stark scoring and atonality provided a sharp contrast to the Romanticism of the 19th century and proved that there was a viable alternative to tonality. ∎

Sprechstimme

Although the vocal line in *Pierrot lunaire* is usually performed by a soprano, Schoenberg did not intend it to be sung but rather recited, like the cabaret songs and melodramas that were popular at the time, in a style he called *sprechstimme* ("speaking voice"). He first used the technique in his cantata *Gurre-Lieder* but realized its full potential in *Pierrot lunaire*. Here, the vocal line is notated conventionally, with precise indications of both rhythm and pitch, but sprechstimme is indicated by small crosses on the stems of the notes. Later, Schoenberg abandoned specific pitch indications for sprechstimme, replacing the five-line staff with a single line and no clef.

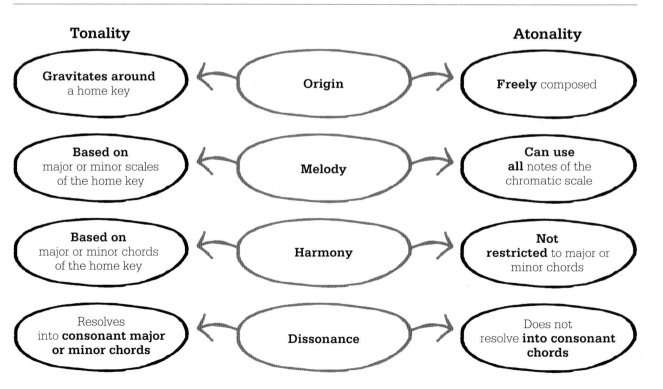

Tonality		Atonality
Gravitates around a home key	Origin	Freely composed
Based on major or minor scales of the home key	Melody	Can use all notes of the chromatic scale
Based on major or minor chords of the home key	Harmony	Not restricted to major or minor chords
Resolves into consonant major or minor chords	Dissonance	Does not resolve into consonant chords

I HAVEN'T UNDERSTOOD A BAR OF MUSIC IN MY LIFE, BUT I HAVE FELT IT

LE SACRE DU PRINTEMPS (1913), IGOR STRAVINSKY

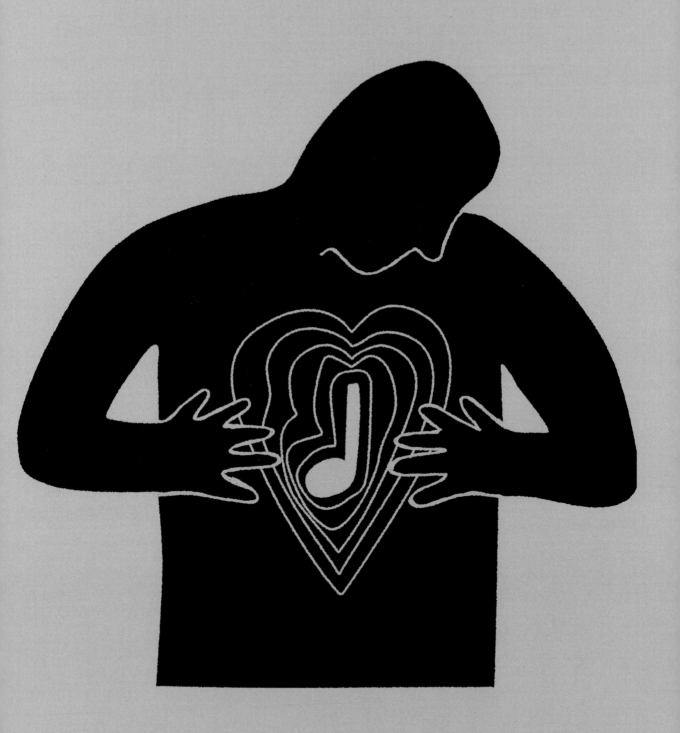

IN CONTEXT

FOCUS
**Primitivism
and modernism**

BEFORE
1889 Debussy is inspired to experiment with the "exotic" sound worlds of non-Western musical traditions after hearing Javanese Gamelan at the *Exposition Universelle*.

AFTER
1923 Darius Milhaud's ballet *La Création du monde*, inspired by African folk mythology, premieres in Paris.

1949 Olivier Messiaen's *Turangalîla-Symphonie*—his most famous large-scale orchestral work—draws inspiration from *Le Sacre du printemps*.

Although the turn of the 20th century saw an increasing fascination with the exotic, no music really prefigured the explosion of violent primitivism that was *Le Sacre du printemps* (*The Rite of Spring*). Igor Stravinsky's ballet portrayed a brutal scenario—a pagan ritual in which a sacrificial virgin danced herself to death to "propitiate the god of spring."

The work was first staged by Sergei Diaghilev's Ballets Russes in Paris in 1913, choreographed by Vaslav Nijinsky—a performance that famously led to a riot. From its plot alone, it is not difficult to see why. Part one introduces a strange and primitive world in which a succession of rituals takes place. These are characterized by wild energy (as in "The Augurs of Spring/Dances of the Young Girls," "Ritual of Abduction," "Spring Rounds," and "Ritual of the Rival Tribes")—until the arrival of the Sage, who stoops to kiss the earth, prompting an orgylike "Dance of the Earth." In part two, as night falls, a sacrificial victim is chosen from among the "Mystic Circles of Young Girls" and then "glorified" by

her peers in another frenzied ritual. Slower pieces follow—"Evocation" and "Ritual Action of the Ancestors," after which the victim dances wildly for the onlookers until she dies of exhaustion.

Folk origins

Stravinsky may have been inspired by Sergei Gorodetsky's poem "Yarila," in which two priestesses sacrifice a young linden tree to a sage. The concept was developed in collaboration with Nikolai Roerich, a leading artist-scholar with expertise in Russian folklore. While many of the details of this scenario have some basis in folk history, its main event is fictitious: human sacrifice was certainly not a feature of Slavic folk religion. The savagery of *Le Sacre* was intended to shock and served to debunk the romanticized notion of ancient folklore so prevalent in the arts by the end of the 19th century.

If the brutality of the subject matter was exaggerated for its shock value, the music was no less so. Stravinsky drew a significant amount of thematic material in the work from existing Lithuanian folk tunes, but these melodies were so

---

Igor Stravinsky

Born near St. Petersburg in 1882, Stravinsky's formative influence was Nikolai Rimsky-Korsakov, his teacher from 1902–1908—however, Stravinsky continually assimilated new styles. His first ballet for Diaghilev, *L'Oiseau de feu*, catapulted him to fame at its Paris premiere in 1910. His early aesthetic was in line with late Romanticism, as was popular in Russia, but his musical language developed from Experimentalism in the 1910s into distinctive Neoclassicism after his wartime exile in Switzerland. Stravinsky and his family settled down in

France in 1920, but after the deaths of his wife, mother, and daughter (shortly before World War II), Stravinsky emigrated to the United States, where his later works would incorporate serial technique. In spite of his failing health, his creative spirit remained strong until two years before his death, in 1971.

Other key works

1910–1911 *Petrushka*
1922–1923 *Octet*
1930 *Symphony of Psalms*
1953–1957 *Agon*

See also: *Prélude à l'après-midi d'un faune* 228–231 ▪ Ives's Symphony No. 4 254–255 ▪ *Parade* 256–257 ▪ *Ionisation* 268–269

Dancers of the Ballets Russes pose in costume for the first performance of *Le Sacre du printemps* at the Théâtre des Champs-Élysées, Paris, in 1913.

reworked as to make the finished product uniquely his. While some of the folk tunes Stravinsky used already contained irregularities of phrase length, rhythm, or meter, he greatly exaggerated these irregularities and introduced many new ones, often fragmenting his melodies into units of unequal length, mixed up and repeated in seemingly unpredictable ways.

Irregularity and brutality

The savagery of Stravinsky's work is most strikingly realized in the composer's use of rhythm, where irregularity is also a defining feature. The rhythms are frequently grouped into bars of differing lengths, but even when the meter looks regular on the page, he often calls for notes to be stressed in unpredictable places, to negate any sense of order and expectation. One

example of this is the opening to the "Augurs of Spring," in which a repeated chord is heavily accented in what seem to be arbitrary places but are actually determined by a mathematical pattern imperceptible to the listener.

Stravinsky's rhythms often take the form of *ostinatos* (short, repeating patterns), made the more compelling by the perpetual driving pulse often underlying them, usually at too fast a speed to be called a beat. "Glorification of the Chosen One," for example, is mostly driven by persistent eighth-note movement, yet in the wildest sections of the "Sacrificial Dance," continuous 16th-note movement is the "motor" behind the music.

Stravinsky also uses dissonance to create a sense of savagery. While the folk melodies woven through the piece are based on recognizable scales (or "modes"), the harmony tends to be dissonant—an effect often achieved by combining two modes (called "bimodality"). This can be heard in the dialogue

between the first two melodies—the opening bassoon melody uses a mode containing only the white notes of the piano, but after around 40 seconds it is juxtaposed against a new melody in a completely unrelated mode (containing mostly black notes). The accompaniment bears little relation to either mode but draws freely upon all the notes. The effect in many ways feels more dissonant than if the piece was completely atonal, because of the clashing of two musical methods.

Percussive techniques

All other features are rendered the more barbaric by Stravinsky's orchestration. He calls upon huge forces—large string, wind, and brass sections are joined by a huge battery of percussion instruments. His tendency toward extremes is explicit from the opening bassoon melody, pitched uncomfortably high in its register. Even more striking is the "percussive" manner in which he writes for the whole orchestra, especially the strings, who are often called upon to play »

[*Le Sacre*] had the effect of an explosion that so scattered the elements of musical language that they could never again be put together as before.
Donald Jay Grout
Music historian

Differences between Romanticism and Modernism

Romanticism   **Modernism**

Composers **built** on historical tradition.

Composers **consciously break** with historical tradition.

Melodies are proportionally **structured**.

Melodies are fragmented or **irregular** and sometimes absent.

Dissonances are **resolved**. Uses one scale at a time.

Dissonances are **freely used**. May employ different scales simultaneously.

Rhythm is **rational** and ordered, following regular meter.

Rhythm is **irregular** and unpredictable, with unexpected emphases.

Orchestra uses **conventional** playing techniques.

Orchestra uses **experimental** playing techniques.

passages of detached notes using repeated, short "down-bows" (essentially hitting rather than stroking the strings); on numerous other occasions, they play *pizzicato* (plucking the strings) or *col legno* (playing using the wood or the hard tip of the bow)—both of which create a more incisive, percussive effect. Apart from this prevalence of staccato, articulated styles of playing, Stravinsky uses many other unusual techniques, such as scraping the metal triangle stick across the surface of the tam-tam, or the French horns playing with their "bells up" in order to increase the volume and impact, and so

on. Conversely, softer passages sometimes call upon mysterious-sounding string harmonics.

Dramatic premiere

The riot that broke out at the premiere in 1913 made the ballet infamous, but this was not just because of the music—in spite of its challenging nature—or even Vaslav Nijinsky's revolutionary choreography, although that certainly shocked, too. At the time, Paris's "high society" attended the ballet expecting stylized elegance. What they got were "knock-kneed and long-braided Lolitas jumping up and down," in Stravinsky's

own words, culminating in the Sacrifical Dance's "ecstatic, irregular jerks" of "primitive hysteria," according to the dance critic André Levinson. Other spectators, not members of Paris's elite, had anticipated the work's novelty and had come for it—some, indeed, courtesy of free tickets handed out by Diaghilev. Hisses from the boxes were quickly and loudly condemned by the supportive faction; before long, the music was all but drowned out by those on both sides. Some spectators claimed that the furore began before the dancers even came on stage. The dancer

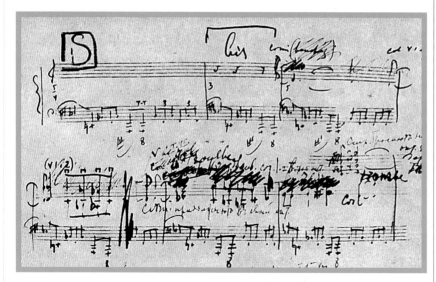

The last page of Stravinsky's handwritten score for *Le Sacre* shows the chaotic nature of the piece, with some huge intervals between notes.

Lydia Sokolova, for example, later reflected: "As soon as it was known that the conductor was there, the uproar began." Some accounts suggest that blows were even exchanged and that as many as 40 audience members were arrested for violence and disorder.

A year later, however, *Le Sacre* was performed in Paris without dancers, and it was the greatest success of Stravinsky's career. This fact may have contributed to the composer's later tendency to prefer *Le Sacre* as a concert piece. For Diaghilev, however, any publicity was good publicity; he later claimed that *Le Sacre*'s premiere was "exactly what [he] wanted."

Stravinskian legacy
The influence of *Le Sacre* on subsequent music is hard to overstate. This is most strikingly seen in Stravinsky's revolutionary use of rhythm, which surpassed anything seen before. Stravinskian "motor rhythms" would drive the minimalism of the 1960s–1980s as much as they permeated film scores and influenced popular styles. Stravinsky's particular style of modernism influenced later composers in the trends of primitivism, exoticism, and experimental composition.

Perhaps because Stravinsky's musical style soon evolved in a neoclassical direction, the "Stravinskian aesthetic" was not only to influence future neoclassical composers but also to reenergize the performing styles of Baroque and Classical music in a way that can still be heard today. ∎

I heard, and I wrote what I heard. I was the vessel through which *Le Sacre* passed.
Igor Stravinsky

Diaghilev and the Ballets Russes

Sergei Diaghilev founded his ballet company in Paris in 1909. For two decades until his death, the Ballets Russes performed regularly in Paris, throughout Europe, and in the Americas. While the company prominently featured highly skilled Russian dancers, and often showcased Russian composers and works, they never performed in Russia.

In stark contrast to the conservative Russian artistic culture from which he hailed, the progressive Diaghilev was responsible for commissioning groundbreaking new work from the leading composers of the day. Chief among them was Igor Stravinsky, whose commissions are among his most significant pieces. He also commissioned works from Sergei Prokofiev, Erik Satie, and three members of the Parisian group of composers known as *Les Six*. Well-known artists often designed sets or costumes for his productions, such as Pablo Picasso, Henri Matisse, and Coco Chanel.

Sergei Diaghilev (right) greets Igor Stravinsky at Croydon Airport, London, UK, in 1926. The pair collaborated on four ballets, including *Le Sacre du printemps*.

STAND UP AND TAKE YOUR DISSONANCE LIKE A MAN

SYMPHONY NO. 4 (1916), CHARLES EDWARD IVES

IN CONTEXT

FOCUS
Collage

BEFORE
1787 Wolfgang Amadeus Mozart simultaneously employs four separate orchestras in different time signatures for *Don Giovanni*.

1912 Igor Stravinsky "pastes" a chord of a dominant seventh on E-flat over a chord of F-flat major in *Le Sacre du printemps* and causes audience outrage.

AFTER
1928 Henry Cowell composes his *Concerto for Piano and Orchestra*, whose three movements are titled "Polyharmony," "Tone Cluster," and "Counter Rhythm."

1967–1969 Luciano Berio composes his *Sinfonia*, the third movement of which is a collage of musical quotations.

Many of the manuscripts of the American composer Charles Ives consist of a patchwork of cutouts pasted over new ideas. Ives often raided his own compositions for inspiration, reusing parts of them or sticking them into others. As a result, many of his compositions sound like collage—different musical fragments layered on top of each other. Many of these were scraps of music that he heard in his youth— hymns of the Pilgrim Fathers, gospel tunes, and brass band music. Ives loved to listen to the amateur

Why tonality as such should be thrown out for good I can't see. Why it should always be present I can't see. It depends, it seems to me … on what one is trying to do.
Charles Ives

music making in his hometown of Danbury, Connecticut—especially the local band and its rivals from nearby towns, which, on national holidays, would assemble within earshot of each other. Ives not only enjoyed the cacophony of different tunes being played simultaneously but later set out to reproduce in his own works exactly what he heard, as in his *Holidays* symphony.

Literary influences
Ives lived a mere 150 miles (240 km) from Concord, Massachusetts—the epicenter of the Transcendentalist literary movement that included Ralph Waldo Emerson, Nathaniel Hawthorne, Louisa M. Alcott, and Henry David Thoreau. Their works promoted the belief that true knowledge could not be attained by studying religion or academia but rather came from reflection and contemplation of the self. Inspired by their ideas, Ives published his Piano Sonata No. 2, "Concord," in 1919, comprising movements named for each of the key writers.

In the early 1920s—during which time Ives worked alongside fellow experimental composers Henry Cowell and Carl Ruggles to spearhead progressive American

See also: *St. Matthew Passion* 98–105 ▪ *Prélude à l'après-midi d'un faune* 228–231 ▪ *Le Sacre de printemps* 246–251 ▪ *A Child of Our Time* 284–285 ▪ Appalachian Spring 286–287

Henry Cowell, who worked with Ives, was one of the most innovative of the experimental composers, as evidenced by his *Mosaic Quartet* (1935).

music—Ives began working on his gigantic Fourth Symphony, the apotheosis of his entire output. The influence of the Transcendentalists continued here, as Ives based the second movement ("Comedy") on Hawthorne's short story "The Celestial Railroad"—a reworking of John Bunyan's allegorical work, *The Pilgrim's Progress.* "The Celestial Railroad" tells of a railway journey from the chaos and mundaneness of everyday life.

Layered complexity

Ives's multilayered composition style was at its best in his Fourth Symphony, in which simultaneous, cacophonous eruptions of sound place the listener alongside the pilgrims as fellow travelers inside that train. Ives also utilized lighter, "offstage" sounds—ethereal flutes, a few strings, harp, a quarter-tone piano, and women's voices. In the second movement, Ives gathered a variety of sources to make his famous layers: hymns, and gospel tunes, brass bands, and popular songs to represent small-town life; as well as atonality, polyrhythms, and grinding dissonances to convey Hawthorne's "iron horse" locomotive heaving into motion.

The first movement, scored for a chamber orchestra, begins boldly—*maestoso*, played with majesty and triumph—before moving into a quieter passage. The first two movements premiered in New York in 1927 and were the only parts of his great symphony that Ives heard performed in concert. The simple third movement (the fugue) and the fourth, a rhythmically challenging piece that required an extra percussion ensemble, did not premiere until 1965, 11 years after the composer's death. ▪

Charles Edward Ives

Born in Danbury, Connecticut, in 1874, Ives was schooled by his father in band music, church hymns, and the music of J.S. Bach. After four years of musical studies at Yale, he joined the Mutual Life Insurance Company and remained in the insurance business for the next 31 years. Ives believed that his insurance work was an important life experience that contributed to his compositions.

Ives also worked part time as an organist in New York City and spent every spare moment composing. In 1908, Ives married Harmony Twichell. Her influence resulted in an outburst of experimental compositions, mostly written before 1915. Many of Ives's pieces, however, did not reach a wider audience until later in his life, after hand tremors and diabetes had forced him to retire from composition. He died of a stroke in 1954.

Other key works

1904–1913 *Holidays* symphony
1906 *The Unanswered Question*
1910–1914 *Three Places in New England*
1911–1915 *Concord Sonata*

I HAVE NEVER WRITTEN A NOTE I DIDN'T MEAN

PARADE (1917), ERIK SATIE

IN CONTEXT

FOCUS
Dadaism in music

BEFORE
1881 *Le Chat Noir* cabaret
club opens in Montmartre,
in Paris. It becomes a meeting
place for avant-garde artists,
writers, and musicians.

1907 Pablo Picasso paints
Les Demoiselles d'Avignon, in
which he develops the ideas
behind Cubism, which will
influence Satie.

AFTER
1924 Satie's ballet *Relâche*
includes a surrealist film
sequence by French director
René Clair.

1930 Jean Cocteau produces
La Voix humaine, a monologue
that Poulenc later turns into
an opera.

At the end of the 19th
century, a new musical
nationalism arose in
France. Young composers sought
to free themselves from European
traditions and imbue their art with
a sense of French, and particularly
Parisian, culture. This led to
two strands of new music: the
impressionist work of composers
such as Debussy and Ravel, which
had parallels in the art of the
period, and the music of Dadaist
composers, which celebrated
the absurd and challenged the
definition of what music might be.

An early example of Dadaism in
music was the work of Erik Satie.
His *Trois Gymnopédies*, the first of
which was published in 1888, with
their focus on repetition of rhythm
and harmony and use of unresolved
dissonances, are both hypnotic
and static. Partly inspired by
medieval French music, they reject
musical development in favor of
the juxtaposition of ideas. Debussy
was so impressed by the pieces
that he orchestrated two of them.

Surrealism in music

Satie was influential among young
French composers and well known
to other artists. When Jean Cocteau
heard his *Trois morceaux en forme
de poire* (*Three Pieces in the Shape
of a Pear*), a piano suite for piano
duet, in 1903, he commissioned
Satie to compose the music to a
ballet that eventually combined the
talents of Sergei Diaghilev's Ballet
Russes, choreographer Léonide
Massine, and Pablo Picasso. The
work, *Parade*, was described in

Inspired by his work as a cabaret
pianist, Satie incorporated jazz
influences into some of his music,
including the Ragtime movement from
"Parade," later transcribed for solo piano.

See also: *Prélude à l'après-midi d'un faune* 228–231 ▪ *Quartet for the End of Time* 282–283 ▪ *4'33"* 302–305 ▪ *In C* 312–313 ▪ *Einstein on the Beach* 321

Noise-making instruments in *Parade*

Ticker tape

Pistol

Typewriter

Satie used a variety of "found sounds" in *Parade* in order to add unusual percussive elements.

Foghorn

Milk bottle

Airplane propellor

Guillaume Apollinaire's program notes as a "kind of surrealism"—three years before the eponymous art movement. Evoking the streets of Paris, the music was scored for "noise-making" instruments, such as a typewriter and a foghorn.

Influential figure

It was after this, in 1917, that Satie formed Les Nouveaux Jeunes, a collective of six young French composers. Under the influence of Cocteau, the group became *Les Six*, whose different styles were united in their opposition to German Romanticism.

Satie also influenced much later composers such as John Cage. In 1963, Cage published Satie's

Vexations (c.1893–1894), a piano piece that may have been a joke—the minimalist music consists of a bass theme and accompanying chords above it—which was never published in Satie's lifetime. Satie's score bore the inscription: "In order to play the theme 840 times in succession, it would be advisable to prepare oneself beforehand, and in the deepest silence, by serious stillness." Played by a relay team of six, the first performance took more than 18 hours, although it has since been performed by a single pianist. Some critics saw the piece as pure experimentation; others as a reaction against Wagner. In the 20th century, it became a key work for conceptual artists. ▪

Erik Satie

Born in Honfleur, France, in 1866, Satie was a natural rebel. He spent two periods at the Paris Conservatoire, first as a pianist and then as a composer, but left to join the military in 1886. Soon discharged, he moved to Montmartre in Paris, where he became a regular patron of *Le Chat Noir* club.

In 1888, Satie published *Gymnopédies*, innovative piano pieces. Always seen in a gray velvet suit (he had seven of them), he lacked a steady income and so resorted to writing and playing cabaret music. By 1912, he began to receive more attention from critics, especially for his earlier piano pieces. Commissions followed, including two ballets and the multimedia *Sports et divertissements*. After his death from cirrhosis of the liver in 1925, a great many unknown works, including *Vexations*, came to light, found in his chaotic apartment.

Other key works

1888 *Gymnopédies*
1914 *Sports et divertissements*
1917 *Sonatine bureaucratique*
1924 *Relâche*

LIFE IS A LOT LIKE JAZZ ... IT'S BETTER WHEN YOU IMPROVISE

RHAPSODY IN BLUE (1924), GEORGE GERSHWIN

IN CONTEXT

FOCUS
Ragtime and jazz influences

BEFORE
1895 Ernest Hogan publishes "La Pas Ma La," the first ragtime sheet music.

1908 Debussy publishes the ragtime-inspired piano piece *Golliwogg's Cakewalk*.

AFTER
1927 Maurice Ravel completes his jazz-inspired Violin Sonata No. 2, which includes a second movement called "Blues."

1971 Polish composer Krzysztof Penderecki and American jazz trumpeter Don Cherry perform the scoreless *Actions for Free Jazz orchestra*.

The start of the 20th century brought new genres and ideas to American music. Many of them came from African Americans, recently freed from enslavement, whose dances contained infectious and lively rhythms that would grow into ragtime piano and marches. African American ideas combined with Caribbean influences to evolve into various forms of jazz.

As jazz spread to Europe, classical composers were drawn to it, but the improvisational nature of this new type of music was not a natural match for the carefully notated and rehearsed world of the concert hall. In the United States, George Gershwin managed to bridge the gap and incorporate jazz on an orchestral scale with *Rhapsody in Blue*. Others followed, including composers who have

See also: *Prélude à l'après-midi d'un faune* 228–231 ▪ *Parade* 256–257 ▪ *Threnody for the Victims of Hiroshima* 310–311

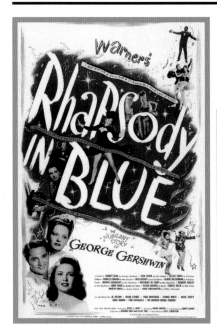

tried to achieve the seemingly impossible by melding composed and improvisational music.

Ragtime reigns

In 1853, the American composer Louis Moreau Gottschalk recreated African American banjo-playing techniques with amazing accuracy in *The Banjo*, a popular virtuoso piano piece. However, it was the rise of ragtime, and especially the work of African American Scott Joplin, that brought an energetic new flavor to classical music in the early years of the 20th century.

The term "ragtime" referred to the music's ragged rhythm, known as "syncopation," in which a steady beat is accentuated by surprising weaker off beats. This unfamiliar style captured the dynamic spirit of the New World and, in discarding the long phrasings and flexible tempos of the 19th century, ushered in the sense of a more modern, mechanized world.

Gershwin's best-known large-scale work was used as the title for a film about his life, made eight years after his death in 1937. Adding to the film's sense of realism, some of Gershwin's friends starred in it as themselves.

Ragtime piano swept America, but it was not until John Philip Sousa, an American of German, Spanish, and Portuguese descent, brought his syncopated brass-band marches across the Atlantic in 1900 that ragtime really had an impact on European music. Coming at a time when young composers were looking for ways to break out of the traditions of Romanticism, the new sound, with its direct and acerbic style, quickly took off among the French avant-garde.

Composers such as Erik Satie and Claude Debussy heard Sousa's music at the 1900 Paris Exposition and responded by experimenting with ragtime. While Satie used it ironically in works such as the song *La Diva de l'Empire*, Debussy pitted it against the *Liebestod* motif from Wagner's *Tristan und Isolde* in his *Golliwogg's Cakewalk*, as if to announce the passing of the old guard. The modernist significance of ragtime, with its implicit »

I frequently hear music in the heart of noise.
George Gershwin

Ragtime and Joplin

For such a popular music form, ragtime was a surprisingly short-lived phenomenon. Although first adopted by musicians unversed in musical notation, it started to spread widely after 1895, when Ernest Hogan published the sheet music for his dance song "La Pas Ma La." Within a few years, ragtime music had become popular across North America, in part thanks to Scott Joplin, whose *Maple Leaf Rag*, published in 1899, earned him the title "King of Ragtime." Joplin, born around 1868, wrote a string of popular ragtime piano pieces, earning him enough from royalties to buy him the time to write two operas, including *Treemonisha* (1911). The newly emerging, more improvisational jazz scene overshadowed ragtime, which by the time of Joplin's death, in 1917, was essentially a part of musical history.

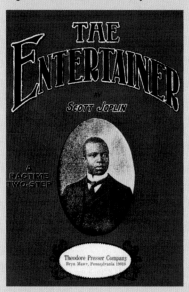

Joplin's 1902 piano piece *The Entertainer* headed a 1970s ragtime revival, led by the pianist and conductor Joshua Rifkin.

rejection of a white European tradition, was also seized on by Igor Stravinsky, recently settled in France, in 1919, when he created his dissonant *Piano-Rag-Music*, which pulls apart and rearranges ragtime like a cubist painting.

Jazz meets classical

By the 1920s, ragtime had been superseded in the United States by more improvisational and flexible styles of jazz, particularly in jazz dance bands. One of the most popular bands was led by Paul Whiteman, who relied on carefully orchestrated arrangements, using a large ensemble, rather than improvisation. He made continued attempts to introduce the concertgoing public to the new jazz style, which he considered to be the first truly American music, giving performances at New York's prestigious Aeolian Hall. It was for one of these events, titled "An Experiment in Modern Music," that Whiteman commissioned a young, successful songwriter named George Gershwin to compose a piano concerto. When first approached, Gershwin turned

You might lose your spontaneity and, instead of composing first-rate Gershwin, end up with second-rate Ravel.
Maurice Ravel
to George Gershwin

down the offer, but Whiteman informed the press that he was writing the concerto anyway, and so Gershwin's hand was forced.

Rhapsody in Blue premiered on February 12, 1924 and was instantly acclaimed by both classical and jazz audiences, which included Sousa, now the elder statesman of ragtime, and the Russian composer Sergei Rachmaninoff. The piece itself was only sketched out by the inexperienced Gershwin, who left the orchestration to Whiteman's

pianist and arranger Ferde Grofé. The unmistakable opening clarinet *glissando* was also not Gershwin's own invention but rather that of Whiteman's clarinetist. Further orchestrations by Grofé, in 1926 and 1942, were to fix *Rhapsody in Blue* firmly in the classical repertoire.

Following the success of his concerto, Gershwin traveled to Paris to study composition. He hoped to work with composers such as Nadia Boulanger and Maurice Ravel, but all potential tutors refused, concerned that such studies would endanger Gershwin's own style. Returning to New York, he started on his most ambitious stage project, the opera *Porgy and Bess*, which had its premiere on Broadway, in 1935. Styled as a "folk opera," it drew heavily on New York jazz and African American folk music such as spirituals and the blues in songs such as *It Ain't Necessarily So* and *Summertime*. The opera also incorporated many classical techniques, such as leitmotifs (themes introduced to identify characters) and recitative (speechlike song), and even elements of the polyrhythms and

African American genres that changed the course of classical music

The cakewalk
Enslaved plantation workers first danced the cakewalk, strutting in couples to syncopated rhythms in parody of their white owners. The dance won European attention when performed at the 1889 Paris Exposition.

Ragtime
The music of African American composer Scott Joplin—such as the famous *Maple Leaf Rag*—and the marches of John Philip Sousa brought the ragtime style out of a purely black idiom and into the mainstream.

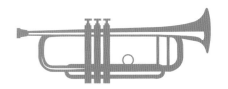

Jazz
Arising from the music of enslaved African Americans in the South, jazz was an improvised form that drew on work songs, marches, and dance rhythms. It was popularized in New Orleans in the 1890s.

George Gershwin

Born the second son of Jewish immigrants in 1898, Brooklyn-born Gershwin became interested in music at the age of 10. By the time he was 15, he had a job as a "song plugger" in New York's Tin Pan Alley, playing the latest sheet music for prospective customers. He published his first song in 1916, but his big break came in 1920 when Broadway star Al Jolson performed the Gershwin song *Swanee*, after which he was invited to collaborate on a number of Broadway musicals. Following the success of *Rhapsody in Blue*, Gershwin focused as much on classical traditions as jazz, with compositions such as the opera *Porgy and Bess* and the Piano Concerto in F running alongside shows such as *Girl Crazy* and *Funny Face,* which he wrote with his lyricist brother Ira, and film scores, including *Shall We Dance*. He died in 1937 of a brain tumor.

Other key works

1925 Piano Concerto in F
1927 *Funny Face*
1935 *Porgy and Bess*
1937 *Shall We Dance*

dissonance that Gershwin admired so much in the work of the Austrian modernist composer Alban Berg.

A closer alliance

In Europe, jazz continued to influence classical composers, most particularly those who skirted the middle-European cabaret scene. In Germany, the Austrian composer Ernst Krenek's 1927 opera *Jonny Plays*, which tells the story of a jazz violinist, was an instant success, with its then-subversive portrayal of jazz as a challenge to European tradition. Similarly, the German composer Kurt Weill used jazz elements in *The Threepenny Opera*—produced in Berlin, in 1928—to such effect that *The Ballad of Mack the Knife* became a jazz standard.

In the 1930s and 1940s, the boundaries between jazz and classical works became more fluid. Jazz clarinetist Benny Goodman commissioned *Contrasts*, a piece for clarinet, violin, and piano, from Bela Bartók in 1938, while Igor Stravinsky's 1945 Ebony Concerto was written for another jazz clarinetist, Woody Herman.

Insistence on a black cast for *Porgy and Bess*—seen here on Broadway in 1942—made Gershwin the subject of criticism and prevented the opera from being performed in opera houses.

This cross-fertilization between jazz and classical did not always meet with approval. In 1957, the American composer Gunther Schuller, wary of unsatisfying classical-jazz collaborations (such as Benny Goodman playing Mozart) and unconvinced by the jazz he found in composers such as Ravel and Shostakovich, suggested a new genre—the "Third Stream." This required performers to be proficient in both classical and jazz so that composed and improvised music could sit side by side. Schuller's ideas influenced jazz musicians, such as John Lewis, Bill Russo, and Charles Mingus, who would go on to lead the avant-garde "free jazz" style of the 1960s, while, in the classical tradition, composers such as Hans Werner Henze, in Germany, and Krzysztof Penderecki, in Poland, took up the challenge, including free jazz in their works. ■

A MAD EXTRAVAGANZA AT THE EDGE OF THE ABYSS
LES BICHES (1924), FRANCIS POULENC

Francis Poulenc's ballet *Les Biches* premiered with the Ballets Russes in Monte Carlo in 1924. Choreographed by Bronislava Nijinska, it consisted of eight dances for 16 female and three male dancers. The title was a play on the word *biche*, which means "doe" or "female deer," but was also 1920s' slang for "coquette." The ballet has no narrative: each dance uses simple melodies to evoke the spirited flirtations of youth with light and whimsical musical language.

Les Six

Simplicity and sharp humor were qualities favored by Poulenc and his fellow composers in the group dubbed *Les Six*—Georges Auric, Louis Durey, Arthur Honegger, Darius Milhaud, and Germaine Tailleferre. Influenced by the avant-garde compositions of Erik Satie and the art and writings of Jean Cocteau, they disdained both the Wagnerian emotionalism of the 19th century and the musical impressionism of Debussy. They sought to be of their time, drawing inspiration from music halls, fairgrounds, and American jazz. Several went on to write for films.

Poulenc's later work lacked this playfulness. Following the success of *Les Biches*, he wrote the song cycle *Figure humaine*. Composed during the Nazi occupation of France, this set to music a defiant ode to liberty and other poems by the surrealist writer Paul Éluard. ∎

Alice Nikitina and Serge Lifar practice for the Ballets Russes' 1924 production of *Les Biches*. The pair also danced together in Henri Sauguet's flirtatious *La Chatte* ("The Cat," 1927).

See also: *The Nutcracker* 190 ▪ *Prélude à l'après-midi d'un faune* 228–231 ▪ *Le Sacre du printemps* 246–251 ▪ *Parade* 256–257 ▪ *Appalachian Spring* 286–287

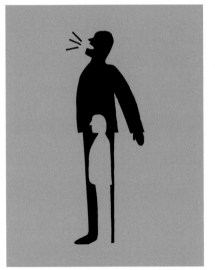

I COME WITH THE YOUTHFUL SPIRIT OF MY COUNTRY, WITH YOUTHFUL MUSIC
SINFONIETTA (1926), LEOŠ JANÁČEK

IN CONTEXT

FOCUS
Czech nationalism

BEFORE
1879 Smetana's cycle of symphonic poems, *Má vlast* (*My Country*), is an expression of musical nationalism, each poem evoking a different Czech place or legend.

1886 Czech and Moravian folk music inspires Dvořák's *Slavonic Dances* for piano duet, whose popularity helps to launch his international career.

AFTER
1938 Janáček's pupil Pavel Haas's opera *Šarlatán* (*The Charlatan*) premieres in Brno, influenced by Moravian folk music and Gregorian chant.

1955 Bohuslav Martinů's chamber cantata, *The Opening of the Wells*, is the first of a cycle of cantatas inspired by his native Moravian highlands.

Czech composer Leoš Janáček's *Sinfonietta* has an unforgettable, rousing start, with more than two minutes of brass fanfares. This then gives way to four further movements— each evoking parts of Janáček's native Brno—that culminate in a final round of fanfares from the orchestra's expanded brass section. Originally titled *Military Sinfonietta*, the piece captures the brash sound and atmosphere of a military band, including a blazing trombone solo and bold solo trumpets.

Musical salute
A sinfonietta is an orchestral work, shorter and lighter in tone than a symphony. The 71-year-old Janáček composed his for a gymnastics festival in Prague in the summer of 1926, two years before his death. For the patriotic Janáček, his work saluted his nation's rebirth as an independent country following centuries of subjugation under the Habsburg Empire. Dedicated to the Czech armed forces, the *Sinfonietta*

My *Military Sinfonietta* with the fanfares will be played at the Sokol rally. Do you remember the Písek fanfares?
Leoš Janáček

celebrated "the contemporary free man, his spiritual beauty and joy, his strength, courage, and determination to fight for victory."

Another source of inspiration, however, was Janáček's passionate friendship with a married woman 37 years his junior, Kamila Stösslová. The composer reportedly had the idea for the fanfares that open and close the *Sinfonietta* after sitting with her in a park listening to a military band give a concert. ∎

See also: *The Bartered Bride* 206 ▪ Dvořák's Symphony No. 9 212–215 ▪ Bartók's String Quartet No. 5 270–271 ▪ *Spartacus* 309

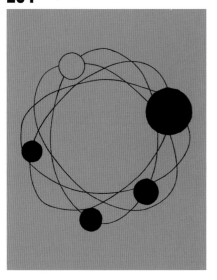

MUSICALLY, THERE IS NOT A SINGLE CENTER OF GRAVITY IN THIS PIECE
SYMPHONIE, OP. 21 (1927–1928), ANTON VON WEBERN

IN CONTEXT

FOCUS
Serialism

BEFORE
1908 Arnold Schoenberg enters new and modernist harmonic territory in the last two movements of his String Quartet No. 2.

1921–1923 In his Suite for Piano, Op. 25, Schoenberg evolves a complete musical statement from a chosen sequence of the 12 notes of the Western chromatic scale.

AFTER
1932 Schoenberg completes the first two acts of the first-ever fully 12-note opera, *Moses und Aron*.

1955 Pierre Boulez's *Le marteau sans maître* ("The hammer without a master") is the first masterpiece of the "post-serial" music championed by the new, Webern-influenced avant-garde generation.

Since Arnold Schoenberg (1874–1951) developed his method of composing works "with 12 notes related only to each other," serial music has remained contentious territory. Although the terms "serial" and "12-note" are sometimes used interchangeably, they emphasize subtle musical differences. "Twelve-tone music" is a mistranslation of the word *Zwölftonmusik*: in German, *Ton* can mean "note," "tone," or "sound." Serialism, on the other hand, means "notes deployed in series." In that sense, argued Anton von Webern, Schoenberg's former pupil, serialism was deeply rooted in the musical tradition. The overlapping repetitions of a "round" song like "Frère Jacques" or "London's burning" are serial music—as are a choral motet by the Renaissance master Palestrina, or a keyboard fugue by Bach.

Webern's method
Twelve-note music first developed from the "atonal" chromatic idiom explored by Webern and his contemporaries. Freedom from traditional tonality had brought exciting new possibilities—and also the risk of musical anarchy, with conventional melody or harmony now abandoned. Webern's instinct was to rationalize the situation. His 12-note method is about creating a musical work out of a "row" consisting of all 12 notes

Anton Webern (right) poses with his fellow student in Vienna, Alban Berg. Webern, Berg, and Schoenberg were the principal composers of the Second Viennese School.

See also: *Canticum Canticorum* 46–51 ▪ *The Art of Fugue* 108–111 ▪ *Pierrot lunaire* 240–245 ▪ *Gruppen* 306–307

of the Western chromatic scale, deployed in a chosen and fixed order, which can also be inverted, or reversed, or both at once. This material determines the music's linear aspect, or melody, and the row's component notes can also be superimposed to create chords, or harmony. These notes can be played for any length and in any rhythm, as long as they are played in the right order.

The short symphony

Schoenberg's 12-note idiom often resembles a modernist take on the Classical musical language of Beethoven or Haydn. Schoenberg's other celebrated pupil, Alban Berg, liked to deploy serialism as one element in an otherwise more freely composed work, as in his nostalgic, Mahler-influenced Violin Concerto (1935). Webern was a more austere composer, drawn to the spiritual purity of Renaissance choral music. The two ultra-concentrated movements of Webern's *Symphonie*, Op. 21, written for a small orchestra without double bass, together last

> Greater coherence cannot be achieved. … The entire movement thus represents in itself a double canon with retrograde motion.
> **George Benjamin**

less than 10 minutes, in a marriage of 12-note chromaticism and the "serial" spareness of Renaissance pieces, such as Palestrina's. It covers just 16 pages of music. Beethoven's First Symphony, by contrast, is more than 60 pages long.

Symphonie's first movement consists of four simultaneous musical lines, deployed in widely spaced points of sound: each line consists of a 12-note row whose last two notes overlap with the first two

of the next so that four unbroken, slowly intertwining musical chains are formed. The second movement presents a fast-moving, tightly compressed sequence of variations on an initial idea, with each of these reversing from its midway point in a mirror-image of itself. The 12-note row used by Webern here is itself symmetrical, creating a complex and self-referential work.

Clear yet complex

Compared to the teeming hyperactivity of Schoenberg's style, the spare, delicate sonorities of Webern's symphony use a similar technical method to achieve a different effect—the distilled essence of musical sound itself. British composer George Benjamin praised the symphony for its kaleidoscope-like intricacy: "Gone is the mono-directional thrust of Classical and Romantic music; in its place a world of rotations and reflections, opening myriad paths for the listener to trace through textures of luminous clarity yet beguiling ambiguity." ▪

Anton von Webern

Born in 1883, Webern was raised in Klagenfurt, in the southern Austrian region of Carinthia. He studied at Vienna University, graduating with a doctoral thesis on the Dutch Renaissance composer Heinrich Isaac. Webern studied composition under Schoenberg from 1904–1908, becoming a lifelong friend of the composer.

After 1908, Webern's work began to combine extreme chromatic harmony with unprecedented concentration

of structure: some of his musical statements were only a few seconds long. He adopted the 12-tone method in 1924 and used it until the end of his life. In 1945, Webern moved to Mittersill, Austria, for his family's safety but was accidentally and fatally shot by a member of the occupying American army.

Other key works

1908 *Passacaglia* for orchestra
1913 *Five Orchestral Pieces*
1927 String Trio, Op. 20
1938–1939 Cantata No. 1

Anton v. Webern
vor der Todeslinie

THE ONLY LOVE AFFAIR I HAVE EVER HAD WAS WITH MUSIC

PIANO CONCERTO FOR THE LEFT HAND (1929–1930), MAURICE RAVEL

During the 19th century, the concerto grew in size and scope in much the same way as the symphony. In fact, some examples, such as Ferruccio Busoni's Piano Concerto in C major, are essentially symphonies with solo parts that enhance the orchestral lines as much as they provide dramatic conflict.

New forms

With the rise of Modernism, the traditions of the concerto and the form itself were challenged, leading some composers to new avenues of expression while others clung to

Great music must come from the heart. Any music created by technique and brains alone is not worth the paper it is written on.
Maurice Ravel

traditionalism. Composers such as Elgar, Richard Strauss, and Rachmaninoff continued to focus on virtuosity in the solo part, which was balanced by a sumptuous orchestration. In contrast, Modernist composers such as Debussy, Stravinsky, and Schoenberg took a different approach. In some cases, they took Classical and Baroque music as their models but used dissonant material to create exciting neoclassical works.

Prokofiev, Bartók, and Ravel continued to write concertos that resembled the Romantic form in terms of length, orchestration, and ethos, with soloists providing dramatic conflict with the orchestra in a structure that showed off their virtuosic abilities. However, in these works, there is a far greater focus on orchestral color and nontraditional accompaniments. Wind and percussion instruments often had equal roles to the strings, and a movement might even omit strings entirely, as in Bartok's Second Piano Concerto.

Restriction and freedom

One composition that broke all conventions was Ravel's *Piano Concerto for the Left Hand*, a one-

See also: C.P.E. Bach's Flute Concerto in A major 120–121 ▪ Saint-Saëns' Piano Concerto No. 2 in G minor 179 ▪ *Pictures at an Exhibition* 207 ▪ Fauré's *Requiem* 210–211

Louis Schwizgebel performs
Ravel's *Piano Concerto for Left Hand*, accompanied by the New York Youth Symphony led by Joshua Gersen, in a 2013 performance in Carnegie Hall.

movement work with a slow-fast-slow structure lasting less than 20 minutes—usually concertos were structurally fast-slow-fast. The piece was commissioned by the Austrian pianist Paul Wittgenstein, who was shot in the elbow and lost his right arm during World War I. Wittgenstein's requirement of a solo part for left hand alone was not as restricting as it might seem. Ravel realized that with the use of his left-hand thumb for melodic material (instead of the right-hand fifth finger), it was possible to create a fuller, more focused, and less Romantic sound. With clever use of the pedal, the restrictions of using only one hand were rarely apparent.

The art of conjuring musical character through orchestration required a thorough understanding of each instrument's qualities and playing techniques and knowledge of how to blend instruments in different ranges and at different volumes. In this, Ravel was one of the great masters.

Left-handed sounds
The concerto features a large orchestra that uses low pitches and darker sounds to give the work an ominous quality—perhaps in memory of the war, the reason for the commission. Ravel's concerto also includes rhythms and harmonies influenced by jazz and blues music. The piano part is rich, spanning the entire keyboard with athletic leaps, and so complex that some pianists, such as Alfred Cortot, angered Ravel by playing with two hands. ▪

Maurice Ravel

Born to a Basque mother and a Swiss father in the Basque region of France in 1875, Maurice Ravel entered the Paris Conservatoire at the age of 14 to study piano. He later focused on composition, studying with Gabriel Fauré and becoming acquainted with Claude Debussy.

Gaining acclaim for early works, such as the *Pavane pour une infante défunte* ("Pavane for a dead princess"), and *Shéhérazade*, Ravel's subsequent failure to win the coveted Prix de Rome in 1905 caused a national scandal. Despite this, he was soon internationally recognized as a great composer. During World War I, Ravel was an ambulance driver, which limited his output. Following a successful tour of North America in 1928, Ravel received a blow to his head. He was left unable to compose, and he died of complications following surgery in 1937.

Other key works

1899 *Pavane pour une infante défunte*
1912 *Daphnis et Chloé*
1928 *Boléro*

SCIENCE ALONE CAN INFUSE MUSIC WITH YOUTHFUL VIGOR
IONISATION (1929–1931), EDGARD VARÈSE

IN CONTEXT

FOCUS
The emancipation of noise

BEFORE
1909 Marinetti publishes the *Futurist Manifesto*, celebrating a new era of speed, machinery, and violence.

1923 Arthur Honegger's *Pacific 231* imitates the sounds made by steam trains.

1926 American composer George Antheil's *Ballet mécanique* premieres in Paris, containing airplane propellors and a siren.

1928 Léon Theremin patents the first electronic musical instrument, the Theremin.

AFTER
1952 *Étude*, a work created from a single sound and its manipulation on audio tape.

The machine age of the early 20th century was an exciting time for avant-garde artists and thinkers. Their "Futurist" manifestos—most famously, Italian painter and composer Luigi Russolo's *Art of Noises* (1913)—advocated making music out of noises that ranged from human shouts and screams to explosions and the sounds of machines in order to give music a new dynamism. Although early Futurist events often ended up as riots and there is little record of the music actually produced, their ideas influenced composers such as Honegger, Prokofiev, and Antheil who variously composed music depicting machine-made sounds.

The new piano
Although the 20th century was full of experiments aiming to turn noise into music, the most successful early attempts came as composers such as Prokofiev and Stravinsky started to treat the piano as a percussive instrument rather than a melodic one. The American composer Henry Cowell was the first to understand the true possibilities of unleashing the "noise" of the piano. In 1917, his

Tides of Manaunaun included tone clusters to be played with the forearm, and he went one stage further in *Aeolian Harp* (1923), where the performer is required to pluck and sweep the strings inside the piano rather than use the keys.

City noise
Edgard Varèse was the first composer to create a complete work scored for a percussion ensemble, in *Ionisation* (1931). He had studied at the Paris Conservatoire under the conservative Charles-Marie Widor, but after moving to New York in 1915, he became fascinated

Our musical alphabet must be enriched. ... Musicians should take up this question in deep earnest with the help of machinery specialists.
Edgard Varèse

See also: Ives's Symphony No. 4 254–255 ▪ *Parade* 256–257 ▪ *Symphonie pour un homme seul* 298–301 ▪ *4'33"* 302–305 ▪ *Six Pianos* 320

by the sounds of urban landscapes. Intrigued by the manifestos of the Futurists, but wishing to refine the cacophony they advocated, Varèse searched for ways in which he could suggest familiar industrial sounds within a tightly controlled compositional outlook.

Ionisation requires 13 players and more than 30 instruments, only three of which can play traditional pitches. Varèse weaves together their intricate textures to create a strange soundscape in which snare drums and claves coexist with a güiro (a scraped gourd) and a cuíca, a Brazilian friction drum. The brash sounds of the city are effectively evoked through the use of a metal anvil as well as the hand-cranked siren—an instrument used in many of Varèse's works.

Dame Evelyn Glennie, the world's most celebrated percussionist, counts *Ionisation* alongside the works of John Cage and Steve Reich as the pinnacle of the entire percussion repertoire.

While the percussion layers create an industrial sound, *Ionisation* is not anarchic noise. The piece has a strong dramatic rhythm; in a letter to composer Carlos Salzedo, Varèse claimed to have written the piece for the flamenco dancer Vicente Escudero. Still, the piece was so difficult to play that percussionists of the New York Philharmonic, engaged to record the piece for its premiere at Carnegie Hall, New York, were dismissed, and Nicholas Slonimsky, who conducted the piece, brought in other performers to play on the recording.

The legacy of Varèse

Ionisation may not be widely performed, but its influence on future music is undeniable. While John Cage denied being influenced by it, it is difficult to listen to Cage's *First Construction (in Metal; 1939)* without hearing parallels to Varèse. The rock guitarist Frank Zappa also counted Varèse as one of his earliest influences. ▪

Edgard Varèse

Born in France in 1883, Varèse studied engineering at the insistence of his father before eventually deciding to study music in Paris. There, he was influenced by composers such as Satie, Debussy, and Busoni. After being invalided out of the army in 1915, he emigrated to New York where he earned his living as a conductor.

It was in the 1920s that his music first started to attract attention, but Varèse wrote sporadically—producing little more than a dozen works as he searched for ways to create truly electronic music. Eventually, in the 1950s, technology had evolved sufficiently to allow him to create *Deserts* for ensemble and tape, and in 1958 his *Poème électronique*, one of the first works created by manipulating magnetic tape, was performed at the Brussels Exhibition through 400 speakers in Le Corbusier's pavilion. Varèse died in 1965.

Other key works

1921 *Amériques*
1923 *Octandre*
1936 *Density 21.5*
1958 *Poème électronique*

A NATION CREATES MUSIC. THE COMPOSER ONLY ARRANGES IT
STRING QUARTET NO. 5 (1934), BÉLA VIKTOR JÁNOS BARTÓK

lthough heavily influenced by German music, Béla Bartók's individual voice became increasingly evident after he began to collect music from his native Hungary in 1904. There is a clear evolution of style between the First Quartet (1909), which included elements of folk music but was influenced by Richard Strauss and Debussy, and his Fifth Quartet (1934), which premiered in 1935.

Musical journey
In 1912, lack of interest in his works from his publishers led Bartók to devote his time to studying folklore and collecting thousands of Eastern European folk songs. In 1913, he also visited North Africa, again finding themes to incorporate in his music. When his health rendered him unfit for military service in World War I, he again began to compose. The success of his fairytale ballet *The Wooden Prince* (1917) led to renewed interest in his opera *Bluebeard's Castle* (1911).

A Transylvanian village receives Bartók (fourth from left) during one of his tours to record folk songs. His interest coincided with a growing pride in traditional national culture.

See also: *Also sprach Zarathustra* 192–194 ▪ *The Bartered Bride* 206 ▪ Dvořák's Symphony No. 9 212–215 ▪ *Finlandia* 220–221 ▪ *The Lark Ascending* 252–253

From the 1920s, Bartók began to experiment with incorporating percussive textures into his music, vividly exemplified in the *pizzicato* (plucked) fourth movement of his Fourth Quartet (1928). In the Fifth Quartet (1934), Bartók combined this technical experimentation with the folk music that he had long been absorbing. The piece begins in a simple 4/4 time signature but soon includes intricate rhythmic mosaics and snatches of folk melodies, accompanied by plucked sounds and dissonant drones. At the climax of the movement, a wild Hungarian dance is conjured out of a melody first heard near the start.

The Fifth Quartet's skeletal second movement, like its fourth movement, includes "night music," comprising eerie dissonances and imitated natural sounds; this style, created by Bartók, is often used in his slow passages. Hushed chords accompany a desperately sad, almost breathlessly stuttering comment from the first violin. After a restrained climax, the music dies out with trills and a slide to silence in the cello.

> With maturity comes the wish to economize—to be more simple. Maturity is the period when one finds the just measure.
> **Béla Bartók**

The time signatures of the highly challenging central fast *scherzo* movement, marked *Alla bulgarese*, features rhythms typical of Bulgarian folk music, with nine quavers in each bar, organized in uneven groups of 4+2+3. A muted soft pattern of notes, performed faster than one can hear, introduces the Trio section—again reflecting a popular folk rhythm of 10 quavers per bar in groups of 3+2+2+3.

The fourth movement is a variation of the second. Plucked sounds replace the bowed strings until an oscillating drone appears in the viola, accompanying an ornate version of the theme. After the restrained climax, Bartok adds a stormy passage with tremolos and loud unison outbursts. Some spectacularly fast and furious music follows, and then the notes of the two violins ascend with tranquil phrases from the viola and cello, creating a heavenly chorale. Soft, guitarlike slides in the cello bring the movement to an end.

Drama to the last

Although the finale recalls the first movement, it is well disguised. Frenzied activity in all instruments, lightning handovers, and strong dissonances are followed by soft scurrying music that becomes louder and more insistent. The culmination is a massively loud, harmonized melody with a resounding ending. The second violin briefly plays the most simple and slow version of the tune with a rolling accompaniment. The first violin then joins in, but in a clashing key. However, this relaxed dissonance is not a conclusion; a crashing interruption brings the work to a chaotic end. ▪

Béla Viktor János Bartók

Born in Nagyszentmiklos, Hungary, in 1881, by the age of 11 Bartók had made public appearances as a pianist and composer. He later studied at the Budapest Academy of Music. Despite the strong German cultural influence of his time, Bartók embraced the new Hungarian nationalism and took to wearing national dress. From 1905, he began a long collaboration with fellow Hungarian Zoltán Kodály to popularize folk songs and gained a practical knowledge of string writing from both folk and classical musicians.

Bartók had a successful career as a pianist, performing throughout Europe and in the United States with musicians such as the jazz clarinetist Benny Goodman. With the rise of fascism, he refused to play in Germany after 1933. In 1940, he left Budapest for the United States and died there in 1945.

Other key works

1911 *Bluebeard's Castle*
1931 *44 Duos for Two Violins*
1936 *Music for Strings, Percussion, and Celesta*
1939 *Divertimento*

I DETEST IMITATION. I DETEST HACKNEYED DEVICES
ROMEO AND JULIET (1936), SERGEI PROKOFIEV

IN CONTEXT

FOCUS
Russian emigrés

BEFORE
1920 Stravinsky's *Symphonies of Wind Instruments*, based on Russian folk music, signals the end of his "Russian phase."

1926 Living in New York, Rachmaninoff writes *Three Russian Songs*, a rare tribute to the music of his homeland.

AFTER
1948 The Central Committee of the Communist Party of the Soviet Union passes a resolution accusing Prokofiev, Shostakovich, Aram Khachaturian, and other composers of "anti-democratic tendencies," and rejecting "the principles of classical music."

1959 In Moscow, the full version of Prokofiev's epic opera *War and Peace* is staged for the first time, six years after the composer's death.

F ollowing Russia's October Revolution of 1917, when the cold reality of Bolshevik rule replaced the euphoria at the end of tsarism, Russian composers faced a choice: whether or not to stay in their homeland. Much depended on social status. Sergei Rachmaninov chose exile, as did the privileged Stravinsky, who was already living in Switzerland. The more lowly born Prokofiev, who was sympathetic to Bolshevism, stayed, but in 1918, frustrated by the post-revolutionary turmoil, Prokofiev accepted an offer to conduct in the United States and remained there for the next 18 years.

Reluctant exile
Prokofiev kept ties with the Soviet Union and, in 1934, wrote *Romeo and Juliet*. The music follows the drama of the story—soft, humorous, and intense in turn—but Prokofiev's ballet was notable in that he gave Shakespeare's star-crossed lovers a happy ending. After two companies pulled out of staging the production (amid concern over the authorities' denunciation of Shostakovich's

opera *Lady Macbeth of Mtsensk*) Prokofiev turned his ballet into orchestral suites.

Despite the Stalinist purges, Prokofiev returned to the Soviet Union in 1936, probably believing that his fame would protect him. The same year, he wrote his most popular work, *Peter and the Wolf*. In 1940, the first full-scale production of the ballet *Romeo and Juliet* took place in Leningrad, but only after Prokofiev was forced to change the orchestration, remove parts, and reinstate the story's sad ending. ∎

The time is past when music was written for a handful of aesthetes.
Prokofiev

See also: *Le Sacre du printemps* 246–251 ∎ *Spartacus* 309

BALINESE MUSIC RETAINED A RHYTHMIC VITALITY BOTH PRIMITIVE AND JOYOUS
TABUH-TABUHAN (1936), COLIN MCPHEE

IN CONTEXT

FOCUS
Gamelan influences

BEFORE
1882 French composer Louis-Albert Bourgault-Ducoudray writes *Rapsodie cambodgienne*, which includes gamelan instruments.

1890 Erik Satie's piano pieces *Trois Gnossiennes* echo the Javanese gamelan music he heard at the Paris Exposition the previous year.

AFTER
1945 John Cage's *Daughters of the Lonesome Isle* is one of many gamelan-inspired pieces written for "prepared piano"—a piano in which the sound is modified by placing objects on or between the strings.

1951 American composer Lou Harrison writes *Suite for Violin, Piano, and Small Orchestra*, which includes movements that reproduce the sounds of a gamelan.

amelan is an orchestra that plays the traditional music of the Indonesian islands of Java and Bali. It is noted for its wide use of percussion, such as drums, gongs, and chimes. The music was first exposed to a wide Western audience at the 1889 Paris Exposition, where a gamelan from Java inspired composers such as Claude Debussy and Maurice Ravel.

Elusive sounds
The freedom and constant variation of gamelan music made it difficult to capture. Therefore, in 1928, the German Odeon and Beka record companies sent agents to Bali to make gamelan recordings. A year later, Colin McPhee, a Canadian-born composer and follower of "absolute music" (music that exists for its own sake), heard one of the recordings. He was so mesmerized, he set off for Bali and spent much of the 1930s there studying the island's music.

McPhee's three-movement symphonic work *Tabu-Tabuhan* was first performed in 1936. In

Gamelan musicians perform in Bali. The pitch of gamelan music varies between instruments, with most orchestras using a five-tone scale rather than the seven tones of Western music.

Balinese, *tabu-tabuhan* refers to the rhythms and sounds of the percussive gamelan instruments, which McPhee sought to recreate using a Western orchestra. In 1941, McPhee and the young Benjamin Britten made a recording of some gamelan transcriptions for two pianos. Britten would continue to draw inspiration from Balinese music, along with other composers, including Olivier Messiaen, John Cage, and Philip Glass. ∎

See also: *Parade* 256–257 ▪ *Quartet for the End of Time* 282–283 ▪ *4'33"* 302–305 ▪ *November Steps* 314–315

REAL MUSIC IS ALWAYS REVOLUTIONARY

SYMPHONY NO. 5 IN D MINOR, OP. 47 (1937), DMITRI SHOSTAKOVICH

IN CONTEXT

FOCUS
Music in the Soviet era

BEFORE
1923 The Russian Association of Proletarian Musicians (RAPM) is founded, decrying modernism in music and claiming that all music should be understood by workers.

1929 A concert performance of Shostakovich's opera *The Nose* is attacked by the RAPM.

1935 Ivan Dzerzhinsky writes the opera *Tikhly Don* (*Quiet Flows the Don*), which, with its patriotic theme and simple melodies, becomes the model of socialist-realist music.

AFTER
1937 Sergei Prokofiev withdraws his *Cantata for the 20th Anniversary of the October Revolution* after criticism from the authorities.

1939 Prokofiev composes *Zdravitsa* ("Hail to Stalin") as part of the celebrations of Stalin's 60th birthday.

1948 Soviet Central Committee secretary Andrei Zhdanov begins a campaign against "formalist" music in which the form of the work is more important than anything it has to say.

1974 Alfred Schnittke's Symphony No. 1, embodying his "polystylism" form of composition, is premiered in Gorky after being turned away from Moscow.

ИДИТЕ В КОММУНИСТИЧЕСКУЮ ПАРТИЮ!

Composers in the Soviet Union worked under severe restrictions during the 1930s. They, like all artists, were expected to serve the people, in terms defined by the communist state, or face punishment. The country's leader, Joseph Stalin, liked patriotic songs and pieces with simple, appealing tunes and conventional harmonies. Music that did not fit this pattern, especially music that was introspective, complex, or difficult to grasp at first hearing, was dubbed "formalist," and its composers were forced into menial jobs, imprisoned, or worse.

Walking a tightrope
Dmitri Shostakovich survived these strictures until the mid-1930s. The authorities were pleased by works such as his Symphony No. 2, written to commemorate the tenth anniversary of the October 1917 revolution, and Symphony No. 3, subtitled "First of May" and premiered in 1930 on the sixth

A poster dated 1920 urges workers to "Join the Communist Party!" and reject the aristocracy, bourgeoisie, and Orthodox Church. Russian composers had little choice but to do the same.

anniversary of Vladimir Lenin's death. But Shostakovich's situation changed on January 26, 1936, when Stalin went to see his opera *Lady Macbeth of Mtsensk* at the Bolshoi Theatre. The work had premiered two years earlier and been an immense success at home and abroad. Stalin, though, took exception to it and left before the final scene. Two days later, an article in the state newspaper *Pravda*, headed "Muddle instead of music," denounced the opera. The anonymous article condemned the musical style of the piece, in which, it alleged, "singing is replaced by shrieking," and objected especially to the lewd "quacks" and "hoots" from the brass during the opera's sex scene. The work was taken off stage immediately.

See also: *Pictures at an Exhibition* 207 ▪ *Romeo and Juliet* 272 ▪ *Spartacus* 309 ▪ *Threnody for the Victims of Hiroshima* 310–311

A campaign began against artists and writers who were not following the party line. Over the next few years, this would result in the deaths of prominent figures, such as the poet Osip Mandelstam and the writer Isaac Babel, both critical of Stalin. Shostakovich himself was labeled an "enemy of the people," and some of his works, including the opera *The Nose* (1928) and the ballet *The Limpid Stream* (1935), were banned. Fearing punishment, he packed a bag and waited for the secret police to knock on his door.

In the end, Shostakovich was spared a visit from the police and went on to complete his next major work, Symphony No. 4, in May 1936. This is a far cry from his previous two "revolutionary" symphonies—a more abstract work, deeply influenced by Gustav Mahler, it is over an hour long and requires a huge orchestra. Like Mahler's symphonies, it is a work of contrasts, setting tradition, in the form of almost banal dance themes (including a Viennese waltz and an Austrian *Ländler*—a kind of slow waltz), against more strident, dissonant music. In the first

> If they cut off both hands, I will compose music anyway holding the pen in my teeth.
> **Dmitri Shostakovich**

movement alone, there are loud onslaughts of brass, a toccata for woodwinds, and a fast virtuoso fugue on the strings. Frightened that this challenging mix might offend the authorities, the composer withdrew the work, which was not heard in public until 1961.

A conflicted symphony
Shostakovich then started from scratch on what became his Symphony No. 5. The work, like its predecessor, features strong contrasts, but it also contains engaging melodies. The first main theme of the opening movement is a lyrical, sad tune, initially played softly on the violins. In the middle of the movement, this gives way to a grotesque march, which gathers in pace and volume, sweeping up the whole orchestra, with loud contributions from the brass and a driving beat from the percussion. The initial, gentle theme returns and the movement ends quietly with a violin solo overlaid with ringing chromatic scales from the celesta (a keyboard instrument that sounds like a glockenspiel, used by Mahler in two symphonies).

The gentle ending of the first movement contrasts strongly with the second movement, a scherzo in the form of a waltz. The third movement, marked *largo*, sees a return to lyrical writing, with long melodies on the strings creating a melancholy mood, punctuated with woodwind solos. The final movement, on the other hand, contains a brass-led return to loud, often aggressive, marchlike music. The piece rises in volume to *fortissimo* (very loud) before it ends resolutely in the triumphant major chord of D. »

Dmitri Shostakovich

For the precociously talented Shostakovich, born in St. Petersburg in 1906, piano lessons began at the age of three, and attendance at the Petrograd Conservatory came a decade later. His three early symphonies, written before he was 33, were well received, and he returned to the form after his first two operas were denounced by the authorities in the 1930s. He also produced a series of emotionally intense string quartets, concertos, and much theatre and film music. In 1960, Shostakovich joined the Communist Party (under extreme pressure), and around the same time he contracted polio and had several heart attacks. This did not stop him composing demanding work, such as Symphony No. 14 (1969). When he died in 1975 Shostakovich was widely regarded as Russia's greatest contemporary composer.

Other key works

1933 Concerto in C minor for piano, trumpet, and strings
1943 Symphony No. 8
1953 Symphony No. 10
1960 String Quartet No. 8 ("To the victims of fascism and war")

Alfred Schnittke and polystylism

In the 1960s, the Russian composer Alfred Schnittke (1934–1998) developed a new way of writing music. He mixed various musical styles in the same piece, such as his Violin Sonata No. 2 (1968) and Symphony No. 1 (1969–1972), and called it "polystylism." Shostakovich had achieved something similar, but in the works of Schnittke the contrasts between musical styles are often more violent and surprising. His Concerto Grosso No. 1 (1977), for example, combines baroque form, an atonal lament, a tango, and pieces of the composer's own film scores, to dramatic and even shocking effect. Schnittke continued to compose polystylistic music into the 1980s, including the String Quartet No. 3 (1983). He also wrote pieces that are less obviously polystylistic, such as Symphony No. 8 (1994), though even this work contains elements taken from Liszt, Wagner, and Russian Orthodox chant.

Schnittke's music was treated with suspicion in the Soviet Union, which he left in 1990 to settle in the German city of Hamburg.

The new work was a resounding success, its triumph at the premiere on November 21, 1937, in Leningrad confirmed by a 40-minute ovation, with many in the audience moved to tears. Through the symphony's series of stark contrasts between gentle, melancholic music and louder, faster passages, often in march-time, Shostakovich had also managed the delicate balancing act of preserving his own lyrical voice while toeing the party line.

The communist authorities, although at first suspicious of the work's rapturous reception, took the brash, closing movement at face value, as an optimistic conclusion using the direct musical language of which they approved. One Soviet reviewer described the symphony's ending as creating "an enormous optimistic lift." Party members had been encouraged to react in this way by an article that appeared in a Moscow newspaper a few days before the concert. The article was signed by Shostakovich, but it was probably written by a journalist working for the Communist Party.

When Germany laid siege to Leningrad in 1941, Shostakovich decided to stay, working as a fireman and finishing his Symphony No. 7, which he dedicated to the city.

In the piece, the symphony is described as "a Soviet artist's creative response to justified criticism". By putting his name to these words, the composer was saying that he had bowed to the will of the party. For men like Stalin, whose rule depended on submission and fear, the fact that Shostakovich had accepted criticism in this way was a victory.

Hidden clues

Although Shostakovich seemed to have caved in to the authorities, for some listeners the symphony carried hints of a more subversive message. It was as though the lyrical music represented freedom and self-expression, while the aggressive outbursts and awkward dances parodied their ruthless obliteration by the triumphant communist state.

Ambiguous meanings in Symphony No. 5

Movement	Overt meaning	Possible meaning
First	A folk tune setting, glorifying the Slavic people and their struggle against oppression.	Use of minor tonality undermines the glorification. Jaunty rhythms in the first theme give way to less assertive rhythms in the second theme, creating an overall sense of ambiguity.
Second	A waltz, suggesting a pleasant and romantic time for relaxation and enjoyment.	An ironic spoof on the traditional form, wittily presenting the waltz as trite, hackneyed, and sometimes brash. It is a satire that creates an unsettling atmosphere.
Third	A lament, reflecting on those who suffered and lost their lives in the battle for liberation from tsarist rule.	Not so much a lament as a piece of nostalgia. References to the Russian Orthodox Requiem hint at a yearning for religion rather than Soviet communism.
Fourth	A celebratory march, with a pensive and peaceful middle section, leading to a triumphant ending.	A bombastic caricature of the military march. A more reflective section underlines the minor tonality of the home key but returns to a militaristic, triumphalist finale aggressively asserting the key of D major.

Shostakovich's Symphony No. 5, on the face of it, is a positive endorsement of the Soviet regime, but subtleties in the music suggest a very different interpretation.

It is likely that Shostakovich also left a particular clue to the deeper meaning of the work hidden in the score. The quiet passage in the final movement of the symphony contains a musical quotation from a song the composer wrote to words by the Russian poet Alexander Pushkin. The song, called "Rebirth," describes someone who overpaints a picture by a great artist; as time passes, the vandal's paint flakes away, and the original image is revealed again as a masterpiece.

The symphony's original audience had no way of knowing of the presence of this quotation, because at the time of the premiere the song had not been performed. But many believe that Shostakovich meant to send a message to the future, when the symphony's real

> Not since the time of Berlioz has a symphonic composer created such a stir.
> **Nicolas Slonimsky**
> *The Musical Quarterly* (1942)

meaning would become clear, and audiences would see the work's martial references and triumphal conclusion as ironic gestures.

Censored again

Shostakovich's acceptance by the authorities lasted only a while. Any lapses into music that seemed to be discordant or introspective were leapt on by Communist Party critics. The composer's Symphony No. 8, written in 1943, was attacked by Soviet officials as "not a musical work at all, repulsive and ultra-individualist," and Shostakovich, denounced again, was forced to resign from the Soviet Composers' Union, although he continued to write symphonies.

After Stalin's death in 1953, the party line softened, but restrictions on artistic creativity continued until the fall of communism in the 1980s. Until then, Soviet composers were unable to express themselves with complete freedom, especially in high-profile works, such as operas and symphonies. As a result, many produced ambiguous works or poured their most personal music into private forms, such as string quartets, which were less likely to attract the authorities' attention. ∎

MY MUSIC IS NATURAL, LIKE A WATERFALL

BACHIANAS BRASILEIRAS (1930–1945), HEITOR VILLA-LOBOS

Brazilian classical composer Heitor Villa-Lobos had two lifelong influences. As a child, he became fascinated by the work of J.S. Bach after his aunt gave him Bach's collection of 48 preludes and fugues, *The Well-Tempered Clavier*. He was also captivated by the traditional music of his own country and traveled widely, collecting folk music in northern and northeastern Brazil and playing alongside musicians in his native Rio de Janeiro. Increasingly, Villa-Lobos sought ways of combining the rich musical traditions of Brazil with elements of Western classical music. In the late 19th century, Latin American composers had begun to explore similar ideas. Composers such as Alberto Nepomuceno used Brazilian folk melodies in works with conventional classical forms.

A truly creative musician is capable of producing, from his own imagination, melodies that are more authentic than folklore itself.
Heitor Villa-Lobos

Integrated styles

With *Bachianas brasileiras*, a collection of nine suites of varying lengths written for different combinations of musicians, Villa-Lobos took this idea much further, integrating folk and classical elements very closely. He did this by applying the contrapuntal techniques of J.S. Bach to Brazilian musical forms, in a bold combination of apparently alien traditions that fit together perfectly.

Like Bach's suites, each of the nine pieces that form *Bachianas brasileiras* has several dance movements. Villa-Lobos gave most of the movements two titles, one drawn from Baroque music (such as Toccata or Fugue) and one a corresponding Brazilian name (such as Desafio or Conversa). In addition to drawing on popular Brazilian forms like the Modinha, a type of sentimental love song, the

See also: *St. Matthew Passion* 98–105 ▪ *The Art of Fugue* 108–111 ▪ Bartók's String Quartet No. 5 270–271

American soprano Lucy Shelton performs *Bachianas brasileiras No. 5*, which is scored for soprano and cellos, at the Symphony Space in New York City, in 2010.

composer also introduces elements of program music, using the instruments of the orchestra to portray scenes such as a small steam train traveling through the Brazilian landscape in *Bachianas brasileiras No. 2*.

Structure and influences

The suites of *Bachianas brasileiras* are very varied in instrumentation. Some are for full orchestra, No. 1 is for an orchestra of cellos, and No. 6 is for just two instruments, flute and bassoon. The most famous of the suites is No. 5, for eight cellos and a soprano soloist whose part combines wordless vocalization with lines from Brazilian poetry. Further Brazilian elements in *Bachianas brasileiras* include music heard by Villa-Lobos on his travels and a street urchin's song from Rio, together with guitarlike pizzicatos on the cello and soulful solos for the saxophone and trombone. The influence of Bach spans not only his suites but also his *Musical Offering*, a collection of canons and fugues, and the Two-part Inventions, short keyboard pieces.

Bachianas brasileiras was part of a wider movement among Latin American composers, combining classical orchestration and forms with certain elements, rhythms, and themes drawn from the old native music of Central and South America. This movement spawned a range of approaches, from the music of composers such as the Mexican Silvestre Revueltas, with its rhythmic drive and vivid orchestration, to the works of Argentinian composer Astor Piazzolla, where classical elements are applied and adapted to the tango. Villa-Lobos led the way in showing how a blend of South American and classical elements could work and popularized its results all over the world. ▪

Heitor Villa-Lobos

Heitor Villa-Lobos was born in Rio de Janeiro, Brazil, in 1887. Resisting family pressure to become a doctor and preferring the company of musicians, he left home to travel through Brazil, supporting himself by playing the cello and guitar.

Between 1923 and 1930, he spent most of his time in Paris, where he absorbed European music and composed prolifically, completing his series *Chôros*, a collection of instrumental and choral pieces in 1929. After returning to Brazil the following year, he produced patriotic pieces for use in music education, as well as the *Bachianas brasileiras*. After 1945, he traveled widely again, building a vast body of work—more than 1,500 pieces, including 12 symphonies and 17 string quartets. Long after his death in 1959, at the age of 72, he has remained Brazil's best-known composer.

Other key works

1919–1920 *Carnaval das crianças*
1920–1929 *Chôros*
1953 Harp Concerto in A minor
1959 *Yerma*

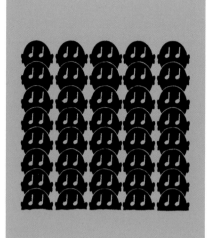

NEVER WAS I LISTENED TO WITH SUCH RAPT ATTENTION AND COMPREHENSION

QUARTET FOR THE END OF TIME (1940), OLIVIER MESSIAEN

IN CONTEXT

FOCUS
Spiritual music in the 20th century

BEFORE
1938 Devout Catholic Francis Poulenc's *Four Penitential Motets* marks the composer's return to sacred music.

AFTER
1962 Benjamin Britten's *War Requiem* combines the antiwar poems of Wilfred Owen with the traditional form of the Requiem Mass.

1971 British composer Sir John Tavener writes *Celtic Requiem*, an early example of his many religious works embodying a sense of timelessness.

1981 Polish composer Henryk Górecki writes *Totus Tuus* to celebrate Pope John Paul II's third official visit to his native Poland.

Early in his career, Olivier Messiaen espoused a musical style that embraced sensuality in music, forming a group called *La Jeune France* (Young France) with several other young composers, in opposition to the neoclassicism of Stravinsky and others who looked back to 18th-century works for inspiration. While Messiaen's music was imbued with references to his Roman Catholic faith, his style was avant-garde. He experimented both with rhythm and what he termed

My faith is the grand drama of my life. I'm a believer, so I sing words of God … I give bird songs to those who dwell in cities … and paint colors for those who see none.
Olivier Messiaen

"modes of limited transposition," such as the whole-tone scale, which can only be transposed up a tone before the same sequence of notes recurs. Messiaen had studied at the Paris Conservatoire with a series of brilliant teachers who inspired him to explore Greek and Hindu modes, while also instilling in him sound principles of harmony, counterpoint, and composition, and encouraging his gift for improvisation.

Apocalyptic inspiration
Within a year of the outbreak of World War II, Messiaen was taken as a prisoner of war and held at a camp in Silesia (now in Poland). Among his fellow inmates, he found three professional musicians, a clarinetist, violinist, and cellist, whose talents he could combine with his own piano keyboard skills. Embracing this rare instrumental combination, Messiaen wrote his *Quartet for the End of Time*, which premiered in the camp itself.

The composer's deep Christian beliefs are clearly indicated in his extensive Preface to the score, which includes quotations from the Book of Revelation. Its title was a homage to the Angel of the Apocalypse, who raises his

See also: *Prélude à l'après-midi d'un faune* 228–231 ▪ *A Child of Our Time* 284–285 ▪ *Gruppen* 306–307 ▪ *Apocalypse* 322 ▪ *In Seven Days* 328

hand toward Heaven saying, "There shall be no more time," in reference to the suffering of the period in which Messiaen was writing.

Reflective and evocative

In the first movement of the piece, two birds, accompanied by a plaintive piano and whistling cello, set the bucolic scene. A loud interruption heralds the second movement with a fast and frenzied unison in the strings, while a distant, slow melody, suspended by soft raindrops in the piano, establishes the pattern of the reflective and unhurried mood that characterizes the work. Cascades of notes end the movement.

In the third movement, the clarinettist plays a sad pastorale, juxtaposed with very long notes moving from silence to ear-piercing volume. Birdsong—something that fascinated Messiaen and absorbed his later years—reappears, adding a surreal note. After a short trio interlude comes the spiritual center of the piece—the fifth movement's slow and expressive cello melody, accompanied by throbbing harmonies on the piano. In the sixth movement, the quartet play in unison to emulate the "seven trumpets" of the Apocalypse, negotiating complex dance rhythms, dynamic contrasts, and fluctuating tempos. A quiet melody follows and others interrupt until a loud unison, accompanied by cascades of piano notes, leads to a brutal, triumphant conclusion. The violinist plays the last notes that slowly rise to a hushed, lonely end.

Within its eight movements, the Quartet contains most of the elements that characterize Messiaen's distinctive style and would later influence his pupils, including Pierre Boulez and Karlheinz Stockhausen. ■

Guards patrol a German POW camp in World War II. Messiaen composed *Quartet for the End of Time* while a prisoner at Camp Stalag VIII-A, premiering the work to 5,000 fellow prisoners outside in freezing weather.

Olivier Messiaen

Born in Avignon, France, in 1908, Messiaen was a highly musical child and studied at the Paris Conservatoire from the age of 11, publishing his eight *Préludes* while still a student. He was also a deeply committed Roman Catholic from childhood onward and combined his two passions as organist of La Trinité in Paris from 1931.

At this time, the composer wrote a number of religious organ pieces and also works for his wife, the violinist and composer Claire Delbos, whom he married in 1932.

In 1941, following his World War II imprisonment in Silesia, Messiaen was appointed professor of harmony at the Paris Conservatoire. During the 1950s and 1960s, he pursued his interest in birdsong with a number of works imitating their sounds. Internationally acclaimed, he died in Paris in 1992.

Other key works

1932 *Thème et variations*
1946–1948 *Turangalîla-symphonie*
1951 *Livre d'orgue*
1959 *Catalogue d'oiseaux*

I MUST CREATE ORDER OUT OF CHAOS

A CHILD OF OUR TIME (1939–1941),
MICHAEL TIPPETT

IN CONTEXT

FOCUS
**English choral tradition
in the late 20th century**

BEFORE
1928 Constant Lambert's *The Rio Grande* premieres in a BBC radio broadcast.

1931 William Walton's cantata *Belshazzar's Feast* launches at Leeds Festival.

1950 Herbert Howell's *Hymnus Paradisi* is sung at Gloucester Cathedral as part of the UK's Three Choirs Festival.

AFTER
1962 The premiere of Britten's *War Requiem* marks the consecration of Coventry Cathedral, in the UK.

1984 Tippett's oratorio *The Mask of Time* premieres in Boston, Massachusetts.

2008 James MacMillan's *St. John Passion* receives its first performance at London's Barbican Center.

A Child of Our Time is performed by the English National Opera in January 2005. Timothy Robinson, seated, sings the tenor solo from the second part: "My dreams are all shattered."

I n the 18th century, frequent performances of Handel's oratorios in Britain established a nationwide tradition of amateur choirs and choral societies. These fueled the production of choral works by British and foreign composers, who often premiered their works at choral festivals.

For many British composers, the production of choral music— for the church or the concert hall—

had continued to be a central activity. During the 20th century, composers began to use the choral tradition to write oratorios or cantatas for soloists, choir, and large orchestra to comment on

See also: *St. Matthew Passion* 98–105 ▪ Dvořák's Symphony No. 9 212–215 ▪ *The Dream of Gerontius* 218–219 ▪ *Peter Grimes* 288–293 ▪ *Einstein on the Beach* 321

social and political events. Michael Tippett's secular oratorio, *A Child of Our Time*, was inspired by the three-part format of Handel's *Messiah*, as well as the structure of J.S. Bach's Passions. However, instead of using chorales, as Bach had, Tippett's work contains American spiritual songs, which Tippett decided to include after hearing the style in a radio broadcast. He believed that these spirituals, with their origins as slave songs, had a universal appeal that traditional hymns did not. For example, 19th-century songs such as "Go Down, Moses" were appropriated for the oppressed Jews of the early 20th century.

Wartime context

Tippett was heavily influenced by his left-wing, pacifist beliefs. He was sentenced to three months in prison in 1943 for non-compliance with rules for conscientious objectors. Tippett's feelings about World War II and its causes were expressed through *A Child of Our Time,* which tells the story of the

> Men were ashamed of what was done. There was bitterness and horror.
> **A Child of Our Time**
> **Narrator, bass solo**

killing of a German diplomat by Herschel Grynszpan—a teenage Polish Jew—in November 1938. The act triggered *Kristallnacht* (the "Night of Broken Glass"), an officially sanctioned Nazi pogrom against German Jews in which Jewish property was destroyed and some 200 Jews died. Tippett saw Grynszpan, who had acted in response to the deportation of his parents by Nazi authorities, as a perfect example of how tyranny

and oppression could drive a marginalized person to commit an unthinkable act.

Protesting inhumanity

Tippett began composing *A Child of Our Time* in 1939, in the days after Britain declared war on Germany. He intended his work to be a protest against the disunity in Europe and the fascist atrocities of the Nazi regime. Tippett wrote both the music and libretto. The work uses choral techniques, such as counterpoint, arias, and triadic harmonies, and utilizes a bass singer as the narrator vocalizing recitatives. While the oratorio has two major moods, anger and grief, it ends on a note of hope, with the spiritual "Deep River": "O don't you want to go to that gospel feast. That promised land, that land where all is peace."

Concern with contemporary events is also shown by Benjamin Britten's *War Requiem*, which added antiwar poems by Wilfred Owen to the standard text of the Requiem Mass. ▪

Michael Tippett

Michael Tippett was born in London in 1905. He studied at the Royal College of Music from 1923 until 1928 and subsequently took lessons from the counterpoint expert R.O. Morris. He then worked as a schoolteacher, first making his mark as a composer with his Concerto for Double String Orchestra (1939); he followed this with the oratorio *A Child of Our Time*, which premiered in 1944.

Perceived as an individual voice in English music, concerned with a variety of social, political, and philosophical issues, Tippett went on to produce a sequence of operas, beginning with *The Midsummer Marriage* (1955). In 1966, he received a knighthood.

In Tippett's later years, his reputation grew internationally, leading to US premieres for *The Mask of Time* (Boston, 1984) and *New Year* (Houston, 1989). Tippett died in London in 1998, after suffering a stroke.

Other key works

1955 *The Midsummer Marriage*
1970 *The Knot Garden*
1991–1992 *The Rose Lake*

THE MUSIC IS SO KNIT ... THAT IT TAKES YOU IN VERY STRONG HANDS AND LEADS YOU INTO ITS OWN WORLD
APPALACHIAN SPRING (1944), AARON COPLAND

IN CONTEXT

FOCUS
Contemporary American nationalism

BEFORE
1911–1915 Inspired by local transcendentalism, Ives composes his *Concord Sonata*.

1928 Virgil Thomson's *Four Saints in Three Acts* celebrates American diversity.

1939 Roy Harris conveys the immensity of the American rural landscape in his Symphony No. 3.

AFTER
1947 Samuel Barber sets his *Knoxville: Summer of 1915* to James Agee's memoir of his childhood in rural Tennessee.

1989 Elliott Carter's *Three Occasions for Orchestra* celebrates the vigor and energy of America.

1999 John Harbison composes *The Great Gatsby* based on F. Scott Fitzgerald's novel.

I n August 1944, the dancer and choreographer Martha Graham first heard the music that Aaron Copland had created for her ballet *Appalachian Spring*, about a young couple ready to embark on married life in a Pennsylvanian farmhouse in the early 1800s. She was pleased with what she heard and praised its power to lead the listener into a singular world. Graham commissioned the work determined that it would be "a legend of American living" and "the inner frame that holds together a people." She had also stipulated that the music should be about

So long as the human spirit thrives on this planet, music in some living form will accompany and sustain it and give it expressive meaning.
Aaron Copland

90 minutes long and scored for only 10 to 12 instruments, but Copland used 13. Graham had also chosen the title *Appalachian Spring*, which came from a verse of "The Dance" by the American poet Hart Crane.

Clarity and simplicity
Copland's music had been heavily influenced by his time as a student in France in the early 1920s, when he had been surrounded by people who represented all that was new in the arts. In Paris, several young composers were newly reworking Classical styles and exploring genres such as Modernism and Impressionism, eschewing the old German Romanticism of Brahms and Wagner. Copland himself was particularly influenced by Igor Stravinsky, who was just entering his neoclassical phase. Stravinsky's *Octet* (1923) impressed Copland with its clean lines, crystal-clear textures, and concise structure.

From this time, Copland's music became more open and its form and instrumentation more tightly controlled. The hardships of World War I compelled him, like Stravinsky, to write for smaller orchestras. With *Appalachian Spring*, he said, he was forced

See also: *Prélude à l'après-midi d'un faune* 228–231 ▪ *Le Sacre du printemps* 246–251 ▪ *Les Biches* 262 ▪ *Romeo and Juliet* 272

Martha Graham performs as the young bride in *Appalachian Spring* at a New York theatre. The music, which Copland also reshaped as an orchestral suite, won him a Pulitzer Prize in 1945.

to say what he had to say "in the simplest possible terms." What Graham had requested was perfectly captured in his skeletal musical language that created a rich sense of space hitherto unknown in American music.

Emotional inspiration

Copland found his theme for the work in the first line of a Shaker hymn: "Tis the gift to be simple." The Shakers were an American Protestant sect known for their plain way of living. The clarity of texture suffuses the ballet, its warmth flooding the entire score, from the opening sense of dawn breaking over a Shaker farmstead. The music perfectly captures the tenderness of young love, the gaiety and buoyant dances of the ensuing wedding, and the most magical moment of all—the ending of the ballet, when the newlyweds, alone for the first time, realize the sheer immensity of what they have done. They are pioneers, about to start their life together in a new country. Although they are safe in their home, they must tame and cultivate the unconquered land stretching out before them.

These mixed feelings of comfort, awe, fear, optimism, vulnerability, and courage were transformed by Copland into pure, deeply moving music. ■

Aaron Copland

The son of Russian immigrant parents, Copland was born in Brooklyn, New York, in 1900. Studying in Paris with the composer Nadia Boulanger, he came under the influence of Prokofiev, Stravinsky, and Poulenc. In collaboration with Roger Sessions, he ran the Copland-Sessions concert series (1928–1931) to encourage young American composers. His own music brought him worldwide fame in the 1940s, although his later serialist works were less well received.

Copland taught at the new Berkshire Music Center in Massachusetts from 1940, and in 1951 he became the first American composer to be appointed as Harvard's Norton Professor of Poetry (poetry in its broadest sense). Around this time, he was falsely accused of communist activities. In 1960, he moved to Rock Hill, New York, where he lived until his death in 1990.

Other key works

1930 Piano Variations
1942 *Fanfare for the Common Man*
1967 *Inscape*

COMPOSING IS LIKE DRIVING DOWN A FOGGY ROAD

PETER GRIMES (1945), BENJAMIN BRITTEN

IN CONTEXT

FOCUS
20th-century British opera

BEFORE
1689 First performance of Henry Purcell's opera *Dido and Aeneas*.

1871–1896 Librettist W.S. Gilbert and composer Arthur Sullivan together produce 14 comic operas, including *HMS Pinafore* and *The Mikado*.

1902 Edward German's opera *Merrie England*, a tale of amorous rivalries at the court of Elizabeth I, opens at the Savoy Theatre in London.

1922 Following the success of his orchestral suite *The Planets*, Gustav Holst composes his one-act opera *The Perfect Fool*.

AFTER
1955 Michael Tippett's first opera, *The Midsummer Marriage,* is performed at Covent Garden.

1966 The one-act opera *Purgatory*, by Hugo Weisgall, premieres at England's Cheltenham Festival.

1968 The Aldeburgh Festival includes the first performance of Harrison Birtwistle's opera *Punch and Judy*.

1984 *Where The Wild Things Are*, by Oliver Knussen to a libretto by Maurice Sendak, receives its first performance at London's National Theatre.

fter Purcell's death in 1695 and on through the 18th and 19th centuries, British music was dominated by European composers, such as Handel, Johann Christian Bach, and Mendelssohn. It was not until the publication of Edward Elgar's *Enigma Variations*, in 1899, that a British composer began almost single-handedly to revitalize the country's music.

At this time, British opera was in an especially perilous state. The comic operas of Gilbert and Sullivan were popular, as was Edward German's operetta *Merrie England,* but there were no serious

The beach at Aldeburgh, the coastal village that inspired *Peter Grimes*. The opera was staged live here in 2013 to mark the centenary of Britten's birth.

successors to Purcell. Elgar would never finish *The Spanish Lady*, his only attempt at opera, while Vaughan Williams labored for years on his first opera, *Hugh the Drover*, working folk songs and idioms into the music in the hope of creating a truly British work. When the opera opened in 1924, it met with little initial success.

The young Benjamin Britten disliked the English pastoral school and wrote of Vaughan Williams, "I am afraid I don't like his music, however much I try." Britten had hoped to pursue postgraduate studies with the Austrian composer Alban Berg, a student of Arnold Schoenberg, whose *Lyric Suite* he admired, but was dissuaded by his parents.

In 1930, the year Britten began his studies at the Royal College of Music in London, the Vic-Wells company was formed in a bid to champion British theatre, opera, and ballet. In 1934, the Old Vic Theatre became the center for spoken drama and Sadler's Wells

Music … has the beauty of loneliness of pain: of strength and freedom. The beauty of disappointment and never satisfied love.
Benjamin Britten

See also: *Dido and Aeneas* 72–77 ▪ *Tosca* 194–197 ▪ *Peer Gynt* 208–209 ▪ *The Wreckers* 232–239 ▪ *A Child of Our Time* 284–285

> I wanted to express my awareness of the perpetual struggle of men and women whose livelihood depends on the sea.
> **Benjamin Britten**

the headquarters for opera and ballet (the Covent Garden Opera Company, later the Royal Opera, was not founded until 1946). Britten felt passionately that his country should have a permanent national opera company and believed the Sadler's Wells Opera Company, which later became English National Opera, was a good first step.

Inspiration for Grimes
During World War II, Britten and his partner, the tenor Peter Pears—a fellow pacifist—spent three years in America. While there, Britten read George Crabbe's poem *The Borough*, published in 1810, in which Crabbe devotes a whole section to the villain Peter Grimes, a murderous outcast, who is hunted down by his community. The long poem depicts the people of the Suffolk town of Aldeburgh, on England's east coast, and describes the local flat landscape, the marshy terrain, the stony beaches, and the suck and surge of the waves. It moved Britten so deeply that not only did he decide to use the story

of Peter Grimes as the subject for opera, but he also determined to return to his native Suffolk.

In spite of the danger and difficulties of crossing the Atlantic in wartime, he and Peter Pears traveled to England on a cargo vessel, the *Axel Johnson*. During the 19-day sea journey, they worked together on the libretto for the new project, surrounded by what Peter Pears described as "callous, foul-mouthed, witless recruits for company." Such a setting for the beginnings of Britten's first serious opera was apt; the sea would form a haunting backdrop in *Peter Grimes*.

Back home in Suffolk, Britten worked further on the libretto with the writer Montagu Slater. Britten, a deeply sensitive man, wanted to explore the character of Crabbe's murderous outcast. Britten felt himself to be an outsider in society and not only because of his pacifism. He had first met Peter Pears in 1937, and the two suffered »

The soprano Joan Cross plays the schoolmistress, Peter Pears is Peter Grimes (center), and Leonard Thompson is the apprentice in the original 1945 production of the opera.

Benjamin Britten
Born in Lowestoft, England, in 1913, Britten played the piano and composed from an early age, studying with the composer and violinist Frank Bridge in his teens. In 1930, he won a scholarship to London's Royal College of Music.

From 1939 to 1942, Britten and the tenor Peter Pears lived in America. On their return to London, Pears joined the Sadler's Wells Opera Company, whose theatre premiered *Peter Grimes,* in 1945. The success of the opera excited interest in every new work by Britten.

Britten and Pears formed the English Opera Group in 1947 and in 1948 launched the Aldeburgh Festival. In 1962, Britten's *War Requiem* was premiered in the newly rebuilt Coventry Cathedral. Britten was made a life peer in 1976, a few months before he died of heart failure. He was the first composer or musician to be made a member of Britain's House of Lords.

Other key works
1946 *The Young Person's Guide to the Orchestra*
1951 *Billy Budd*
1961 *War Requiem*

The main characters in *Peter Grimes*

Foes

Mrs. Sedley (mezzo soprano)
Town gossip

Auntie (contralto)
Landlady of the pub

Swallow (bass)
Lawyer

Bob Boles (tenor)
A fisherman and a Methodist

The Townspeople
(chorus)

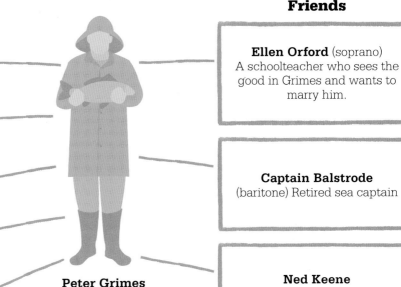

Peter Grimes
The antihero, he is violent,
solitary, and an outsider.

Friends

Ellen Orford (soprano)
A schoolteacher who sees the
good in Grimes and wants to
marry him.

Captain Balstrode
(baritone) Retired sea captain

Ned Keene
(baritone) Apothecary

because of their love for one another—homosexuality being illegal in Britain until 1967.

Ovations for a masterpiece

The first performance of Britten's *Peter Grimes* took place at the Sadler's Wells Theatre on June 7, 1945. The composer and conductor Imogen Holst, who was later a codirector of the Aldeburgh Festival, recalled the thrill of the occasion: "No one in the audience will ever forget the excitement of that evening," she wrote. When the tragedy had reached its quiet end and the opera was over, she sensed that the audience knew they had been listening to a masterpiece: "They stood up and shouted and shouted."

The popularity of the opera lay partly in its psychological drama and depth of characterizaton. A complex, lonely, and tormented

fisherman, Peter Grimes has just been cleared of the death of an apprentice but is warned not to seek a replacement. Faced with the townspeople's hostility, Grimes yearns in vain for love and simple domesticity with his friend Ellen Orford, a widowed schoolmistress,

He wished for one to
trouble and control;
he wanted some obedient
boy to stand and bear the
blow of his outrageous hand.
Peter Grimes

but the relationship is halting. In the prologue's duet "The truth … the pity … and the truth," Ellen sings in the bright E major chord while Grimes begins in F minor. Gradually, Grimes gives way to Ellen, and the pair are in unison, but it does not last.

In defiance of local opinion, Grimes procures a new apprentice, and his fate is sealed. When Ellen spots a bruise and accuses him of mistreating the boy, local people see Grimes strike her then leave. Forming a lynch mob, they advance on Grimes's clifftop hut to a drum beat suggesting impending doom but find nothing amiss as Grimes is away fishing. His apprentice, however, has fallen down the cliff to his death. His jersey is later found washed ashore, and the mob advances on the hut once more. Doomed, Grimes rows out to sea and sinks his boat. The opera ends

the next morning when, to the mournful sound of a foghorn, reports emerge of a sinking vessel too far out to be rescued.

Building tension

The music of *Peter Grimes* has astonishing tensile strength, what Peter Pears called "The bare minimum of notes to convey the maximum effect." Such economy of style, already apparent in Britten's early works, such as *A Boy was Born* (1933) and *Les Illuminations* (1939), was skeletal compared to the English pastoral school of composition. In *Peter Grimes*, the music expresses the drama at all times. In the quartet "Hi! Give us a hand!" in the first scene of Act One, for example, all four characters sing at the same time, mimicking an argument, while the mix of song, speech, and laughter in the chorus's "Assign your prettiness to me" in Act Three conveys the natural simplicity of the villagers. Conversely, at the end of the opera, the canon of the chorus evokes the menace of the crowd.

Orchestral interludes are also employed to great effect between acts, especially in the Four Sea Interludes ("Dawn," "Sunday Morning," "Moonlight," and "Storm"), which are often performed on their own. They serve to set the scene, evoke the emotions of the characters, and foreshadow the building drama, from gentle violins and flutes depicting a coastal dawn to an upsurge in the brass denoting an approaching storm.

Britten went on to write other operas, including *Billy Budd* (1951) based on Herman Melville's novella *Billy Budd, Sailor*, and *Death in Venice* (1973), from the novel by Thomas Mann. In addition to carving a place for modern British opera in the international repertoire, Britten actively promoted music and fellow composers. He also upheld the traditional elements of opera, such as a good story, evocative atmosphere, and a large and stirring chorus. Essentially, he reclaimed the concept of opera as entertainment in an age when minimalism ruled. ∎

Britten is memorialized in a window by John Piper in Aldeburgh Parish Church. *The Burning Fiery Furnace*, depicted here, evokes Britten's three "church parables."

The English Opera Group carry props into the Jubilee Hall for Britten's *Let's Make An Opera* during Aldeburgh's 1949 festival.

Music festivals

Aldeburgh Festival, launched by Britten and his friends in 1948, gained international status within a few decades. It became the latest in a growing number of international music festivals, including the Bayreuth Festival founded by Richard Wagner in 1876 to stage his own operas, and Salzburg's festival of Mozart's music, founded by its citizens in 1877. In Italy, it was the centenary in 1913 of Verdi's birth that prompted the first operas at the Arena di Verona, where the city's annual festival is held in summer.

As in Europe, classical music festivals in the US flourished in the 1870s, though the Handel and Haydn Society in Boston held its first triennial festival as early as 1858. In the 20th century, the composer Henry Kimball Hadley staged concerts in 1934 that evolved into the celebrated Tanglewood Festival.

CONTEM

PORARY

Pierre Schaeffer
and **Pierre Henry**
create *Symphonie
pour un homme
seul* from
recorded sounds.

In France, **Iannis
Xenakis** composes
Pithoprakta, a
piece inspired by
mathematical and
engineering principles.

Polish composer
Krzysztof Penderecki's
*Threnody for the Victims
of Hiroshima* explores
sonorism with a 52-piece
string orchestra.

1950

1956–1957

1960

1956

1958

1964

In the Soviet Union,
Aram Khachaturian's
ballet *Spartacus*, about
the first-century slave
revolt against Rome, wins
the Lenin Prize.

Three orchestras
simultaneously
bring **Karlheinz
Stockhausen's** *Gruppen*
to life at its premiere
in Cologne, Germany.

Terry Riley writes
In C—one of the
first minimalist
compositions, with
no set number of
performers or duration.

I
n the wake of World War II,
classical music became
increasingly experimental,
as composers searched for more
adventurous ways to rework the
language of music. Turning their
back on the past, they looked to
new sources of inspiration, such
as mathematics and physics, and
overturned former concepts of
structure. They even questioned
fundamental aspects of music,
such as what constituted a musical
instrument, the necessity of a
"performer," and what music
itself can be.

In Europe, the postwar
generation pushed the serial
method of composition pioneered
by Arnold Schoenberg in the 1920s
further by applying the technique
to volume and duration as well
as pitch. Encouraged by Olivier

Messiaen, their teacher at the
Paris Conservatoire, Pierre Boulez
and Karlheinz Stockhausen
became the leading lights of
serialism, while Iannis Xenakis
used it as a starting point for a
music that was based on a
combination of mathematical
and acoustic theories. Composers
also found rich inspiration in
technology, which provided access
to a whole new sound world. In
Paris, Pierre Henry and Pierre
Schaeffer pioneered a technique
known as *musique concrète*, using
sounds recorded onto magnetic
tape as their building blocks.

At the same time, a young
American composer, John Cage,
explored music determined by
chance, or aleatory music, and
examined the musical potential
of silence. He determined key

elements of his compositions by
tossing coins and sorting yarrow
sticks or giving ambiguous graphic
instructions to performers. One
of his works (*4'33"*) specified four
minutes and 33 seconds of silence,
in which only the ambient sounds
of the auditorium could be heard.

Ideas spread

After the death of Joseph Stalin
in 1953, news of these fresh
developments began to reach
composers behind the Iron Curtain,
where the Soviet-dominated
regimes had censored music
that it considered degenerate or
subversive. György Ligeti, born
in communist Romania, made
his way to the West via Hungary
in 1956 and developed an
idiosyncratic style after coming
across the music of Stockhausen

Luciano Berio uses collage and quotation to compose a kaleidoscope of musical texture in *Sinfonia*.

With minimal words and no intervals, **Philip Glass's** *Einstein on the Beach* subverts the traditional narrative of opera.

Witold Lutosławki's 25-minute *Fourth Symphony* is performed as one continuous movement of two sections.

The American composer **Eric Whitacre** adapts his instrumental work *October* to a choral setting in *Alleluia*.

1968   **1976**   **1993**   **2011**

1967   **1969**   **1977**   **2000**

Toru Takemitsu juxtaposes Eastern and Western musical traditions in the orchestral work *November Steps*.

Eight Songs for a Mad King by **Peter Maxwell Davies**, based on the words of King George III, presents a new type of "music theatre."

Canadian composer **Raymond Murray Schafer's** biblically inspired *Apocalypsis* features multiple choirs, conductors, and orchestras.

Jennifer Higdon composes and premieres *blue cathedral*, a work that epitomizes a return to lyricism.

and his contemporaries, eventually finding inspiration in chaos theory and fractal mathematics.

As restrictions on the arts lifted in Poland, Krzysztof Penderecki and others leapt at the chance to create a new musical language, composing pieces for conventional instruments in "blocks" of sound reminiscent of electronic music or, like Witold Lutosławski, they introduced elements of chance into their work. This eclectic approach to musical composition, incorporating elements of different styles, was also a feature of the music of Luciano Berio, who embraced musical collage.

The birth of minimalism

Much of this new music perplexed and alienated listeners, and in 1960s America, there was a reaction against it. In place of complexity, some young composers advocated simplicity, or minimalism. Pioneered by Terry Riley and given fresh impetus by Philip Glass and Steve Reich, the style was characterized by repetition and the most basic of harmonies, partly inspired by the hypnotic qualities of some African and Asian music. A number of composers encouraged improvisation by the performers. In Riley's *In C*, the order, duration, and tempo of the composition are determined by the musicians.

Cross-cultural trends

In the late 1960s, as political, social, and technological horizons widened, the fusion and cross-fertilization of musical cultures became increasingly evident, as in the work of Toru Takemitsu, who composed for Western and Japanese instruments, and the cross-cultural music of Kaija Saariaho. Classical composers also absorbed ideas from popular culture, incorporating elements of pop and rock music as well as jazz into their work, while also embracing the possibilities of new technology. British composer Thomas Adès's *In Seven Days*, for example, is a multimedia work, while American composer Eric Whitacre has explored the possibility of "virtual" ensembles, assembled via the Internet.

It is too early to say which direction classical music will take in the 21st century, or what the next musical movement will be. But history suggests that composers will continue to find many new means of musical expression. ∎

SOUND IS THE VOCABULARY OF NATURE

SYMPHONIE POUR UN HOMME SEUL (1949–1950), PIERRE SCHAEFFER/ PIERRE HENRY

IN CONTEXT

FOCUS
Electronic music and *musique concrète*

BEFORE
1939 The first example of electroacoustic music, John Cage's *Imaginary Landscape No. 1*, uses variable-speed turntables, frequency recordings, muted piano, and cymbal.

1948 Made entirely from recordings of steam trains, Pierre Schaeffer's *Étude aux chemins de fer* is broadcast alongside his other early studies in sound.

AFTER
1952–1953 Olivier Messiaen composes his only electronic work, *Timbres-durées*, although he later withdraws it.

1954 Edgard Varèse's *Déserts,* which alternates sections of *musique concrète* with others scored for an orchestra of wind and percussion, is broadcast from Paris on December 2.

1956 In *Gesang der Jünglinge,* Stockhausen mixes sounds derived from the voice of a treble choirboy with manipulated electronically generated tones.

1958 Edgard Varèse writes *Poème électronique* for the futuristic Philips Pavilion, a building designed by Le Corbusier, at the World's Fair in Brussels.

In the aftermath of World War II, composers were among the many creative figures who sensed a need for a new aesthetic. They sought to create works that would not be tainted—as they felt complex state-sponsored orchestral music and opera were—by any connections with previous regimes, particularly the Third Reich, its allies, and the countries it had occupied. Some turned to forms of serialism (in which notes are repeated in a specific order) developed from the organic structures of Anton Webern, an earlier exponent of serial music and one of the composers whose work had been denounced as "degenerate" by the Nazi Party.

Others found a new beginning by recording ordinary, everyday sounds and putting them together into collagelike compositions that merely needed to be played on a disk or a tape, rather than interpreted by live musicians in a concert hall. This was the origin of *musique concrète*, an early form of electronic music.

It was at the Studio d'Essai de la Radiodiffusion Nationale that Pierre Schaeffer began work on the

Something new has been added, a new art of sound. Am I wrong in calling it music?
Pierre Schaeffer

Pierre Henry, in concert in Paris in 1952, used four large circular receiver coils to show how sound transmitted through four loudspeakers could be shifted around a listening space.

Symphonie de bruits ("Symphony of sounds"). Founded in 1942 by theatre director Jacques Copeau and his pupils as the center of the Resistance movement in French radio, the studio subsequently became the cradle of musique concrète. In collaboration with Pierre Henry, who joined the electronic studio in 1949, Schaeffer developed his original *Symphonie* into the *Symphonie pour un homme seul* ("Symphony for a lone man"), premiered at the École Normale de Musique in Paris, in 1950. Henry went on to run what was eventually called the Groupe de Recherche de Musique Concrète—the body that studied and developed musique concrète from 1951 to 1958.

The sounds of a life
In its original form, the *Symphonie* consisted of 22 movements using turntables and mixers. For a broadcast in 1951, this number was reduced to 11, but then »

Pierre Schaeffer and Pierre Henry

Born in 1910 in Nancy, Schaeffer grew up in a family of musicians. He, however, studied engineering and received a diploma in radio broadcasting from the École Polytechnique before joining the French radio and TV broadcasting company Radiodiffusion-Télévision française, in 1936. In 1949, Schaeffer met Pierre Henry, a composer and percussionist, born in Paris in 1927, who had studied at the Paris Conservatoire with the composers Nadia Boulanger and Olivier Messiaen. Together they formed the Groupe de Recherche de Musique Concrète, remaining close collaborators until 1958 when the more prolific Henry left to found his own independent studio called Applications de Procédés Sonores en Musique Electroacoustique.

Henry continued to write electronic scores for films and ballet, as well as his incomplete *La Messe de Liverpool*, an electronic mass commissioned for the opening of Liverpool Cathedral in the UK in 1968. Schaeffer composed little more, although he continued writing and teaching; his pupils included Jean-Michel Jarre, a pioneer of electronic music. Schaeffer died in Aix-en-Provence in 1995 aged 85. Henry died in Paris in 2017, at the age of 89.

Other key collaborations

1950 *La course au kilocycle* (radio score)
1953 *Orphée 53*
1957 *Sahara d'aujourd'hui*

The soundtracks and effects for most programs made by the BBC were mixed in the control room at Alexandra Palace, London, until the early 1950s.

increased to 12 for Henry's 1966 revision, which has become accepted as the official version. The symphony is an explorative work utilizing recorded sounds and new techniques in a relatively simple and also somewhat crude manner, when compared with what would later be achieved in the field of electronic music.

The first and seventh of the 12 movements of Henry's 1966 revised version are titled *Prosopopée 1* and *Prosopopée 2,* from the Greek rhetorical term *prosopopeia*, in which a speaker communicates in the guise of someone else. Other movements are given musical terms, such as Valse and Scherzo, two are evocatively named Erotica

and Eroïca, and a further two—Collectif and Apostrophe—suggest verbal exchanges. Strette, the title of the last and longest movement, like the Italian term *stretto*, which is often used to describe fugues or operatic finales, indicates a faster speed or richness of texture as earlier sounds are reprised.

In his 1952 work, *À la recherche d'une musique concrète* (*In search of a Concrete Music*), Schaeffer described the individual nature of the work and also listed some of its sonic elements. He declared that a man could be his own instrument, using many more than the 12 notes of the singing voice: "He cries, he whistles, he walks, he thumps his fist, he laughs, he groans. His heart beats, his breathing accelerates, he utters words, launches calls, and other calls reply."

The choreographer Maurice Béjart, who sensed the further expressive potential of the *Symphonie,* used it as a score for the dance piece that was also called *Symphonie pour un homme seul,* which he created in 1955. It was Béjart's first success and has been revived several times.

A musical legacy

Although Schaeffer was appointed professor of electronic composition at the Paris Conservatoire in 1968, he composed few works after 1962. He continued, however, to pursue a vast range of artistic interests and concepts, especially creative writing, theoretical studies in musique concrète and other electronic techniques, and the organization and running of groups dedicated to the new genres.

Henry went on to explore the medium he had helped to invent in collaboration with Béjart, the choreographer Alwin Nikolais, his fellow composer Michel Colombier,

Sounds used in the 12 movements of *Symphonie pour un homme seul*

1. Prosopopée I	Knocking, shouts, humming, whistling, and wordless singing.
2. Partita	Mostly someone playing a prepared piano.
3. Valse	Made up of the distorted sounds of an orchestra playing fragments of a waltz with various voices over the top.
4. Erotica	A woman's voice laughing and purring with pleasure.
5. Scherzo	Conversational speaking voices played at various speeds and alternating with detached sounds from the piano.
6. Collectif	Relaxed voices over soft, sustained piano chords.
7. Prosopopée II	The sound of footsteps alternates with various pitches from the piano.
8. Eroïca	Busy clattering sounds with a voice played backward.
9. Apostrophe	Male and female voices repeat lyrical phrases against short rhythmic ideas on the piano.
10. Intermezzo	Sounds like fragments of a collective prayer against a tense, percussive accompaniment.
11. Cadence	Sounds of knocking on wood and metal.
12. Strette	A loud, eruptive opening, then a summary of what has gone before, with percussive sounds, crowd noises, and sirens.

and the British rock band Spooky Tooth. His work also influenced composers of multiple electronic music styles, including the British musician and producer William Orbit, Mat Ducasse of the UK-based band Skylab, and the UK music producer and DJ Fatboy Slim.

Other composers who worked briefly at the Groupe de Recherche de Musique Concrète included Karlheinz Stockhausen, Pierre Boulez, and the veteran Edgard Varèse, who recognized the advent of a medium that he had longed for all his life. However, the main contributions to the genre born in Paris were made elsewhere.

In 1952, the German theorist and composer Herbert Eimert inaugurated a department for electronic music at the radio studios in Cologne. Stockhausen joined him there and their focus moved from sounds recorded in diverse contexts (as in musique concrète) to sounds that were electronically produced. Between 1953 and 1954, Stockhausen wrote two influential studies in pure electronics before going on

An opera for blind people, a performance without argument, a poem made of noises, bursts of text, spoken or musical.
Pierre Schaeffer
Describing the Symphonie in La musique concrète (1973)

to combine real sounds with electronics in his masterly *Gesang der Jünglinge* (1955–1956).

New experimental spaces

Studios similar to those in Cologne began to open across the world in New York, Tokyo, Munich, and in Milan, where the Italian composers Luciano Berio and Bruno Maderna founded Europe's third electronic music facility. In London in 1958,

the BBC launched its Radiophonic Workshop, which began to develop atmospheric music for radio and television, such as the *Dr Who* theme (1963), written by the Australian composer Ron Grainer and realized by Delia Derbyshire. Important works by Varèse (his *Poème electronique*) and the Greek Iannis Xenakis were created in European studios at this time.

In 1977, the Institut de Recherche et Coordination Acoustique/ Musique (IRCAM) opened in Paris. Boulez was its head, and such figures as Berio and the French-Slovenian composer and trombonist Vinko Globokar were among its staff. Since then, many composers have experimented and realized compositions at IRCAM, using electronics and latterly computers. The organization has remained influential in making such techniques part of classical composition today. Major figures to develop work there include Jonathan Harvey, Harrison Birtwistle, George Benjamin, Kaija Saariaho, Unsuk Chin, Gérard Grisey, and Tristan Murail. ∎

The biblical tale of Hebrew youths surviving in a furnace, depicted here on a Bible study card (c.1900), was a potent inspiration for Stockhausen.

Gesang der Jünglinge

Karlheinz Stockhausen's *Gesang der Jünglinge* ("Song of the Youths") was created in the studios of West German Radio between 1955 and 1956. Its text comes from the biblical Book of Daniel where Nebuchadnezzar had the Hebrew youths Shadrach, Meshach, and Abednego cast into a fiery furnace for refusing to worship his image. Remaining miraculously unharmed, they sang God's praise from the flames.

Some regard the work as the first masterpiece created using the sound techniques developed from the experiments of Schaeffer

and Henry. It also reflects the strong spiritual basis that Stockhausen's work almost always possessed. Using electronically generated tones and pulses, filtered white noise, and the voice of 12-year-old choirboy Josef Protschka, Stockhausen created a fiery whirlwind of rich and complex textures, operating at different speeds and dynamic levels, and utilizing the space around the audience via four-channel (originally five-channel) sound. The result is a virtuoso creation that maintains a consistent momentum due to its perfectly planned overall structure.

I CAN'T UNDERSTAND WHY PEOPLE ARE FRIGHTENED OF NEW IDEAS; I'M FRIGHTENED OF THE OLD ONES

4'33" (1952), JOHN CAGE

IN CONTEXT

FOCUS
Indeterminacy, aleatory music, and silence

BEFORE
1787 Mozart is thought to write "Instructions for the composition of as many waltzes as one desires with two dice, without understanding anything about music or composition."

1915 Marcel Duchamp composes *Erratum musicale* for three voices, written by drawing cards out of a hat.

AFTER
1967 Cornelius Cardew completes *Treatise*, a large graphic score with no musical parameters.

1983 Morton Feldman completes String Quartet No. 2, his longest work exploring the slow unfolding of music.

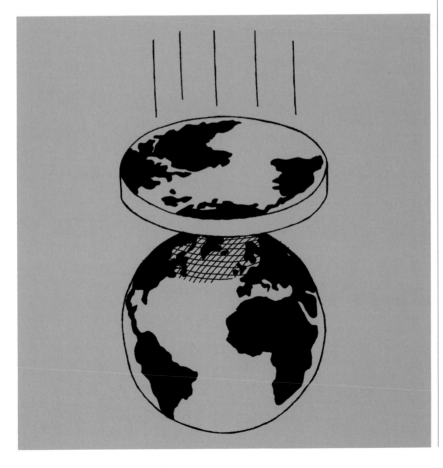

F or centuries, "indeterminacy" has been a compositional feature of classical music—from Baroque works with a figured bass that trusts the keyboard player to fill in the harmony in a manner not stipulated by the composer, to the "musical dice games" that were popular in the 18th century, in which players threw dice to decide on the order of a series of musical ideas given by a composer. A version of the game attributed to Mozart, for example, has the possibility of creating as many as 45,949,729,863,572,161 waltzes.

In the 20th century, avant-garde composers pushed the concept further, and the term "aleatory

Cage's experiments in sound led to his invention of the "prepared piano," in which the piano has its sound altered by the placement of objects on or between the strings.

view, espoused by Stravinsky, that even interpretation was unnecessary. The performer's only concern, it claimed, was to reproduce the score without interference. This attitude reached its apogee with the advent of integral, or total, serialism, in which virtually all the musical parameters were controlled by the compositional system.

Cage the anarchist

For the American composer John Cage, this imbalance of power toward the composer created a musical hierarchy in opposition to his socialist and anarchist beliefs. The only way this hierarchy could be undermined, he thought, was if either the composer were less or the performer more a part of the compositional process. »

John Cage

Born in Los Angeles in 1912, John Cage studied music under Arnold Schoenberg and Henry Cowell and used serial techniques in his early works. By 1939, he had started to experiment with the prepared piano, tape recorders, and other technology. His concert at the New York Museum of Modern Art in 1943 brought him to the attention of a wider musical community.

In the years that followed, Cage explored Buddhism and other eastern philosophies and became fixated on the nature of music and its absence. His compositions brought fame and infamy. Although he never fully abandoned notated scores, his experimentalism led to him becoming an icon of the Fluxus movement, espousing "found" sound and materials. Plagued by poor health, Cage suffered a fatal stroke in 1992 at the age of 80.

Other key works

1946–1948 *Sonatas and Interludes*
1958 *Concert for Piano and Orchestra*
1974–1975 *Études Australes*
1987 *Europeras I and II*

music" was coined to describe compositions in which chance plays a significant role. Early on, Dadaists—an avant-garde art movement—saw that chance could form a part of a new aesthetic. French-American artist Marcel Duchamp composed two aleatory works between 1913 and 1915, while Frenchmen Francis Picabia and Georges Ribemont-Dessaignes wrote works for performance at the Festival Dada in Paris, in 1920.

The composer's role

Although aleatory music originated in pure experimentalism, it was considered a serious concept by the mid-20th century, a reaction to what had gone before. Ever since composers had moved from figured bass to full notation, performers had gradually lost a sense of being actively creative musicians, and as improvised ornamentation fell by the wayside, and scores became more detailed, there had been a

If you develop an ear for sounds that are musical, it is like developing an ego. You begin to refuse sounds that are not musical and that way cut yourself off from a good deal of experience.
John Cage

This concept is particularly evident in Cage's *Imaginary Landscape No.4 for 12 radios* (1951), in which the "performers" manipulate short-wave radios and so require no proficiency in an instrument. Cage remains the composer, as the various frequencies that the operators must find are detailed in the score, but the sounds received by the radios depend on when and where the concert takes place and are therefore unpredictable. The result is white noise interrupted by snatches of speech and music.

Musical silence

Cage's seminal work, *4′33″*, in which the performers sit in silence for the duration (four minutes and 33 seconds), was inspired by the idea of silence as a part of music. Musicians had long used silence in music—Beethoven is reputed to have said that the music was in the silences—but for Cage this was an engagement with the Japanese idea of *Ma*, which

examines the human perception and experience of the space between things as a focus in its own right. Cage became fascinated by the idea of silence and went to Harvard University to experience its anechoic chamber, in which all sound is absorbed. Cage was shocked to find that even there, he could still hear two sounds—one high, one low—which turned out to be the sounds of his own body.

In *4′33″*, Cage sought to portray his realization that even in musical silences, there was no true silence. While audiences new to *4′33″* tend to think the work is absurd, the experience of hearing the ambient noises of the concert hall against which music is usually played is an enlightening one. Curiously, the duration of the work, roughly the length of the 78 rpm record, was a direct challenge to the commodification of music, particularly pop music, which was a neatly packaged predictable product. In publishing the score

> The first question I ask myself when something doesn't seem to be beautiful is why do I think it's not beautiful. And very shortly you discover that there is no reason.
> **John Cage**

(which includes instructions for the performers), and in saying that the piece "may be performed by any instrumentalist," Cage is still allied to the Classical tradition.

Defining music

The first performance of *4′33″* in 1952 opened the doors to further speculation and experimentalism into what actually constitutes music. An extreme example was written by one of Cage's students, La Monte Young, whose 1960 *Piano Piece for David Tudor #1* (the American pianist and composer David Tudor had also premiered *4′33″*) gives only the following instructions: "Bring a bale of hay and a bucket of water onto the stage for the piano to eat and drink. The performer may then feed the piano or leave it to eat by itself. If the former, the piece is over after the piano has been fed. If the latter, it is over after the piano eats or

An anechoic chamber in Bell Laboratories, New Jersey, in the 1950s, is lined with wedge-shaped pieces of fibre-glass, which was commonly used in such chambers to absorb echoes.

One of John Cage's aleatory methods

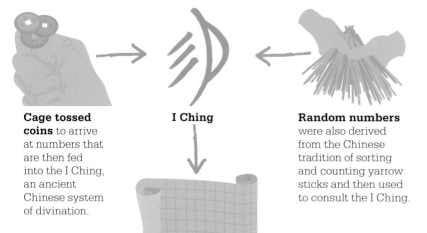

Cage tossed coins to arrive at numbers that are then fed into the I Ching, an ancient Chinese system of divination.

I Ching

Random numbers were also derived from the Chinese tradition of sorting and counting yarrow sticks and then used to consult the I Ching.

Cage created a series of charts to translate the results of his findings into sounds (including silence), duration, and volume.

decides not to." Equally challenging to musical orthodoxy were some of American composer Morton Feldman's works, which sought to redefine the act of listening by unfolding music very slowly on a very large scale. Some listeners used to classical works, which average 25 to 30 minutes, were dismayed by his Second String Quartet (1983), which lasts some five hours in performance and defies conventional development. In music on such a scale, which is seldom loud and never fast, and where changes are subtle, each sound takes on its own meaning.

Graphic scores

Composers also sought to create notation that might empower rather than enslave the performer. In his notation for *Projections and Intersections* (1950–1953), Feldman allowed the players to choose pitches and rhythms themselves. The most important new form of

notation was the graphic score. This generally presented very few parameters for the performers and instead proffered a visual provocation against which they could create music. Some of these were a set of visual instructions defining the broad shape of the music, such as Cage's *Aria* (1958), but others presented complex and subtle imagery that bore little relation to a performable sound.

The preeminent example of a graphic musical score was British composer Cornelius Cardew's *Treatise* (1963–1967), a 193-page graphic score that allows total interpretative freedom but expects the performers to decide on the meaning of certain features in the score beforehand. Indeed, as traditions of performance began to coalesce, graphic scores were seldom used as inspirations for improvisation but as a way for performer and composer to have equal responsibility for the work. ∎

Music of Changes

In 1951, Cage was given a copy of the *I Ching* by the American composer Christian Wolff. Also known as the *Book of Changes*, this ancient Chinese text used for divination inspired the title of Cage's *Music of Changes* and came to inform much of its content. Enthralled by the concept of chance music, Cage wrote the piece by making charts that, when used in conjunction with the *I Ching*, generated pitches, note durations, dynamics, tempi, silences, and even determined how many layers of sound would be used. The resulting rhythms were too complex to notate. Cage therefore used proportional notation, in which the distance between notes on the page determined how long they were. In addition to this, some parts of the composition were to be played on the piano strings directly, and the pianist used beaters to create percussive sounds on the piano's exterior. The result was a piece for solo piano in four books, which posed demanding challenges for David Tudor, Cage's customary pianist.

Every something is an echo of nothing.
John Cage

HE HAS CHANGED OUR VIEW OF MUSICAL TIME AND FORM
GRUPPEN (1955–1957), KARLHEINZ STOCKHAUSEN

In 1955, Westdeutscher Rundfunk (WDR, the Studio for Electronic Music of the West German Radio) commissioned a new work from the German composer Karlheinz Stockhausen. That August, he rented a room in Paspels, eastern Switzerland, and planned a large and ambitious new piece. Although he initially aimed to write an electronic piece, he abandoned this idea in favor of conventional instrumentation, eventually conceiving a large-scale work for three orchestras playing simultaneously. Titled *Gruppen* ("Groups"), it became well known,

Repetition is based on body rhythms, so we identify with the heartbeat, or with walking, or with breathing.
Karlheinz Stockhausen

both for the way it developed compositional technique and for its huge orchestral soundscape.

Structure and space

The key compositional technique of *Gruppen* lies in its structure. In the 1920s, composers such as Arnold Schoenberg had devised a way of writing music based on set rows of 12 pitches. Later composers, such as Pierre Boulez and Stockhausen, took this technique further, using series or groups of notes that determined not only pitch but also musical elements such as the notes' volume and duration—a method often known as total serialism. The title of *Gruppen* refers to this technique, as the work is based on 174 formulae (short groups of notes). Yet this was not the only influence on its structure: the contours of the mountains that Stockhausen saw from his window in Switzerland inspired his organizational diagrams for the piece.

Stockhausen scored the work for three orchestras, each with its own conductor and playing at a different tempo, thereby transforming the usual conception of musical time. The orchestras are arranged in a

See also: *Pierrot lunaire* 240–245 ■ Webern's *Symphonie,* Op. 21 264–265 ■ *Quartet for the End of Time* 282–283 ■ *Symphonie pour un homme seul* 298–301

The BBC Symphony Orchestra performs *Gruppen* for three orchestras on a designated "Stockhausen Day" at the BBC Proms in 2008, with Martyn Brabbins, David Robertson, and Pascal Rophé conducting.

horseshoe shape, with one in front of the audience, one to its left, and one to its right. A huge variety of sounds comes from these three locations—delicate high woodwind, passages of plucked strings, and powerful assaults from the brass. The three-orchestra format also allows the composer to use musical space dramatically, with the focus of the audience's interest passing from one orchestra to another. Material played by one ensemble can be picked up by another or tossed around between all three.

Deviations from form

The most dramatic moments in *Gruppen* occur when Stockhausen disregards the rigorous rules of total serialism. Three passages in particular abandon serial control of tempo and range of notes in order to produce musical climaxes—one highlighting violin solos by the three orchestral leaders, another involving percussive or plucked sounds that bounce from one orchestra to another, and a third, near the end of the work, featuring prominent brass chords and a piano cadenza. Despite these deviations, Stockhausen became known for his formulaic composition—as well as his experiments with spatialization, which culminated in his *Helicopter String Quartet* (1992–1995). ■

Whenever I felt happy about having discovered something, the first encounter … with other musicians, with specialists, etc, was that they rejected it.
Karlheinz Stockhausen

Karlheinz Stockhausen

Stockhausen was born in the Cologne region of Germany in 1928 and studied at Cologne University of Music. He later took lessons in Paris with Olivier Messiaen, whose serial compositional technique impressed him, and with Pierre Schaeffer, from whom he learned about musique concrète. In 1953, he began working at the electronic music studio of WDR. This led to wide-ranging works, from *Gruppen* to electronic works such as *Kontakte* (1958–1960). His last great work before his death in 2007 was *Licht,* a cycle of seven operas.

Other key works

1955–1956 *Gesang der Jünglinge* ("Song of the Youths")
1958–1960 *Kontakte* ("Contacts")
1968 *Stimmung* ("Voice")
1977–2003 *Licht* ("Light")

THE ROLE OF THE MUSICIAN ... IS PERPETUAL EXPLORATION
PITHOPRAKTA (1955–1956), IANNIS XENAKIS

IN CONTEXT

FOCUS
Music and mathematics

BEFORE
1742–1750 J.S. Bach writes the Art of Fugue comprising 14 fugues and four canons.

1912 Arnold Schoenberg writes the hyperstructured *Pierrot lunaire*.

1933 *Ionisation* by Edgard Varèse is premiered in New York. Xenakis greatly admired Varèse's originality.

1936 Béla Bartók composes *Music for Strings, Percussion, and Celesta*, incorporating symmetrical design.

1950–1952 Pierre Boulez extends the scope of Schoenberg's 12-tone method by creating serial music.

AFTER
1960 Krzysztof Penderecki creates blocks of sound in *Threnody for the Victims of Hiroshima*.

I t was Olivier Messiaen who suggested that Iannis Xenakis should apply mathematical and engineering principles to musical composition. Xenakis, who had studied engineering, was working in Paris for the avant-garde designer and architect Le Corbusier after fleeing the anti-communist regime in postwar Greece.

Scientific basis

Pithoprakta, an early work whose title comes from the Greek for "actions through probabilities," is typical of Xenakis's technique, which he called "stochastic," a term relating to probability. Scored for 46 stringed instruments, two trombones, a xylophone, and a wood block, the work was inspired by the scientific theory that a gas's temperature derives from the movement of its molecules through space. Compiling a sequence of imaginary temperatures and pressures, Xenakis translated the theory to stringed instruments moving through their pitch ranges, using a series of *glissandi* (rapid

The role of the musician must be this fundamental research: to find answers to phenomena we don't understand.
Iannis Xenakis

slides through different pitches) for each instrument. Punctuated by the wood block, trombones, and xylophone, the effect is of a seething, gaslike "sound mass."

Outlined in his book *Musiques formelles* (*Formalized Music*, 1963), Xenakis's style has had a lasting impact. Among others who cite his influence, Richard Barrett, a Welsh composer who studied genetics, says the book helped him decide to become a composer. ∎

See also: *Pierrot lunaire* 240–245 ▪ *Quartet for the End of Time* 282–283 ▪ *Gruppen* 306–307 ▪ *Threnody for the Victims of Hiroshima* 310–311

CLOSE COMMUNION WITH THE PEOPLE IS THE NATURAL SOIL NOURISHING ALL MY WORK
SPARTACUS (1956, REV. 1968), ARAM KHACHATURIAN

IN CONTEXT

FOCUS
Ballet in Soviet Russia

BEFORE
1921 Mikhail Gnessin, who later taught Khachaturian, writes the opera *Abraham's Youth*, one of several works on Jewish themes.

1927 Backed by the Kremlin, *The Red Poppy*, a ballet with music by Reinhold Glière, premieres at the Bolshoi Theatre in Moscow.

1940 Prokofiev's *Romeo and Juliet* is widely regarded as the greatest ballet written during the Soviet period.

AFTER
1976 Armenian composer Edgar Hovhannisyan bases his opera-ballet *Sasuntsi Davit* on a ninth-century Armenian epic poem.

The ballet *Spartacus*, known best in its revised 1968 version, is a spectacle on a grand scale. Unlike most ballets, its theme is not romantic but heroic—a slave rebellion led by Spartacus against his Roman masters.

The ballet won Khachaturian a Lenin Prize in the year of its composition. The Soviet regime felt it symbolized the Russian people's victory against tsarist oppressors. Others, however, now see it as referencing Soviet repression. In 1948, together with Prokofiev and Shostakovich, Khachaturian had been denounced for bourgeois "antidemocratic" music, but he had regained official favor, especially after Stalin's death in 1953.

Childhood influences
Khachaturian had grown up in Georgia, steeped in the folk music of Armenia and the Caucasian region. The melodies and harmonic inflections of the composer's childhood, along with his commitment to "close communion"

with ordinary people and their music, were key inspirations in his music. The hauntingly exultant "Adagio of Spartacus and Phrygia," from *Spartacus*, and the "Sabre Dance" from the ballet *Gayane*, have been widely used in television and film. The full 1968 version of *Spartacus* remains a staple of Russian ballet repertoire. ■

Aram Khachaturian, photographed in later years at the height of his fame, won worldwide acclaim for his highly popular ballets, *Spartacus* and *Gayane*.

See also: *The Nutcracker* 190–191 ■ *Romeo and Juliet* 272 ■ Shostakovich's Fifth Symphony 274–279

I WAS STRUCK BY THE EMOTIONAL CHARGE OF THE WORK

THRENODY FOR THE VICTIMS OF HIROSHIMA (1960), KRZYSZTOF PENDERECKI

IN CONTEXT

FOCUS
Music behind the Iron Curtain

BEFORE
1946 Stalin-appointed Andrei Zhdanov imposes a policy of "socialist realism," championing conventional music in eastern Europe and shunning avant-garde compositions.

1958 Russian composers such as Edison Denisov and Sofia Gubaidulina begin to emulate western experimental music and are dubbed dissidents by the authorities.

AFTER
1961 Hungarian-born, Austrian-resident György Ligeti composes *Atmosphères* for orchestra, with its sliding and combining note clusters.

1970 Witold Lutosławski's *Cello Concerto* is premiered, bringing him international success in the wake of social unrest in his native Poland.

For many contemporary listeners, Polish composer Krzysztof Penderecki's 1960 piece *Threnody for the Victims of Hiroshima* signaled an innovative new phase of music in communist eastern Europe. Until then, much of the region's music had adhered to a traditional, socialist-realist style. In Penderecki's *Threnody*, however, audiences were exposed to an unprecedented soundscape of strings, wails, and whispers.

It is scored for a string orchestra of 52 players, each one with their own individual line and with the string sections also divided into groups. The 24 violins, for example, are split into four groups of six each, to experiment with locations of sound.

The cenotaph in Hiroshima's Peace Park, Japan, commemorates those who lost their lives in the atomic bombing of Hiroshima, from which *Threnody* takes its title.

See also: Shostakovich's Fifth Symphony 274–279 ▪ *Spartacus* 309 ▪ Lutosławski's Fourth Symphony 323 ▪ Ligeti's *Études pour piano* 324

> A profoundly disturbing piece of apparently hopeless cataclysmic atmosphere in a highly individual technique of composition.
> **Karl H. Wörner**
> *Author*

As the piece begins, these four groups all play a note cluster near the top of their registers. From there, and throughout the piece, the group members play at different pitches just a quarter step apart from each other in clusters of notes, causing a sense of unease that permeates the piece.

Playing with technique

The *Threnody* is not structured conventionally but around blocks of sound—some of them based on the opening note cluster, others on thinner textures, instrumental lines, or other material. Much of the piece sounds striking because of Penderecki's instructions that players produce unusual timbres by means of irregular techniques. These include bowing the strings on the bridge of the instrument, along the fingerboard, or between the bridge and the tailpiece, or hitting the body of the instrument with the bow, or their fingers. The result is a composition quite unlike any of its time. Penderecki conceived of the work as abstract

music and planned to call it 8'37", in reference to its length. However, even though the work had not been inspired by the detonation of the atomic bomb, he retitled the work *Threnody for the Victims of Hiroshima* to increase the piece's emotional impact before entering it for a UNESCO prize in composition.

Penderecki also devised a unique, graphic way of notating his music. Instead of bar lines, the composer gave timings in seconds at regular points in the score to denote tempo. Blocks of quarter steps are shown on the score as horizontal bands. Penderecki also created additional symbols, such as a note stem that instructs the player to bend the pitch up or down a quarter step and wavering lines indicating a pitch-bending vibrato. *Threnody* made Penderecki's name and influenced other eastern European composers, such as Henryk Górecki and Kazimierz Serocki, in Poland, and the Hungarian György Ligeti, to explore new sounds and textures and ways of writing music based on blocks of sound. ▪

> This was not really political music … but it was music that was totally appropriate to the time during which we were living.
> **Krzysztof Penderecki**

Krzysztof Penderecki

Born in Dębica, Poland, in 1933, Krzysztof Penderecki was educated at the Krakow Academy of Music. Within two years of graduating in 1958, he became well known for *Threnody for the Victims of Hiroshima*. Many of his subsequent pieces also employed unconventional instrumentation, such as the typewriter and musical saw. Still more popular was Penderecki's *St. Luke Passion* (1966), which combined unusual textures with a traditional form and Christian theme.

In the 1970s, Penderecki became a professor at the Yale School of Music. His output returned to a more conventional musical style in pieces such as his Symphony No. 2 (1980). With a catalogue of works in various forms, Penderecki, who is still composing music, is widely regarded as Poland's greatest living composer.

Other key works

1960 *Anaklasis, for 42 strings and Percussion*
1970–1971 *Utrenja*
1984 *Polish Requiem*
1988–1995 Symphony No. 3

ONCE YOU BECOME AN ISM, WHAT YOU'RE DOING IS DEAD
IN C (1964), TERRY RILEY

IN CONTEXT

FOCUS
Minimalism

BEFORE
1893 Erik Satie composes "Vexations," a piano piece that is widely recognized as being a forerunner of minimalism.

1958 La Monte Young writes his *Trio for Strings*, considered to be the original work of musical minimalism.

1960–1962 In *Mescalin Mix,* Riley develops the technique of repetitions using tape delay.

AFTER
1967–1968 Philip Glass writes a succession of minimalist pieces, including *Gradus* (for solo saxophone) and *1 + 1* (for amplified tabletop).

1971 The Who's song "Baba O'Riley," dedicated to Terry Riley, opens with a keyboard riff inspired by trademark minimalist repetition.

I n 1950s' America, a generation of artists, such as Donald Judd, Richard Serra, and Frank Stella, championed a new kind of minimalist art. Inspired partly by Piet Mondrian and other artists of the Dutch De Stijl movement founded in 1917, it relied on plain, often industrial, materials and was free of any explicit meaning or influence. In music, too, American composers, including La Monte Young, Steve Reich, and Terry Riley, looked to strip notation, instrumentation, and rhythm to their barest essentials. To this they added

In C is revolutionary. It introduces repetition as a primary constructive force into Western music.
Robert Davidson
Composer and student of Riley

a new set of materials, including sound "samples" recorded on magnetic tape and played on a repeated "loop."

Breaking new ground
In C was the work in which Terry Riley defined the musical style that became known as minimalism. It features a steady pulse, gradual transformation, and the repetition of short phrases or musical cells, focusing the attention, not on a goal toward which the music is progressing, but on a continuous process of change.

Riley did not begin with the aim of writing a "minimalist" piece. *In C* emerged partly from his experimentation with tape loops, particularly when he collaborated with trumpeter Chet Baker on the music for a theatre production, called *The Gift*, in Paris in 1963. He recorded Baker and his musicians then made loops from the tapes and played them back simultaneously but starting at different times so they repeated out of sync.

In C uses a similar technique but with live players rather than tapes. The piece consists of 53 musical phases of varying length (none longer than 32 beats) that

See also: *4′33″* 302–305 ▪ *Six Pianos* 320 ▪ *Einstein on the Beach* 321

Seated at his keyboard, Terry Riley accompanies the Lahore-born musician Pandit Pran Nath—one of his earliest mentors—in a concert at Le Palace Theatre, Paris, in 1972.

can be played by any number of instruments and ensembles of any size, although Riley prefers a group of between 25 and 30 musicians. The performers play the phrases in a set order but can repeat each phrase as many times as they like, creating a piece that can vary in length from 20 minutes to several hours. The musicians also start the phrases at different times, so they are not always synchronized.

The work is anchored by a rhythmic pulse provided by one musician who repeats the C note throughout—acting as a kind of metronome. This is usually played on the piano or a percussion instrument, such as a marimba.

A lasting presence

Although *In C* has been called the first truly minimalist work, it followed a number of earlier experiments from the late 1950s and displays major differences from many other works in the genre. In most minimalist pieces, the composer typically controls the material much more tightly than Riley, who leaves crucial decisions, such as the instrumentation and the number of repetitions, to the performers. This is known as "aleatory," or chance-driven, music (from the Latin *alea*, meaning "game of dice").

Riley has rejected the "minimalist" label—and resisted being limited by any kind of "ism." In spite of this, his work has been hugely influential on composers such as Michael Nyman and Gavin Bryars in Britain, Americans Steve Reich and Philip Glass, and the Estonian Arvo Pärt, who have all embraced elements of minimalism in their work. Riley's hypnotic musical approach also influenced the rise of "ambient" music in the 1970s. ▪

Terry Riley

Born in California in 1935, Terry Riley met La Monte Young, with whom he was to forge a new and radical approach to music, while studying composition at the University of California. In the 1960s, as well as pioneering the use of tape loops, Riley embraced electronic overdubbing, especially on the album *A Rainbow in Curved Air* (1969), on which he played all the instrumental parts himself—a major influence on Mike Oldfield's similarly virtuosic album *Tubular Bells* (1973). In the 1970s, Riley studied Indian classical music, which he has continued to combine with his interest in avant-garde Western music and jazz. In the same decade, Riley began a long-lasting collaboration with the Kronos Quartet, producing many works, including *Sun Rings*, which features sounds gathered from space.

Other key works

1969 *A Rainbow in Curved Air*
1971–1972 *Persian Surgery Dervishes*
1989 *Salome Dances for Peace*
2002 *Sun Rings*

I DESIRE TO CARVE ... A SINGLE PAINFUL TONE AS INTENSE AS SILENCE ITSELF

NOVEMBER STEPS (1967), TORU TAKEMITSU

IN CONTEXT

FOCUS
East meets West

BEFORE
1903 Inspired by East Asia, and the European trend of exoticism, Claude Debussy mimicked Chinese and Japanese melodies in *Pagodes*, the first movement of his *Estampes* (*Engravings*).

AFTER
1991 In his *Quotation of Dream*, subtitled "Say Sea, Take Me," from a poem by Emily Dickinson, Takemitsu quotes Debussy's *La Mer*.

1998 Chinese American composer Tan Dun dedicates his *Water Concerto for Water Percussion and Orchestra* to the memory of Takemitsu.

Takemitsu composed *November Steps* in his secluded private cottage on Mount Asama in central Honshu, Japan's main island. The only materials he had with him were Debussy's original manuscript piano scores of *Prélude à l'après-midi d'un faune* and *Jeux*, with their multicolored notation and handwritten commentaries.

In *November Steps,* Takemitsu employs traditional Japanese instruments—the *shakuhachi* (an end-blown flute) and *biwa* (a short-necked lute). His aim in this piece was not to blend their sounds into the Western orchestra but to contrast their timbre with those of a Western ensemble. He succeeded in reviving the essential nature of the Japanese instruments, creating a striking intensity against the orchestra's sound stream, couched in a unique tone language.

A cosmic world of music
Takemitsu was first exposed to Western Classical music, represented by such figures as Debussy, Alban Berg, and Olivier Messiaen, during military service in World War II. He would later create his own cosmic world of music that infused these influences with Eastern and Japanese sensitivity. Inspired by Debussy's rare intuition, Takemitsu came to recognize the "light and

The traditional *biwa*, used in *November Steps*, is played here in 2007 in New York by Junko Tahara to music by Joji Yuasa, an early member of Takemitsu's experimental workshop.

See also: *Das Lied von der Erde* 198–201 ▪ *Prélude à l'après-midi d'un faune* 228–231 ▪ *Quartet for the End of Time* 282–283 ▪ *4'33"* 302–305

> I am a gardener of time.
> I want to create a garden
> connecting to infinite time.
> **Toru Takemitsu**

shade of sound" and what he called a "density of tones." From Messiaen, Takemitsu learned "the conception of the form and color of time," as he put it, and in fact wrote his piano piece *Rain Tree Sketch II* (1992) in memory of the composer.

Unlike Messiaen, Takemitsu did not belong to a particular religion but considered himself a religious person. The act of composing was for him a prayer: he likened it to "taking out a part of an eternal 'river of sound' running through the world surrounding us." Like his close friend John Cage, who was fascinated with fungi, and Messiaen, a passionate bird lover, Takemitsu related deeply to the natural world. As the titles of many of his works indicate, he felt his music was intimately linked to both nature and the universe.

Silence and sound

Takemitsu had a profound interest in the relationship between silence and sound. The Eastern concept of "Ma," an intense silence between sounds, was for him contrary to the Western idea of a musical "rest"— literally, a resting silence. In the East, too, according to Takemitsu,

"one tone of the *shakuhachi* can become *Hotoke* [God]." That is, a single tone can embody cosmic nature. In the West, by contrast, tones are joined together into melodies, rhythms, and harmonies. Takemitsu never used conventional Western musical forms. Most of his works are short, reflecting characteristics of Japanese literature, such as Haiku poetry.

Colorful sonorities are one hallmark of Takemitsu's music. As the Western orchestra possesses perhaps the greatest capacity to create different tone colors, it is no coincidence that he wrote a large number of orchestral works. Takemitsu also devised unique compositional techniques, later adopted by younger Japanese composers. In the piano piece *Les yeux clos* ("Eyes closed," 1979), he created layers of simultaneous melodies with slightly different note values so that each note makes a tiny anticipation, or delay, erasing the sense of beats and creating a fluidlike texture. Takemitsu's music is wholly original—a unique juxtaposition of Japanese and Western musical traditions. ▪

> A Western tone walks
> horizontally but a tone
> of the *shakuhachi* rises
> vertically like a tree.
> **Toru Takemitsu**

Toru Takemitsu

Born in Tokyo, Japan, in 1930, Takemitsu briefly studied composition with Yasuji Kiyose in 1948 but was essentially self-taught. In 1951, he organized the experimental workshop "Jikken Kobo" with the poet Shuzo Takiguchi and others pursuing avant-garde methods. Takemitsu's *Requiem for Strings* (1957), written after the death of composer Fumio Hayasaka whom he adored, was praised by Stravinsky. A decade later, the success of *November Steps* established his international reputation as the leading Japanese composer. From the 1970s, he used fewer Japanese instruments in his works, preferring conventional Western instruments and more tonal sonorities, as in pieces such as *A String around Autumn* (1989). He composed a large number of works with Western idioms and wrote music for more than 90 Japanese films. Takemitsu died in Tokyo in 1996.

Other key works

1957 *Requiem for Strings*
1979 *In an Autumn Garden*
1994 *Archipelago S.*

IN MUSIC ... THINGS DON'T GET BETTER OR WORSE: THEY EVOLVE AND TRANSFORM THEMSELVES
SINFONIA (1968–1969), LUCIANO BERIO

IN CONTEXT

FOCUS
Quotation and collage

BEFORE
1906 American composer
Charles Ives writes "Central
Park in the Dark," an early
example of musical collage.

1952 *Imaginary Landscape
No. 5* by John Cage creates an
unpredictable collage using 42
records as its source materials.

AFTER
1977 Alfred Schnittke
composes his Concerto Grosso
No. 1 in an example of the
collage technique that he
called "polystylism."

1981 *The Adventures of
Grandmaster Flash on the
Wheels of Steel* showcases
the virtuoso DJ mixing
techniques that were a
foundation of early hip-hop.

The 1960s—a decade of
profound social change—
reached its height in 1968,
the year in which Luciano Berio's
Sinfonia had its first performance.
These changes—the Civil Rights
Movement, student protests, new
mass media channels, and the
clash of high art and popular
culture—were happening on
streets and in homes around the
world, and all made their way into
Italian composer Luciano Berio's
dismantling and reconstruction
of classical music history.

The Swingle Singers perform in
1965, typically with only drums and
double bass as accompaniment. The
French group made jazzy covers of
both popular and classical pieces.

Sinfonia—the title of which is
a deliberate allusion to the old-
fashioned symphony genre—
established Berio as one of the
most inventive composers of his
generation. Commissioned by
Leonard Bernstein and the New
York Philharmonic Orchestra, it is
best known for its extraordinary

See also: *Magnus liber organi* 28–31 ▪ Ives's Symphony No. 4 254–255 ▪ *Symphonie pour un homme seul* 298–301 ▪ *Gruppen* 306–307

third movement, which consists of a whirl of musical quotations from Bach to Pierre Boulez. Running throughout its 12 minutes is the largest quotation of all: the dancing, spinning Scherzo from Mahler's Symphony No. 2, "Resurrection."

The quotation technique

Composers had used quotation and even collage techniques before; as early as 1906, and before artists such as Picasso and Braque had painted visual collages in the early 1910s, Charles Ives had layered different melodies and musical styles in "Central Park in the Dark." More recently, John Cage had begun experimenting with playing records and differently tuned radios simultaneously. In a way, quotation had been a part of classical music since the masters of organum used Gregorian chants to make their polyphonic church music in the 12th century. However, *Sinfonia* was the first time quotation had been used to such an extent: it was a whole movement for full orchestra, created almost entirely from borrowed materials.

On top of all of this are the vocal lines. Eight singers perform from a text in which passages from Samuel Beckett's *The Unnamable* are mixed with extracts from James Joyce, Paul Valéry, musical directions, and slogans from the Paris protests. In order for the singers to be heard, their voices needed to be amplified, and Berio turned to the Swingle Singers, a popular group in their day, because of their familiarity with microphone technique.

Sinfonia is a five-part meditation on the past and the future. The first part was originally intended

to stand alone. "O King," the work's second movement, was written in 1967 as a tribute to the Reverend Martin Luther King Jr. After King's assassination in April 1968, Berio decided to incorporate it into *Sinfonia*, expanding that into a work for four singers and full orchestra and serving now as a memorial to the Civil Rights leader. Its text simply repeats King's name, separated into "phonemes" (the smallest individual sounds of a word) and stretched across wide intervals of time, as though evaporating into the air.

Other influences

Sinfonia's fourth movement is also a lament, in which Berio mourns all of the lost heroes and ideas of movements two and three. Unlike these, the first movement is a study in Brazilian origin myths, drawing on text extracted from Claude Lévi-Strauss's revolutionary, and recently published study in mythology, *The Raw and the Cooked* (1964). The fifth and final movement, which Berio added only after the work's premiere, synthesizes and reflects upon the previous four. ∎

Using Mahler was a tribute to Leonard Bernstein, who has done so much for his music.
Luciano Berio

Luciano Berio

Berio was born in the town of Oneglia, Italy, in 1924. His father and grandfather, who were both organists, taught him to play the piano. After World War II, he went to study at the Milan Conservatory, but an injury to his hand forced him to give up piano studies for composition. He married the American singer and composer Cathy Berberian in 1950, writing several works for her before their divorce in 1964.

Berio's interest in the avant-garde movement began in the 1950s, and he became Italy's leading composer in the genre. In 1955, he established an electronic studio in Milan—one of the world's first—with Bruno Maderna. Berio was also a respected teacher of composition, particularly at the Juilliard School in New York. His pupils included Steve Reich and Grateful Dead guitarist Phil Lesh. Berio died in Rome in 2003.

Other key works

1958 *Thema (Omaggio a Joyce)*
1966 *Sequenza III*
1977 Coro

IF YOU TELL ME A LIE, LET IT BE A BLACK LIE

EIGHT SONGS FOR A MAD KING (1969), PETER MAXWELL DAVIES

IN CONTEXT

FOCUS
Theatre and radicalism in English music

BEFORE
1912 Arnold Schoenberg's song-cycle melodrama *Pierrot lunaire* launches the concept of the avant garde.

1968 The ritualistic violence of Harrison Birtwistle's opera *Punch and Judy* disconcerts listeners at the UK's Aldeburgh Festival, including its founder, Benjamin Britten.

AFTER
1972 Maxwell Davies's opera *Taverner*, an ambitiously dramatic portrait of the Tudor composer John Taverner, is first performed at the Royal Opera House, Covent Garden.

1986 Birtwistle's "lyric tragedy" *The Mask of Orpheus*, a theatrical representation on an immense scale of multiple versions of the Orpheus legend, premieres in London.

With some exceptions—such as the areas of psychology and imagination explored in the operas of Benjamin Britten and Michael Tippett—British classical music after World War II was generally in thrall to convention. Prominent new works, such as *Sinfonia antartica* (1952) by Ralph Vaughan Williams, or William Walton's Cello Concerto (1956), were seen as looking back to a traditional past rather than pointing toward an exciting new future. As the 1960s arrived, however, with their release of long pent-up desires for social and political change, a similar revolution in classical music was about to erupt.

New blood

When Peter Maxwell Davies entered the Royal Manchester College of Music in 1952, he found a number of like-minded radical fellow-students: composers Harrison Birtwistle and Alexander Goehr, trumpeter and conductor Elgar Howarth, and pianist John Ogdon. This new "Manchester School" was an informal group of very different artistic personalities. While Goehr's music related to the modern Austro-German tradition of the inter-war years, with its roots in the style and technical method of Arnold Schoenberg, Birtwistle looked to reconnect with ancient theatrical ritual, particularly Greek

The ravings of the mentally afflicted George III (1738–1820), King of Great Britain and Ireland, provided the disconcerting basis for the libretto of *Eight Songs for a Mad King*.

See also: *Pierrot lunaire* 240–245 ▪ *A Child of Our Time* 284–285 ▪ *Peter Grimes* 288–293 ▪ *In Seven Days* 328

theatre. Davies meanwhile rebelled against conventional teaching methods in the quest for a modern composing idiom developed from the musical techniques and structures of Renaissance Europe.

Music theatre

In the 1960s, the avant-garde genre of "music theatre" provided Davies with a vehicle for his modernist style. In music theatre, musicians shared the stage with vocal and theatrical performers, all taking part equally in the drama. The idea had its origins in Schoenberg's groundbreaking atonal work *Pierrot lunaire* (1912), with its new kind of part-singing, part-spoken vocal performance and strong theatrical elements.

In 1967, Davies and Birtwistle founded a chamber group to perform *Pierrot lunaire* and more contemporary pieces. It was called the Pierrot Players, after the Schoenberg work, and in 1970 reformed as The Fires of London. The group set out to stage provocatively subversive dramatic works in small venues. Among these was *Eight Songs for a Mad King*, portraying the unhinged psychological world of the British monarch King George III. Some of the group's players were deployed on stage in cages to represent the caged birds that the king liked to talk to. Alongside the traditional instruments used, such as violin, cello, and clarinet, were unusual examples, including a railway whistle, steel bar, didgeridoo, and toy bird calls.

The vocal part, written for the South African baritone Roy Hart, exploited an extraordinary range of sounds, from singing to screaming and screeching, extremely high or low notes, and even simultaneous notes sung together in chords.

Fusion sounds

Although the work was a huge success, Davies soon moved away from composing purely avant-garde pieces. From 1972, he turned his attention to classical forms and went on to write 10 orchestral symphonies, many of which were inspired by his new home of Orkney, Scotland.

Over the course of his career, Davies gained a reputation for polystylism—combining disparate genres in one piece. By the turn of the 21st century, classical music in Britain had similarly moved far beyond the dominance of any one set of stylistic values. The music of Jonathan Harvey mastered the fusion of vocal, instrumental, and electronic sounds, whereas John Tavener successfully absorbed the music of Eastern Orthodox Christianity into the Western concert hall. The music of Mark-Anthony Turnage, meanwhile, has boldly incorporated elements of jazz into classical pieces. ▪

Sometimes I suspect that Davies himself may be a little bit mad.
Peter G. Davis
Music critic (1983)

Peter Maxwell Davies

Born in Salford, Lancashire, in 1934, Davies won a place at the Royal Manchester College of Music. After further study in Italy, he taught music at Cirencester Grammar School, starting a lifelong commitment to musical education. After spells studying and teaching in the US and Australia, he returned to England in 1966, where he gained a reputation as a controversial figure in contemporary music.

A visit to the Orkney Islands in Scotland in 1970 began a deep involvement with the islands and their culture. He settled on Hoy in 1974, later moving to another island, Sanday. In 1976, he founded the St. Magnus International Festival, named after Orkney's patron saint, involving local people alongside professional musicians. Davies was Master of the Queen's Music from 2004 until his death in 2016.

Other key works

1960 *O Magnum Mysterium*
1962–1970 *Taverner*
1969 *Worldes Blis*
1976–1977 *The Martyrdom of St Magnus*

THE PROCESS OF SUBSTITUTING BEATS FOR RESTS
SIX PIANOS (1973), STEVE REICH

IN CONTEXT

FOCUS
Late minimalism

BEFORE
1958 American composer
La Monte Young completes
his pioneering minimalist
work, *Trio for Strings*.

1964 Terry Riley's *In C* is an
influential minimalist work; it
uses simple musical fragments
to create a wavelike sound.

AFTER
1978 Brian Eno's *Ambient 1:
Music for Airports* introduces
minimalism into popular
music, helping to create the
new genre of ambient music.

1982 Minimalism and
medieval Gregorian chant
influence the Estonian Arvo
Pärt in works such as his
St. John Passion.

First performed in New York
in 1973, Reich's *Six Pianos*
employs the "phasing"
technique the American composer
had developed in the 1960s. The six
pianists play the same repeated
eight-beat rhythmic pattern, but
each strikes different notes. The
repeated pattern produces richly
textured, shifting waves of sound
as the pianists move in and out of
phase with each other.

Rhythm and repetition
Reich was an early adherent of
the minimalist style that began to
emerge in the United States in the
late 1950s. Pioneered by La Monte
Young and Terry Riley, soon joined
by Philip Glass and Reich, it was a
reaction against the serialism of
European composers such as
Arnold Schoenberg and Pierre
Boulez. In contrast to melodies and
harmonies based on the 12-tone
chromatic scale, minimalism used
repeated chords or sequences that
changed only by tiny increments
over the course of a piece. It was
also marked by strong rhythms.

Although his style was initially
controversial, by 1976 Reich's *Music
for 18 Musicians* was well received.
In the 1980s, he moved away from
strict minimalism, developing
richer harmonies and melodies.

Notable later works by Reich,
whose style has influenced both
classical and popular music,
include *Different Trains* (1988)
and *The Cave* (1993), a multimedia
opera created with his wife, the
video artist Beryl Korot. ∎

Reel-to-reel tapes and other
recording equipment enabled Reich,
shown here in 1982, to perfect the
phasing techniques that he would
then apply to live instruments.

See also: *Pierrot lunaire* 240–245 ▪ *Gruppen* 306–307 ▪ *Threnody for the Victims
of Hiroshima* 310–311 ▪ *In C* 312–313 ▪ *Einstein on the Beach* 321

WE WERE SO FAR AHEAD ... BECAUSE EVERYONE ELSE STAYED SO FAR BEHIND
EINSTEIN ON THE BEACH (1976), PHILIP GLASS

IN CONTEXT

FOCUS
Minimalism and opera

BEFORE
1954 Glass visits Paris and sees films by Jean Cocteau that later become the basis for his operas, *Orphée* (1993), *La Belle et la bête* (1994), and *Les Enfants terribles* (1996).

1965 In an early involvement with avant-garde theatre, Glass writes music for Samuel Beckett's one-act *Play*.

AFTER
1977 David Bowie's albums *Low* and *"Heroes,"* created with Brian Eno, will later inspire Glass's symphonies No. 1 (1992) and No. 4 (1996).

1990 Glass and Indian musician Ravi Shankar release *Passages*, an album of chamber music that they have composed together.

Created in collaboration with the avant-garde theatre director Robert Wilson, Philip Glass's opera *Einstein on the Beach* was first performed in 1976, in Avignon, France. Inspired by the life of the physicist Albert Einstein, it has no plot but works through image, dance, and music, using recurring projected images to evoke aspects of Einstein's world. There is no orchestra but only an ensemble of electronic keyboards and wind instruments. Words are sparse and incantatory. The work has no intervals and lasts five hours, during which the audience can come and go as they please.

Powerful, hypnotic music
Einstein on the Beach was the fruit of a decade of experimenting. Glass was classically trained, but like Reich and others in the emerging minimalist movement, he rejected earlier styles. After transcribing some of Ravi Shankar's Indian sitar music and traveling in India and North Africa in the 1960s, he began to develop a style of his own based,

I was in that generation of people who could look beyond the borders of Europe and North ... and South America.
Philip Glass

in his words, "on repetitive and cyclic structures." The result was often hypnotic—arpeggio and harmonic motifs repeated for long stretches virtually unchanged.

His success with *Einstein on the Beach* was followed by *Satyagraha* (1980), *Akhnaten* (1984), and a number of other operas, film scores, symphonies, and other works. Glass influenced musicians such as David Bowie, Brian Eno, and the band Pink Floyd; their music also influenced his own. ∎

See also: *Gruppen* 306–307 ▪ *In C* 312–313 ▪ *Eight Songs for a Mad King* 318–319 ▪ *Six Pianos* 320

THIS MUST BE THE FIRST PURPOSE OF ART ... TO CHANGE US

APOCALYPSIS (1977) R. MURRAY SCHAFER

IN CONTEXT

FOCUS
Sonic ecology

BEFORE
1912 Mahler writes his Eighth Symphony, a bid "to imagine the whole universe beginning to ring and resound."

1966 Schafer begins *Patria*, a cycle of large-scale music theatre works conceived for special (often outdoor) spaces.

AFTER
1994 *The Apocalypse* by John Tavener is premiered at the BBC Proms.

2003 With *Sonntag*, Karlheinz Stockhausen completes his seven-opera cycle *Licht*.

2006 John Luther Adams's *The Place Where You Go To Listen,* a sound and light installation reflecting natural rhythms, opens in Alaska.

Conceived on the grandest scale, with multiple ensembles, singers, and instrumentalists, Schafer's musical spectacle *Apocalypsis* (1977) is part of a long tradition in Western art music that extends back to Monteverdi's *Vespers*. An even earlier inspiration is Tallis's motet *Spem in alium*, whose immersive use of eight five-voice choirs influenced the 12 spatially arranged choirs used in the second part of *Apocalypsis*, "Credo."

Opposing sound pollution

Schafer, who founded the study of acoustic ecology in the 1960s, pursues ecological themes in his work, opposing the gradual masking of the natural soundscape by man-made noise. Such themes are the subject of *Apocalypsis*.

The first part, "John's Vision," tells of the destruction of the world using texts from the Bible's Book of Revelation and a new Antichrist's vision of good (cities, jet aircraft, computers, and "the habit of energy") and evil (museums, feminism, sentiment, and art). This vision, clearly opposed to Schafer's ethics, is vanquished in the second part, "Credo." Here, Schafer adapts 12 meditations from Giordano Bruno's cosmological treatise *De la causa, principio et uno* of 1584. Each starts, "Lord God is universe," creating a cumulative, ritualistic effect. The last proclaims "Universe is one: one act, one form, one soul, one body, one being, the maximum, and only," encapsulating Schafer's spiritual and ecological beliefs. ∎

Schafer's *Apocalypsis* is inspired by the vision in Revelation in which four horsemen, depicted here in a woodcut by Christoph Murer (1558–1614), are the harbingers of the Last Judgment.

See also: *Spem in alium* 44–45 ▪ Monteverdi's *Vespers* 64–69 ▪ *St. Matthew Passion* 98–105 ▪ *Elijah* 170–173 ▪ *The Dream of Gerontius* 218–219

I COULD START OUT FROM THE CHAOS AND CREATE ORDER IN IT

FOURTH SYMPHONY (1993)
WITOLD LUTOSŁAWSKI

IN CONTEXT

FOCUS
"Controlled aleatory" composition

BEFORE
1958 John Cage composes his *Concert for Piano and Orchestra*.

1961 After hearing a snippet of Cage's *Concert* on the radio, Lutosławski uses "controlled aleatory" for the first time in his *Jeux vénitiens*.

AFTER
2003 Lutosławski's Polish colleague Wojciech Kilar composes *September Symphony* (Symphony No. 3) to commemorate the 9/11 attacks in New York City.

2011 Liza Lim's *Tongue of the Invisible* is one of many contemporary works since Lutosławski's death that combine controlled improvisation with passages in conventional notation.

The life of Polish composer Witold Lutosławski coincided with a turbulent period in Eastern Europe. At the time of his birth in 1913, Poland was partitioned between Austria, Prussia, and Russia. In World War II, the composer was briefly imprisoned by the Nazis, and after the war, he was hounded by the communist authorities. Only in his last years was Poland free.

While Lutosławski believed in the autonomy of art, critics often perceive the reflection of outside tensions in his music. Like many of his pieces, his Fourth Symphony, whose composition spanned the fall of communism, has two halves—a halting introduction, followed by a decisive and conclusive statement.

An element of chance
From the early 1960s, a consistent feature of his music was his use of "controlled aleatory" passages, in which the coordination between instrumental parts is partially governed by chance. They may be fully written out, but how they line up is only partly predictable—they may start at different times, for example. The method is evident in the Fourth Symphony's first section: at three points, rhythmic music dissolves into disarray, like a false start to a race, creating a sense of anticipation that is resolved in the work's more assertive second half.

The Fourth Symphony was Lutosławski's last work. He died in 1994, a year after conducting its Los Angeles premiere. ■

It [music] always fascinated me, and I couldn't imagine any other profession than musician, and even composer.
Witold Lutosławski

See also: Webern's *Symphonie*, Op. 21 264–265 ▪ Shostakovich's Fifth Symphony 274–279 ▪ *4'33"* 302–305 ▪ *Gruppen* 306–307

VOLCANIC, EXPANSIVE, DAZZLING—AND OBSESSIVE
ÉTUDES (1985–2001)
GYÖRGY LIGETI

The term "fractal" was first used in 1975 by the mathematician Benoit Mandelbrot, though the concept is much older. It describes images, surfaces, sounds, or other patterns made up of mini-versions of the whole, which they continue to resemble however tiny they are and however often subdivided.

The composer György Ligeti first came across fractals in 1984, in images by the mathematician Heinz-Otto Peitgen. Ligeti recognized that the principle of internal symmetry had been present in his music for years. He had used a technique he called "micropolyphony," overlaying multiple closely related versions of the same musical line to create dense, shimmering textures.

Studies in fractal style
Ligeti began to employ ideas derived from mathematics and the broader theory of chaos. He had also become interested in Central African music, the pianola studies of Conlon Nancarrow, and the jazz piano music of Bill Evans and Thelonius Monk. To synthesize these influences, he turned to the piano study, or *étude*, a form used by Chopin, Liszt, and Debussy.

Ligeti's 18 *Études* all employ rhythmic and melodic processes that interact, conflict, and even cancel each other out. Their titles, such as *Disorder* and *Vertigo*, reflect the images their streams of notes evoke. Works of fantasy, they are a major contribution to the late 20th-century repertoire. ∎

In my music one finds … a unification of construction with poetic, emotional imagination.
György Ligeti

See also: *The Art of Fugue* 108–111 ▪ Chopin's *Préludes* 164–165 ▪ *Prélude à l'après-midi d'un faune* 228–231 ▪ *Pithoprakta* 308

MY MUSIC IS WRITTEN FOR EARS
L'AMOUR DE LOIN (2000), KAIJA SAARIAHO

IN CONTEXT

FOCUS
Opera into the 21st century

BEFORE
1992 Peter Sellars stages Olivier Messiaen's opera *Saint François d'Assise*, in Salzburg, Austria; Saariaho finds it inspiring.

AFTER
2003 The opera *Rasputin* by Finnish composer Einojuhani Rautavaara receives its world premiere in Helsinki.

2008 *The Minotaur* by Harrison Birtwistle to a libretto by poet David Harsent is premiered at the Royal Opera House in London.

2015 Jennifer Higdon's grand opera, *Cold Mountain*, premieres in Santa Fe, New Mexico, United States.

F innish composer Kaija Saariaho's opera, *L'Amour de loin* (2000), was one of the first new operas of the 21st century. The lavish production, premiered at the Salzburg Festival, Austria, renewed excitement in the genre of grand opera involving large casts and orchestras; in the late 20th century, inexpensive chamber operas had been more popular.

Love from afar
Written to a French libretto by Amin Maalouf, *L'Amour de loin* is based on a sketch of Jaufré Rudel, a 12th-century French troubadour, and his love for Clémence, a woman he has idealized from a distance— hence the title, meaning "love from afar." The small solo cast is complemented by a chorus and sizeable orchestra that features accessible, consonant harmony, with electronic elements and attention to tone color—all hallmarks of Saariaho's style.

Following the opera's world premiere at the Salzburg Festival in Austria, critics praised its lyricism.

Kaija Saariaho works on a score in Paris, France, her home since 1982, when she first studied at IRCAM, the acoustic music research institute that strongly influenced her early style.

Since then, it has become one of the most frequently performed operas in the 21st century, with productions in Paris, London, New York, and Toronto.

The success of *L'Amour de loin* led to renewed interest in grand opera and further commissions. Saariaho's second grand opera, *Adriana Mater*, followed in 2005. ∎

See also: *Peer Gynt* 208–209 ▪ *The Wreckers* 232–239 ▪ *Peter Grimes* 288–293 ▪ *Einstein on the Beach* 321–322

BLUE ... LIKE THE SKY. WHERE ALL POSSIBILITIES SOAR

BLUE CATHEDRAL (2000), JENNIFER HIGDON

IN CONTEXT

FOCUS
Return to lyricism

BEFORE
1984 The New York Philharmonic programs "Horizons '84: The New Romanticism—a Broader View" draw mass public attention to Neo-romanticism.

1991 John Corigliano's opera *The Ghosts of Versailles* premieres at the Metropolitan Opera, New York City. It is the company's first new opera since the 1960s.

AFTER
2009 Film composer, John Williams's *On Willows and Birches* (Concerto for Harp and Orchestra) premieres with the Boston Symphony Orchestra.

2017 *The (R)evolution of Steve Jobs*, by Mason Bates, opens at Opera Santa Fe, Santa Fe, New Mexico.

T he unifying theme of Jennifer Higdon's music is her compositional philosophy of communicating effectively. Her work *blue cathedral* achieves this through her characteristic exploration of tone color (the quality that gives an instrument its distinct sound), combined with expressive lyricism.

In the latter half of the 20th century, many artistic ensembles were struggling financially. Contemporary music had been associated with trends such as post-minimalism, electronic works,

I don't think you should have to know anything about my music, or anything about music in general, to enjoy it ... I look at music as a mirror.
Jennifer Higdon

and experimental music that had often alienated the general public. To attract audiences, ensembles therefore chose to perform older works that entailed little risk. Higdon's *blue cathedral*, however, with its warmth, lyricism, and emotion, demonstrated that modern music could appeal to audiences of all ages and demographics, opening the door for an exciting period of new music in the 21st century.

Love, life, and death

Higdon was commissioned to write *blue cathedral* to mark the 75th anniversary of the American conservatory, the Curtis Institute of Music. Although initially conceived as a celebration, the composer was at the time mourning the death of her younger brother, Andrew Blue Higdon. Both events informed the title: "blue," in memory of her brother Andrew, to whom the score is dedicated, and "cathedral" to represent Curtis as a place of learning and growth.

In this tone poem, Higdon's heavenly music suggests a cathedral in the sky. It features numerous solo instruments, most prominently the flute and the clarinet, to represent the

See also: *Symphonie fantastique* 162–163 ▪ Saint-Saëns' Piano Concerto No. 2 in G minor 179 ▪ *Das Lied von der Erde* 198–201 ▪ *Prélude à l'après-midi d'un faune* 228–231 ▪ *The Lark Ascending* 252–253 ▪ *Appalachian Spring* 286–287

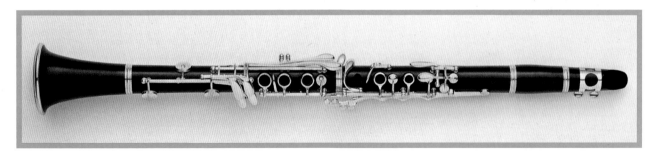

Higdon siblings who played those instruments. As Higdon is the older sibling, the flute appears first, followed by the clarinet. This duet briefly returns near the end, before the flute ceases, leaving the clarinet (Andrew) to continue its journey alone.

Additional extended solos are presented by the English horn and a violin; both are complemented by smaller instrumental melodies that represent the lives a single person touches in his or her journey. In the introduction and coda, Higdon also experiments with the percussion section, utilizing some unorthodox orchestration, such as crystal glasses and Chinese bells, to create an ethereal atmosphere.

The work premiered on May 1, 2000, in Philadelphia, Pennsylvania, with Robert Spano as conductor. Musicians and critics lauded Higdon's ability to communicate the universal themes of love, life, and death. The work's strong lyricism, exploration of orchestral color, and programmatic content made it a great success, and it became one of the 21st century's most popular compositions, with some 600 productions (at all levels) performed across the world.

The Atlanta School

Following *blue cathedral*'s premiere, Higdon began a long and fruitful association with the Atlanta Symphony Orchestra led by Spano.

The solo clarinet features prominently in *blue cathedral*. It was the instrument played by Higdon's brother, who died of skin cancer shortly before Higdon composed the piece.

The conductor initiated what would become known as the Atlanta School of Composers, a group comprising Higdon, Christopher Theofanidis, Osvaldo Golijov, Michael Gandolfi, and Adam Schoenberg. Although diverse in musical style, the composers are unified by their dedication to tonality and melody, as well as their incorporation of world music and popular culture. Together, they have redefined the genre of contemporary music. ▪

Jennifer Higdon

Jennifer Higdon was born in Brooklyn, New York, in 1962, and then moved with her family first to Atlanta and then to the Appalachian Mountains in Tennessee. After teaching herself to play the flute at the age of 15, she began formal music studies at 18 and went on to pursue composition studies at graduate level alongside two of America's most significant composers of the 20th century, Ned Rorem and George Crumb.

Higdon has received many awards, including the Pulitzer Prize in Music for her *Violin Concerto*, Grammy Awards for her *Percussion Concerto* and *Viola Concerto*, and an International Opera Award for her first opera, *Cold Mountain*, based on the bestselling novel of the same name by Charles Frazier. Her popularity allows her to compose exclusively on commission.

Other key works

2005 *The Percussion Concerto*
2008 *The Singing Rooms*
2009 *Violin Concerto*
2015 *Cold Mountain*

THE MUSIC USES SIMPLE BUILDING BLOCKS AND GROWS ORGANICALLY FROM THERE ...
IN SEVEN DAYS (2008), THOMAS ADÈS

IN CONTEXT

FOCUS
Music and multimedia

BEFORE
1910 In *Prometheus: The Poem of Fire*, Alexander Scriabin calls for a "color organ" to fill the concert hall with colored light.

1952 John Cage's Theatre Piece No. 1, with paintings by Robert Rauschenberg and dance by Merce Cunningham, is staged in North Carolina.

2003 Olga Neuwirth combines video, music, and theatre in her adaptation of David Lynch's film *Lost Highway*.

AFTER
2010 Michel van der Aa's *Up-close* combines video opera (incorporating video images) and cello concerto.

2016 *Everything Is Important* by Jennifer Walsh uses music and film to explore modern life.

Visual accompaniments to music have been known for centuries, becoming ubiquitous and infinitely more varied in recent times. In British composer Thomas Adès's *In Seven Days*, a depiction of the biblical creation story, his collaborator Tal Rosner's video illustrates, enriches, and expands on the music—a set of variations on two themes, for piano and orchestra. Adès adds an unusual twist. His themes are not introduced at the beginning but at the end, in a short final movement, which distills the core essence from the earlier six movements corresponding to the six days described in Genesis. In this music, creation evolves from chaos into order.

Images enhancing sound

In Rosner's visual accompaniment to *In Seven Days*, images dance and spin in time with the sounds, echoing the music's kaleidoscopic depiction of the balance between chaos and order. The video is mostly abstract, with geometrical shapes, patterns, waves, and flows, yet these are actually derived from pictures of London's Royal Festival Hall and the Los Angeles Walt Disney Concert Hall, which jointly commissioned the work.

Adès and Rosner call their work a "visual ballet," and when used, the video is generally projected on screens above the orchestra. The music can also be played alone, but together the two create a powerful multimedia experience. ∎

The better you play it, and the closer you come to his idiosyncratic vision, the more wonderful it sounds.
Simon Rattle

See also: Ives's Symphony No. 4 254–255 ▪ Janáček's *Sinfonietta* 263 ▪ *Pithoprakta* 308 ▪ Ligeti's *Études pour piano* 324

THIS IS THE CORE OF WHO WE ARE AND WHAT WE NEED TO BE
ALLELUIA (2011), ERIC WHITACRE

Eric Whitacre, one of the most popular 21st-century composers, is an advocate for the uplifting power of choral music. The majority of his works are choral, including *Alleluia* (2011), though the origins of that piece are instrumental—a composition titled *October* evoking the colors and radiance of autumn. Inspired by the 20th-century pastoralism of English composers such as Ralph Vaughan Williams, Whitacre had written *October* for wind orchestra (actually school bands) in 2000.

A decade later, Nevada-born Whitacre, who describes himself as spiritual rather than religious, decided to set liturgical text to music for the first time, choosing the words "Alleluia" and "Amen" and uniting them with *October,* whose simplicity and elegance transferred well to a choral setting.

Alleluia retains many aspects from the choral tradition that make it just as gratifying to sing as to listen to: richly ringing harmonies, phrases that fit well with natural breath, and allusions to ancient chant and Renaissance polyphony. Yet in its mysterious folklike opening, and the way harmonies are used as resonating chambers for the solo lines, it also achieves a contemporary sound. ∎

Eric Whitacre, pictured here in 2011 at Sidney Sussex College, Cambridge, Britain, while Composer in Residence, was inspired to write *Alleluia* by his work with the chapel choir.

See also: *Canticum Canticorum* 46–51 ▪ Monteverdi's *Vespers* 64–69 ▪ *St. Matthew Passion* 98–105 ▪ *Elijah* 170–173 ▪ *The Dream of Gerontius* 218–219

DIRECT

ORY

DIRECTORY

In addition to the composers covered in the preceding chapters in this book, numerous others have also made an impact on the development of classical music. The music represented by those listed here—many of whom were also teachers, scholars, and virtuoso soloists—is diverse, ranging from the choral works of the great Spanish composer of the Renaissance, Tomás Luis de Victoria, to the loud and unsettling symphonies of Anton Bruckner, while the particular impact of Mily Balakirev was in leading the circle of composers known as Russia's "Mighty Handful," or "Five." What unites them is the way they have enriched the lives of their audiences and influenced the compositions of their peers with new ideas or refinements of existing ones.

JOHANNES OCKEGHEM
c.1410–1497

Born in Flanders, Johannes Ockeghem made his name in Paris at the court of King Charles VII and his successors, becoming one of the most celebrated composers of early Renaissance Europe. Much of his work has been lost, but surviving compositions include 14 Masses and 10 motets (religious choral works) along with 20 secular chansons. Ockeghem introduced richer, more sonorous harmonies to Renaissance music, exploring the lower reaches of the bass part for the first time. His works are contrapuntal, weaving together two or more melodic lines.

ORLANDO DI LASSO
1532–1594

As a boy chorister in Mons (in modern Belgium), Orlando di Lasso was so renowned for the beauty of his voice that he was kidnapped three times by those keen to have him in their choirs. In 1556 he moved to Munich, where he remained for the rest of his life, serving as *kapellmeister* (director of music) to Duke Albrecht V of Bavaria. As a composer, he was both versatile and prolific, writing more than 2,000 works. His secular pieces include songs in Italian (madrigals), French (chansons), and German (Lieder). His sacred music includes settings of the psalms, notably a sequence of penitential psalms, *Psalmi Davidis poenitentiales* (published in 1584). His music has an emotional intensity, reflecting the words he set to music, that preempts the Baroque style of the 18th century.

TOMÁS LUIS DE VICTORIA
c.1548–1611

Spain's greatest Renaissance composer, Tomás Luis de Victoria, was born near Ávila in central Castile. He enjoyed royal patronage from an early age, and in his late teens, King Philip II sent de Victoria to Rome, where he was ordained a priest but also practiced as a musician—probably studying under the composer Giovanni Pierluigi da Palestrina. He returned to Spain around the age of 40, becoming director of music and later organist at the wealthy convent of Las Descalzas Reales in Madrid. His work is dramatic and sometimes vividly pictorial, as in the motet *Cum Beatus Ignatius*, where the music evokes the wild beasts tearing at the Christian martyr Ignatius of Antioch. His deep spirituality is expressed in settings of the psalms and several Masses, including the *Missa O quam gloriosum* and the *Missa Ave Regina coelorum*.

JAN PIETERSZOON SWEELINCK
1562–1621

Dutchman Jan Pieterszoon Sweelinck was the most influential performer and composer of organ music before J.S. Bach. Before the age of 20, he succeeded his father as organist at Amsterdam's Oude Kerk (Old Church), where he would later be succeeded by his own son. He wrote vocal music, both sacred and secular, but is remembered for his innovative organ works, in which, among other things, he developed the fugue form. As an organist, he was famous for his virtuoso improvisations before and after services. His many pupils spread across Protestant northern Germany, themselves influencing the young Handel and Bach.

CARLO GESUALDO
1566–1613

A man of passionate and often melancholy temperament, Neapolitan nobleman Carlo Gesualdo, Prince of Venosa, is believed to have been personally responsible for the revenge murder of his first wife and her lover, the Duke of Andria. Gesualdo also published three books of motets (religious choral works) and six of madrigals. The later books of madrigals, in particular, show

an innovative use of harmony, unparalleled in Renaissance music, which won him many admirers in later centuries.

ORLANDO GIBBONS
1583–1625

Orlando Gibbons came from a musical English family. A celebrated keyboard player, he was appointed organist of London's Chapel Royal at the age of 21 and later became organist at Westminster Abbey. His sacred compositions included popular anthems, such as "O clap your hands together" for Church of England services. Among his secular works, he won the greatest fame for songs such as "The Silver Swan" and "What Is Our Life" written in the madrigal style of which he was a master. His volume *Parthenia* with pieces for the virginals (a smaller version of the harpsichord) was the first collection of keyboard music published in England.

GIROLAMO FRESCOBALDI
1583–1643

Born in Ferrara in northern Italy, Girolamo Frescobaldi moved to Rome while still in his teens and was appointed organist at St. Peter's Basilica in 1608. Apart from a period as court organist to the Medici rulers of Florence, he remained at St. Peter's for the rest of his life. His music, mostly for organ, has a strongly contemplative, mystical quality. Even his toccatas (pieces written to allow performers to show off their skills) are remarkable, less for virtuoso display than for dramatic intensity. One of his most famous publications was *Fiori musicali* (*Musical Flowers*, 1635), a collection of organ pieces for church services.

HEINRICH SCHÜTZ
1585–1672

Widely credited as the greatest German composer before J.S. Bach, Heinrich Schütz was a major figure in introducing the new styles of the Italian Baroque to Germany. An early patron, Maurice of Hesse-Kassel paid for him to study in

Venice under Giovanni Gabrieli. In 1617, following his return to Germany, he was appointed kapellmeister at the court of the electors (rulers) of Saxony in Dresden. His settings of biblical and sacred texts transformed Lutheran church music, ranging from early psalm settings, *Psalmen Davids* (1619), to the great *Christmas Oratorio* (1664), and three a cappella *Passions* (1665), dramatizing the trial and death of Jesus.

JOHANN HERMANN SCHEIN
1586–1630

Alongside Schütz, Johann Hermann Schein was a key figure in bringing Italian Baroque influences into German music. A native of Saxony, in 1616 he was appointed to the prestigious post of cantor at Leipzig's Thomas Church. An early publication, *Banchetto musicale* ("Musical banquet," 1617), was one of his few instrumental collections. His vocal music includes both secular and sacred works. An outstanding work is *Israelsbrünnlein* ("Fountains of Israel") (1623), a collection of 26 motets based on Old Testament texts written in the style of Italian madrigals.

JOHANN JAKOB FROBERGER
1616–1667

Born in Stuttgart, Johann Jakob Froberger introduced Italian and French keyboard styles into German music. He studied in Rome with Frescobaldi before being appointed organist at the court of the Habsburg emperor in Vienna in 1641. An organist as well as harpsichordist, he was the first German composer to write important works for the harpsichord. Most influential were his dance suites, with pieces drawing on French tradition in which each movement is inspired by a different dance form.

BARBARA STROZZI
1619–1677

The Venetian Barbara Strozzi was known as a singer as well as composer. Her mother was Isabella Garzoni, a

servant to the wealthy dramatist and poet Giulio Strozzi, who adopted Barbara and may well have been her biological father. Strozzi studied under the composer Francesco Cavalli and was a member of the Accademia degli Unisoni (Academy of the Like-Minded), a group of intellectuals founded by Giulio Strozzi. She published eight volumes of music, mostly arias and cantatas for solo voice. Most are settings of poems dealing with love and its pains, including the cantata *Lagrime mie* ("My tears") and the aria "Che si può fare" ("What can I do").

MARC-ANTOINE CHARPENTIER
1643–1704

From a family of painters, French composer Marc-Antoine Charpentier switched his allegiance to music after being influenced by the composer Giacomo Carissimi in Rome. On his return to Paris, he held various posts, including that of composer to Louis XIV's cousin, the Duchesse de Guise. He worked with the dramatist Molière, writing music for plays, including *Le Malade imaginaire* (1673), and wrote a successful opera, *Médée* (1693), based on a play by Pierre Corneille. His best-known sacred works are dramatic motets (or short oratorios) written for the Jesuit community. His reputation suffered from comparisons with his archrival Jean-Baptiste Lully until his work was rediscovered in the 20th century.

JOHANN CHRISTIAN BACH
1735–1782

The youngest of J.S. Bach's surviving sons, Johann Christian Bach studied in Berlin and Italy, where he was briefly organist at Milan cathedral and had his first opera, *Artaserse*, performed in Naples. In 1762, he was appointed composer at the King's Theatre in London, remaining in Britain for the rest of his life. He became a dominant figure in English musical life, partly through the series of highly popular concerts he organized each year with his countryman Carl Friedrich Abel. Apart from his operas, he was known for his

piano concertos, which were an important influence on the young Mozart, who met Bach in London.

CARL DITTERS VON DITTERSDORF
1739–1799

Carl Ditters von Dittersdorf was a boy prodigy as a violinist in Vienna, but as an adult he made his name with light-hearted operas. His most productive years followed his appointment as court composer to Philipp Gotthard von Schaffgotsch, Prince-Bishop of Breslau, whose castle was an important cultural and intellectual hub. Dittersdorf's greatest operatic success, *Doktor und Apotheker* (1786), helped to define the Singspiel genre (mingling songs and choruses with spoken dialogue), which his friend Mozart would take to new heights in *Die Zauberflöte* (*The Magic Flute*) in 1791.

LUIGI BOCCHERINI
1743–1805

Born in Lucca in central Italy, Luigi Boccherini had studied and worked in both Rome and Vienna by the age of 20. He became composer to the Spanish king's music-loving brother, Don Luis de Borbón, in Madrid, then later was court composer to King Frederick William II of Prussia. A cellist by training, Boccherini wrote symphonies and concertos (mostly for cello) but is best remembered for more than 300 chamber works, string quintets in particular.

ANTONIO SALIERI
1750–1825

The Venetian-born Antonio Salieri went to Vienna at the age of 16 and remained there for the rest of his life, as court composer to the Habsburg emperor and later imperial Kapellmeister. He made his name as a composer of operas—of which the best regarded is *Tarare* (1787), written for a Parisian theatre—but in 1804, he abandoned opera and began writing sacred music and teaching.

The latter was his most important legacy. His pupils included Beethoven, Schubert, and Liszt.

JAN LADISLAV DUSSEK
1760–1812

As the Classical movement gave way to Romanticism, the pianist and composer Jan Ladislav Dussek was a major musical figure. Born in Caslav (in the modern Czech Republic), he traveled widely in Europe before settling in London in 1789. Bankruptcy after the failure of his music publishing business forced him to leave London in 1799, and he ended his days in the household of the French statesman Prince of Talleyrand. Dussek is best remembered for his piano sonatas, which inspired Beethoven.

GIACOMO MEYERBEER
1791–1864

Born into a wealthy Jewish banking family in Berlin, Giacomo Meyerbeer won acclaim as a pianist while in his early 20s, but his real ambitions lay in composition. After a period of study in Venice, where he came under the sway of Rossini's music, he had some success with the opera *Romilda e Costanza* (1817), but his breakthrough work was *Robert le diable*, based on a libretto by the French playwright Eugène Scribe. First performed at the Paris Opéra in 1831, it was a massive hit. Alongside Meyerbeer's *Les Huguenots* (1836) and *Le Prophète* (1849), it helped to define the emerging genre of grand opera, appealing to the audience's love of spectacle. His influence was noticeable in the operas of Verdi and even Wagner.

GAETANO DONIZETTI
1797–1848

Gaetano Donizetti, born in Bergamo, is regarded as the most important Italian opera composer between Rossini and Verdi. Starting with *Enrico di Borgogna*, first performed in Venice in 1818, his output was prolific, with 65 completed

operas in total. His serious works include *Lucrezia Borgia* (1833) and *Linda di Chamounix* (1842). His comic works include *L'elisir d'amore* (The elixir of love; 1832) and *Don Pasquale* (1843). A major influence on Verdi, Donizetti is credited with introducing northern European Romanticism into Italian opera.

VINCENZO BELLINI
1801–1835

The Sicilian-born Vincenzo Bellini wrote 10 operas, of which the masterpieces are *La sonnambula* (1831), *Norma* (1831), and *I Puritani* (1835). In 1827, *Il pirata*— the first of six collaborations with the librettist Felice Romani—won him international acclaim at La Scala in Milan. Encouraged by Rossini, he moved to Paris where *I Puritani* was premiered. With a gift for vocal melody, Bellini was the master of the Italian bel canto ("beautiful singing") style, expressed, for example, in the famous song "Casta diva" ("Chaste goddess") from *Norma*.

MIKHAIL GLINKA
1804–1857

Mikhail Ivanovich Glinka came from a wealthy Russian landowning family and abandoned a civil service career to study music in Italy and Berlin. Back in Russia, his first opera, *A Life for the Tsar* (or *Ivan Susanin*, 1836), based on the story of a 17th-century Russian hero, was well received in St. Petersburg. In this and later works, Glinka drew upon folk songs to create music that was authentically Russian. In 1845, Hector Berlioz conducted a concert in Paris with excerpts from Glinka's works; this was the first time Russian music had been played in the West.

CLARA WIECK SCHUMANN
1819–1896

A child prodigy, Clara Wieck won Europe-wide fame while still in her teens. Around that time, she fell in love with Robert Schumann, one of the pupils of her father, who was a well-known

piano teacher. She and Robert married in 1840, defying her father's opposition. Despite having eight children, Schumann maintained an active musical career of performing and teaching. Her works, all of which date from before her husband's early death in 1856, include collections of *Lieder*, chamber music, an early piano concerto, and what is generally regarded as her finest work, the Piano Trio in G minor, Op. 17 (1846).

CÉSAR FRANCK
1822–1890

In his teens, the Belgian-born César Franck was already studying at the Paris Conservatory and performing as a concert pianist. In his late 20s, however, following the poor reception of an oratorio he had composed, he abandoned his career as a composer and performer and started to earn his living as an organist and teacher. Only in his 50s did Franck resume a more public profile, after accepting the post of organ professor at the Paris Conservatoire. He became an influential composition teacher and started writing again. His works include a symphony, organ pieces, and a series of chamber works, notably the Piano Quintet in F minor (1879), Violin Sonata in A major (1886), and String Quartet in D major (1889).

ANTON BRUCKNER
1824–1896

The Austrian Anton Bruckner was a bold, if unlikely, musical innovator, best known for his nine symphonies and his religious works. Bruckner worked as a teacher until 1855, when he was made chief organist at Linz Cathedral. In Linz, following years of intensive study of composition, he wrote his first major works: three Mass settings and a symphony. In 1868, he took up a teaching post at the Conservatory in Vienna, where he lived for the rest of his life. An admirer of Wagner, he expanded the scope of the late Romantic symphony with complex harmonies, dissonances, and the rich weaving together of the different instrumental parts.

ALEKSANDR BORODIN
1833–1887

The illegitimate son of a Georgian nobleman and an army doctor's wife, Aleksandr Borodin trained as a scientist. In 1864, he became professor of chemistry at the Imperial Medical and Surgical Academy in St. Petersburg. As an enthusiastic amateur musician, he was also a member of a group of young composers, called "The Five," determined to fashion a truly Russian tradition of classical music. He wrote two symphonies, two string quartets, and a tone poem, *In Central Asia* (1880). His greatest work, the opera *Prince Igor*, based on a medieval Russian epic, was unfinished when Borodin died of a heart attack. It was completed by Nikolay Rimsky-Korsakov, another of the Five, with his pupil Aleksandr Glazunov.

MILY BALAKIREV
1836–1910

Demanding, often tyrannical, Mily Alekseyevich Balakirev was the driving force behind "The Five"—a group of ardently nationalist young Russian composers who came together in St. Petersburg in the 1860s. He was also a founding member of the Free School of Music, which was set up as a less academic alternative to the St. Petersburg Conservatory. He suffered a nervous breakdown in the 1870s and withdrew from the musical world for five years, working as a railway clerk. When he returned, he had lost much of his former spirit. His works include a piano piece, *Islamey* (1869), and a symphonic poem, *Russia* (1887), but his major achievement was to have brought together "The Five," who collectively transformed Russian classical music.

GEORGES BIZET
1838–1875

The French composer Georges Bizet wrote a symphony when he was 17, and his first opera was performed the next year. He then spent three years studying

in Rome, but back in Paris, his early successes did not continue, and his opera *Les pêcheurs de perles* (*The Pearl Fishers*; 1863) was disappointingly received. A one-act piece, *Djamileh* (1872), was more successful and led to a commission to write an opera based on a novel by Prosper Mérimée. The result, *Carmen*, opened in March 1875, drawing unenthusiastic reviews until Bizet's sudden death of an undiagnosed heart condition in June, when the critics abruptly reversed their verdicts. *Carmen* became a landmark of French opera—tautly dramatic with a strongly realist focus on ordinary working people.

NIKOLAY RIMSKY-KORSAKOV
1844–1908

A naval officer who turned to music, Rimsky-Korsakov had the most lasting impact of the Russian composers known as "The Five." In 1871, he was appointed professor of composition and orchestration at the St. Petersburg Conservatory. Unlike his fellows in "The Five," he had a high regard for the academic disciplines of composition, which he passed on to his pupils. After the deaths of Mussorgsky and Borodin, he edited and completed their works. His own talent for colorful orchestration is seen in pieces such as *Capriccio español* (1887) and *Scheherazade* (1888), as well as his operas, notably *Sadko* (1897) and *The Golden Cockerel* (1909).

RUGGERO LEONCAVALLO
1857–1919

The Neapolitan opera composer Ruggero Leoncavallo is remembered for one great work, *Pagliacci* ("The players"), which was first staged at La Scala in Milan in 1892. The son of a police official, Leoncavallo had written other operas with no success. For *Pagliacci*, he turned to a new Italian school of opera known as *verismo* (literally, "truth-ism" or "realism"), characterized by sensational plots drawn from everyday life. His short, two-act work—supposedly inspired by a case his father was involved in—tells

the story of love and jealousy among a troupe of actors, culminating in murder. Leoncavallo wrote several more operas, but none had the success of *Pagliacci*.

FREDERICK DELIUS
1862–1934

The son of a German wool merchant, Frederick Delius started studying music in his spare time while managing an orange plantation in Florida. Once back in Europe, he continued his studies in Leipzig then settled in France. His works included six operas, only two of which, *Koanga,* composed in 1895–1897, and *A Village Romeo and Juliet* (1900–1901), were staged in his lifetime. His most successful pieces—introduced to British audiences by the conductor Sir Thomas Beecham—were *Sea Drift* (1904), a setting of a Walt Whitman poem, and a series of orchestral idylls and tone poems, including *Brigg Fair* (1907), *In a Summer Garden* (1908), and *North Country Sketches* (1914).

PIETRO MASCAGNI
1863–1945

Pietro Mascagni's one-act opera *Cavalleria rusticana* ("Rustic chivalry"), premiered in 1890, was the earliest major success of the Italian school of *verismo* ("realism"). Based on a short story by Giovanni Verga, it tells a tale of passion and betrayal in a Sicilian village, climaxing in a fatal duel between two rival lovers. As with Leoncavallo's *Pagliacci*, with which it is often performed as a double bill, it was the Tuscan-born Mascagni's only major hit.

CARL NIELSEN
1865–1931

Danish composer Carl Nielsen was one of the great symphonic writers of the early 20th century. He completed his First Symphony in 1892, but it was the Third (titled *Sinfonia espansiva*, 1911) that started to establish his reputation as a composer with an original use of tonality and harmony. The Fourth (*The Inextinguishable*, 1916) and Fifth (1922) were responses to the brutality of World War I. The Sixth and last (*Sinfonia semplice*, 1925) was the most challenging, perhaps reflecting Nielsen's fatal heart condition. He also wrote operas, but his best works, outside the symphonies, are a Wind Quintet (1922) and two concertos, for flute (1926) and clarinet (1928).

FERRUCCIO BUSONI
1866–1924

Partly Italian, partly German, Ferruccio Busoni gave his first piano recital aged 10 in Vienna. After studying in Leipzig, he became professor of piano in Helsinki and later took up posts in Moscow, Boston, and Berlin. He was renowned as one of the great pianists of the time but was also a teacher, musical theorist, and composer. His book, *The New Aesthetic of Music* (1907), was a key inspiration for figures such as the avant-garde French composer Edgard Varèse. His compositions include operas, orchestral pieces, and solo piano works, notably *Fantasia after J.S. Bach* (1909) and *Fantasia contrappuntistica* (1910–1921).

GUSTAV HOLST
1874–1934

An influential teacher and composer, Gustav Holst was one of the fathers of the English school of the 20th century that gave rise to figures such as Benjamin Britten and Michael Tippett. Holst was interested in both English folk music and Hindu mysticism, reflected in his *Choral Hymns from the Rig-Veda* (1912). His most famous work is the orchestral suite, *The Planets* (1916). His vocal works include operas, song cycles, the choral piece *The Hymn of Jesus* (1917), and *Ode to Death* (1919), based on a Walt Whitman poem.

ZOLTÁN KODÁLY
1882–1967

Zoltán Kodály was a pioneer in the field of ethnomusicology (the study of music in its ethnic and cultural context) and in modern methods for teaching music to children. Born in Hungary, he studied at Budapest's Academy of Music alongside Béla Bartók, with whom he went on expeditions into the countryside to collect folk music. The techniques they devised were influential for those who followed in the study of indigenous music traditions. Later, Kodály also developed a method to teach children to sight-read music when singing. As a composer, his major works are *Psalmus Hungaricus* (1923) for tenor, chorus, and orchestra and a comic opera, *Háry János* (1926).

ARTHUR HONEGGER
1892–1955

Born to Swiss parents living in France, Honegger belonged to "Les Six," a group of young composers who emerged in Paris in the 1920s, including Francis Poulenc and Darius Milhaud. He is remembered for his five symphonies, collectively regarded as one of the most impressive symphonic oeuvres of the 20th century. His other works include *Pacific 231* (1923) and *Rugby* (1928), in which he sought to express in music the impressions of a locomotive and a rugby match, respectively. Honegger's dramatic works included film scores, ballets, and an oratorio *Jeanne d'Arc au bûcher* (*Joan of Arc at the Stake*) (1935), with a libretto by the writer Paul Claudel.

DARIUS MILHAUD
1892–1974

With more than 400 works to his credit, Darius Milhaud was one of the most prolific 20th-century composers. From a Jewish family living in Provence, he studied in Paris and, in 1917–1918, traveled to Brazil with the poet, dramatist, and diplomat Paul Claudel. He was a member of the group of composers known as "Les Six," through whom he met the surrealist writer and designer Jean Cocteau. His collaboration with Cocteau produced the ballets *Le Boeuf sur le toit* (1919) and *Le Train bleu* (1924), while his work with Claudel yielded musical dramas, including *Les Choéphores* (1915), *Christophe Colomb*

(1928), and *David* (1954). During the 1940s, he taught composition at Mills College, California. One of his pupils was the pioneer of minimalism, Steve Reich.

PAUL HINDEMITH
1895–1963

Paul Hindemith taught composition at Berlin's School of Music until he was forced to resign in 1937, due to his opposition to the Nazi regime. He went to the United States, teaching at Yale from 1940 to 1953 before returning to Germany. His textbooks, starting with *The Craft of Musical Composition* (1941), are still widely studied. His compositions include chamber works, symphonies, and operas, most famously *Mathis der Maler* ("Matthias the painter"), which premiered in Zurich in 1938. Telling the story of German painter Matthias Grünewald, who joined a peasants' uprising in 1525, it concerns an artist living in troubled times and trying to follow his conscience in the face of an oppressive regime.

HENRY COWELL
1897–1965

In the 1920s and 1930s, the Californian composer, pianist, and teacher Henry Cowell toured North America and Europe, shocking audiences with works such as *The Tides of Manaunaun* (1912), *The Aeolian Harp* (1923), and *The Banshee* (1925). These involved creating "tone clusters" by placing his fist or forearm on the keyboard while the other hand played the notes as normal or placing one hand inside the piano and strumming the strings like a harp. Cowell was eclectic, drawing inspiration from his own Irish roots, hymns, or Japanese or Indian music. Through his periodical, *New Music*, he was an active promoter of other people's works.

KURT WEILL
1900–1950

German composer Kurt Weill is best known for his collaborations with the left-wing dramatist and poet Bertolt Brecht. These included the two satirical operas *Die Dreigroschenoper* (*The Threepenny Opera*; 1928), adapted from an 18th-century English ballad opera, and *Aufstieg und Fall der Stadt Mahagonny* ("Rise and fall of the city of Mahagonny"; 1930). Drawing inspiration from cabaret and jazz as well as his classical training, Weill created bitingly surreal numbers, such as the famous "Ballad of Mack the Knife" from *Die Dreigroschenoper*. In 1933, following Hitler's appointment as chancellor, the Jewish Weill fled Germany, first for Paris, then the United States, where he wrote a series of Broadway musicals before his death in 1950.

JOAQUÍN RODRIGO
1901–1999

Blind from the age of three, Joaquín Rodrigo nonetheless studied music in Paris. He returned to his native Spain in 1939 after the end of the civil war there. His most famous piece, the *Concierto de Aranjuez* for guitar and orchestra, inspired by the gardens of the royal palace of Aranjuez, premiered the next year. Other works include 11 concertos; another guitar piece, *Fantasia para un gentilhombre* ("Fantasia for a gentleman"; 1954), and an opera, *El hijo fingido* ("The false son"; 1964).

ELISABETH LUTYENS
1906–1983

For much of her life, Elisabeth Lutyens's uncompromising Modernism drew blank incomprehension from her fellow Britons. Lutyens studied in Paris and at the Royal College of Music in London. Her early works included a *Concerto for Nine Instruments* (1939), composed in a style individual to her but somewhat akin to the serialism developed by Arnold Schoenberg. Vocal works included literary settings, notably a motet using texts from the philosopher Ludwig Wittgenstein (1952). Among her stage works were the chamber opera *Infidelio* (1954) and *Isis and Osiris* (1969–1970). Her best-known orchestral pieces include *Six Tempi* (1957), *Quincunx*

(1959), and *Music for Orchestra II* (1962). She also worked with Hammer Film Productions, writing scores for horror movies to earn money.

ELLIOTT CARTER
1908–2012

In the 1930s, New Yorker Elliott Carter was one of many Americans who studied under Nadia Boulanger in Paris. Back in the United States, he developed his own style, with different instrumental parts following different lines, interacting with one another like characters in a play. Carter's important orchestral works included his Cello Sonata (1948), two String Quartets (1950–1951 and 1959), a Double Concerto for Harpsichord and Piano (1961), and a Piano Concerto (1964–1965), a response to the building of the Berlin Wall. From the 1970s, he turned to vocal music, with settings of contemporary North American poets, such as Elizabeth Bishop in *A Mirror on Which to Dwell* (1975).

SAMUEL BARBER
1910–1981

Samuel Barber was born in Pennsylvania in 1910 and became one of the most celebrated American composers of the century. His most popular work was one of his earliest—the *Adagio for Strings* (1938), an orchestration of the Adagio movement from a String Quartet he had written two years earlier. An alumnus of Philadelphia's Curtis Institute of Music, Barber was later known for vocal works, such as *Knoxville: Summer of 1915* for solo soprano (1948), the *Hermit Songs* cycle (1952–1953), and two operas: *Vanessa* (1958), and *Antony and Cleopatra* (1966), which was written for the inauguration of the Metropolitan Opera's new theatre at New York's Lincoln Center in 1966.

MILTON BABBITT
1916–2011

The avant-garde American composer, teacher, and theorist Milton Babbitt had a background in both mathematics and

music. Babbitt was a firm proponent of serialism, as well as a pioneer of electronic music. His most important works include *Three Compositions for Piano* (1947), *Ensembles for Synthesizer* (1962–1963), and *Philomel* (1964) for solo soprano with electronic accompaniment.

LUIGI NONO
1924–1990

The Venetian Luigi Nono was a radical in music and politics alike, and often combined the two. His *Il canto sospeso* ("The interrupted song"; 1955–1956)— for solo voices, chorus, and orchestra— excerpts letters written during World War II by members of the anti-Nazi resistance awaiting execution. Nono's Marxist beliefs are also clear in his first opera, *Intolleranza* (1960), about an Italian migrant looking for work. In the 1960s, he began staging pieces, such as *La fabbrica illuminata* ("The illuminated factory"; 1964), in factories and other places of work.

PIERRE BOULEZ
1925–2016

The avant-garde French composer Pierre Boulez was a hugely influential figure in the late 20th century. One of his most admired early works was *Le Marteau sans maître* (*The Hammer without a Master*; 1954), a setting of poems by the surrealist René Char. A decade later, he composed the successful *Pli selon pli* ("Fold upon fold"; 1964) for soprano and orchestra. Among his later works was *Répons* (1985), for chamber orchestra with six percussive soloists and live electronics. Boulez had an international career as a conductor, including periods with the New York Philharmonic and the BBC Symphony Orchestra in London.

MORTON FELDMAN
1926–1987

Born in Queens, New York, Morton Feldman was notable for the slow, deliberate quietness of his music and the exceptional length of his later works.

The quietness, he said, meant that audiences could hear the sounds. In 1977, he composed *Neither* for soprano and orchestra, a setting of a monologue by the playwright Samuel Beckett. His later works, such as the *String Quartet II* (1983), which lasts for five hours without break, were immersive, almost mystical experiences for listeners.

HANS WERNER HENZE
1926–2012

A German living in Italy, Hans Werner Henze is known for a shimmering lyrical style that drew inspiration from traditions as varied as Romanticism, neoclassicism, and jazz. Highly prolific, he wrote 10 symphonies as well as solo instrumental, chamber, and orchestral music. He found fame, above all, for his operas, including two collaborations with the English poet W.H. Auden: *Elegy for Young Lovers* (1961) and *The Bassarids* (1966).

HARRISON BIRTWISTLE
1934–

Harrison Birtwistle was part of a group of students at the Royal Manchester College of Music in northern England, who became known as the Manchester School. Modernists, they also drew inspiration from medieval and early Renaissance music. Birtwistle came into his own in the 1960s with works such as *Tragoedia* (1965) for wind quintet, harp, and string quartet and his first opera, *Punch and Judy* (1968). Operas remain an important part of his output, including *The Mask of Orpheus* (1986), *Gawain* (1991), and *The Minotaur* (2008); his instrumental works include *Exody* (1997) for orchestra, *The Cry of Anubis* (1994) for tuba and orchestra, and *Harrison's Clocks* (1998) for solo piano.

HELMUT LACHENMANN
1935–

The German Helmut Lachenmann's goal as a composer is to open up new "sound worlds." A Modernist who studied under

Luigi Nono, he coined the term "*musique concrète instrumentale*" ("concrete instrumental music"). In *Pression* (1970) for solo cello, he uses not only the sounds the cellist has been trained to produce but also other more mechanical sounds, as when the bow is pressed down hard on the strings. He also incorporates recordings (often distorted) of well-known pieces, such as Mozart's Clarinet Concerto, into his compositions, as in his work for clarinet, orchestra, and tape, *Accanto* (1976). Other pieces include *NUN* (1999) for flute, trombone, male chorus, and orchestra, and an opera, *Das Mädchen mit den Schwefelhölzern* ("The little match girl") in 1997.

ARVO PÄRT
1935–

The Estonian-born Pärt's early works include unmistakably Modernist pieces, such as *Nekrolog* (1960) and his first two symphonies (1963 and 1966). From 1968, however, he almost completely ceased composing for eight years, partly in response to the repressive censorship in his still Soviet-controlled homeland, but also in the light of his devout Russian Orthodox faith. His new style emerged in a short solo piano piece, *Für Alina* (1976), remarkable for its pared-back minimalism and the bell-like quality of the sound. A stream of works followed, including *Tabula Rasa* (1977), *Summa* (1977), the *Cantus in memoriam Benjamin Britten* (1977), and a *St. John Passion* (1982).

ARIBERT REIMANN
1936–

Aribert Reimann, a Berlin-born composer, pianist, and teacher, has written chamber works, concertos, and orchestral pieces but is mainly known for his deft use of the human voice— Reimann had a long, close association with the baritone Dietrich Fischer-Dieskau, for whom he often acted as accompanist. Reimann wrote a series of successful operas, mostly based on the works of famous dramatists. *Lear*, adapted from the Shakespeare play, is

widely seen as his most successful work. A Modernist in style, Reimann is also influenced by Indian music.

JOHN TAVENER
1944–2013

With influences including Stravinsky and Messiaen, John Tavener found fame in 1970 when his cantata, *The Whale*—based on the biblical tale of Jonah—was released by the Apple record label. The London-born Tavener's conversion to Russian Orthodox Christianity in 1977 was the fruit of a long-standing spiritual quest that gave rise to richly mystical pieces, including *Ikon of Light* (1984), *The Protecting Veil* (1989), and *Song for Athene* (1993). In 2003, he wrote *The Veil of the Temple*: a huge choral work intended to last all night in an Orthodox vigil service and regarded by Tavener as his "supreme achievement."

JOHN ADAMS
1947–

Younger than his fellow minimalists, Steve Reich and Philip Glass, the New England–born Adams made his name with pieces such as *Shaker Loops* (1978) and *Grand Pianola Music* (1982). His music is often humorous, referencing popular culture. Adams is arguably more concerned than most minimalists with harmony and progression. This can be seen in his *Harmonielehre* (1985), a three-movement orchestral work, and his first opera, *Nixon in China* (1987), inspired by President Richard Nixon's 1972 visit. In addition to two more operas, his later works have included concertos for violin (1993), clarinet (1996), and piano (1997) and *Scheherazade.2* (2014), a "dramatic symphony" for violin and orchestra.

JUDITH WEIR
1954–

Born in England to Scottish parents, Weir is known above all for her operas—from her high-spirited debut work, *A Night at the Chinese Opera* (1987), to *Miss Fortune* (2011), a Sicilian folktale

updated to the urban world of the 21st century. Inspired by composers such as Janáček and Stravinsky, Weir draws on the folk traditions not only of her native Scotland and Europe but also of South Asia. Weir's work pays particular attention to narrative; *King Harald's Saga* (1979), for solo soprano, is a medieval historical drama compressed into less than 15 minutes. Meanwhile, her instrumental works include her 15-minute Piano Concerto (1997), another gem of distillation, and *The Welcome Arrival of Rain* (2001). In 2014, Weir was appointed Master of the Queen's Music in succession to Sir Peter Maxwell Davies.

MAGNUS LINDBERG
1958–

The orchestra is the Finnish composer Magnus Lindberg's first love, and he has established himself as one of the world's most popular composers of ambitious orchestral pieces. His beginnings were avant-garde, as seen in works such as *Action–Situation–Signification* (1982) and *Kraft (Power*; 1985). Later his music became more eclectic, drawing on classical tradition (including the works of his Finnish predecessor, Sibelius) and with richer melodies and color. His major pieces from the 1990s were *Aura* (1994) and *Arena* (1995), and his works since 2000 have included concertos for clarinet (2002) and violin (2006), as well as his first vocal work for a soloist, *Accused; three interrogations for soprano and orchestra* (2014).

JAMES MACMILLAN
1959–

Catholic spirituality, progressive politics, and Scottish folk tradition have been inspirations for the Scottish Modernist James MacMillan. His first big success was with an orchestral work, *The Confession of Isobel Gowdie*, which was first performed at the BBC Proms in 1990. Two years later, he wrote *Veni, Veni, Emmanuel*—a concerto for percussion and orchestra—for the great Scottish percussionist Evelyn Glennie.

His vocal works, which constitute a large proportion of his output, have included *Cantos Sagrados* (1990), a setting of poems by the Latin American writers Ariel Dorfman and Ana Maria Mendosa; the cantata *Quickening* (1998); two operas; and settings of liturgical texts and the Catholic Mass.

MARK-ANTHONY TURNAGE
1960–

British composer Mark-Anthony Turnage's first opera, *Greek*, is based on a version of Sophocles's tragedy *Oedipus Rex*, set in London's East End. The opera was an instant success when premiered at the Munich Biennale in 1988. Drawing on jazz and rock as well as the classical tradition, Turnage's music is streetwise, expressionistic, and often humorous. His stage works have included two further operas—*The Silver Tassie* (2000) and *Anna Nicole* (2011)—and the ballets *UNDANCE* (2011), *Trespass* (2012), and *Strapless* (2016). Among his instrumental works are *Three Screaming Popes* (1989), inspired by paintings by the artist Francis Bacon; the trumpet concerto *From the Wreckage* (2005), written for Swedish trumpeter Håkan Hardenberger; and a violin concerto, *Mambo, Blues, and Tarantella* (2008).

GEORGE BENJAMIN
1960–

One of the elderly Messiaen's last and best loved students, Benjamin is unusual among British composers for his affinity with French avant-garde music. His output has been remarkable for its combination of precision with color and sensuousness. His breakthrough came at the age of 20, when his orchestral piece, *Ringed by the Flat Horizon*, premiered at the BBC Proms in 1980. His works since then have included *At First Light* (1982) for chamber orchestra; *Upon Silence* (1990) for soprano and string ensemble, and *Palimpsests* (2002) for full orchestra. He has also written three operas with the playwright Martin Crimp: *Into the Little Hill* (2006), *Written on Skin* (2012), and *Lessons in Love and Violence* (2018).

GLOSSARY

A cappella Unaccompanied singing by a soloist or group.

Alto The highest male and lowest female voice; also a term describing an instrument that is lower in pitch than a treble instrument.

Aria A vocal piece for one or more voices in an opera or oratorio.

Atonal Without a recognizable key; the opposite of tonality.

Baritone The male voice between tenor and bass, or an instrument within this tonal range.

Baroque Music composed between 1600 and 1750; describes pieces from the period before the Classical.

Bass The lowest in tone: describes the lowest male voice; the lowest part of a chord or piece of music; or the lowest instrument in a family.

Basso continuo Harmonic accompaniment, usually by a harpsichord or organ and bass viol or cello, extensively used in the Baroque period.

Bel canto Meaning "beautiful song" in Italian; an 18th- and early 19th-century school of singing characterized by a concentration on beauty of tone, virtuosic agility, and breath control.

Cadence The closing sequence of a musical phrase or composition. A "perfect cadence" creates a sense of completion; an "imperfect cadence" sounds unfinished.

Cadenza Originally an improvised solo by the soloist in a concerto; from the 19th century, it became more formalized, less spontaneous.

Canon A contrapuntal composition in which the separate voices enter one by one. In a strict canon, each part repeats the melody exactly.

Cantata A programmatic piece, generally for voice and orchestra, designed to tell a story; a *cantata da camera* is a secular piece, while *cantata da chiesa* is a sacred one.

Chamber music Pieces for small groups of two or more instruments, such as duets, trios, and quartets.

Chord A simultaneous combination of notes. The most frequently used are called "triads," which consist of three distinct notes built on the first, third, and fifth notes of a scale. For example, in the key of C major, the notes of the scale are C, D, E, F, G, A, and B; the C major triad consists of the notes C, E, and G.

Chromatic Based on the scale of all 12 semitones in an octave, as opposed to diatonic, which is based on a scale of seven notes.

Classical The post-Baroque period, approximately 1750–1820; also a term used to distinguish Western music written for a formal context, such as a church or concert hall, from informal music styles.

Clef A symbol placed at the beginning of a musical staff to determine the pitch of the notes on the staff; a treble clef, for example, marks the bottom line of a staff as being an E, whereas a bass clef means it should be read as a G.

Coda Literally "tail" in Italian; a final section of a piece of music, distinct from the overall structure.

Concerto A large piece for solo instrument and orchestra, designed to showcase the soloist's skills; the Baroque concerto grosso, however, has a more equal interplay between the smaller orchestra (*ripieno*) and a group of soloists (*concertino*).

Consonance A chord or interval, such as a third or fifth, that sounds pleasing; opposite of dissonance.

Consort An instrumental ensemble popular during the 16th and 17th centuries in England; the term is also used to describe the music played by these ensembles as well as the performance itself.

Contralto Term describing the lowest of the female voices (alto) in an opera context.

Contrapuntal Using counterpoint: the simultaneous playing or singing of two or more melodic lines.

Counterpoint see **Contrapuntal**.

Diatonic Based on a scale of seven notes with no sharps or flats, only the white piano keys.

Dissonance Notes played together to create discord (sounds unpleasing to the ear); opposite of consonance.

Dynamics Differences in volume of a piece or section of music; also refers to the notation system of markings on sheet music that instruct players on volume.

Flat A note that has been lowered by a half step (B lowered by a half step is B-flat); also describes an instrument or voice that is out of tune by being lower than the intended pitch.

Fugue From the Italian *fuga*, "to chase"; a highly structured contrapuntal piece, in two or more parts, popular in the Baroque era. The separate voices or lines enter one by one imitatively.

Harmony The simultaneous playing of different (usually complementary) notes. The basic unit of harmony is the chord.

Interval The difference in pitch between two notes, expressed numerically to show how many half steps apart they are; can be called "major," "minor," or "perfect," for example, a "minor third" is an interval of three semitones, while a "major third" is an interval of four.

Key The tonal center of a piece of music, based on the first note (or tonic) of the scale.

Key signature A written indication of which key to play in, shown by a group of accidentals— sharps or flats—at the beginning of a staff. Rather than writing in a sharp for each F and C in a piece in D major, for example, the two sharps would be included on the staff.

Leitmotif Literally "leading motif" in German; a short musical phrase that recurs through the piece

to indicate the presence of its associated character, emotion, or object.

Libretto The text of an opera or other vocal dramatic work.

Lied Traditional German song, popularized by Schubert.

Madrigal Secular "a cappella" song that was popular in Renaissance England and Italy; often set to a love poem.

Major A term applied to a key signature or any chord, triad, or scale in a major key. The intervals in a major key consist of two whole steps followed by a half step, then three whole steps followed by a half step. Major keys are often described as sounding happy, while minor keys are subdued and sad.

Mass Main service of the Roman Catholic Church, highly formalized in structure, comprising specific sections—known as the "Ordinary"—performed in the following order: Kyrie, Gloria, Credo, Sanctus with Hosanna and Benedictus, and Agnus Dei and Dona nobis pacem.

Measure A segment of musical time containing a fixed number of beats, depending on the time signature; measures are visualized by vertical lines on a score.

Melody A series of notes that together create a tune or theme.

Mezzo-soprano Literally "half soprano"; the lowest soprano voice; one tone above contralto.

Minimalism A predominantly American school of music from the mid-20th century, which favored a

sound-world involving an almost hypnotic texture of repeated short patterns.

Minor A term applied to a key signature or chord, triad, or scale in a minor key; has a relative major key. Different to its relative major in that the third note (and sometimes sixth and seventh) are flatted, leading to a darker sound.

Mode Seven-note scale inherited from Ancient Greece via the Middle Ages, in which they were most prevalent; they survive today in folk music and plainsong.

Modulation A shift from one key to another—for example, from C major to A minor.

Monody Vocal style developed in the Baroque period with a single, dominant melodic line; can be accompanied or unaccompanied.

Monophonic Describes music written in a single line, or melody without an accompaniment.

Motet A polyphonic choral composition based on a sacred text, usually unaccompanied.

Movement A self-contained section of a larger work; so called because each has a different, autonomous tempo indication.

Musique concrète Electronic music comprising instrumental and natural sounds, often altered or distorted in the recording process.

Natural A note that is neither sharp nor flat. A natural symbol can be used following a sharp or flat introduced earlier in a measure, to indicate that the player not flat

or sharp the note anymore, or to override sharps or flats in the work's key signature.

Obbligato An accompaniment that is important (and therefore "obligatory"); often describes a countermelody played by an instrument in an ensemble or a Baroque keyboard accompaniment written out in full rather than with the standard figured bass notation.

Octave The interval between one pitch and another with double or half its frequency—for example, on a piano, there is an octave between high C and the next highest C note.

Opera Drama in which all or most characters sing and in which music is an important element; usually all dialogue is sung.

Opera buffa Type of comic opera popular in the 18th century; opposite of opera seria.

Opéra comique An exclusively French type of opera that, despite its name, is not always comic, nor particularly light; also includes spoken dialogue.

Opera seria Literally "serious opera," the direct opposite of opera buffa; characterized by heroic or mythological plots and formality in both music and action.

Operetta Italian for "little opera," and sometimes known as "light opera"; a lighter 19th-century style including spoken dialogue.

Oratorio A work for vocal soloists and choir with instrumental accompaniment; differs from an opera in that an oratorio is a concert piece, not a drama.

Ornamentation Embellishment of a note or chord with, for example, a trill or a short fragment such as a turn—the note above the main note, the main note, and the note below, played in quick succession.

Ostinato Repeated musical figure, usually in the bass part, providing a foundation for harmonic and melodic variation above.

Overture French for "opening"; an instrumental introduction to an opera or ballet; presents some of the main thematic material.

Pianola A self-playing piano in which the keys are operated by air that is pumped through perforated paper fed by a roller.

Pitch The position of one sound in relation to the range of tonal sounds—how high or low it is— which depends on the frequency of sound waves per second (hertz).

Plainsong Medieval church music also known as plainchant; consists of a unison, unaccompanied vocal line in free rhythm, like speech, with no regular measure lengths.

Polyphony Meaning "many sounds," this refers to a style of composition in which all parts are independent and of equal value.

Program music Any music written to describe a nonmusical theme, such as an event, landscape, or literary work.

Recitative Style of singing in opera and oratorio closely related to the delivery of dramatic speech in pitch and rhythm; often used for dialogue and exposition of the plot between arias and choruses.

Requiem A piece written as a memorial; also specifically a setting of a Catholic Requiem Mass, which celebrates the dead.

Rhythm The pattern of relative durations of and stresses on notes in a piece, commonly organized in regular groups or measures.

Romantic The cultural epoch heralded in music by Beethoven, which dominated the 19th century; characterized by the abandonment of traditional forms, inspiration by extra-musical subjects, an increase in the scale of composition, and use of chromaticism.

Rondo Piece or movement of music based on a recurring theme with interspersed material; follows a form such as ABACADAE.

Sarabande A slow court dance in triple time, popular in Europe from the 17th century.

Scale A series of notes that define a tune and, usually, the key of the piece. Different scales give music a different feeling and "color."

Scherzo Lively dance piece (or movement) in triple time.

Semitone Also known as a half step or half tone; the smallest musical interval between notes in Western tonal music. There are two semitones in a whole tone and 112 semitones in an octave. On a keyboard, a semitone is found where two keys are as close together as possible—for example, E to F is a semitone. See also **Tone**.

Serial music System of atonal composition developed in the 1920s by Arnold Schoenberg and others,

in which fixed sequences of music are used as a foundation to create a more complex whole work.

Sharp A note that has been raised by a half step—for example, F raised by a half step is F-sharp; also describes an instrument or voice that is out of tune by being higher than the intended pitch.

Singspiel Literally "song play" in German, a type of comic opera with spoken dialogue rather than recitative; typified in Mozart's *The Magic Flute*.

Sonata Popular instrumental piece for one or more players; originated in the Baroque period, when the term referred to a short piece for a solo or small group of instruments accompanied by a basso continuo.

Sonata da camera "Chamber sonata" in Italian; a type of chamber piece—usually for two violins with basso continuo—from the late 17th and early 18th century.

Sonata da chiesa "Church sonata"; a multi-instrumental piece similar to the sonata da camera, usually comprising four movements: a slow introduction, a fugal movement, a slow movement, and a quick finale.

Sonata principle A musical form made up of the exposition (two subjects linked by a bridge section, the second of which is in a different key), the development (expounding upon the exposition), and the recapitulation, an altered restating of the exposition in the tonic key.

Song cycle A group of songs that tells a story or shares a common theme; designed to be performed in a sequence as a single entity.

Soprano The highest of the four standard singing voices—above alto, tenor, and bass; term for a female or a young boy singing in this vocal range.

Staff The grid of five horizontal lines on which music is written; also called a "stave."

Suite Multimovement work—generally instrumental—made up of a series of contrasting dance movements, usually all in one key.

Symphony Large-scale work for full orchestra; Classical and Romantic symphonies both contain four movements—traditionally an allegro, a slower second movement, a scherzo, and a lively finale. Later symphonies can contain more or fewer—the first movement is often in sonata form, and the slow movement and finale may follow a similar structure.

Temperament Tuning an instrument by adjusting intervals between notes to enable it to play in different keys. Most keyboard instruments are tuned using "equal temperament" based on an octave of 12 equal half steps.

Tempo The pace of a work; indicated on sheet music with terms such as *allegro* ("quickly") or *adagio* ("slowly").

Tenor The highest natural adult male voice; also a term describing an instrument in this range.

Timbre The particular quality (literally "stamp"), or character, of a sound that enables a listener to distinguish one instrument (or voice) from another; synonymous with "tone color."

Tonality System of major and minor scales and keys; forms the basis of all Western music from the 17th century until Schoenberg in the early 20th century. Tonal music adheres to the principles of tonality.

Tone Two half steps; equal to the interval of a major second, comprising two adjacent positions on a staff. See also **semitone**.

Tone poem Extended single-movement symphonic work, usually programmatic, often describing landscape or literary works; also called a "symphonic poem."

Tonic The first note, or degree, of any diatonic (major or minor) scale; most important note of the scale, providing the focus for the melody and harmony of a piece of music; also describes the main key of a piece of music.

Treble The highest unchanged male voice, or the highest instrument or part in a piece of music; also the name for the symbol (clef) used to indicate notes above middle C on the piano.

Triad A three-note chord that consists of a root note plus the intervals of a third and a fifth. There are four types: major (e.g. C–E–G), minor (e.g. C–E-flat–G), augmented (e.g. C–E–G-sharp), and diminished (e.g. C–E-flat–G-flat).

Vibrato The rapid, regular variation of pitch around a single note for expressive effect.

12-tone music Works in which each degree of the chromatic scale is ascribed the same degree of importance, eliminating any concept of key or tonality.

INDEX

Page numbers in **bold** refer to main entries; those in *italics* refer to captions.

P

Q R

QUOTE ATTRIBUTIONS

EARLY MUSIC

22 St. John of the Ladder
24 Guido d'Arezzo
26 Hildegard of Bingen
28 St. Augustine
32 Walther von der Vogelweider
36 Guillaume de Machaut

RENAISSANCE

42 Johannes Tinctoris
43 Josquin des Prez
44 Thomas Tallis
46 Giuseppe Verdi
52 John Irving
54 John Milton
55 Thomas Coryat
56 Sir Thomas Wyatt

BAROQUE

62 John Evelyn
64 Claudio Monteverdi
70 Évrard Titon du Tillet
72 Henry Playford
78 Martin Luther
80 Angelo Berardi
82 François Couperin
84 George Frideric Handel
90 Domenico Scarlatti
92 Antonio Vivaldi
98 Johann Sebastian Bach
106 Johann Mattheson
107 Alexis Piron
108 Frédéric Chopin

CLASSICAL

116 Christian Friedrich Daniel Schubart
118 Romain Rolland
120 Carl Philipp Emanuel Bach
122 Joseph Haydn
128 Richard Wagner
132 William Dean Howells
134 *The Magic Flute*
138 Ludwig van Beethoven

ROMANTIC

146 Yehudi Menuhin
148 Gioachino Rossini
149 Carl Maria von Weber
150 Franz Schubert
156 Ludwig van Beethoven
162 Hector Berlioz
164 Frédéric Chopin
166 Robert Schumann
170 London *Times* reviewer, 1846
174 D.H. Lawrence
176 Faust
178 Heinrich Heine
179 Camille Saint-Saëns
180 Vincenzo Bellini
188 Clara Wieck Schumann
190 Robert Caro
192 Gustav Mahler
194 Giacomo Puccini
198 Gustav Mahler

NATIONALISM

206 Bedřich Smetana
207 Havelock Ellis
208 Edvard Grieg
210 Gabriel Fauré
212 Antonín Dvořák
216 Edward MacDowell
218 Ralph Vaughan Williams
220 Jean Sibelius
222 Isaac Albéniz
223 London *Times* reviewer, 1918

MODERN

228 Stephane Mallarmé
232 Ethel Smyth
240 Peter Maxwell Davies
246 Igor Stravinsky
252 George Meredith
254 Charles Ives
256 Erik Satie
258 George Gershwin
262 Maurice Sachs
263 Leoš Janáček
264 Anton von Webern
266 Maurice Ravel
268 Edgard Varèse
270 Mikhail Glinka
272 Sergei Prokofiev
273 Colin McPhee
274 Dmitri Shostakovich
280 Heitor Villa-Lobos
282 Oliver Messiaen
284 Michael Tippett
286 Martha Graham
288 Benjamin Britten

CONTEMPORARY

298 Pierre Schaeffer
302 John Cage
306 Pierre Boulez
308 Iannis Xenakis
309 Aram Khachaturian
310 Krzysztof Penderecki
312 Terry Riley
314 Toru Takemitsu
316 Luciano Berio
318 Peter Maxwell Davies
320 Steve Reich
321 Philip Glass
322 R. Murray Schafer
323 Witold Lutosławski
324 Richard Steinitz
325 Kaija Saariaho
326 *blue cathedral* program notes
328 Thomas Adès
329 Eric Whitacre

ACKNOWLEDGMENTS

Dorling Kindersley would like to thank Smita Mathur, Riji Raju, and Nonita Saha for editorial assistance, and Hansa Babra for design assistance.

PICTURE CREDITS

The publisher would like to thank the following for their kind permission to reproduce their photographs:

(Key: a-above; b-below/bottom; c-center; f-far; l-left; r-right; t-top)

22 The Metropolitan Museum of Art: Gift of J. Pierpont Morgan, 1917 (bc). **23 Getty Images:** DeAgostini (br); Universal History Archive (tl). **24 Alamy Stock Photo:** Music-Images (cr). **25 Getty Images:** DEA / Veneranda Bilblioteca Ambrosiana / De Agostini (r). **26 Getty Images:** Fine Art Images / Heritage Images (cr). **27 Wellcome Images** http://creativecommons.org/licenses/by/4.0/: William Marshall (tr). **29 Alamy Stock Photo:** Steve Hamblin (tl). **Getty Images:** Imagno (br). **30 Alamy Stock Photo:** Paul Fearn (tr). **31 Alamy Stock Photo:** Paul Fearn (br). **33 Lebrecht Music and Arts:** culture-images (tl). **34 Getty Images:** Prisma / UIG (bl). **36 Alamy Stock Photo:** Lebrecht Music and Arts Photo Library (crb). **37 Alamy Stock Photo:** Music-Images (tr). **42 Alamy Stock Photo:** Granger Historical Picture Archive (crb). **44 Alamy Stock Photo:** Music-Images (cb). **45 Alamy Stock Photo:** James Hadley (tr). **48 Getty Images:** DeAgostini (br). **49 Alamy Stock Photo:** Marka (tr). **51 Alamy Stock Photo:** Artokoloro Quint Lox Limited (b). **52 Getty Images:** Culture Club (br). **53 Getty Images:** Mansell / The LIFE Picture Collection (tr). **55 Getty Images:** Fine Art Images / Heritage Images (cb). **57 Getty Images:** Leemage / Corbis (tl). **SuperStock:** A. Burkatovski / Fine Art Images (bl). **62 Alamy Stock Photo:** Art Collection 2 (cr). **63 Getty Images:** DEA Picture Library (tr). **66 iStockphoto.com:** Clodio (br). **67 Getty Images:** Imagno (tr). **68 Getty Images:** DeAgostin (bl). **The Metropolitan Museum of Art:** Bequest of Gwynne M. Andrews, 1931 (tc). **69 Alamy Stock Photo:** Granger Historical Picture Archive (bl). **71 akg-images:** (t). **The Metropolitan Museum of Art:** Harris Brisbane Dick Fund, 1917 (tc). **74 Getty Images:** 19th era (tr). **75 Alamy Stock Photo:** Lebrecht Music and Arts Photo Library (tr). **Getty Images:** DEA / Veneranda Biblioteca Ambrosiana / De Agostini (bl). **76 Getty Images:** Historical Picture Archive / Corbis (tl). **77 Alamy Stock Photo:** Lanmas (bl). **79 akg-images:** (t). **80 Alamy Stock Photo:** AM Stock (br). **81 Getty Images:** DeAgostini (tr). **83 Getty Images:** DEA / G. Dagli Oorti / De Agostini (bl); Leemage / Corbis (tr). **86 Getty Images:** DEA / G. Dagli Oorti / De Agostini (bl). **87 Getty Images:** Bettmann (tr). **88 Alamy Stock Photo:** Chronicle (bl). **89 Getty Images:** Angelo Hornak / Corbis (tr). **90 Alamy Stock Photo:** Artokoloro Quint Lox Limited (br). **91 Getty Images:** De Agostini / A. Dagli Orti (tr). **94 Getty Images:** DEA / A. Dagli Orti / De Agostini (tr). **95 Getty Images:** Stefano Bianchetti / Corbis (bl). **96 Alamy Stock Photo:** Music-Images (tr). **Getty Images:** Adam Berry / Redferns (bl). **100 Getty Images:** Fine Art Images / Heritage Images (br). **101 Getty Images:** DeAgostini (tr). **103 Getty Images:** Stefano Bianchetti / Corbis (bl). **104 Alamy Stock Photo:** DPA picture alliance (b). **105 Getty Images:** DEA Picture Library / De Agostini (tr). **107 Getty Images:** Eric Cabanis / AFP (cr). **109 Alamy Stock Photo:** LOOK Die Bildagentur der Fotografen GmbH (br); Music-Images (tr). **111 Getty Images:** Gordon Parks / The LIFE Picture Collection (bl). **116 Getty Images:** Imagno (cr). **117 Alamy Stock Photo:** Paul Fearn (tr). **119 Getty Images:** Imagno (bl, tr).

120 Alamy Stock Photo: Science History Images (cb). **124 Getty Images:** De Agostini / A. Dagli Orti (bl). **125 Getty Images:** Imagno (tr). **127 Getty Images:** DEA / A. Dagli Orti / De Agostini (bl). **129 Getty Images:** DeAgostini (bl); Imagno (tr). **130 Getty Images:** De Agostini Picture Library (tr); DEA / A. Dagli Orti / De Agostini (bl). **132 Alamy Stock Photo:** Music-Images (br). **133 Getty Images:** De Agostini / A. Dagli Orti (tr). **135 Alamy Stock Photo:** Westend61 GmbH (t). **136 Alamy Stock Photo:** Interfoto (tl). **137 Rex Shutterstock:** Alfredo Dagli Orti (tr). **139 Alamy Stock Photo:** GL Archive (cb). Library of Congress, Washington, D.C.: LC-USZC4-9589 (tr). **140 Getty Images:** Imagno (tl). **141 Rex Shutterstock:** Gianni Dagli Orti (br). **147 Alamy Stock Photo:** Chronicle (tr). **Getty Images:** De Agostini Picture Library (bl). **149 Alamy Stock Photo:** Music-Images (c). **152 Alamy Stock Photo:** DeAgostini (b). **153 Alamy Stock Photo:** North Wind Picture Archives (tr). **154 Alamy Stock Photo:** Lebrecht Music and Arts Photo Library (bl). **155 Alamy Stock Photo:** Music-Images (br). **158 Alamy Stock Photo:** Granger Historical Picture Archive (tr). **161 123RF.com:** Mikhail Markovskiy (b). **163 Alamy Stock Photo:** Granger Historical Picture Archive (bl). **Getty Images:** Pierre Petit / Hulton Archive (tr). **164 Getty Images:** Fine Art Photographic Library / CORBIS (br). **165 Getty Images:** DeAgostini (tr). **167 Getty Images:** Universal History Archive (bl); Roger Viollet Collection (tr). **169 Getty Images:** DeAgostini (tr) **171 Alamy Stock Photo:** Paul Fearn (tr). Getty Images: SSPL (tl). **172 Alamy Stock Photo:** Music-Images (tl). **173 Getty Images:** Mansell / The LIFE Picture Collection (tr). **174 Getty Images:** Bertrand Langlois / AFP (cr). **175 Getty Images:** De Agostini Picture Library (bl). **176 Alamy Stock Photo:** Paul Fearn (c). **177 Getty Images:** Imagno (br). **Rex Shutterstock:** Alfredo Dagli Orti (ca). **178 Dreamstime.com:** Ershamstar (br). **182 Getty Images:** Fine Art Images / Heritage Images (tr). **183 Alamy Stock Photo:** North Wind Picture Archives (bl). **185 Alamy Stock Photo:** Granger Historical Picture Archive (tl). **Getty Images:** DeAgostini (br). **186 Rex Shutterstock:** John Alex Maguire (tr). **188 Getty Images:** DeAgostini (br). **189 Getty Images:** DEA / A. Dagli Orti / De Agostini (cla). **191 Getty Images:** Ole Jensen - Corbis (bl); Universal History Archive / UIG (tr). **192 Alamy Stock Photo:** Prisma Archivo (bc). **193 Getty Images:** DEA / A. Dagli Orti / De Agostini (cb). **Library of Congress, Washington, D.C.:** LC-B2- 3747-11 [P&P] (tr). **195 Alamy Stock Photo:** Chronicle (tr). **Getty Images:** Culture Club (bl). **196 Alamy Stock Photo:** Lebrecht Music and Arts Photo Library (bl). **Getty Images:** Christophel Fine Art / UIG (t). **199 Getty Images:** Culture Club (tl); Fine Art Images / Heritage Images (tr). **201 Getty Images:** Imagno (br). **207 Alamy Stock Photo:** World History Archive (crb). **208 Alamy Stock Photo:** Granger Historical Picture Archive (cr). **209 Getty Images:** DEA / A. Dagli Orti / De Agostini (tr). **210 Alamy Stock Photo:** Music-Images (cr). **211 Getty Images:** The Print Collector (tr). **213 Alamy Stock Photo:** Music-Images (tl, tr). **214 Alamy Stock Photo:** Granger Historical Picture Archive (bl). **215 NASA:** (tl). **217 Alamy Stock Photo:** The Granger Collection (tr). **Getty Images:** Robert W. Kelley / The LIFE Images Collection (bl). **219 Alamy Stock Photo:** Chronicle (bl). **220 Getty Images:** Alex Robinson / AWL Images Ltd (br). **221 Getty Images:** Hulton-Deutsch Collection / CORBIS (tr). **223 Getty Images:** PHAS / UIG (t). **229 Getty Images:** Fine Art Images / Heritage Images (tr, bl). **230 Getty Images:** Vibrant Pictures (br). Getty Images: DEA / G. Dagli Oorti / De Agostini (tl). **234 Alamy Stock Photo:** Music-Images (bl). **235 Alamy Stock Photo:** Paul Fearn (cr). **Getty Images:** Hulton

Archive (bl). **236 Getty Images:** Universal History Archive (t). **238 Alamy Stock Photo:** Chris Fredriksson (bl); Heritage Image Partnership Ltd (tc). **239 Getty Images:** Robbie Jack / Corbis (b). **242 Getty Images:** PhotoQuest (br). **243 Getty Images:** Imagno (tr). **244 Alamy Stock Photo:** Lebrecht Music and Arts Photo Library (bl). **245 Getty Images:** Imagno (tl). **248 Alamy Stock Photo:** Heritage Image Partnership Ltd (bl). **249 Alamy Stock Photo:** Granger Historical Picture Archive (tl). **251 Alamy Stock Photo:** Granger Historical Picture Archive (tl). **Getty Images:** Apic (br). **252 Getty Images:** Universal History Archive / UIG (b). **253 Alamy Stock Photo:** Music-Images (tl). **255 Getty Images:** Bettmann (bl, tr). **256 Getty Images:** DEA / A. Dagli Orti / De Agostini (bc). **257 SuperStock:** Fototeca Gilardi / Marka (tr). **259 Alamy Stock Photo:** Everett Collection, Inc. (tl); Granger Historical Picture Archive (br). **261 Alamy Stock Photo:** Music-Images (tr). **Getty Images:** George Karger / Pix Inc. / The LIFE Images Collection (tl). **262 Getty Images:** Fine Art Images / Heritage Images (crb). **264 Getty Images:** DEA / A. Dagli Orti / De Agostini (bc). **265 Alamy Stock Photo:** Granger Historical Picture Archive (br). **267 Getty Images:** Hiroyuki Ito (tr); Albert Harlingue / Roger Viollet (bl). **269 Getty Images:** Fred Stein Archive / Archive Photos (tr); Ken Hively / Los Angeles Times (bl). **270 Getty Images:** DEA / A. Dagli Orti / De Agostini (br). **271 Getty Images:** Bettmann (tr). **273 Alamy Stock Photo:** Michele Burgess (cr). **276 Getty Images:** Fine Art Images / Heritage Images (tr). **277 Alamy Stock Photo:** Music-Images (tr). **278 Getty Images:** Fine Art Images / Heritage Images (tr); Frans Schellekens / Redferns (bl). **281 Getty Images:** Hiroyuki Ito (tr); Time Life Pictures / Pix Inc. / The LIFE Picture Collection (bl). **283 Getty Images:** Erich Auerbach / Hulton Archive (tr); Hulton Archive (bl). **284 Lebrecht Music and Arts:** Tristram Kenton (cr). **285 Getty Images:** Hulton-Deutsch Collection / Corbis (bl). **287 Getty Images:** Mary Delaney Cooke / Corbis / Martha Graham in "Appalachian Spring" Choreographed by Martha Graham / Martha Graham Dance Company (tl); Leonard M. DeLessio / Corbis (br). **290 Getty Images:** Geography Photos / UIG (tr). **291 Alamy Stock Photo:** Everett Collection Inc (tr). **Getty Images:** Hulton-Deutsch Collection / Corbis (bl). **293 Alamy Stock Photo:** Stan Pritchard (tr). **Getty Images:** Kurt Hutton / Picture Post / Hulton Archive (bl). **299 Getty Images:** Maurice Lecardent / INA (ca). **300 Getty Images:** George Konig / Keystone Features (tl). **301 Getty Images:** Donaldson Collection / Michael Ochs Archives (bl). **303 Alamy Stock Photo:** Pierre Brye (tl); Granger Historical Picture Archive (tr). **304 Alamy Stock Photo:** Science History Images (bl). **307 Alamy Stock Photo:** Interfoto (cb). **TopFoto.co.uk:** Sisi Burn / ArenaPAL (tr). **309 Alamy Stock Photo:** ITAR-TASS News Agency (crb). **310 Alamy Stock Photo:** Lucas Vallecillos (br). **311 Alamy Stock Photo:** DPA Picture Alliance (tr). **313 Alamy Stock Photo:** Philippe Gras (tr). **Getty Images:** Jack Vartoogian (bl). **314 Getty Images:** Hiroyuki Ito (bc). **315 Getty Images:** Jack Mitchell (tr). **316 Getty Images:** Claude James / INA (cr). **317 Rex Shutterstock:** Camilla Morandi (tr). **318 Getty Images:** Photo 12 / UIG (bc). **319 Getty Images:** Eamonn McCabe / Redferns (tr). **320 Getty Images:** Nancy R. Schiff / Hulton Archive (crb). **322 Alamy Stock Photo:** Artokoloro Quint Lox Limited (br). **325 Getty Images:** Raphael Gaillarde / Gamma-Rapho (cr). **327 Lawdon Press:** J. Henry Fair (bl). **329 Rex Shutterstock:** Rob Scott (br)

All other images © Dorling Kindersley
For further information see:
www.dkimages.com